Tim Powell

GIGABIT ETHERNET NETWORKING

David G. Cunningham, Ph.D.
& William G. Lane, Ph.D.

MACMILLAN
TECHNICAL
PUBLISHING
U·S·A

Gigabit Ethernet Networking

By David G. Cunningham, Ph.D. & William G. Lane, Ph.D.

Published by:
Macmillan Technical Publishing
201 West 103rd Street
Indianapolis, IN 46290 USA

Printed in the United States of America 1 2 3 4 5 6 7 8 9 0

Library of Congress Cataloging Number: 98-84223

ISBN: 1-57870-062-0

Universal Product Code: 619472700624

Warning and Disclaimer

This book is designed to provide information about Gigabit Ethernet networking. Every effort has been made to make this book as complete and as accurate as possible, but no warranty or fitness is implied.

The information is provided on an "as is" basis. The authors and Macmillan Technical Publishing shall have neither liability nor responsibility to any person or entity with respect to any loss or damages arising from the information contained in this book or from the use of the disks or programs that may accompany it.

Trademark Acknowledgments

All terms mentioned in this book that are known to be trademarks or service marks have been appropriately capitalized. Macmillan Technical Publishing cannot attest to the accuracy of this information. Use of a term in this book should not be regarded as affecting the validity of any trademark or service mark.

The list of goals and non-goals of the original Ethernet Specification proposal is provided courtesy of Intel Corporation (Copyright © 1980 Intel Corporation. All rights reserved. Intel Corporation, 2200 Mission College Blvd., Santa Clara, CA 95052-8119, USA.)

Table 4.1 and Figure 14.1 reproduced from Internetworking Technologies Handbook; Cisco Press (courtesy of Cisco Systems, Inc. All rights reserved)

Content from the IEEE 802.3 Standard is reprinted by permission of the Institute of Electrical and Electronics Engineers, Inc. The IEEE disclaims any responsibility or liability resulting from the placement and use in the described manner.

PUBLISHER
Jim LeValley

EXECUTIVE EDITOR
Linda Engelman

ACQUISITIONS EDITOR
Karen Wachs

MANAGING EDITOR
Patrick Kanouse

DEVELOPMENT EDITOR
Christopher Cleveland

PROJECT EDITOR
Jen Nuckles

COPY EDITOR
Lunaea Hougland

TECHNICAL REVIEWERS
Del Hanson
Charlie Catlett
Christopher T. DiMinico

TEAM COORDINATOR
Amy Lewis

MANUFACTURING COORDINATOR
Brook Farling

BOOK DESIGNER
Anne Jones

COVER DESIGNER
Brainstorm Technologies

GRAPHICS IMAGE SPECIALISTS
Shelley Norris
Laura Robbins

PRODUCTION TEAM
Argosy

PROOFREADER
Megan Wade

INDEXER
Chris Wilcox

About the Authors

David G. Cunningham holds a B.S. in Physics and a Ph.D. in Laser Physics from The Queen's University in Belfast, Northern Ireland. After graduation, he spent two years at British Telecom Research Laboratories before joining Hewlett-Packard Laboratories in Bristol, England, where he is a principal scientist and project manager responsible for Link Technology. David has more than 14 years experience with communication systems design and has personally conducted much of the basic research on the use of optical fibers for longer distance Gigabit transmission. He is cited as a key inventor on many patents and has authored numerous journal papers. He has been involved with the development of LAN/MAN standards for more than 10 years, including serving as a sub-task force editor for the IEEE 802.12 Demand Priority standard. David was given an award by the Gigabit Ethernet task force (IEEE 802.3z) for his critical contributions to the Gigabit Ethernet standard.

William G. Lane holds a B.S. in Electrical Engineering from Stanford University, an M.S. in Electrical Engineering from the University of Southern California, and a Ph.D. in Electrical Engineering from the University of California at Davis. He was a design engineer in industry for eight years before joining the California State University, Chico, Electrical Engineering faculty in 1960. Bill was the founder of their computer science program and later was a co-founder of their computer engineering program. Bill served nine years as department chair, six years as dean, and is currently Professor Emeritus of computer science and computer engineering. He has 32 years of teaching experience and has been a computer and communications systems consultant for both government and industry, including approximately 10 years with one of the larger U.S. Navy laboratories. Most recently, Bill has been a participant in the IEEE 802 standards development process for more than five years, during which he co-authored and served as technical editor of the Ethernet-compatible IEEE 802.12 Demand Priority standard. He has also closely followed development of the Gigabit Ethernet standards.

Dedication

To Shirley, whose belief, support, encouragement, and tolerance enabled me to complete this book. Also, to my son Adam, for the many times I didn't play with him.

David

To Jeanne, who after 52 years of marriage, still has the patience, love, and sense of humor to enable me to take on yet another project before our house remodeling is finished and the landscaping is completed.

Bill

Acknowledgments

Writing this book has been an interesting experience in long-distance communications. David Cunningham lives near Bristol, in the west of England, and Bill Lane lives near Sacramento, in northern California. We couldn't have done it without the help of a number of people on both sides of the Atlantic.

We would like to extend our sincere thanks to Hewlett-Packard's Laboratories in Bristol (HPLB) for their encouragement, time, equipment, and support during the preparation of this book. Special thanks go to Steve Wright, David's manager at HPLB, for making it possible for us to have regular telephone conversations and several face-to-face visits on weekends following David's company meetings in California.

Special thanks also to Del Hanson at HP's Fiber Components Division for believing we could write this book, for putting us in contact with Macmillan, for encouraging us throughout the writing, and for being a brilliant reviewer.

To Jim LeValley of Macmillan Technical Publishing (MTP) for accepting Del's seemingly mad suggestion that we could write the book and then convincing us that we should. Chris Cleveland, development editor at MTP, deserves a great deal of credit for the quality of this book. Amy Lewis and Karen Wachs, also of MTP, helped greatly by taking care of many details. Thanks also for providing part of the funding for Bill to attend the Spring 1998 IEEE 802 plenary meeting.

Ken Deroucher, Bill's dean at CSU, Chico, provided the remainder of the funding for Bill to attend the Spring 1998 plenary meeting and made a processor available for his use while this book was being written.

Chris DiMinico and Charlie Catlett provided excellent technical reviews for the book. Their insight and suggestions really made a fantastic difference to the quality.

Mark Nowell, formerly of HPLB, provided most of the experimental data for the graphs and figures, and Alistair Coles of HPLB supplied electronic versions of the 3B4B, 5B6B code tables in Chapter 8 and the 8B10B code tables in Appendix B. Thanks to both of them for numerous helpful suggestions and discussions.

And finally, to the members of the IEEE 802.3z, the EMBI, the MBI, and the TIA FO 2.2 committees: it was a great privilege working with you all, and we hope this book is a true reflection of your great contribution to Gigabit Ethernet and LAN/MAN technology.

About the Technical Editors

Del Hanson is Principal Engineer in the Fiber Optic Communications Division of Hewlett-Packard Company, responsible for network standards development and related strategic component product planning. He worked on microwave subsystem development at Bell Laboratories and HP prior to starting fiber optic LAN technology development at HP Laboratories in 1974. He has participated in the development of numerous fiber optic LAN link standards and has presented many papers and seminars on fiber optic networks and link performance. He received a B.S. in electrical engineering from the University of Wisconsin and a Ph.D. in electrical engineering from the University of Michigan. Dr. Hanson is a Senior Member of IEEE and was co-chairman of the 1987 Optical Fiber Communication (OFC) Conference. He was chairman of the OFC Networks and Switching Subcommittee and the IEEE 802.3z Gigabit Ethernet Optical PMD Link Subcommittee.

Charlie Catlett is Chief Technology Officer for the National Center for Supercomputing Applications (NCSA), located at the University of Illinois at Urbana-Champaign. He was a member of the original NSFNET backbone project in 1987 and has designed, built, and supported large wide area, campus, and local area networks since the early 1980s. During the past decade, he has worked on the DARPA/NSF Gigabit Testbeds initiative and the NSF vBNS project, and is a founding principal investigator for the National Laboratory for Applied Network Research. During the last several years, he has focused on long-range strategic planning for NCSA in supercomputing, storage, component software technologies, information security, and networking. Charlie holds a B.S. in computer engineering from the University of Illinois at Urbana-Champaign.

Christopher T. DiMinico is the Director of Network Systems Technology with Cable Design Technology (CDT) Corporation. Christopher is a member of the IEEE, TIA TR41.8.1, and the U.S. advisory group for international cabling standards development.

OVERVIEW

CONTENTS

INTRODUCTION

The primary focus of this book is Gigabit Ethernet and its use in multispeed LANs. The Ethernet protocol quickly rose to the forefront when it was first proposed and has since become the preferred LAN protocol for computer users. This does not mean that there has not been competition. A number of other LAN technologies, including Token Ring, FDDI, 100VG-AnyLAN, and most notably ATM, have all attempted to eclipse Ethernet within the LAN marketplace. However, they have all been spectacular in their failure to achieve that goal. Ethernet is now used on 80 to 85 percent of the world's LAN-connected PCs and workstations because of its demonstrated capability to respond to the ever-increasing need for more and more bandwidth.

The Ethernet protocol has been able to successfully incorporate a number of new capabilities because its developers, manufacturers, and standards committees have remained true to the initial Ethernet goals and design principles of simplicity, interoperability, robustness, and low cost. In short, Ethernet has remained viable precisely because it has been adapted to meet the changing needs of its customers while remaining easy to use, easy to install, easy to maintain, and economical to own.

Gigabit Ethernet is the most important recent addition to the Ethernet protocol. The capability for priority-based transmission at 1,000 Mbps in both directions (full-duplex operation) over a single link plus associated improvements in network addressing methodology (VLAN tagging) and in switching/routing hardware will ensure that Ethernet remains well ahead of other LAN technologies.

Gigabit Ethernet has a very important role to play in existing LANs that are implemented with a combination of twisted pair copper and multimode optical fiber cabling. However, transmission through these cables at Gigabit rates presented some very challenging problems and at one point even threatened the Gigabit Ethernet goal of being able to operate over long-established standard link lengths. In contrast with other books on Gigabit Ethernet, we have not shied away from these issues, but have included in-depth discussions of both the problems encountered and their solution development.

We took the time to write this book because we passionately believe that you should understand the recent capability additions to Ethernet: why they were developed, how they work, what the cabling limitations are, how Gigabit Ethernet fits into existing Ethernet (and other) LANs, how it should be installed, and how all of this will affect future LAN/MAN development.

Like other books on Gigabit Ethernet, we have included a discussion of the protocol, but at greater depth than most, and we have also included discussions on the following:

- Layered architectures (a concept that we have found is not well understood by many of the people in the field)

- The concepts and nuances of signal transmission through optical fiber (explained in a diagrammatic way that does not require higher level mathematics to be understood)

- Systems considerations and practical planning methods for new networks and network upgrades (how you would actually develop a network plan)

- Network topologies that provide improved chances for rapid recovery in case of equipment or link failure (where and why you should install alternate paths and redundant equipment or cables)

- Cable plant installation and management (including a few anecdotal examples of what not to do)

- Integrating Gigabit Ethernet with other LAN technologies (such as ATM)

These are all areas where experience has shown that there is a definite need, but that are often not well-covered in technical books on the Ethernet protocol.

Our Approach

Several people we talked to when we first considered writing this book told us that they didn't need "just another Gigabit Ethernet book." What they did need was a book that contained technical information in sufficient detail to provide them with the background knowledge that would allow them not only to understand the current state of the protocol, but to be better prepared for future changes, as well.

Our approach throughout the book has been to provide an essentially non-mathematical treatment to each subject and to use conceptual diagrams and graphs to explain what is going on in each part of the system. For example, the coverage of baseband transmission through optical fiber links is very diagrammatic and, based on reactions from people who have seen it, should be readily understandable, even to readers not previously familiar with the physics of light transmission through optical fiber.

Our Target Audience

This book was written for several broad audiences, including but not limited to:

- Networking systems product developers: engineers, computer scientists, and marketing personnel working for companies that design and manufacture network equipment (such as switches and routers) and components (such as laser transceivers, LAN interfaces, networking software, and optical fiber cables and connectors)

- Network implementers: network planners, managers, buyers, installers, and maintenance personnel who work for organizations that currently need, or soon will need, to upgrade or better understand their particular networks

- Students and faculty in electrical and computer engineering and computer science for coursework at the senior or first-year graduate level

While we assume that you may be familiar with LANs and Ethernet, we have provided enough information in the book to enable you to understand all aspects of Gigabit Ethernet networking without prior experience with high speed digital communications and network bridges, routers, and switches.

In addition, this book can be used as a companion to the Gigabit Ethernet standards documentation. In this role, it contains a lot of previously unpublished information that provides context and will help you understand why the specification is how it is.

Organization

The book is organized in six parts, in a fashion that allows you to skim or even skip individual sections or chapters, depending on your interest or need at the moment. We recommend, however, that you review the table of contents to determine the topics included in each chapter before you decide to go on. Backward and forward references are included throughout the text to help you find related information on specific topics.

Part I: Introduction

Chapter 1, "Ethernet Development: The Need for Speed," documents the creation, development, and evolution of Gigabit Ethernet networking. This chapter also introduces the CSMA/CD transmission and reception procedures and provides an overview of the components and topology of a Gigabit Ethernet network.

Chapter 2, "The OSI and Gigabit Ethernet Standard Reference Models," introduces both the ISO and IEEE 802.3 Ethernet reference models as a precursor to detailed discussion of layered architectures and the logical requirements of the interfaces between the different protocol layers of the model.

Part II: Network Access and Control

Chapter 3, "Media Access Control," details the Ethernet media access control (MAC) layer functions and responsibilities, the MAC frame format and format options, frame generation and transmission in both full- and half-duplex mode (including collision filtering, carrier extension, and frame bursting in CSMA/CD mode), and frame reception and error control.

Chapter 4, "Gigabit Repeaters, Bridges, Routers, and Switches," introduces reference models for Gigabit repeaters and bridges and describes functions/responsibilities of repeaters, bridges, routers, and switches, including port buffering, speed handling, and flow control.

Part III: Transmission Fundamentals

Chapter 5, "Fundamentals of Baseband Transmission," is essentially a non-mathematical introduction to baseband digital transmission. All key concepts required to understand the underlying thinking, design procedures, and trade-offs that led to the final specifications for the 1000BASE-X Gigabit Ethernet physical layers are covered.

Chapter 6, "Fundamentals of Fiber Optic Communication," is also a self-contained, essentially non-mathematical tutorial that introduces the basic optical fiber definitions, concepts, components, and technology relevant to Gigabit Ethernet. This chapter provides important background information for anyone implementing optical fiber networks.

Part IV: The Common 1000BASE-X Physical Layers

Chapter 7, "The Common Physical Sublayers: Reconciliation and the GMII," introduces the Gigabit Media Independent Interface that provides a simple, inexpensive, and easy-to-implement interconnection between the Gigabit Ethernet media-independent layer and the media-dependent physical layers, and between the physical layers and the network management processor.

Chapter 8, "Physical Coding, Physical Medium Attachment, and Auto-Negotiation for 1000BASE-X," introduces the concepts and operation of the Physical Coding Sublayer (PCS), Physical Medium Attachment Sublayer (PMA), and Auto-Negotiation unit that are common to all 1000BASE-X systems.

Part V: The 1000BASE-X Media Dependent Layers

Chapter 9, "The Gigabit Ethernet Optical Link Model," documents the Gigabit Ethernet optical link model, a tool developed by the Gigabit Ethernet task force to aid development of the 1000BASE-X physical sublayer specifications. The link model is currently (1999) the state of the art as far as laser-based data communication standards are concerned.

Chapter 10, "The Gigabit Ethernet Modal Bandwidth Investigation," discusses the resolution of some long-standing fundamental issues regarding laser-based multimode optical fiber transmission by Gigabit Ethernet: modal noise and unpredictable bandwidth performance.

Chapter 11, "1000BASE-X: Optical Fiber and Copper PMDs," discusses the functions, components, and specifications for baseband Gigabit Ethernet optical and short-haul copper PMDs. The Gigabit Ethernet optical link model is used with techniques discussed in Chapter 5 to illustrate and derive the PMD specifications.

Part VI: Network Installation and System Considerations

Chapter 12, "The Cable Plant: Installation and Management," introduces basic concepts of structured cabling relevant to Gigabit Ethernet and discusses installing conduit and cable. As-built drawing and database content requirements for effective cable plant management are also defined.

Chapter 13, "Upgrading Ethernet LANs: System and Topology Considerations," reviews the Ethernet system and compatibility considerations and defines planning procedures for implementing Gigabit Ethernet in network upgrades and/or new networks.

Chapter 14, "Gigabit Ethernet in Context with Other LAN Technologies," reviews some non-Ethernet technologies currently deployed in LANs (Token Ring, FDDI, 100VG-AnyLAN, and ATM) and then considers the use of Gigabit Ethernet as a network upgrade.

Chapter 15, "The Future: Gigabit Ethernet and Beyond," begins with a review of 1000BASE-T Gigabit Ethernet and link aggregation. It then moves on to discuss the use of Gigabit Ethernet in MAN/WAN networks and as part of WDM-based virtual MANs/WANs. Ten Gigabit Ethernet is also discussed.

Reader Guidelines

We are very aware that not everyone needs, nor should they be expected, to know and understand all the information that is contained in each chapter of this book. We also realize that while the table of contents provides some insight into each chapter's contents, a few suggestions might also be in order.

First, because development of 1000BASE-T (Gigabit Ethernet over four pair Category-5 or better, unshielded twisted pair copper cable) was not complete until most of the chapters had been written, we included it in Chapter 15. We recommend that you go to section 15.1 after you have completed Chapter 11, "1000BASE-X: Optical Fiber and Copper PMDs." The 1000BASE-T and 1000BASE-X physical sublayers are very different from each other, and should be considered in sequence.

Second, the following table suggests possible approaches for several different categories of readers.

Reader Work Assignment or Interest	Chapters Containing Background Material	Chapters Containing Essential Material
Network consultants, planners, and implementers	1, 2	3–15
Network managers	1, 2, 7–11	3–6, 12–15
Network installers and maintenance personnel	1–4, 7–11, 14–15	5–6, 12–13
Designers of network equipment and components	1, 12	2–11, 13–15
Components designers (for example, network interface cards, transceivers)	1, 12, 14	2–11, 13, 15
Cable and cable components designers, (for example, cable, connectors, cross-connect panels)	1–4, 7–8	5–6, 9–15
Electrical/Computer Engineering students	1	2–15
Computer Science students	1, 8–11	2–7, 12–15

Course Materials

Bill Lane is planning to use this book as the text for a High Speed Data Communications Networks course for Computer Science and Electrical/Computer Engineering majors (senior/graduate level) during the fall of 1999. Course materials will be available after the end of the course and will include a syllabus, suggested assignments, and additional discussion topics. You can receive this material by sending an email to *bill_lane@ieee.org*.

Contacting the Authors

If you have comments or suggestions about the book, you may contact either of us by email or at the address shown below. While we cannot guarantee an immediate response to questions and comments, we will certainly try to get back to you in a timely fashion.

William G. Lane, Prof. Emeritus
Dept. of Electrical and Computer Engineering
California State University, Chico
Chico, CA 95929
bill_lane@ieee.org

FOREWORD

Over the past five years, we have witnessed two dramatic improvements in LAN technology. Ethernet, already well-established as the world's most popular network, was reborn as Fast Ethernet. The idea of providing a tenfold increase in bandwidth while retaining all of the important characteristics of a mature and well-understood technology proved to be an irresistible combination for a market that perpetually demands ever faster and ever larger capacity for information exchange. Thus, when Fast Ethernet appeared on the scene in 1995, it rapidly became the network of choice.

This phenomenon hardly went unnoticed. Indeed, with many other technologies contending for the honor of succeeding Ethernet, every step of the evolution of Fast Ethernet was monitored and reported with interest and no small amount of sensationalism. The spectacular success enjoyed by those who invested in Fast Ethernet attracted the attention of the venture capital community, which was smarting from the poor returns it had received on investments in other, more complicated, networking technologies. Fast Ethernet quickly acquired a golden reputation as a simple and reliable technology, with broad appeal and tangible benefits. It required a fairly small investment, both to develop and to deploy, yet it yielded dramatic returns. Whether you were a venture capitalist putting money into a startup company, or a Management Information Systems manager purchasing the network infrastructure for your enterprise, Fast Ethernet was the smart place to put your money.

And then, just five months after the Institute of Electrical and Electronic Engineers completed its work on the formal standard for Fast Ethernet, they began work on a standard for Gigabit Ethernet. Against the backdrop of Fast Ethernet's success, the ordinarily dull and dry exercise of writing an IEEE standard became a closely watched event. Once again, the ink and the money started flowing. In the space of just one year, twenty startup companies were funded to develop Gigabit Ethernet products. The founders of these companies became celebrities, and the companies achieved lofty valuations on the basis of little more than the market potential of Gigabit Ethernet.

While all this attention raged about them, a relatively small group of engineers applied themselves to the task of defining just what Gigabit Ethernet was, and how it would work. This group banded together under the auspices of the IEEE 802.3 Working Group, the committee responsible for the development of Ethernet standards. For the most part, they were volunteers, taking time away from their normal jobs to work side-by-side with engineers from rival companies. The standards writing process took two and a half years from start to finish, and along the way there were numerous technical challenges to address and resolve. This process took place under the harsh glare of attention from the industry press, and the constant pressure to deliver the standard on schedule. This last point is significant in that few, if any, standards projects commit to and publish a target schedule for completion.

No one took on a larger responsibility or produced a larger contribution to the IEEE standard for Gigabit Ethernet than Dr. David Cunningham. At a critical point in the development of the standard, Dr. Cunningham assumed the leadership role in addressing a critical technical issue which threatened to delay the progress of the standards project. This issue was referred to as Differential Mode Delay, and it was resolved by the Modal Bandwidth Investigation, which was chaired by Dr. Cunningham. By applying his extensive knowledge of laser physics and fiber optics, and his exceptional leadership and communication skills, Dr. Cunningham became one of the heroes of Gigabit Ethernet, for which the industry owes him profound thanks.

Together, Dr. Cunningham and Dr. William Lane have authored a definitive work on the subject of Gigabit Ethernet. Their long experience with the development of standards in the IEEE 802 LAN/MAN Standards Committee gives them unique insight into the inner workings of this exciting technology. Both of these gentlemen are acknowledged experts in the development of networking standards, and both share an insider's view of the process by which an industry standard turns a concept into a formal specification. *Gigabit Ethernet Networking* provides more than just a comprehensive explanation of the contents of the IEEE 802.3z standard for Gigabit Ethernet. It provides the background knowledge necessary to understand how Gigabit Ethernet works, why it works, and where to use it to the best advantage.

Technical professionals at all levels will benefit from reading this work. Whether one seeks to learn the physical principles that underlie the technology of high-speed fiber optic communications, or wishes to acquire a detailed knowledge of the protocols and algorithms specified in the IEEE 802.3z standard for Gigabit Ethernet, or desires to understand how Gigabit Ethernet can and should be deployed in a modern data communications network infrastructure, *Gigabit Ethernet Networking* by Dr. Cunningham and Dr. Lane is the authoritative source of information.

Howard M. Frazier, Jr.
Former Chairman, IEEE P802.3z Gigabit Task Force

PART

I

Introduction

The two chapters in this part are included to provide the background information needed to understand the rest of the book. The Ethernet operational concepts, goals, and history are covered in Chapter 1 and can easily be skimmed if you are somewhat familiar with the Ethernet protocol (backward references are provided in later chapters to call your attention to a concept that may be unfamiliar or that may need reinforcing).

Chapter 2 introduces layered architectures and the use of abstract service primitives to define not only what services are to be provided by the layer, but also when they are to be provided and what information is to be passed across layer interfaces. This chapter should be read for background knowledge not only because several later chapters in the book assume an understanding of this concept, but also because the material introduced in this chapter is equally applicable to both hardware and software specification. Layered architecture definitions have the potential to save considerable time during product development and testing.

Chapter 1: Ethernet Development: The Need for Speed

Chapter 2: The OSI and Gigabit Ethernet Standard Reference Models

CHAPTER

1

Ethernet Development: The Need for Speed

We will continually find new things for microchips to do that were scarcely imaginable a year or two earlier. [Andrew Grove, Intel CEO and *Time*'s Man of the Year, 1997—Isaacson, 1997]

Which came first, the chicken or the egg? It is a philosophical conundrum that often provokes heated discussions regarding the evolution of the species. A similar question can be asked about the evolution and development of computing, and by extension, of data communications. Which came first, increases in computing power, expanded applications software, or higher-speed data networks?

In his book on the early history of computing, Herman Goldstine, a colleague of von Neumann's, noted that advances in the state of the art and the development of radical new machines are usually the result of the convergence of two very different concepts. One is the recognition of a need for an advance. The other results from someone seeing how to adapt technology to meet that need [Goldstine, 1972].

Consider the case, in the early 1980s, of a large U.S. Navy research lab with several mainframe processors and hundreds of minicomputers. Part of their long-range planning effort needed to consider possible network architectures that would be able to carry all of their voice, data, and video communications traffic into the next century.

A major problem arose. No one could predict the level and type of traffic that would be needed even in the next year or two, let alone what would be needed in 20 years. The research staff had no experience with the computational capabilities of computers and workstations or video equipment that were yet to be developed. They didn't know what would be possible in 20 years, and they were reluctant to do anything that would jeopardize their options that far into the future.

This is not a unique problem. It is one that is continually faced by network designers. Much has changed in the past two decades, and if history is a metric, even greater changes will occur in the future.

Moore's 1965 observation (it is now known as Moore's Law) that the number of transistors on a chip, and the resulting performance, doubles in power and halves in price approximately every 18 to 24 months has been amazingly accurate over the last three and a half decades [Isaacson, 1997]. This is also supported by Michael Slater of MicroDesign Resources with his recent observation that "Moore's Law can be sustained certainly for five years, and probably for ten years . . . after that, things could slow down without new and different technologies" [O'Malley, 1998]. Similar evaluations have been made by various people during recent years, and they have typically been followed shortly after with the development of an appropriate new technology.

Hardware advances have resulted in personal computers and workstations that rival the computing power of earlier-generation mainframes. The Internet and World Wide Web are becoming as necessary as the telephone. Data files have grown much larger, often include embedded color graphics, and are being downloaded more frequently. Multimedia, while still in the early stages of development, shows indications of early acceptance and rapid future growth that adds a requirement for real-time large-file transfers.

These improvements in computing capability plus large growth in the user base have had major impacts on many data networks, particularly for closely located facilities on single sites. Transmission speeds of 10 Mbps (megabits per second) were sufficient for most local area networks (LANs) from the 1980s through the early 1990s. About 1993, however, it became obvious that data traffic loads would soon be approaching LAN saturation. This led to the development of 100 Mbps networks. The rapid acceptance and implementation of the 100 Mbps networks, even before the 100 Mbps standards had been officially approved, pointed to a large potential market for even higher speed transmission rates. Design activity for 1,000 Mbps LANs began in late 1995.

Note

In their attempt to be first on the market, manufacturers often begin releasing products for production when draft standards appear to be reaching stability, and before the final draft has been agreed upon by all levels in the approval process.

The trend is obvious. Moore's Law is definitely at work. Traffic loads will continue to increase and probably at much greater than a linear rate.

The purpose of this book is to provide you with the knowledge and understanding that will enable you to make technically informed, cost-effective decisions about how your particular network can be designed and implemented to meet current/near-term traffic loads while also ensuring capability for easy upgrade and future growth.

This chapter begins with a discussion of Ethernet fundamentals and a brief review of the major milestones in the continuing development of the Ethernet standard as transmission speeds increased from 10 Mbps through 100 Mbps to 1,000 Mbps.

1.1 Ethernet Fundamentals

The Ethernet protocol has its roots in an experimental network designed to support 3 Mbps interconnection of "Alto" personal computers at the Xerox Palo Alto Research Center [Metcalfe and Boggs, 1976]. Experience with that network formed the basis of a formal 1980 proposal by DEC, Intel, and Xerox for an Ethernet protocol standard [Intel, 1980]. These companies proposed a network with a 10 Mbps baseband transmission rate over a shared media that would interconnect up to 1,024 closely located computers and other digital devices (2.5 km maximum station separation).

The targeted environment included office automation, distributed data processing, and other activities that would typically generate bursty traffic at high data rates. No provision was made for situations requiring real-time guarantees or hostile environments such as those that are found in manufacturing or process control applications.

The DEC-Intel-Xerox proposal set down a series of assumptions (goals and non-goals) that, with few exceptions, still govern the design of today's networks. Together, they defined a set of rules that governed the Ethernet design and that restricted several functional capabilities that they specifically chose not to include. These assumptions will be revisited in detail in later sections of this chapter as well as in several later chapters.

1.1.1 The Original Ethernet Goals

The original goals provided a definition of the capabilities and functional characteristics that were to be included in the Ethernet design.

- **Simplicity**. Features that would complicate the design without substantially contributing to the meeting of the other goals have been excluded.

- **Low Cost**. Because technological improvements will continue to reduce the overall cost of stations wishing to connect to the Ethernet, the cost of connection itself should be minimized.

- **Compatibility**. All implementations of the Ethernet should be capable of exchanging data at the data link level. For this reason, the specification avoids optional features in order to eliminate the possibility of incompatible variants of the Ethernet. (This goal is also known as the interoperability requirement.)

- **Addressing Flexibility**. The addressing mechanisms should provide the capability to target frames to a single node, a group of nodes, or to all nodes on the network.

- **Fairness**. All nodes should have equal access to the network when averaged over time.

- **Progress**. No single node operating in accordance with the protocol should be able to prevent the progress of other nodes.

- **High Speed**. The network should operate efficiently at a data rate of 10 Mbps.

- **Low Delay**. At any given level of offered traffic, the network should introduce as little delay as possible in the transfer of a frame.

- **Stability**. The network should be stable under all loads, in the sense that the delivered traffic should be a monotonically non-decreasing function of the total offered traffic.

- **Maintainability**. The Ethernet design should allow for network maintenance, operation, and planning.

- **Layered Architecture**. The Ethernet design should be specified in layered terms to separate the logical aspects of the data link protocol from the physical details of the communication medium.

1.1.2 The Ethernet Non-Goals

The original proposal also included several possibly desirable capabilities that were not to be included in the Ethernet design. These were stated as non-goals, which included the following:

- **Full-Duplex**. At any given instant, the Ethernet can transfer data from one source station to one or more destination stations. Bidirectional communication is provided by rapid exchange of frames, rather than full-duplex operation.

Note
Full-duplex operation allows a station to send and receive data frames at the same time. The full-duplex non-goal meant that when the DEC-Intel-Xerox group proposed Ethernet for development as a standard, they felt that full-duplex operation was not necessary, and that half-duplex bidirectional communication, one direction at a time, would be sufficient.

- **Error Control**. Error handling at the data link level is limited to the detection of bit errors in the physical channel, and the detection and recovery from collisions. Provision of a complete error control facility to handle detected errors is relegated to higher layers of the network architecture.

- **Security**. The data-link protocol does not employ encryption or other mechanisms to provide security. Higher layers of the network architecture may provide such facilities as appropriate.

- **Speed Flexibility**. This specification defines a physical channel operating at a single fixed data rate of 10 Mbps.

- **Priority**. The data-link protocol provides no support of priority station operation.

- **Hostile User**. There is no attempt to protect the network from a malicious user at the data link level.

The DEC-Intel-Xerox proposal implemented the lower two architectural layers of the new ISO open systems reference model [Zimmermann, 1980; ISO/TC97/SC16 N227, 1979]. They envisioned variable-length data frames being transmitted over a bus-connected coaxial cable (see Figure 1.1) with a "best effort" delivery policy. Detection of lost frames and recovery from transmission errors was left to higher-level layers of the ISO model.

Figure 1.1   The Basic Ethernet Bus

1.1.3   CSMA/CD Operational Principles

The Ethernet CSMA/CD (carrier-sense, multiple-access/collision-detect) protocol has three definitive rules:

- **Carrier Sense**. All active stations must continually listen to the network. If a signal carrier is present, the network is busy. If no carrier is present, the network is quiet and presumed not busy.

- **Multiple Access**. Any station may transmit a frame whenever it detects that the network has been quiet for a short period of time.

- **Collision Detect**. If two or more stations begin transmitting during one quiet period, the transmitted bit streams will interfere (collide) with each other. Each station must be able to detect bit-stream collisions during transmission.

The network itself is a passive broadcast media. There is no central network controller. Every station can listen to transmissions from every other station on the network, and every station is responsible for controlling its own transmission and reception.

The transmission unit is the Ethernet frame that consists of a synchronizing preamble, a Start-of-Frame Delimiter (SFD), destination and source addresses, a Length/Type indicator, Data and Pad fields, and a frame check sequence that provides for error detection. Frame size may be any integral number of octets (bytes) between a specified minimum and maximum. Destination addresses may be either the address of an individual station or the address of a previously defined group of stations.

1.1.3.1 Basic Transmission Methods

There are two basic, commonly used techniques for transmitting digital signals over a cable: baseband and broadband. Both transmission systems can use the same cable types, and both support shared use of the media.

In *baseband* systems, a stream of encoded digital pulses representing the data is transmitted directly onto the cable. The frequency spectrum of the pulse stream can extend from zero to some high value, depending on the bit rate, although the data encoder is often designed to remove the DC component and to attenuate the low frequencies. A cable can support only one baseband electromagnetic signal stream at a time. Shared use of the media can be accomplished by allocating a specific fixed segment of a time period to each user (this is known as time division multiplexing [TDM]) or by providing a way for the users to contend for exclusive short term use.

In *broadband* systems, the digital pulse stream is first modulated onto a sinusoidal carrier signal and the modulated carrier is then transmitted onto the cable. Bandpass filtering constrains the modulated carrier to occupy only a specific small band of frequencies in the spectrum. A number of modulated carriers can use the same cable if their assigned center frequencies are separated enough to ensure that the frequency bands do not overlap (this is known as frequency division multiplexing [FDM]). The other frequency bands may also be used for other signal purposes, such as audio or TV.

Baseband transmission is used for all modern Ethernet systems. A broadband option was specified during the early years, but received little acceptance in the marketplace.

1.1.3.2 *Ethernet Frame Transmission*

The CSMA/CD protocol allows any station to begin frame transmission any time after a brief interframe delay whenever the network becomes quiet (when no carrier is sensed). The station constructs the frame from the data supplied by the upper layers in the protocol stack, appends a preamble and Start-of-Frame Delimiter, and begins transmitting the bit stream onto the cable, but it does not yet know whether the transmission will be successful. Consider the example transmission sequence shown in Figure 1.2.

Figure 1.2   CSMA/CD Access Interference and Recovery Sequence

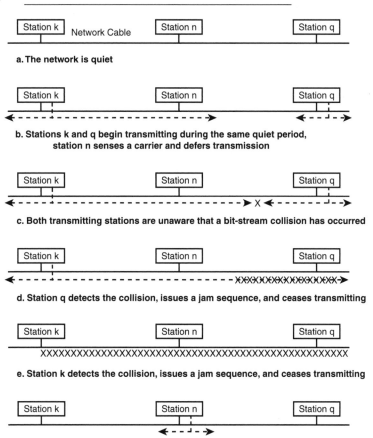

a. The network is quiet

b. Stations k and q begin transmitting during the same quiet period, station n senses a carrier and defers transmission

c. Both transmitting stations are unaware that a bit-stream collision has occurred

d. Station q detects the collision, issues a jam sequence, and ceases transmitting

e. Station k detects the collision, issues a jam sequence, and ceases transmitting

f. Station n detects that the network is quiet and begins transmitting before either station k's or station q's wait time expired

◄ - - - ►   transmitted bit stream
XXXXXXX   corrupted bit stream

If stations k and q both begin transmitting a frame during the same quiet period, the two bit streams will collide with each other at some time during the initial portion of the transmission (during the sequence depicted in parts [a], [b], and [c] of Figure 1.2). The combined bit stream will be different from either original stream, and will propagate in both directions back toward the two transmitting stations. When the received bit stream at a transmitting station is different from the bit stream being sent, the station knows that a collision has occurred. A short "jamming" sequence is sent to ensure that the collision will also be detected by all other involved transmitting stations and then the transmission is terminated (during the sequence shown in parts [c], [d], and [e] of Figure 1.2).

Indication of successful frame transmission requires a frame length long enough to ensure that a collision can be detected before the entire frame has been sent. The worst case occurs when the two stations are at opposite ends of the longest path in the network, and when the second station doesn't begin transmitting until just before the frame from the first station arrives. In this case, the time between transmit initiation and collision detection by the first station is twice the maximum propagation delay for the network. This period is known as the *collision window*.

The set of paths between all possible pairs of stations is called the *collision domain*. The length of the longest path in the collision domain is the collision domain diameter. When the collision window has expired, the transmitting station can assume that the frame will be correctly received. All other stations in the collision domain will have sensed the carrier and will be waiting until the network is quiet again before attempting transmission.

The rule allowing every station to begin transmission any time after the network goes quiet is modified for each station that is involved in a collision (see part [f] of Figure 1.2). To decrease the probability of repeated collisions between the same transmitting stations or with other stations attempting to send a frame, each colliding station delays its retransmission attempt for a randomly selected time period. If additional collisions still occur, the range of values from which the random wait time is selected is expanded after each successive collision until either the retransmission succeeds or the station reaches the established limit for the number of successive transmission attempts.

1.1.3.3 Ethernet Frame Reception

When the beginning of an incoming frame is detected, each station checks the destination address of the frame to determine whether or not it matches that station's individual or group address. If there is a match, the station receives the remainder of the incoming frame and checks the frame for transmission errors. Frames that have been involved in a collision are processed in the same manner as collision-free frames, but are detected as incomplete frames by the error checking procedures and are discarded. Complete frames received with detected transmission errors are also discarded without notification to the sending station. Recovery from transmission errors, including notification of the sending station, is the responsibility of upper layers in the ISO Open Systems Reference model protocol stack (Chapter 2, "The OSI and Gigabit Ethernet Standard Reference Models," provides a description of the ISO Open Systems Reference model and its relationship to the Ethernet layered architecture).

1.1.4 The Elements of an Ethernet Network

Internally, an Ethernet network consists of network stations (called DTEs, for data terminal equipment, in the standard), repeaters, bridges, and their interconnecting network media (buses and links).

1.1.4.1 Network Stations (DTEs)

DTEs are typically personal computers, workstations, or network servers such as printers and storage devices. Each DTE is equipped with all the necessary hardware and software to implement the functional requirements of the CSMA/CD protocol. There can be up to 1,024 DTEs on a network.

1.1.4.2 Repeaters

Repeaters allow the length and topology of the network to be extended beyond the limits of a single segment. Repeaters are the active connecting element between LAN segments, but are essentially passive from a network control standpoint. Only two of the three definitive Ethernet CSMA/CD protocol rules, carrier sense and collision detect, are implemented. Repeaters detect incoming frames from one segment (carrier sense), restore the signal characteristics of the received bit streams, and then repeat (transmit) the bit streams on the other connected segment. When a collision is detected on either segment, a jam signal is transmitted on both segments. A repeater is not a DTE and does not count toward the 1,024 overall station limit for a network.

1.1.4.3 Bridges

Bridges are special DTEs that are used to interconnect one LAN with another. They provide both protocol and speed translation, as needed, for frames originating in one network and being sent to a station on the other. The Ethernet connection to a bridge is the same as other Ethernet DTEs.

All incoming frames are checked for transmission errors, and are passed on only if they are error free. If the other connected LAN is also an Ethernet network, the bridge buffers and then retransmits the incoming frame at the transmission speed of the other LAN. If the other LAN is not an Ethernet network, the bridge also translates the incoming frame into the appropriate format for the other LAN's protocol. Bridges learn and store the source addresses of each station on both connected networks and forward only those frames addressed to stations known to be on the other network.

1.1.4.4 *Buses and Links*

The physical media connecting DTEs, repeaters, and bridges in an Ethernet network can be configured as either a bus or a link, depending on the media type, the transmission speed, and the cable's position in the network. Current media types include coaxial cable, twisted-pair copper cable, and optical fiber cable. There can be one, and only one, transmission path between any two stations on an Ethernet network.

1.2   *The Development of Ethernet*

The primary purpose of a communications network is to transfer information between network stations when it is needed and in a form that is both readable and error free. The primary purpose for a local area network standard is to establish physical and functional interoperability requirements that will ensure fully compatible operation in networks built with elements from different manufacturers.

The Ethernet protocol first became an official IEEE standard in 1985 and has since undergone a number of revisions and additions. All are published under the IEEE 802.3 and/or ISO/IEC 8802-3 number series.

ISO/IEC and IEEE Standards
The ISO/IEC publication dates typically lag one to two years behind publication as an IEEE standard because the international review and approval process usually does not begin until after IEEE approval is complete. Revisions are issued as supplements identified by a letter suffix appended to the number of the standard. When published, ISO/IEC standards can incorporate several IEEE supplements into the same document, and these documents always supersede the original IEEE publications. Only the latest ISO/IEC or IEEE versions of the standard should be used when implementing new or upgrading existing networks.

Sections 1.2.1–1.2.5 trace the development of Ethernet as it progressed from a 10 Mbps coaxial-bus-based network to star-configured networks that can support not only 10 Mbps, but also 100 Mbps and 1,000 Mbps transmission rates. However, because this discussion also includes a number of different Ethernet type names, you should first understand how to decode them.

The first generation Ethernet was not given the version name 10BASE5 until alternate cable types and transmission methods were defined. The first naming convention used a concatenation of the transmission data rate (in Mbps), followed by the transmission method (BASE for baseband; BROAD for broadband), followed by a numerical suffix that indicated either the length of the coaxial segment or the diameter network (in 100s m, rounded). For example:

- **10BASE5** = 10 Mbps, baseband, 500 m coaxial cable

- **10BASE2** = 10 Mbps, baseband, 185 m (approximately 200 m) coaxial cable

- **10BROAD36** = 10 Mbps, broadband, 3,600 m CATV cable (round trip 1,800 m maximum from the furthest point to the head end)

One early Ethernet element, the fiber optic inter-repeater link (FOIRL), retained its original name. Subsequent optical fiber links were identified by the naming convention.

Beginning with 10BASE-T, the third designator in the concatenation was separated from the first two designators by a dash and was changed to indicate the media type and, in some cases, the signal encoding. Examples of this later convention are as follows:

- **10BASE-T** = 10 Mbps, baseband, over two twisted-pair cable

- **100BASE-T4** = 100 Mbps, baseband, over four twisted-pair cable

- **100BASE-FX** = 100 Mbps, baseband, over fiber cable

- **1000BASE-CX** = 1,000 Mbps, baseband, over balanced copper jumper cable

- **1000BASE-LX** = 1,000 Mbps, baseband, long wavelength over fiber optic cable

- **1000BASE-SX** = 1,000 Mbps, baseband, short wavelength over fiber optic cable

The "X" suffix in the 100BASE series has a different meaning from the "X" in the 1000BASE series. The 100BASE-X series implementations use a 4B5B encoding scheme where each 4-bit half of a data octet is encoded as a 5-bit transmission symbol. The 1000BASE-X series implementations use an 8B10B encoding scheme where each 8th-bit data octet is encoded as a 10-bit transmission symbol. Transmission signal encoding is discussed in Chapter 5, "Fundamentals of Baseband Transmission."

The glossary contains a full list of Ethernet standard type names that were current at the time this book was published. Appendix A also includes a list of the applicable IEEE 802.3 Ethernet standards and both the Web site location and the address of the IEEE publications office.

1.2.1 First Generation Ethernet: 10 Mbps Over Coaxial Cable

First generation Ethernet (later known as 10BASE5) was defined in 1985 and was published as IEEE Std 802.3-1985. This Ethernet LAN was relatively expensive and somewhat difficult to install. The coaxial cable used for the Ethernet bus was large, almost a third of an inch in diameter, and stiff, with a 10-inch minimum bend radius. The interface cable between the coax bus and the DTE required seven shielded twisted-pair cables plus an outside shield. Connections to the coax bus could be made only at specified points on the cable, as shown in Figure 1.3.

Figure 1.3   Basic Coaxial Bus Segment Configuration

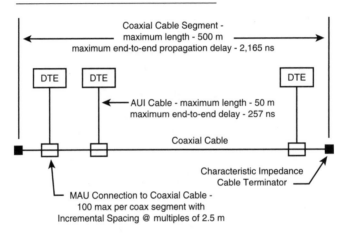

While the single-segment network was satisfactory in smaller installations, building layout restrictions and/or larger work forces could require networks configured with multiple segments. This required the definition of network building blocks and a list of bus/link configuration restrictions to ensure that the maximum path lengths did not violate the collision window.

Note

The Ethernet standard uses the term "segment" when referring to either coax bus segments or coax link segments. We use the added descriptors "bus" and "link" here to avoid confusion between the two segment types. After the definition of the 10BASE-FP passive star, coax bus segments were also called *mixing segments*.

1.2.1.1 *Coax-Based Network Building Blocks and Cable Restrictions*

The basic intersegment connection was a repeater set shown in Figure 1.4 and was used whenever the two coax bus segments were located within reach of the repeater's two Attachment Unit Interface (AUI) cables.

Figure 1.4   Basic Two-Segment Repeater-Set Interconnect

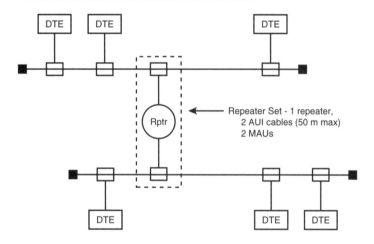

In cases where the two coax bus segments were further apart, the interconnect required two repeater sets connected by a coax link segment, as shown in Figure 1.5.

Figure 1.5   Two-Repeater-Set Remote Interconnect

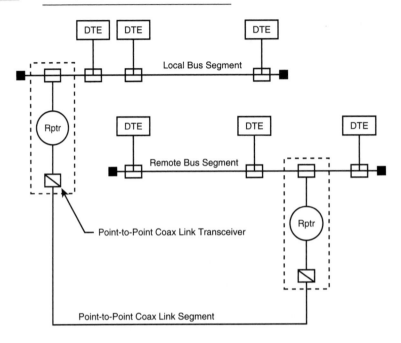

The repeater sets could be located at any Medium Attachment Unit (MAU) position on a coax bus segment, and the repeater's MAU counted toward that segment's 100 MAU allowance.

1.2.1.2 *Configuring Larger Coax-Based Networks*

Figures 1.3–1.5 provide the basic architectural building blocks needed to create much larger networks. The limiting factor is the length of the collision window, which is determined by the end-to-end propagation delay of all the elements in the transmission path. The collision window can be viewed as a propagation delay budget to be apportioned as worst-case delays among the stations and their AUI cables, the repeater sets, and the coax segments.

The delay values allocated represent a series of trade-offs between and among the desire for a geographically large network, the need to maintain network transmission efficiency and to minimize the probability of collisions during transmission attempts, and the physical limitations of the network elements. The end result was a list of network configuration restrictions like those shown in Table 1.1 for coax-based networks.

Table 1.1   Coax Network Configuration Restrictions

Network Connections	
Maximum number of MAUs per coax bus segment (DTE and repeater MAUs)	100
Maximum number of DTEs per collision domain	1,024
Coax Bus Segments	
Maximum number of MAUs per coax bus segment (DTE and repeater MAUs)	100
Maximum length of a coax bus segment	500 m
Maximum end-to-end propagation delay for a coax bus segment	2,165 ns
Coax Link Segments	
Maximum length of a coax link segment	not specified, but > 500 m
Maximum end-to-end propagation delay for a coax link segment	2,570 ns
Transmission Paths	
Maximum number of segments (coax bus + coax link) in a transmission path between any two stations on the network	5
Maximum number of coax bus segments in a transmission path	3
Maximum number of repeater sets in a transmission path	4

The definition of network building blocks plus the establishment of network configuration restrictions provided a guide for configuring much larger networks. Figure 1.6 shows an example of a central bus segment that is connected to other local and remote bus segments in a topology that limits the transmission path between any two stations on the network to no more than three bus segments, two link segments, and four repeaters.

Figure 1.6   A Large Network with Maximum Transmission Paths

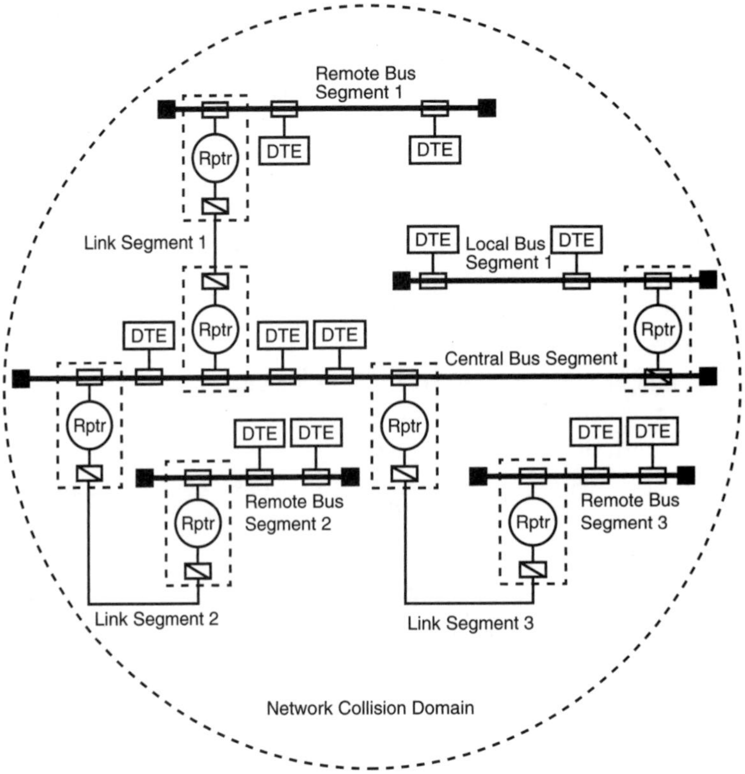

Note: If the entire network contains only two link segments and they are adjacent, a repeater set joining the two coax link segments is not required

The practice of using network building blocks and system restriction definitions plus attention to propagation delay budgets continues to be the primary guide for configuring new and/or upgrading existing networks.

The first generation of Ethernet networks was a major step forward. In spite of the cost and the installation difficulties, it accomplished the following objectives:

- It proved that the protocol was definitely viable.

- It established an easy network configuration methodology.

- It showed that there was a large market potential for the protocol.

However, the 10BASE-T generation proved to be the key to the marketplace.

1.2.2   10BASE-T Ethernet: 10 Mbps Over Voice-Grade Twisted-Pair Telephone Cable

Ethernet development continued down several different paths after the first-generation coax-based system was standardized; however, the most significant milestone by far in early LAN development and standardization was the introduction of 10BASE-T in 1990.

10BASE-T was the first truly mass market version of Ethernet. Its success was due to the use of multiport repeaters and structured telephone wiring, pioneered by StarLAN, to create the shared medium. The popularity of the 10BASE-T Ethernet and the IEEE 802.5 Token Ring LAN also fueled the development of several national and international structured cabling standards that have since become fundamental to LAN standardization.

The principle change for 10BASE-T was to the physical layer. The protocol and signaling method stayed the same, but new network building blocks, cable restrictions, and installation procedures were required.

1.2.2.1   10BASE-T Building Blocks and Cable Restrictions

10BASE-T represented three major changes in the basic Ethernet structure:

- The coax bus segments and their interconnecting repeaters were replaced with a new multiport repeater (that was also known as a hub). The coax bus segment was reduced to an internal connection within the repeater, and the segment's MAU positions became connection ports at the repeater interface. With the proper MAU configuration, a 10BASE-T repeater port could also be connected to other bus and link segments.

- The 10BASE-T station's AUI and MAU were made an internal part of the DTE interface.

- A new twisted pair telephone-cable link segment was defined for connection between the hub and the DTEs (see Figure 1.7). The typical office installation followed common telephone building wiring practice. 10BASE-T hubs are typically installed in wiring closets near the cross connect (patch) panels and the DTEs are connected to the link at a telephone wall jack.

Figure 1.7   10BASE-T Twisted-Pair Link

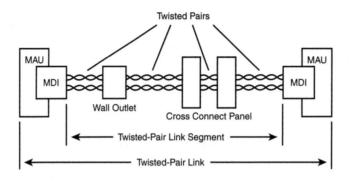

MDI - Medium Dependent Interface, with the connector jack in the MAU and
the connector plug attached to the twisted pair link segment

The result of these changes was the basic star-topology network building block shown in Figure 1.8 and the network configuration restrictions listed in Tables 1.2 and 1.3.

Figure 1.8   Basic 10BASE-T Single Repeater Network Configuration

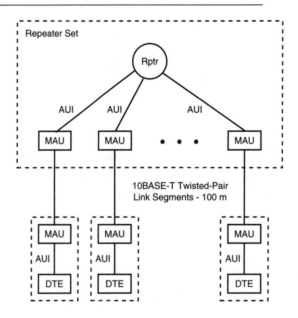

Note: The MAUs and AUIs are internal in both the repeater and the DTEs

Table 1.2   Network Media Segment Length Limits

Media Segment Type	Maximum Number of MAUs per Segment	Maximum Segment Length
Mixing Segment		
10BASE5 coax bus	100	500 m
10BASE2 coax bus	30	185 m
Non-Coax Links		
FOIRL fiber optic link	2	1,000 m
10BASE-T twisted-pair link	2	100 m[a]
10BASE-FB fiber optic bus	2	2,000 m
10BASE-FL fiber optic link	2	2,000 m

[a]The actual maximum length depends on the cable characteristics.

Table 1.3   10BASE-T Transmission Path Configuration Restrictions

Maximum Transmission Path between Any Two Stations on the Network	4 Repeater Sets and 5 Segments
4 repeater-set transmission paths	
Allowable number of mixing[a] segments	0–3
Allowable number of non-coax link segments (twisted-pair or optical fiber)	5 minus the number of mixing segments
Maximum FOIRL length in a 5-segment transmission path	500 m
3 repeater-set transmission paths	
Maximum FOIRL length	1,000 m

[a]A mixing segment could be a coax bus or an optical fiber passive star.

1.2.2.2 Configuring Larger 10BASE-T Networks

Considerable flexibility is allowed during configuration of a 10BASE-T network. The path between any pair of DTEs may include up to four repeaters and all three types of links: twisted-pair, coaxial cable, and optical fibers. The path is also called the collision domain. Figures 1.9 and 1.10 show two examples of maximum-diameter 10BASE-T collision domains.

Figure 1.9 Four-Repeater 10BASE-T Maximum-Transmission-Path Network with Twisted-Pair, Coaxial-Cable, and Fiber Optic Links

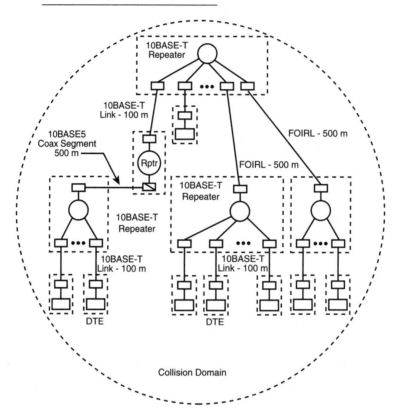

Figure 1.10 Three-Repeater 10BASE-T Network with Maximum Transmission Paths

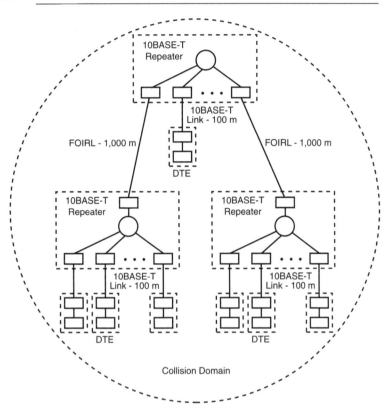

1.2.3 100BASE-X Fast Ethernet: 100 Mbps Over Copper and Optical Fiber Cables

Development of Fast Ethernet began in late 1993 and 100BASE-X became a standard in 1995. The foundations remained the same as those for 10BASE-T: Ethernet frame format, multiport repeaters, bridges, and structured wiring, but with ten times the transmission speed. Some trade-offs were required, however.

The telephone cable used for 10BASE-T will not support the transmission rates required for Fast Ethernet. First, there is too much signal degradation in telephone cable for 100 Mbps operation and second, the level of electromagnetic radiation allowed by the FCC and European regulatory bodies is exceeded during transmission. If appropriate unshielded twisted-pair (UTP) cable is not already available, new cable must be installed. The currently specified UTP cable is as follows:

- **100BASE-T4** uses four pairs of Category-3 or Category-5 balanced, UTP cabling.

- **100BASE-TX** uses two pairs of Category 5 UTP or shielded twisted-pair (STP) cable.

Note

Twisted-pair cabling for data transmission service is defined by EIA/TIA Standard 568. Several categories of UTP cables are available:

- **Category-1 and Category-2.** These cables are not covered by EIA/TIA 568. They are typically used for telephone service.

- **Category-3.** The characteristics of these cables are specified up to 16 Mbps. They are typically used for voice and data transmission rates up to 10 Mbps.

- **Category-5.** The characteristics of these cables are specified up to 100 Mbps. They are typically used for voice and data transmission rates up to 100 Mbps.

Well-designed signal encoding plus the use of multiple pairs can allow Category-3 cables to be used for transmission rates up to 100 Mbps.

The most severe trade-off with Fast Ethernet is with size of the network collision domain. Recall that any two DTEs on the network must be able to contend for network access at the same time, and that each station must be able to receive a returned collision signal within the time allotted by the collision window, regardless of where on the network the collision occurred. Also recall that the collision window is equal to the round-trip propagation time for the maximum transmission path and that the collision window must be shorter than the bit-stream transmit time for a minimum-length frame. Because the cable propagation velocity is constant and the transmission time for minimum-length frame now takes only one tenth the time required for the same length 10 Mbps stream, the length of the maximum transmission path must be reduced accordingly.

1.2.3.1 Fast Ethernet Building Blocks and Cable Restrictions

The three basic building blocks that have been defined for 100 Mbps networks are as follows:

* The DTE-to-DTE link shown in Figure 1.11 allows dedicated service between two high-traffic entities. Because this configuration will support two, and only two, DTEs, it is a complete collision domain.

* The single-repeater configuration shown in Figure 1.12 uses a Class I repeater and either 100BASE-FX fiber or twisted-pair links. Class I repeaters are used to connect different physical signaling systems (100BASE-T4 transmission uses a different signaling method than either 100BASE-TX or 100BASE-FX). Longer internal delays require that only one Class I repeater be used in a collision domain where maximum-length cables are implemented.

* The two-repeater configuration shown in Figure 1.13 uses Class II repeaters that have shorter internal delays and typically allow only one method of signal generation, either 100BASE-T4 or 100BASE-TX/FX, but not both.

Figure 1.11   100BASE Dedicated DTE-to-DTE Interconnect

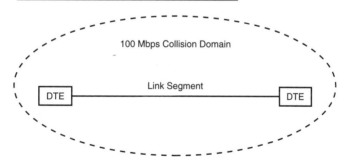

Figure 1.12   100BASE Single-Repeater Collision Domain

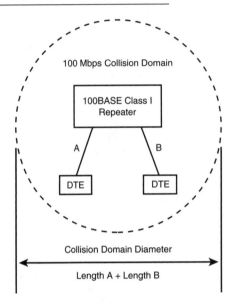

Figure 1.13   100BASE Two-Repeater Collision Domain

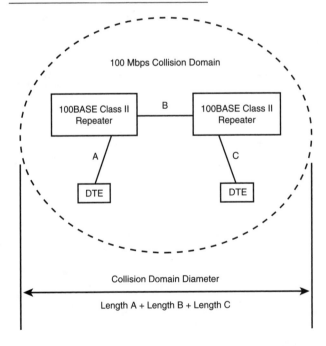

100BASE-X networks may be configured with either UTP copper or optical fiber links. The cable limits and network configuration restrictions for Fast Ethernet collision domains are listed in Table 1.4. The difference in allowable link lengths between UTP and optical fiber results from transmission over UTP copper links being limited by the characteristics of the link rather than the diameter of the collision domain.

Table 1.4   Fast Ethernet Maximum Collision-Domain Diameters[a]

Domain Configuration	Copper Links Only	Optical Fiber Links Only	Mixed T4 and FX Links	Mixed TX and FX Links
DTE-DTE	100 m	412 m	N/A	N/A
Single class I repeater	200 m	272 m	231 m[b]	260.8 m[b]
Single class II repeater	200 m	320 m	N/A	308.8 m[b]
Two class II repeaters	205 m	228 m	N/A	216.2 m[c]

[a]The diameters indicated are the maximum allowed. No margin is provided.

[b]Assumes one 100 m link of balanced copper cable and one fiber optic link.

[c]Assumes one 100 m link plus a 5 m jumper of balanced copper cable and one fiber optic link.

1.2.3.2 *Configuring Larger Fast Ethernet Networks*

Because the basic 100BASE building blocks already represent maximum collision domains, steps must be taken when it is necessary to extend network boundaries. One way is to interconnect several 100 Mbps collision domains with a bridge, as shown in Figure 1.14.

Figure 1.14 100 Mbps Multiple-Collision-Domain Topology Interconnected with a Multiport Bridge

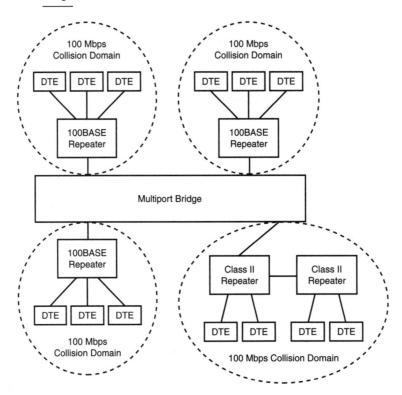

Another way to extend network boundaries is to analyze the bandwidth needs of the individual users. Many users may not need the higher-speed transmission rates. If this is the case, the network can be configured with both 10 Mbps and 100 Mbps collision domains. However, an even better way is to use a switch instead of a bridge.

1.2.4 Ethernet Switches: A Fast Ethernet Alternative

When it became apparent in 1994 that the collision domain for Fast Ethernet would be much smaller than the collision domain for 10BASE-T networks, development of switched alternatives was intensified.

Conceptually, a switch is just a next-generation multiport bridge that has been implemented in hardware. Each port on the switch appears to the connected DTE as just another DTE, and each port is equipped with multiple frame buffers. When the switch begins to receive a frame at one of its ports, it decodes the destination address and checks to determine whether the destination DTE's port is busy. If that port is not busy, and a non-busy internal path is available, the connection is made and the frame is transferred. If the destination port is busy, or no internal non-busy paths are available, the frame is held in the receiving port's buffer until the connection can be made.

Consider the basic 10BASE-T switch shown in Figure 1.15.

Figure 1.15 10BASE-T Basic Switch Configuration

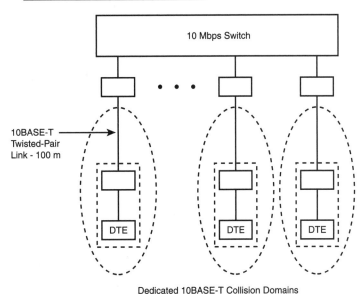

Dedicated 10BASE-T Collision Domains

Switches can be used to replace both repeaters and bridges in the network star topology. Switched networks have several advantages over repeater-based networks, some of which include the following:

- Dedicated collision domains between each port and its connected DTE reduces media contention and the probability of a collision during frame transmission.

- Multiple paths through the switch allow multiple frames to be transferred at the same time.

- Multiple switch-to-switch connections allow multiple frames to be transferred between switches at the same time (this is known as link aggregation or trunking—which will be discussed in Chapter 15, "The Future: Gigabit Ethernet and Beyond").

- A failure in one link is isolated from the rest of the network.

The net result of a switched network is increased effective bandwidth with no change in transmission speed, no change to the DTE interface, and no need to decrease the collision domain diameter or to replace part or all of the cable plant.

The next step in switch technology was the definition of a 10/100 switch equipped with 100 Mbps internal buses and universal ports that could accept either 10 Mbps or 100 Mbps links. The 10/100 switch provides increased network configuration flexibility because it allows high-traffic devices such as file servers to be assigned dedicated 100 Mbps service while most individual users are provided with 10 Mbps service (see Figure 1.16). The 10/100 switch also allows fiber optic link lengths to be increased to the DTE-to-DTE link limits shown in Table 1.4.

Figure 1.16   Dual Transmission Rate Switched Network

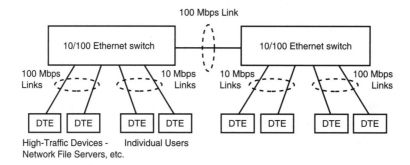

1.2.5   *Gigabit Ethernet: 1,000 Mbps Over Copper and Optical Fiber*

Gigabit Ethernet provides the data rate increase required to take Ethernet into a new, high-speed era. Gigabit Ethernet is founded on key principles of 10BASE-T, Fast and Switched Ethernet, and the Ethernet frame format over either shared or switched media in a network using standardized structured cabling.

The development of Gigabit Ethernet turned out to be a classic example of Goldstine's observation that advances in the state of the art result from someone seeing how to adapt technology to meet a need.

The Gigabit development team took the physical layer technology originally developed for the Fibre Channel Standard, improved it, and incorporated it into the physical layer of Gigabit Ethernet. The result is another tenfold increase in Ethernet data rate, at a lower cost, and in less time than would have been required to develop a new technology. Gigabit Ethernet was approved as a standard in 1998.

The primary longer-distance Gigabit Ethernet link media is single-mode optical fiber (SMF) with a 10 μm core diameter or multimode optical fiber (MMF) with either a 50 μm core diameter or 62.5 μm core diameter. Two transmission wavelengths, 850 nm (SX—short wavelength) and 1300 nm (LX—long wavelength) are supported. Four-pair Category-5 UTP copper cable can be used for distances up to 100 m.

> **Note**
>
> Single-mode optical fiber is also known as mono-mode optical fiber, but for brevity, the rest of the book will refer to it as single-mode or SMF.

1.2.5.1 *Gigabit Building Blocks and Cable Restrictions*

The basic Gigabit Ethernet building blocks use the same model as the 100BASE dedicated DTE-to-DTE interconnect in Figure 1.11 and the 100BASE single-repeater collision domain in Figure 1.12. Tables 1.5 and 1.6 list the cable limits and collision domain diameters defined for Gigabit Ethernet.

Table 1.5 Cable Limits for Gigabit Ethernet Networks Defined by the Standard

Media Type	Maximum Segment Length[a]
1000BASE-T Balanced Category-5 UTP copper link	100 m
1000BASE-CX TW-style copper link	25 m
1000BASE-SX short wavelength, 62.5 μm multimode fiber optic link	275 m
1000BASE-SX short wavelength, 50 μ multimode fiber optic link	550 m[b]
1000BASE-LX long wavelength, 62.5 μm multimode fiber optic link	550 m[b]
1000BASE-LX long wavelength, 50 μm multimode fiber optic link	550 m[b]
1000BASE-LX,long wavelength, 10 μm single-mode fiber optic link	5,000 m[b]

[a]May be limited by the maximum qualified transmission distance of the link.

[b]The actual distance may be shorter or longer, depending on the bandwidth of the fiber (see Chapter 11, "1000BASE-X: Optical Fiber and Copper PMDs").

Table 1.6   Gigabit Ethernet Maximum Collision-Domain Diameters[a]

Domain Configuration	Category-5 Copper Links Only	TW-Style Copper Links Only	Optical Fiber Links Only	Mixed Category-5 & Optical Fiber Links	Mixed TW-Style & Optical Fiber Links
DTE-DTE	100 m	25 m	320 m[b]	N/A	N/A
Single repeater	200 m	50 m	220 m	210 m[c]	220 m[d]

[a]The diameters indicated are the maximum allowed. No margin is provided.

[b]May be limited by the maximum qualified transmission distance of the link.

[c]Assumes one 100 m of Cat-5 link and one 110 m fiber optic link.

[d]Assumes 25 m of TW-style cable and one 195 m fiber optic link.

1.2.5.2 Configuring Larger Gigabit Ethernet Networks

Larger Gigabit Ethernet networks can be configured with bridges in the same manner as Fast Ethernet networks; however, 10/100/1,000 Ethernet switches offer the greatest flexibility. Figure 1.17 shows an example of a network that has been periodically upgraded that might be found in a research and development facility.

Figure 1.17 Large Triple Transmission Rate Network

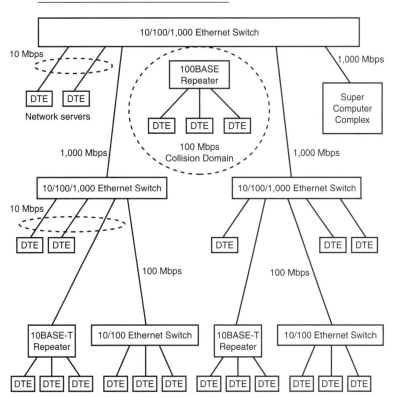

1.3 The Evolution and Current State of Ethernet

Ethernet will soon be entering its third decade. Much has changed since the original proposal and the number of options available for configuring Ethernet networks has grown markedly. The following chapters address, in detail, the improvements and changes that have been made to various aspects of Ethernet.

1.3.1 Transmission Rate

The most obvious change in Ethernet networks over the past decade has been two tenfold increases in the transmission data rate. As shown in Table 1.7, however, these increases have also had a severe impact on the maximum diameter of the collision domain.

Table 1.7   Maximum Collision Domain Diameters

Network Configuration	Maximum Collision Domain Diameter[a]
10BASE5 Coax	3,000 m
10BASE-T, three repeaters	1,700 m[b]
10BASE-T, four repeaters	2,200 m[b]
100BASE-X, DTE-to-DTE	100 m (copper), 412 m (optical fiber)
100BASE-X, single repeater	200 m (copper), 320 m (optical fiber)
100BASE-X, dual repeater	205 m (copper), 228 m (optical fiber)
1000BASE-X, DTE-to-DTE	25 m (copper), 316 m (optical fiber)
1000BASE-X, single repeater	50 m (copper), 220 m (optical fiber)
1000BASE-T, DTE-to-DTE	100 m (Category-5 UTP copper)

[a]Approximate, based on maximum segment/link length plus AUI cables. The actual diameter depends on the limit of the total end-to-end propagation delay.
[b]FOIRL repeater-to-repeater and twisted-pair repeater-to-DTE links.

1.3.2 Switches

The development of multi-speed switches has been an equally significant factor in the market acceptance of higher-speed Ethernet networks. Switches offer the following improvements to Ethernet networks:

- Switches are the key to configuration flexibility that allows overall network diameters to be restored and expanded.

- Switches provide a greater total network bandwidth than is allowed by the same technology in shared media configurations.

1.3.3 The Star Topology and Its Effect on Network Installation

The market acceptance of the 10BASE-T star topology not only made Ethernet the major LAN protocol, it also led to the development of building cabling standards that are now accepted by the entire industry. This, plus the development of better cable types and new techniques for data transmission, have resulted in physical cable plants that are easier to install and less costly to maintain. Each user station is wired directly to a cross-connect panel in a centrally located communication wiring closet similar to those used for ordinary telephone service. Repeaters, bridges, and/or switches typically occupy rack space in the same closet as the cross-connect panels. This setup, in turn, has centralized most network maintenance, including moves and changes, which can be made by simply disconnecting and reconnecting jumper cables.

1.3.4 New Functional Capabilities

Other link options have been defined for 10 Mbps and 100 Mbps networks. (See the "Numerics" section of the Glossary.) These have not been discussed because they either have had little acceptance in the marketplace, or didn't play an important role in the developments leading up to Gigabit Ethernet.

Full-duplex operation, flow control, and VLAN tag are three new functional capabilities that deserve mention. All will be described in Chapter 3, "Media Access Control," and then discussed in several later chapters.

1.3.4.1 Full-Duplex Operation

Full-duplex operation allows simultaneous two-way transmission in DTE-to-DTE configurations, such as switch-to-switch and switch-to-server. The possibility of collisions is eliminated and the effective bandwidth of the link is doubled.

1.3.4.2 Flow Control

The optional MAC Control capability provides a way to control the flow of traffic on the network and to reduce the probability the frames would be lost because of buffer overflow in bridges and switches.

1.3.4.3 VLAN Tagging

VLAN tagging is an optional capability that is designed to allow creation of a separate virtual network for group users based on a logical identification rather than their physical addresses. This, in turn, reduces both the number of addresses that must be maintained in switch address tables and the time required to track adds, moves, and changes in the network configuration. But equally important for local Ethernet LANs, VLAN tagging also allows assignment of a user priority, which can be used to indicate transmission priorities for time-critical frames such as those for multimedia and process control.

1.3.5   Perspective on the Original Ethernet Goals

All but two of the original goals for Ethernet remain solidly in place. One of the changes was recognized as a need from the beginning. Reluctantly, the other change has only recently been agreed upon.

- **High Speed**. The proposed goal was for a network that would operate at 10 Mbps. This goal was modified in the first edition of the standard. It limited specification and parameter value definition to those required for 10 Mbps operation, but stated, "This standard is intended to encompass several media types and techniques for signal rates from 1 Mbps to 20 Mbps." Subsequent editions of the standard have added definitions for 1 Mbps, 100 Mbps, and 1,000 Mbps operation with no change to the Ethernet protocol.

- **Compatibility**. The original goal stated, "All implementations of the Ethernet should be capable of exchanging data at the data link level. For this reason, the specification avoids optional features, to eliminate the possibility of incompatible variants of the Ethernet." VLAN tagging will require adding four octets to the frame format.

1.3.6   Perspective on the Original Ethernet Non-Goals

Three original non-goals (specific capabilities that were not to be included in the original Ethernet) have been included in later versions of the standard. Speed, flexibility, and full-duplex operation did not require any change to the protocol. Priority capability required a change in the MAC frame format and, as such, constitutes a change in the protocol that affects interoperability. (Network devices without VLAN tagging capability will not be able to recognize priority assignment, and could reject a maximum-length VLAN-tagged frame as being oversized.) All three capabilities, which are laid out in the following list, represent improvements for network operation.

- **Speed Flexibility**. The non-goal of defining only a single fixed data rate of 10 Mbps was eliminated during the 1980s with the definition of the 1BASE5 1Mbps protocol, which never gained market acceptance. The real changes were from 10 Mbps to 100 Mbps to 1,000 Mbps.

- **Full Duplex**. Full-duplex operation (simultaneous two-way transmission over a link) is now possible for dedicated link configurations.

- **Priority**. VLAN tagging allows the assignment priority levels 000 (no priority) through 111 (highest priority). Priority recognition can allow a switched-media network to also be used for time-sensitive applications, such as process control and multimedia applications.

1.4 A Cautionary Conclusion

You should not assume that the forgoing discussion immediately qualifies you to plan and install or manage a Gigabit Ethernet network. There are still a number of concepts and details to be discussed, particularly with respect to high-speed data transmission and signal recovery in both copper and optical fiber media; the qualification of network transmission path lengths; the use of the added capabilities such as flow control, full-duplex operation, and VLAN tagging; and the configuration of multi-speed networks.

CHAPTER 2

The OSI and Gigabit Ethernet Standard Reference Models

> The term 'open' denotes the capability of an end-system of one manufacturer (or design) to connect with any other end-system conforming to the reference model and the associated standard protocols. [Harold C. Folts, discussing the Open Systems Interconnection Model—Folts, 1981]

Until the late 1970s, most data communications networks only allowed data exchange between computers produced by the same manufacturer, but not between computers from different manufacturers. The most notable exception was the Advanced Projects Research Agency Network (ARPANET) developed by the U.S. Department of Defense (DoD). DoD needed a way to provide for data communications between projects located at government R&D labs and at some of the country's major research universities.

A similar situation was emerging in Europe. European companies and national labs also needed to exchange data, but here, too, there was often no system commonality between organizations.

The competing manufacturers' design emphasis was on *implementation* and not on cooperation. Everyone wanted to lead and no one wanted to follow.

Consistency was clearly needed, and in 1977, the International Organization for Standardization (ISO) established a committee to develop an architecture that could be a *framework* for defining standard protocols for linking heterogeneous computer systems. The committee's emphasis was on communication systems *architecture*, on its logical parts, and on how these parts communicated with each other. Their effort resulted in the seven-layer Open Systems Interconnection (OSI) model, which became an ISO standard in 1979. That model has since become the architectural reference model for all the local and metropolitan area network (LAN and MAN) standards that have been developed by the IEEE 802 LAN/MAN committee and its working groups (including IEEE 802.3) during the last two decades.

The primary purpose of the OSI model was to establish clear architectural divisions of responsibility (architectural layers) for the various communication tasks. A second purpose was to provide flexibility for the definition of competing lower-layer transmission protocols that could still be compatible at higher layers.

The purpose of this chapter is to introduce the concept of layered architectures and the use of abstract service primitives to define both the functions (services) provided within each layer and the information flow between adjacent layers of the model.

Our reason for including this material is based on our experience during development of the IEEE 802.12 Demand Priority LAN standard. We found that a number of the 802.12 working group members did not understand the purpose or appreciate the power of using abstract service primitives as part of an internal functional definition. The cost was the time to bring everyone to a working understanding of the concept, plus the additional time to convince them that the concepts really worked.

Layered architectures and the use of service primitives are concepts that are necessary for a full understanding of both the Ethernet standard and several later chapters of this book. We will begin with a brief description of the OSI model and an introduction to the use of primitives to control information flow across the layer-to-layer interfaces.

2.1 The ISO/OSI Reference Model

The protocol functions of the OSI reference model are divided into seven distinct functional groups (layers) that are essentially independent of each other (see Figure 2.1). The upper three layers (application, presentation, and session) relate to application issues, while the lower four layers (transport, network, data link, and physical) deal with network control and data transmission/reception.

Until recently, the bottom two layers (data link and physical) were implemented in hardware and software, and the other layers in software only. With the development of application specific integrated circuits (ASIC) chips and the supporting software applications packages for computer aided design (CAD) and circuit simulation, hardware implementation of the second and third layers is becoming more and more common.

Figure 2.1   The OSI Seven-Layer Reference Model

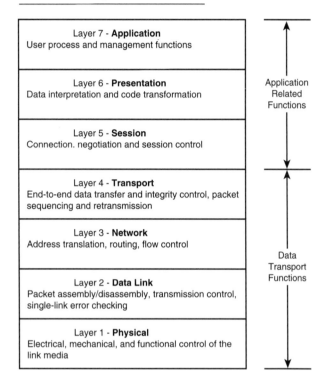

The functional units within each layer establish what is to be done, but not how to do it. The specific functions provided by each layer may vary somewhat, depending on the requirements of the particular protocol implemented for the layer. (Ethernet, for example, adds carrier sense and collision detect to the physical layer functions.) The following list describes typical functions in each layer of the model.

- **Application Layer**. Functions as the user's network interface. This layer typically handles login and password authentication, provides directory service, sets up associations between named peers, performs message handling, and handles concurrency and recovery.

- **Presentation Layer**. Negotiates the transfer syntax and performs any necessary data conversions, such as character set and text stream translations and any encryption/decryption that are required to allow the two end nodes to communicate with each other.

- **Session Layer**. Establishes and manages the communication session. This layer maps addresses to names, decides when to start and stop a communication, and controls when each device transmits and for how long.

- **Transport Layer**. The highest layer directly concerned with data transfer across the network. The transport layer is responsible for ensuring reliable communication between the transmitting and receiving devices. This layer handles end-to-end error detection and recovery, provides flow control, monitors the quality of service, and may disassemble/ reassemble the session data and/or reorder out of sequence packets.

  OSI transport layers provide for up to five transport protocol classes. TP0 through TP3 all require connection-oriented network service (see section 2.1.1). TP4 allows either connection-oriented or connectionless network service.

- **Network Layer**. Sets up the network routing, translates addresses, recognizes packet (frame) priorities, sends packets in proper priority order, and handles internetworking. The network layer may also disassemble and reassemble transport data structures if the data length is too long for the maximum frame size of the local area network protocol. An important network layer protocol for Ethernet systems is the Internet Protocol (IP).

- **Data Link Layer**. Provides access to the LAN and ensures reliable transfer across a single link. For transmission, this layer formats data frames, generates frame check sequences for error detection, and initiates transmissions. On frame reception, this layer filters destination addresses and checks for transmission and frame format errors. The data link layer provides indication of, but not recovery from, transmission errors. Recovery from transmission errors is the responsibility of higher layers in the protocol stack.

- **Physical Layer**. Responsible for all electrical, optical, and mechanical requirements for connection to the communication media. This layer provides bit stream encoding/decoding, synchronization, clock recovery, and transmission/reception.

2.1.1 *Types of Network Services*

There are two types of network service, connection-oriented and connectionless. The connection-oriented service is patterned after telephone service, where a dedicated communication path (the connection) is set up and is maintained until all the data has been transmitted. The connection may be either actual or virtual, and once the path has been set up, packets may be sent with minimal header information attached. Successive data packets will be received in the order they are sent.

Connectionless service (also known as *datagram* service) is patterned after telegraph service, where each data packet contains all the addressing information necessary to transfer the packet from source to destination without a communication path being first set up. Because there is no fixed connection, and because the routing may vary from packet to packet, datagram packets may be received in a different order than they are sent.

2.1.2 *Network Service Primitives*

The functions in any layer (n) of the OSI model provide a set of services which can be performed for the next higher layer ($n+1$) or which may be used for the exchange of information with its peer layer (n) in the associated network entity. The functions of layer (n) are built on the services it requires from the next lower layer ($n-1$).

The services in each layer are specified by the information flow between adjacent layers. The information flow is described by an abstract set of primitives that identify the particular service that is requested or that has been provided. Each primitive may have one or more parameters that convey any information required to provide the service, and a particular service may have one or more primitives that are related to the desired function.

The primitives that we are most interested in are those defined for the lower layers of the model. They fall into four generic categories:

- **Request**. A primitive that is passed from a layer (n) to a lower layer ($n-1$) to request that a service be initiated.

- **Indication**. A primitive that is passed from a lower layer (n) to an upper layer ($n+1$) to indicate an event or condition significant to layer ($n+1$). The event may be logically related to a remote request primitive or it may have been caused by a condition that is internal to the layer (n).

- **Response**. A primitive that is passed from a layer (n) to a lower layer ($n-1$) to complete a procedure previously invoked by an indication primitive.

- **Confirmation**. A primitive that is passed from a lower layer ($n-1$) to an upper layer ($n+1$) to provide the results from one or more previously invoked request primitives.

There are a number of possible relationships among the four types of primitives, as shown in Figure 2.2. A dotted linear line connecting two primitives indicates a logical relationship between the primitives and the internal processing delay of the layer. A dotted curved line in the shape of a tilde (~) connecting two primitives indicates that both primitives must occur within a finite period of time, but that it is impossible to predict which will occur first.

Figure 2.2   Service Primitive Time/Sequence Relationship Examples

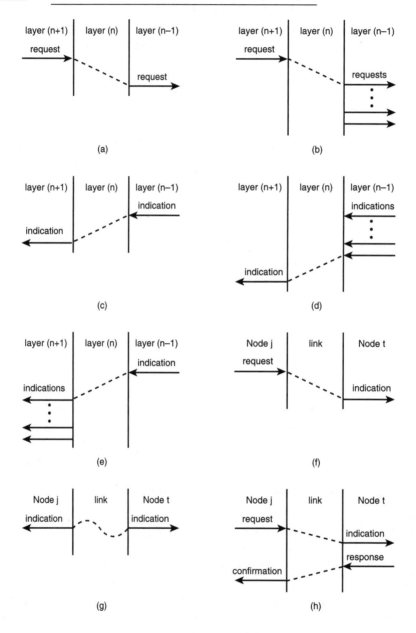

Within a specific layer, receipt of a single request primitive may result in the generation of one or more request primitives being generated and passed to the next lower layer, as

shown in parts (a) and (b) of Figure 2.2. A request to transfer a data file from the transport layer, for example, may result in the later generation of several requests by the network layer to transmit several smaller data packets across the network.

Similarly, one or more indications received at a lower layer may result in one or more indications being later generated to an upper layer, as shown in parts (c), (d), and (e) of Figure 2.2. In the previous file transfer example, the data link layer might indicate the valid reception of each packet, whereas the network layer would only indicate the valid reception of the entire file.

Part (f) of Figure 2.2 is a little more abstract because the link is a passive device and cannot interpret primitives and parameters. The bit stream that is passed between the transmitting physical layer and the link, however, can be viewed as a request by the physical layer of the transmitting entity, which becomes an indication when it reaches the physical layer of the receiving entity. Part (g) of Figure 2.2 is an example of a link condition or event, such as the presence of a carrier or a bit stream collision, that causes the generation of an indication at each end of the link. Finally, part (h) of Figure 2.2 might be an upper layer requesting the establishment of a connection and later receiving confirmation that it has been done.

2.1.3   Network Communication Under the OSI Model

In the peer-to-peer mode, communication between networks may be with either its associated peer layer in the destination node or with a peer layer in an intermediate network entity, as shown in Figure 2.3.

Figure 2.3   Peer-to-Peer Communication Paths Over an Extended Network

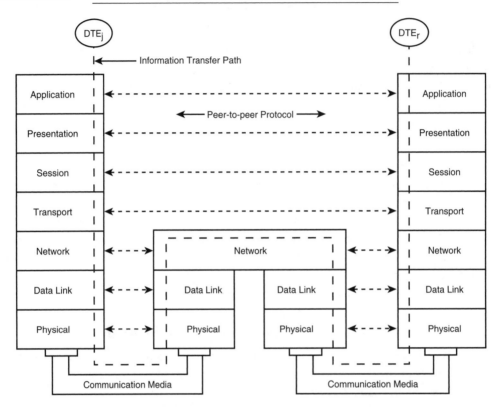

Data transfer begins with the sender's request to the application layer for a data structure transfer, progresses down through lower layers, crosses over the link media, and then rises as data indications through all the layers of the receiving device (see Figure 2.4).

Figure 2.4   OSI Layer-to-Layer Data Transfer

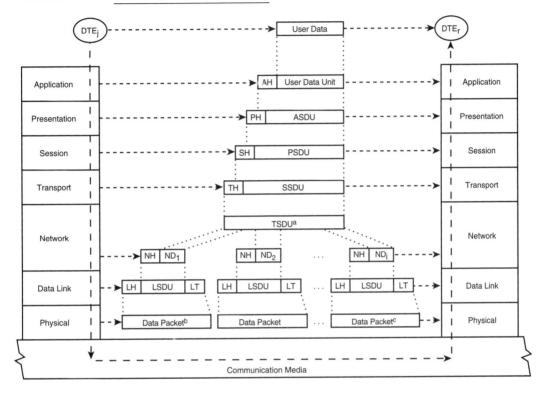

AH = Application Header
PH = Presentation Header
SH = Session Header
TH = Transport Header
NH = Network Header
LH = Link Header
LT = Link Trailer

ASDU = Application Service Data Unit
PSDU = Presentation Service Data Unit
SSDU = Session Service Data Unit
TSDU = Transport Service Data Unit
ND = Network Service Data Unit
LSDU = Link Service Data Unit

Notes: [a] The TSDU is disassembled into transmission protocol lengths by the network layer
       in the transmitting DTE and reassembled by the network layer in the receiving DTE
       [b] Data Packet = (LH+LSDU+LT) after encoding for transmission
       [c] The length of the last data packet is typically less than the maximum packet length

In the sending mode, each layer accepts the data unit from above, adds a layer header, and transfers that layer's data unit (the header plus the data unit from the layer above) to the layer below. The length of upper layer's data unit is checked at both the transport and network layers and, if the length is longer than the next lower layer's maximum data unit length, the received data unit is separated (disassembled) into lengths that can be handled by the next lower layer.

In the example shown in Figure 2.4, the network layer receives a transport service data unit (TSDU) that is longer than the maximum allowed for a link service data unit (LSDU):

- The network layer then disassembles the TSDU into a sequence of separate transmission protocol length data segments and adds a network header (NH) to each, forming a series of LSDUs that are passed to the data link layer.

- The data link layer adds its own protocol header (LH) plus an error detection trailer (LT—a frame check sequence called the FCS) to each LSDU. The concatenated sequence—data link header, LSDU, and data link trailer—is then passed to the physical layer.

- The physical layer then encodes the octets in the LSDU into transmission symbols and transmits the packet in serial fashion over the link. The transmitted data packet is depicted in Figure 2.4 as being longer than the LSDU to emphasize the fact that some encoding schemes require more than 8 bits for the transmitted character symbol (in Gigabit Ethernet, each 8-bit data octet is encoded as 10-bit transmission symbol).

All the packets that make up the TDSU are transmitted at the maximum length allowed by the protocol except the last, which is typically less than maximum (few files are exactly an integer multiple of maximum length packets).

In the receiving mode, each associated layer interprets and strips the layer header, and if no errors are indicted, passes the received data up to the next higher layer. In the example shown, the physical layer decodes the incoming bit stream as it is received to restore the data octets. The data link layer then strips and interprets the received header and generates its own frame check sequence, which is checked against the transmitted FCS. If no errors are detected, the received LSDU is passed to the network layer, where it is reassembled into a TSDU.

The content of each service data unit header is transparent to all lower layers and will vary from layer to layer. The header content may also vary according to the implemented protocol for any particular layer.

Not all network configurations implement all seven layers of the OSI model because many networks do not provide the services defined for the upper layers. Standalone Ethernet LANs, for example, implement only the lowest two layers, data link and physical. Access to the Internet from an Ethernet LAN requires the addition of the network and transport layers to implement the TCP/IP protocols of the Internet Protocol Suite.

Additional information about the various protocols that are implemented in the upper five layers, including expanded definition of transport protocol classes TP0 through TP4 and TCP/IP, is available in Ford et al, 1997. This chapter concentrates on the Ethernet implementation of the lower two OSI layers and their relationship with the network layer.

2.2   *The Gigabit Ethernet Reference Model*

The Gigabit Ethernet reference model, defined in IEEE 802.3z and shown in Figure 2.5, represents a continuing evolution in the Ethernet logical structure. In the early Ethernet versions, the functions in the OSI data link layer were separated into two IEEE 802 sublayers, the Logical Link Control (LLC) and the Media Access Control (MAC). Later versions rename the LLC sublayer as the MAC Client sublayer and expand its definition to include bridges and other undefined entities as well as the LLC. The OSI physical layer functions are also separated into several sublayers, and the model, as shown, includes all the physical layer variations that have been defined since 1985.

Figure 2.5   The IEEE 802.3 Ethernet Reference Model

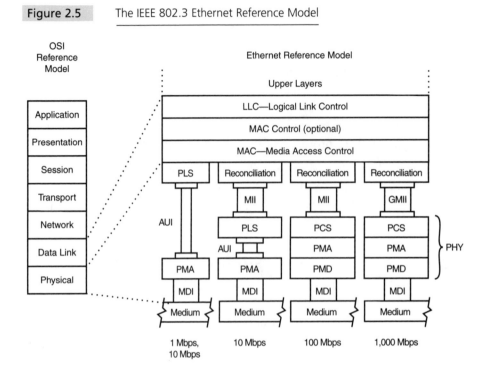

AUI = Attachment Unit Interface
GMII = Gigabit Media Independent Interface (optional)
MDI = Medium Dependent Interface
MII = Media Independent Interface (optional)
MAU = Medium Attachment Unit

PCS = Physical Coding Sublayer
PHY = Media Dependent PHY Group
PLS = Physical Layer Signaling Sublayer
PMA = Physical Medium Attachment Sublayer
PMD = Physical Medium Dependent Sublayer

An actual implementation, however, would contain the MAC Client, the MAC and its optional sublayers, and only those physical layer elements that are needed for its particular transmission rate and communication medium. Because we are primarily interested in Gigabit operation, the model can be redrawn as shown in Figure 2.6.

Figure 2.6   A Gigabit Ethernet Implementation Model

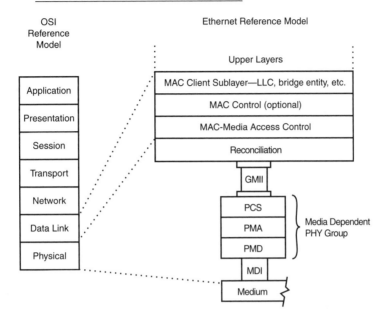

GMII = Gigabit Media Independent Interface
MDI = Medium Dependent Interface
PCS = Physical Coding Sublayer
PMA = Physical Medium Attachment Sublayer
PMD = Physical Medium Dependent Sublayer

Separation of the data link layer into the MAC Client and the MAC Group sublayers adds another layer to the data transfer diagram shown in Figure 2.4. IEEE 802 MAC Client sublayers also add a header before they transfer the MAC service data unit (MSDU) to the MAC Group sublayers, as illustrated in Figure 2.7.

Figure 2.7 Ethernet Layer-to-Layer Data Transfer

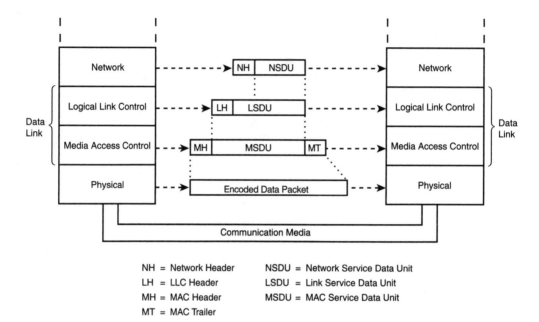

NH = Network Header   NSDU = Network Service Data Unit
LH = LLC Header   LSDU = Link Service Data Unit
MH = MAC Header   MSDU = MAC Service Data Unit
MT = MAC Trailer

The MAC Client sublayer is the only sublayer of the Ethernet model that is not defined in the IEEE 802.3 standard. The IEEE 802 LAN/MAN Standards Committee has separately defined the LLC and bridge entities in a manner that allows them to be common to all IEEE 802 protocols. We will begin our discussion of the Ethernet model with the LLC sublayer, which is common to end stations and network servers. Chapter 4, "Gigabit Repeaters, Bridges, Routers, and Switches," will cover the intermediate network devices— bridges and their derivatives (switches and routers).

2.2.1 *Logical Link Control (LLC) Sublayer*

The LLC sublayer is defined as ISO/IEC 8802-3:1994 (IEEE Std 802.2-1994). This sublayer provides services to allow the local network layer entity to exchange protocol data units (PDUs) with remote peer network entities in any of the following three ways:

- **LLC Type 1 Operation**. Unacknowledged connectionless-mode service where the network entities can exchange link service data units (LSDUs) without establishing a link connection. Data transfer is point-to-point and may be unicast (addressed to one receiving station only), multicast (addressed to a defined group of receiving stations), or broadcast (addressed to the group that includes all stations on the network).

- **LLC Type 2 Operation**. Connection-mode service where the LLC is able to establish, use, reset, and terminate data link layer connections.

  - Connection establishment allows the network entity to request or to respond to a request for the establishment of a data link layer connection.

  - Connection-oriented data transfer allows PDUs to be sent and received over the network. This service also provides LSDU sequencing, flow control, and error recovery of unacknowledged LSDUs.

  - Connection flow control provides a way to control the flow of packets associated with a specific connection between the LLC and the network layer.

  - Connection reset provides a way to return an established connection to its initial state.

  - Connection termination allows the LLC to request or to respond to a request for connection termination.

- **LLC Type 3 Operation**. Acknowledged connectionless-mode service where the network entities can exchange LSDUs that are acknowledged by the receiving entity without establishing a link connection. Data transfer is point-to-point.

The IEEE 802 standard mandates that all LLCs must support at least Type 1 operation and may also support either or both Type 2 and Type 3 operations in one of the specific LLC implementation classes shown in Table 2.1.

Table 2.1   LLC Implementation Classes

Supported LLC Operation Types	LLC Class I	LLC Class II	LLC Class III	LLC Class IV
1. Unacknowledged connectionless mode	x	x	x	x
2. Connection mode		x		x
3. Acknowledged connectionless mode			x	x

Because Ethernet currently only supports LLC Class I operation, the discussion here is limited to that class only. The last three chapters of the book revisit connection-mode operation.

2.2.2   *The Media Access Control Sublayer Group*

The MAC group currently consists of two sublayers: one mandatory sublayer and one optional sublayer. (Chapter 15, "The Future: Gigabit Ethernet and Beyond," discusses a third MAC group sublayer, link aggregation, which is currently under development.)

The MAC is the only mandatory sublayer in the MAC group. This is the primary control entity for access to the network. On receipt of an MA_UNITDATA.request primitive from the LLC, the MAC formats a data frame from the information in the provided parameters, adding its own header and error check trailer. When the link goes quiet, it initiates and controls the transmission. When a frame is received, the MAC checks it for validity, strips the header and trailer, and, if no errors are detected, generates an MA_UNITDATA.indication primitive that is passed to the LLC.

The optional MAC Control sublayer allows implementation of flow control procedures and contains provisions for adding other control functions in the future.

2.2.3   *LLC/MAC Service Primitives*

Figure 2.8 shows the primitives that are required for the basic MAC implementations (a MAC that is implemented without any optional provisions) and for implementations that also include optional provisions, such as the MAC Control sublayer.

Figure 2.8   LLC/MAC Group Service Primitives

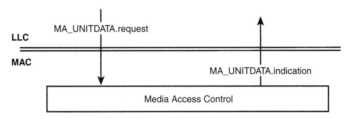

(a) Without the Optional MAC Control Sublayer Implemented

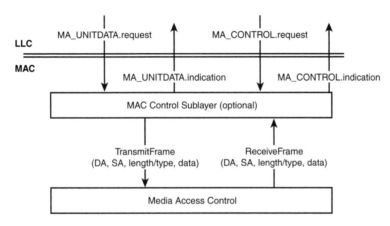

(b) With the Optional MAC Control Sublayer Implemented

The MA_UNITDATA.request and MA_UNITDATA.indication primitives are mandatory. The MAC_CONTROL.request and MAC_CONTROL.indication primitives are required only if the MAC Control sublayer is implemented. TransmitFrame and ReceiveFrame are internal pass-through MAC-group primitives that are required for transferring information between the MAC and the MAC Control sublayers. TransmitFrame and ReceiveFrame are content equivalent to the MA_UNITDATA.request and the MA_UNITDATA.indication primitives. Table 2.2 lists the parameters associated with each of LLC/MAC service primitives. Figure 2.8 shows parameters associated with TransmitFrame and ReceiveFrame.

Table 2.2 LLC/MAC Group Service Primitives and Parameters

Primitive	Source Address Parameter	Destination Address Parameter	Data Parameter	Other Parameters
MA_UNITDATA. request		x	x	service_class
MA_UNITDATA. indication	x	x	x	reception_status
MA_CONTROL. request		x		opcode, request_operand_list
MA_CONTROL. indication				opcode, indication_operand_list

2.2.4 Service Primitive Definition

The primitives defined for the interface between the LLC and MAC sublayers provide a good example of how the services in an individual layer or sublayer are specified.

The procedure used for specifying a primitive requires more than just identification of the primitive and a list of parameters. It also requires a statement of the function (purpose) of the primitive, its semantics (the associated parameters and the order in which they are typically passed), when the primitive is generated, and the effect that the primitive will have when it is received, plus any additional information that will impact the implementation of the primitive.

If the layers on either side of the interface are included in the same standard, the primitives are typically defined in the specification for the lower, service-providing layer. However, if the two layers are described in different standards, the same service primitive is often defined in both standards.

Service primitives are specifications of the services provided by one architectural layer for the layer immediately above. Descriptions for each primitive include:

• The name of the primitive and its function (purpose)

• Its semantics (the associated parameters and the order in which they are typically passed)

• When the primitive is generated

- The effect that the primitive will have when it is received

- Any additional information that impacts the implementation of the primitive

If the layers on either side of the interface are included in the same standard, the primitives are typically defined in the specification for the lower, service-providing layer. However, if the two layers are described in different standards (for example, the MAC client sublayer in one and the MAC sublayer in another), the same service primitive is often defined in both standards. If this is the case, both definitions must be considered before the primitive is implemented.

2.2.4.1 The MA_UNITDATA.indication Primitive: Function and Semantics

Consider, for example, the MA_UNITDATA.indication primitive and its definitions in IEEE 802.2 (the LLC standard) and IEEE 802.3 (the Ethernet standard) shown in Table 2.3. The stated purpose of the primitive is functionally the same in both documents: to define the transfer of an incoming data frame from the MAC sublayer to the LLC sublayer.

Table 2.3   Contrasting Semantic Definitions for the MA_UNITDATA.indication MAC Service Primitive

LLC Primitive (IEEE 802.2)	MAC Primitive (IEEE 802.3)
MA_UNITDATA.indication (source_address destination_address routing_information data, reception_status priority, service_class)	MA_UNITDATA.indication (destination_address source_address m_sdu, reception_status)

The semantic definitions for MA_UNITDATA.indication are obviously different in the LLC and Ethernet documents. The LLC definition includes more parameters than the Ethernet definition, and the order of the destination_address and source_address parameters is reversed. However, this does not mean that there is an inconsistency between the two standards.

The LLC standard was defined as a universal LLC sublayer for all 802 LAN protocols. Not all MA_UNITDATA.indication parameters are required by all 802 MACs. Parameter fields for features not supported by a particular 802 LAN protocol are set to null (for example, basic Ethernet MACs do not support priority frame transfer, but as you will see in Chapter 3, "Media Access Control," this parameter is also required when the optional VLAN capability is implemented).

The order of the source address and the destination address was inadvertently reversed when one of the two standards (probably the LLC) was written. The Ethernet order is the same as the frame format order (which is also consistent with several other 802 LAN protocol definitions). It just means that the person designing the software driver needs to make sure that the addresses passed across the LLC/MAC interface are consistent.

Note

We have periodically been asked why standards are often hard to read and why inconsistencies or oversights are allowed to remain in subsequent versions, even after they have been identified. (For example, IEEE 802.1D defines M_UNITDATA.request and M_UNITDATA.indication primitives for the case where the MAC client is a bridge entity. These primitives are not even mentioned in the IEEE 802.3 documents—everyone is expected to understand that they are essentially the same as MA_UNITDATA.requests and MA_UNITDATA.indications, and to act accordingly.)

It may seem a bit arrogant, but if the inconsistency has not presented much of a problem in implementation of the standard, it is typically allowed to stand (usually because no one wants to spend the time identifying all instances of the problem, proposing the corrections, and shepherding the changes through the approval process).

2.2.4.2   When the MA_UNITDATA.indication Primitive Is Generated

An MA_UNITDATA.indication is passed by the MAC sublayer to the LLC sublayer to indicate that a data frame has arrived at the local MAC sublayer and that it is being transferred to the LLC. An MA_UNITDATA.indication is generated only if the frame's destination address designates the local MAC entity and it is both correctly formed and received without any detectable errors.

Note

Incoming frames whose destination addresses do not match the local MAC entity's individual or assigned group addresses are never passed on to the LLC. This is the MAC's address filtering function.

2.2.4.3 Effect of Receipt

Because the MAC is a service provider to the LLC, the MAC cannot tell the LLC what to do with the results of the service the MAC provided. The local MAC has delivered a frame to the LLC that is an exact copy of the MSDU passed by the peer LLC to the MAC in the transmitting entity. The receiving LLC now has the responsibility to determine whether or not the original MSDU was valid.

2.2.4.4 Additional Comments

As stated earlier, we have periodically been told that standards are written in a manner that is sometimes difficult to translate. The additional comments section for the MA_UNITDATA.indication primitive in IEEE 802.3 provides an excellent example of standardese:

> If the local MAC sublayer entity is the designated *destination_address* parameter of an MA_UNITDATA.request, the indication primitive will also be invoked by the MAC entity to the local LLC entity. The full-duplex characteristic of the MAC sublayer may be due to unique functionality within the MAC sublayer or full-duplex characteristics of the lower layers (for example, all frames transmitted to the broadcast address will invoke MA_UNITDATA.indication primitives at all stations in the network including the station that generated the request).

We never claimed that standards were easy reading. This statement just means that if you are sending a data frame to a group address, and the address of your workstation is also in that group, the MAC in your workstation will tell your LLC that the frame you just sent has also been received.

2.2.5 The Physical Sublayer Group

The higher-speed Ethernet implementations divide the OSI Physical layer into four sublayers and two physically defined interfaces. The Reconciliation Sublayer and the Gigabit media independent interface (GMII) are common to all media types. The remaining three sublayers (the PHY group) and the medium dependent interface (MDI) are dependent on the particular link media and data encoding method. Figure 2.9 shows the media dependent sublayers for 1000BASE-X implementations.

Figure 2.9   1000 BASE-X Ethernet Reference Model and Media Options

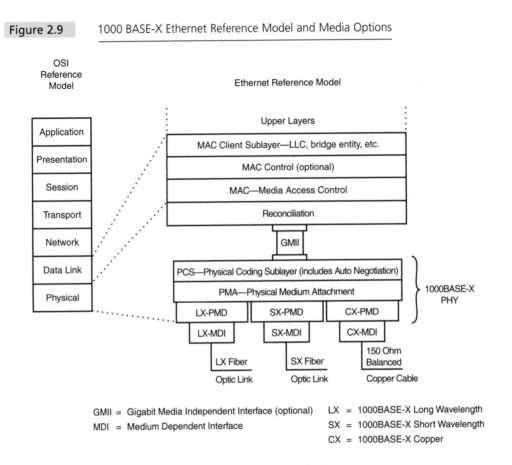

GMII = Gigabit Media Independent Interface (optional)   LX = 1000BASE-X Long Wavelength
MDI = Medium Dependent Interface   SX = 1000BASE-X Short Wavelength
                                                         CX = 1000BASE-X Copper

2.2.5.1   *The Reconciliation Sublayer and GMII*

The purpose of the GMII is to provide an easy-to-implement, fully defined interface that allows a clean separation between the MAC and PHY Group sublayers. The function of the Reconciliation Sublayer is to map the GMII signal set to the PLS service primitives at the MAC/PHY interface as illustrated in Figure 2.10.

Figure 2.10   MAC/Reconciliation Sublayer Service Primitives and Primitive-to-GMII Signal Mapping

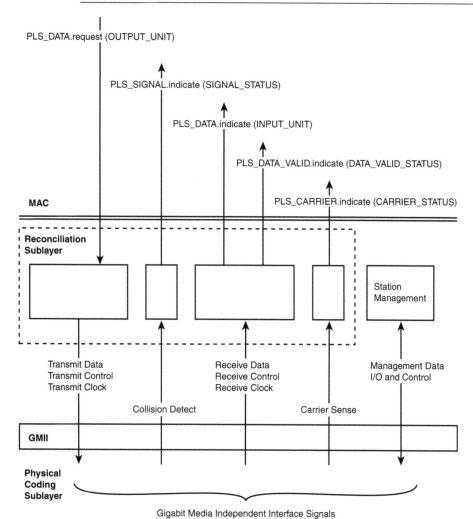

The GMII is defined to be a physically exposed interface for connecting the MAC and Reconciliation Sublayers to the PHY Group. The GMII may optionally be hidden as a completely internal interface.

The GMII provides separate 8-bit transmit and receive data paths plus the necessary control and clocking signals to allow simultaneous bidirectional data transfer (full-duplex) operation. Two additional signals provide data management information transfer and control.

The GMII signal set is based on the 100 Mbps MII signal set. Signal names are the same, and the functions of most signals are consistent although some additional signal combinations have been defined for 1,000 Mbps operation. PHY implementations that provide a physically exposed GMII must support operation at 1,000 Mbps and may optionally also support operation at 100 Mbps or both 10 Mbps and 100 Mbps (through an MII).

2.2.5.2   1000BASE-X PHY Sublayer Group

The 1000BASE-X Physical sublayer group consists of the physical coding sublayer (PCS), the physical medium attachment sublayer (PMA), and the physical medium dependent sublayer (PMD). The PCS and PMA are common to all 1000BASE-X PMDs, and the 1000BASE-X PMDs are dependent on the particular medium (copper or optical cable) and in case of optical fiber cable, the transmission wavelength (short—850 nm, or long—1300 nm).

The Physical Coding Sublayer (PCS)

During transmission, the PCS sublayer is responsible for encoding outgoing data octets from the GMII into 10-bit tx_code_groups that are passed to the PMA sublayer by PMA_UNITDATA.request primitives as illustrated in Figure 2.11. In the receive mode, the PCS decodes the incoming 10-bit rx_code_groups from PMA_UNITDATA.indication primitives back into data octets for forwarding to MAC through the GMII.

| Figure 2.11 | 1000BASE-X PCS/PMA Service Primitives |

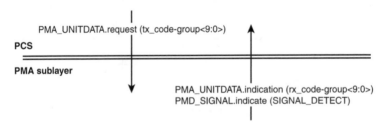

The PCS also manages the auto-negotiation process to allow the devices at each end of a link to exchange functional capability information and to select the highest common operational mode (such as half- or full-duplex, and so forth).

The Physical Medium Attachment (PMA) Sublayer

During data transmission, the PMA serializes the 10-bit tx_code_groups (passed down from the PCS as PMA_UNITDATA.request primitives) into tx_bits and forwards them unaltered to the PMD for transmission over the link, as illustrated in Figure 2.12.

Similarly, during data reception, the PMA recovers the RX clock and deserializes the incoming rx_bit stream into 10-bit rx_code_groups for transfer to the PCS. The PMA also checks the first bits received in an incoming frame and may adjust (slip) the initial code-group boundaries to ensure proper code-group alignment.

Figure 2.12   1000 BASE-X PMA/PMD Service Primitives

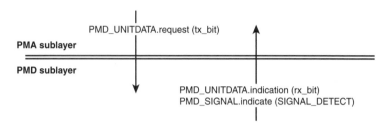

The Physical Medium Dependent (PMD) Sublayer and MDI

The PMD sublayer is responsible for the actual transmission (reception) of bit streams sent (received) over the link. During frame transmission, the PMD translates the tx_bits received from the PMA sublayer into a form (the appropriate pulse shape, power, light intensity, voltage level, and so forth) that allows them to be impressed directly onto a maximum-length link and to be correctly received by a peer PMD at the other end of the link.

The reverse occurs during frame reception. The PMD shapes the pulses and translates them into rx_bits that are passed to the PMA sublayer. The PMD also monitors the signal power being received on the link. If the signal power falls below a specified value, the PMD generates a PMD_SIGNAL.indicate (SIGNAL_DETECT) to inform the PMA/PCS that the incoming signal is too weak to allow code detection.

The MDI is the electrical or optical connector that allows the link to be connected to the DTE or repeater.

2.3   *Summary*

We have spent a number of pages describing the layered architectures, primitive defini-tions, and the OSI and Gigabit Ethernet reference models. We also made the bold state-ment that an understanding of the service primitives defined for the various layer interfaces would also convey considerable information about the functions in each layer.

2.3.1 The OSI Model Revisited

The introduction to the OSI model stated that the upper three layers all related to application issues and that the lower four layers dealt with network control and packet transmission/reception. However, since the Ethernet model appears to relate to only the bottom two layers of the OSI model, you might be wondering about now whether the other five layers of the OSI model are really needed and why, after all these years, the OSI model is still used as a reference point for Ethernet LANs. These are both good questions and they will be addressed in order.

2.3.1.1 Is a Seven Layer Model Really Necessary?

Kreshav makes a valid case that the four lower layers are necessary, but that the functions of the upper three layers could be bundled into a single, more comprehensive application layer [Kreshav, 1997]. Network protocols (for example, Ethernet, Token Ring, and Demand Priority) that reside in the lower two (data link and physical) layers are the province of the IEEE 802 LAN/MAN standards group. After their documents are approved and published as IEEE standards, they are submitted to ISO for review and acceptance as an ISO/IEC standard (a process that can take many months and that seldom results in any substantive change).

The third (network) and fourth (transport) layers are a different matter. Development of an ISO standard is a very slow, contentious process and according to Kreshav, sometimes fraught with "endless politically motivated bickering." ISO standards have been published for the Network and Transport protocols, but they have not gained wide acceptance. Definition of these two layers has been co-opted by a less formal and more active group known as the Internet Engineering Task Force (IETF).

IETF developed the widely accepted TCP/IP (Transport Control Protocol/Internet Protocol). These two layers are commonly coupled with the IEEE 802.2 MAC client standards and the IEEE 802.3 MAC and physical layers to form a 4-layer protocol "stack" that has become the *de facto* standard for Ethernet networks, as shown in Figure 2.13. (TCP/IP will be introduced in Chapter 4 and will be discussed in greater detail beginning with Chapter 13.)

Figure 2.13   The de Facto Protocol Stack for Ethernet Networks

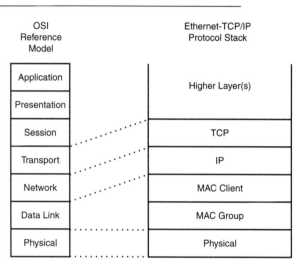

2.3.1.2   So Why Do the IEEE 802 Standards Continue to Use the ISO Reference Model?

The ISO Open Systems Interconnect (OSI) standard is the only official, internationally recognized model available, and there appears to be little or no interest in changing it. The OSI model does not specify how any layer will be implemented. It also puts little restriction on the protocol developers, a fact that has been amply demonstrated by the number of competing LAN protocols that have been developed over the years by the 802 standards group.

The ultimate success of any protocol stack is determined by how it is accepted in the marketplace, not by which architectural model is used during the definition process. The OSI model has accomplished its most important purpose to be a framework and definition technique for protocol development.

2.3.2   Service Primitives Revisited

Consider the example frame reception sequence in Figure 2.14.

Figure 2.14 Primitive Generation During Frame Reception

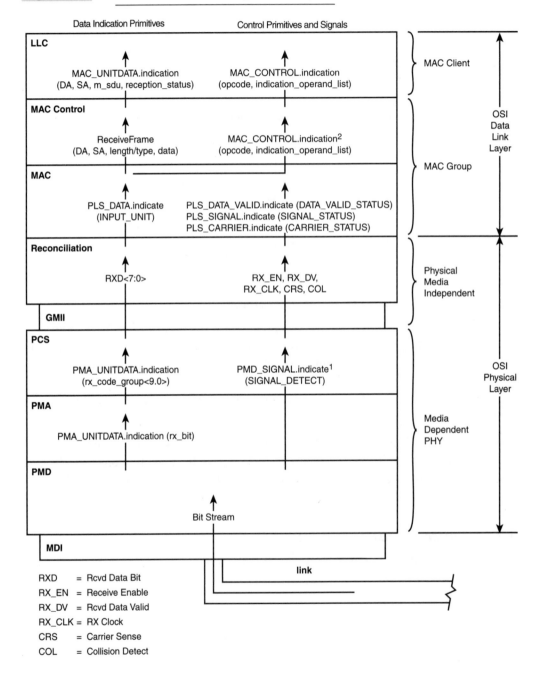

RXD	= Rcvd Data Bit
RX_EN	= Receive Enable
RX_DV	= Rcvd Data Valid
RX_CLK	= RX Clock
CRS	= Carrier Sense
COL	= Collision Detect

Reception of a bit stream will result in the generation of two primitive stacks, one to pass the data values and the other to pass the associated control information. The complete process is as follows:

1. The PMD sublayer detects the bits in the incoming bit stream and passes a PMD_UNITDATA.indicate (rx_bit) to the PMA for each bit detected. If the signal level drops too low, a PMD_SIGNAL.indicate will be generated and passed directly through the PMA to the PCS. The PMD may continue generating PMD_UNITDATA.indicates, but they will be ignored by the PCS until a PMD_SIGNAL.indicate shows SIGNAL_STATUS=OK.

2. The PMA converts each sequence of 10 rx_bits into a 10-bit rx_code_group and generates a PMA_UNITDATA.indicate to the PCS sublayer for each 10 PMD_UNITDATA.indicates received (as in part [d] of Figure 2.2).

3. The PCS sublayer decodes the 10-bit rx_code_groups into data octets 8-bit code that are transferred across the GMII as RXD<7:0. The RX_DV signal indicates data status and RX_CLK synchronizes the transfer. The CRS signal verifies the existence of a carrier, and COL indicates that a collision has not been detected.

4. The Reconciliation Sublayer maps the GMII signal set into a PLS_UNITDATA.indicate primitive, transfers the data octet to the MAC, and generates a PLS_DATA_VALID.indicate defining data status.

5. The MAC adds the octet to those previously received and continues checking for transmission errors.

    *   If there are no detected errors after the last octet has been received, and if the Length/Type field indicates that this is a data frame, the MAC generates a ReceiveFrame primitive and passes it to the MAC Control sublayer.

    *   If the Length/Type field indicates that this is a MAC Control frame, the MAC generates a MAC_CONTROL.indication primitive and passes it to the MAC Control sublayer.

    The PLS_DATA_VALID.indicate, PLS_CARRIER.indicate, and PLS_SIGNAL.indicate control primitives tell the MAC whether the transferred octet is valid, whether a carrier is being sensed, and whether a collision has been detected. The latter two primitives provide information required by the MAC to properly control the CSMA/CD protocol.

6. If the received primitive is a ReceiveFrame, the MAC Control sublayer then changes the information in the Length/Type and data fields into an m_sdu, adds a valid *reception_status* parameter and passes the MA_UNITDATA.indication to the LLC. If the MAC Control is not implemented, the MAC skips ReceiveFrame step and then generates the MA_UNITDATA.indication directly to the LLC.

   If the received primitive is a MAC_CONTROL.indication, the MAC Control sublayer decodes the primitive's associated parameters and performs the indicated control operation. It also passes the MAC_CONTROL.indication primitive to the LLC sublayer.

That was fairly straightforward, and, except for possibly the last step, you should now be able to construct a similar sequence of data-transfer primitives for frame transmission. If you are wondering how we knew that the MAC accumulated a sequence of octets before generating the primitive to the LLC to indicate that an entire frame had been received without any detectable transmission errors, the answer lies in section 2.2.4.2. The reverse happens during transmission. The MAC receives an entire m_sdu for the LLC, constructs the frame, and then sends individual octets to the Physical sublayer group until the entire frame has been transferred.

The control primitives are a little more difficult. You'll need more information about the individual primitives than was covered in the preceding sections. MAC Control will be discussed in Chapter 3.

The next task is to show how this all ties into the functions that are contained in each of the various sublayers. Chapter 3 starts near the top with a more in-depth look at the MAC group.

Media Access Control

> All implementations of the Ethernet should be capable of exchanging data at the data-link level. [The computability goal in the original Ethernet specification—Intel, 1980]

This chapter presents an architectural view, rather than an implementational view, that will build on the material already presented in Chapter 2, "The OSI and Gigabit Ethernet Standard Reference Models". Toward that end, the chapter emphasizes not only the functions of the MAC, but also the logical differences and similarities of the various MAC configurations. The chapter concludes with a discussion of the question of whether or not you need to include all MAC options in Gigabit Ethernet.

If you are already familiar with some or all of the MAC frame formats and the currently defined MAC options, you may wish to skim or even skip section 3.3. It is recommended, however, that you at least review the remaining sections of the chapter because they represent a view of the MAC's functionality that is consolidated from additions and changes that until the publication of IEEE Std. 802.3-1998 had been spread across the base standard, IEEE 802.3-1996, and several supplements (IEEE 802.3u-1995, IEEE 802.3x&y-1997, IEEE 802.3z-1998, and IEEE 802.3ac-1998).

3.1 MAC Overview

Figure 3.1 shows the dimensions of the two types of compatibility in an Ethernet network, link compatibility and access compatibility. Link compatibility requires the media-dependent physical layers in the entities at *each end of the link* to be compatible with both the link media and with each other. Link compatibility is determined on a link-by-link basis and, as you have already seen in Figures 1.9 and 1.19 in Chapter 1, "Ethernet Development: The Need for Speed," link compatibility does not require that the entire network be configured with the same media or be operated at the same transmission speeds.

Figure 3.1 Basic Network Compatibility Dimensions

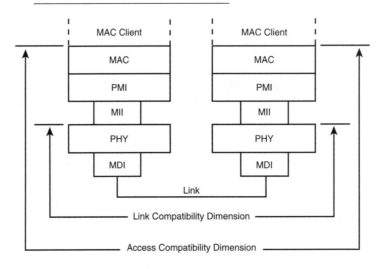

PMI = Physical Medium Independent Sublayer
MII = Medium Independent Interface
PHY = Physical Sublayer
MDI = Medium Dependent Interface

Access compatibility is more restrictive than link compatibility. The MAC is responsible for network access control during frame transmission and for format control during frame assembly and disassembly. Access compatibility requires not only that MACs in the entities at each end of a link be compatible with each other, but also that they be compatible with all intermediate MACs in the transmission path between the two entities.

Until 1997, all Ethernet MACs were logically the same and, except for the speed differences between 10 Mbps systems and 100 Mbps systems, were functional equals. However, that is no longer the case. Several optional capabilities have recently been defined for Ethernet MACs:

- Full-duplex operation allows the MAC to transmit and receive packets at the same time, so long as there are exactly two nodes on the network (a configuration that is common in switched networks—one node is the network station, the other is a switch port). [IEEE Std. 802.3x-1997]

- MAC Control was defined to allow the local MAC (or the peer entity at the other end of the link) to request that the peer entity (or the local MAC) inhibit further frame transmission for an indicated period of time. This option also provides the structure and framework for the future definition of additional control functions.

- VLAN tagging allows the assignment of transmission priorities and the designation of defined extended-network routing paths for individual packets. VLAN is the acronym for virtual-bridged local area networks. [IEEE Std. 802.3ac-1998]

The result of these optional capabilities is that all standards-compliant Ethernet MACs are no longer functionally equal. Each of the previously listed options impacts the MAC in one way or another, including the following:

- Full-duplex operation requires that the MAC have fully separate transmit and receive paths and that the paths are able to operate independently of each other.

- MAC Control adds a second logical sublayer to the MAC. The basic Ethernet frame format is not changed, but an alternate interpretation of the length and data fields must be provided. The currently defined control actions also require the affected MACs to have full-duplex capability.

- VLAN tagging requires changes to the frame format.

Networks cannot take full advantage of the optional MAC capabilities unless the affected MACs are implemented with the desired option set. However, this does not mean that the network stations will not be able to communicate with each other. It just means that some of the advanced features may not always be useable and that network operation may have to be in a fall-back mode.

So, what does that mean for Gigabit Ethernet MACs? The optional MAC capabilities were defined before Gigabit Ethernet became a standard. You might find yourself asking, "Can't I just assume that Gigabit Ethernet MACs will be implemented with all the optional capabilities?"

The answer is a resounding "maybe." Unfortunately, to implement or not to implement all MAC options is not the only issue. A MAC is required in each end station and in each intermediate network entity port (see Figure 3.2). For the foreseeable future, Ethernet LANs will have to operate as multispeed networks (see Figure 3.3) that typically have a mix of old and new end stations that may or may not be equipped with the latest MAC options.

Note

IEEE 802.3 refers to end stations as DTEs (data terminal equipment) because they are at either the sending or receiving end of a frame transmission. A DTE may be a workstation (or PC) or a network server such as a printer or a disk drive. Throughout this chapter and the book, you'll see the terms "end station" and "network server" instead of DTE.

Repeaters, bridges, switches, and routers are sometimes called DCEs (data communications equipment). DCEs will be referred to throughout the rest of the book either by their specific functional names (repeater, bridge, switch, or router) or as intermediate network devices when they are referred to as a group.

Figure 3.2   Basic Network Entity Models

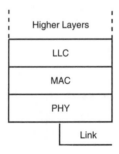

(a) End Station Model

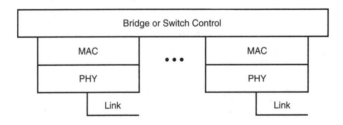

(b) Multiport Bridge/Switch Model

Part (a) of Figure 3.2 illustrates the end station model in which the MAC client sublayer is implemented as an LLC. Part (b) of the figure illustrates an intermediate network device where the MAC client is a bridge entity.

Figure 3.3   A Typical Multispeed Network

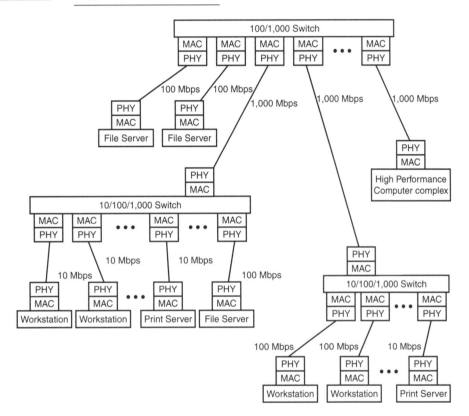

3.2   MAC Frame Formats

Both current MAC group options require modifications to two or more of the fields in the basic frame format as defined in sections 3.2.1 through 3.2.3.

3.2.1   The Basic MAC Frame Format

Figure 3.4a shows the basic Ethernet MAC frame format. The frame length and the frame check sequence coverage include all fields except the Preamble, Start-of-Frame Delimiter (SFD), and the Extension fields. The frame must also be an integral number of octets in length.

Note

The terms "octet" and "byte" both represent groups of eight contiguous bits, and for purposes of this book, the terms are interchangeable.

Figure 3.4a   The Basic MAC Frame Format and Transmission Order

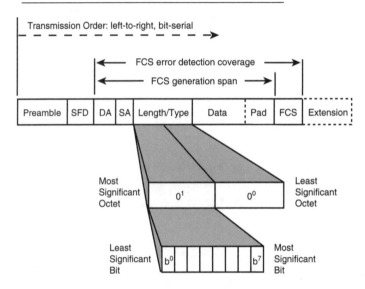

SFD = Start-of-Frame Delimiter
DA = Destination Address
SA = Source Address
FCS = Frame Check Sequence

Note: The octet and bit order shown is typical for all fields except the FCS, the FCS is formatted with the high order bits to the left.

The octet-order within each field of the format is most significant octet on the left, least significant on the right, as shown in Figure 3.4a. The bit-order within each octet is reversed. The least significant bit is on the left, the most significant on the right. The octet- and bit-orders are typical for all fields except the FCS, which is treated as a special 32-bit field (with the high order bits on the left) rather than as four individual octets.

Figure 3.4b shows the size and content of the individual fields. Sections 3.2.1.1 through 3.2.1.7 describe the functionality and characteristics of the fields in a basic MAC frame.

Figure 3.4b   The Basic MAC Frame Format Field Size and Content

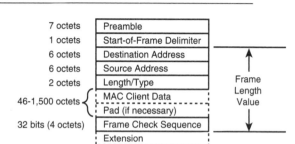

3.2.1.1 The Preamble

The purpose of the Preamble is to allow the physical layer to detect a carrier and to reach steady-state synchronization with an incoming frame before the actual Start-of-Frame Delimiter has been received. The Preamble is the following 7-octet sequence of alternating bits where the last bit is a zero:

```
Preamble = 10101010 10101010 10101010 10101010 10101010 10101010 10101010
```

3.2.1.2 The Start-of-Frame Delimiter (SFD)

The purpose of the Start-of-Frame Delimiter (SFD) is to identify the beginning of the MAC frame and to synchronize format octet boundaries. The SFD is a 1-octet field that continues the alternating bit pattern of the Preamble. The two 1s in the last two bit positions identify the end of the Preamble sequence. The next received bit will be both the first bit in the MAC frame and the first bit of the first octet of the Destination Address:

```
SFD = 10101011
```

3.2.1.3 The Address Fields

Figure 3.5 shows the format for the two address fields: Destination Address (DA) and Source Address (SA). Early versions of the standard allowed both 16-bit and 48-bit addresses, but because no conforming implementation of the standard uses 16-bit addresses, the 16-bit address option was deleted. IEEE Std. 802.3x-1997 now requires that all Address fields be a full six octets.

Figure 3.5 The MAC Frame Address Field Format

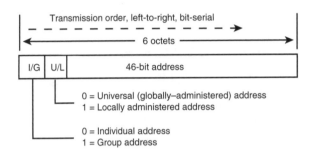

Each Address field contains two address type identifiers plus a 46-bit address. The leftmost bit in the Address field indicates whether the address is an individual or a group address (1 identifies a group address, 0 an individual address). The second bit is used to distinguish between globally and locally administered addresses (0 indicates globally administrated, 1 locally administrated).

The leftmost bit in the Source Address field is reserved and is always set to 0. The Destination Address of all 1s is reserved as the broadcast address and indicates all stations on the network. Additional information on the use of MAC addresses is available in IEEE Std. 802-1990.

3.2.1.4 The Length/Type Field

The Length/Type field indicates either the number of MAC client data octets in the Data field or the type of frame:

- If the Length/Type field value is ≤ 1,500, the data field contains LLC data (the LSDU in Figure 2.4 from Chapter 2) and the number of LLC data octets in the Data field is equal to the Length/Type field value.

- If the Length/Type field value is ≥ 1,536 (0600 hexadecimal), the frame is a Type-Frame and the value in the Length/Type field identifies the particular type of frame being sent or received.

The Length/Type field values for the optional MAC Control and VLAN-Tagged Type-Frames are discussed in sections 3.2.2 and 3.2.3. Section 3.4.4 details frame type determination during frame reception.

3.2.1.5 The Data and Pad Fields

The Data field contains a sequence *n* individual octets that may be any arbitrary value, allowing full data transparency for the transmitted frame. The length of the Data field may be any value $n \leq 1,500$. However, if $n < 46$, the Data field must be extended by adding a filler (a pad) to bring the actual Data field length to the minimum length shown in Figures 3.4a and 3.7. Since the value of the Length/Type field indicates the number of LLC data octets in the Data field (but not the length of the field), the length value is not changed when a pad is added to the Data field.

3.2.1.6 The Frame Check Sequence Field (FCS)

Figure 3.6 shows the format for the 32-bit cyclic redundancy check sequence that is generated over the DA, SA, Length/Type, and Data + Pad fields before transmission. The transmitted FCS value is compared against the new FCS value that is computed as the frame is being received and that provides error detection over the DA, SA, Length/Type, Data + Pad, and the Frame Check Sequence (FCS) fields. The FCS field is transmitted from left-to-right, most significant bit first.

Figure 3.6   The FCS Field Format

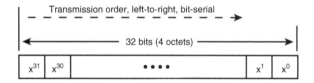

3.2.1.7 The Extension Field

At Gigabit transmission rates, the *slotTime* may be greater than the time required for packet transmission. In this case, the length of the frame is extended by appending a sequence of extension bits to the end of the frame, after the FCS field. The length of the Extension field is determined at transmission time and is discussed in 3.2.2.1 below.

> **Note**
>
> *slotTime* is the parameter name used in the standard for the collision window. The values *slotTime* and all other italicized parameters in sections 3.2 through 3.4 are defined in Table 3.1 in the chapter summary.

You will see later in this chapter that the Extension field is only required for MACs operating at 1,000 Mbps data rates and only when operating in half-duplex mode.

3.2.2 The MAC Control Frame Format

The differences between MAC Control and basic MAC frames are the interpretation of the Length/Type field, the replacement of the Data and Pad fields with a MAC Control Opcode, a MAC Control Parameters field, and a Reserved field. The Preamble, SFD, DA, SA, FCS, and Extension field formats are the same as in the basic MAC frame. Figure 3.7 compares the format for MAC Control frames (shown in part (b)) to the basic MAC frame format (part (a)) and also illustrates the specific format used for MAC Control PAUSE frames (part (c)).

Figure 3.7   The MAC Control and MAC Control PAUSE Frame Formats

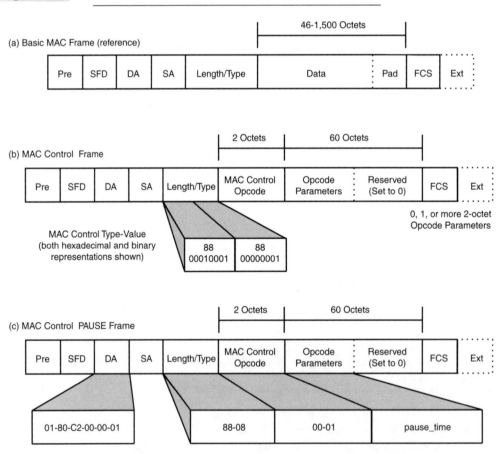

The MAC Control frame format was defined in a manner that will allow definition of other, as yet to be determined, control operations spanning one or more links. The only control operation that is currently defined is the PAUSE operation, which is used to provide fast response, short term flow control over a single link.

Receipt of a MAC Control PAUSE frame causes the MAC Control sublayer in the receiving entity to cease frame transmission for a defined period. The capability of one link partner to request the other link partner to stop frame transmission for a selected period of time is known as *flow control*. This type of flow control may only be invoked on a link-by-link basis and should not be confused with end-to-end flow control that is the function of higher layers in the protocol stack. (Chapter 4, "Gigabit Repeaters, Bridges, Routers, and Switches," provides detailed examples on the use of the MAC Control PAUSE operation.)

3.2.2.1 An Assigned Destination Address for MAC Control PAUSE Frames

The globally assigned hexadecimal destination address 01-80-C2-00-00-01 has been reserved for exclusive use with MAC Control PAUSE frames. Because the PAUSE operation is restricted to frame transmission between two devices connected by a single link, frames with the destination address value 01-80-C2-00-00-01 are filtered out by the receiving MAC and are not forwarded by switch or bridge ports, even if the ports are equipped with MACs that are not implemented with the MAC Control option.

3.2.2.2 The MAC Control Length/Type Field

The Length/Type field in a MAC Control frame is assigned the exclusive type-field identifier decimal value of 34,824 (88-08 hexadecimal). This Length/Type field value will also be used to identify future, as yet undefined, MAC Control type-frames.

3.2.2.3 The MAC Control Opcode Field

The MAC Control Opcode is contained in the first two octets following the Length/Type field. The MAC Control Opcode field contains exactly one MAC Control Opcode that defines the type of control operation to be performed.

The MAC Control Opcode for the PAUSE operation is the hexadecimal value 00-01.

3.2.2.4 The MAC Control Parameters and Reserved Fields

The MAC Control Parameters field may contain zero, one, or more parameters, as required by the particular MAC Control Opcode. The parameters in this field are opcode-specific and define the semantics of the desired control operation.

The length of the MAC Control Parameters and Reserved fields is always 60 octets. If the length of the Parameters field is less than 60 octets, the Parameters field is extended by adding a sequence of reserved octets (zeros) at the end of the last Opcode parameter so that the length of the (Parameters+Reserved) is equal to 60 octets.

The MAC Control Opcode requires one parameter to designate the pause_time to indicate the number of pause_quanta requested for the frame delay. One pause_quanta = 512 bit_times for the transmission rate being used. The requested delay may be from 0–65,535 pause_quanta.

3.2.3 The VLAN-Tagged MAC Frame Format

The difference between the VLAN-tagged format and the basic MAC (non-tagged) frame format is the addition of the QTag (short for 802.1QTag) Type and Tag Control Information fields between the Source Address field and the MAC client Length/Type field as shown in Figure 3.8. The Preamble, SFD, DA, SA, Data, Pad, FCS, and Extension field formats are the same as in the basic MAC frame, except the minimum length of the (Data+Pad) fields is four octets shorter in a VLAN-tagged frame.

Figure 3.8   The VLAN-Tagged MAC Frame Format

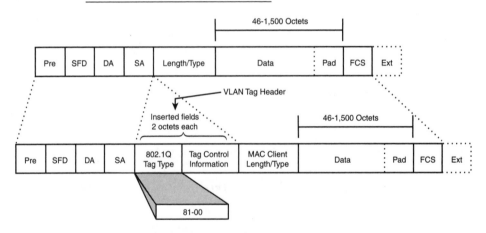

3.2.3.1 The VLAN-Tagged 802.1QTag Type Field

The VLAN-tagged 802.1Q Tag Type is in the format location normally occupied by the Length/Type field in the non-tagged MAC frame. The 802.1Q Tag Type field is assigned the exclusive type-field identifier hexadecimal value 81-00.

3.2.3.2 The VLAN-Tagged Tag Control Information Field

Figure 3.9 shows the IEEE 802.1Q (part a) and IEEE 802.3 (part b) representations of the 2-octet Tag Control Information field.

Figure 3.9   Tag Control Information Field Format

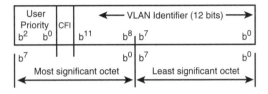

(a) IEEE 802.1Q Representation

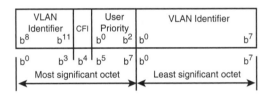

(b) IEEE 802.3 Representation

The 2-octet Tag Control Information field contains three designators as follows:

- User Priority indicates the desired level of transmission priority (0–7, where 7 is the highest priority)

- CFI is the canonical format indicator that is used to indicate the presence or absence of a routing information field (RIF) in the MAC Client Data field.

- VLAN Identifier is the identification number of the VLAN being used for the frame transfer.

When introducing the Ethernet frame format octet bit-order earlier, it was stated that the bit-order was reversed from the frame octet-order. However, there was no comment on the possible confusion that this can cause when comparing the frame field contents from two different protocols representing the same field value. IEEE 802.1 and IEEE 802.5 (Token Ring), for example, define their octet bit-order with the high-order bits on the left. Comparing the 802.1Q representation of the Tag Control Information fields with the 802.3 representation in Figure 3.9 shows that this can result in some apparently strange juxtapositions, particularly if an octet is packed with more than one field value. This is not a problem, however, unless you are one of the people who must work with the actual bit patterns in the frame.

VLAN tagging became a standard in the fall of 1998. Chapter 4 revisits this option in conjunction with bridges and switches. Chapter 13, "Upgrading Ethernet LANs: System and Topology Considerations," discusses system considerations and the use of VLAN tagging. For the moment, however, you need to consider how the MAC operates.

3.3 Frame Transmission

The basic MAC provides frame construction, transmission, and reception services for its MAC client by accepting, acting on, and generating the data transfer and control service primitives indicated in Figure 3.10 and as shown in the functional flow chart of Figure 3.11.

Figure 3.10 Data and Control Communication Paths, with MAC Control Not Implemented

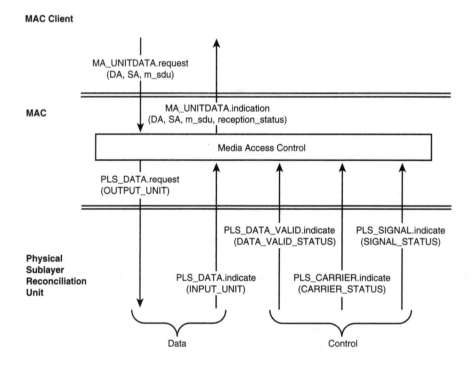

Figure 3.11   Gigabit Ethernet Frame Transmission

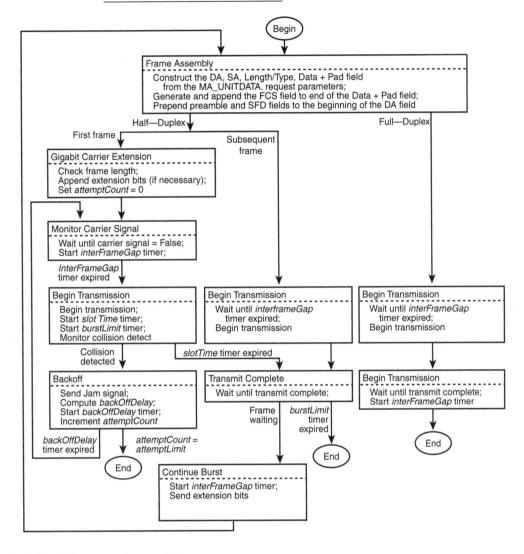

3.3.1 *Frame Assembly*

Upon receipt of an *MA_UNITDATA.request* from the MAC client, the MAC constructs a frame from the client-supplied data. The DA, SA, and Data fields of the MAC frame are set to the DA, SA, and *m_sdu* parameter values in the request primitive, the length of the Data field is checked, and a pad is added if necessary to ensure that the frame length ≥ *minFrameSize*. The Length/Type field value is set to the number of data octets provided by the MAC client. An FCS value is then generated and appended to the end of the Data field, and the Preamble and SFD are both prepended to the DA field.

Transmission of the assembled frame depends on whether the MAC is operating in half- or full-duplex mode. Half-duplex mode and CSMA/CD operation are equivalent in Ethernet networks (half-duplex means that the link can support data transfer in both directions, but only one direction at a time). Before transmission can begin, the link must be quiet, and if a collision is detected, the MAC must go into backoff mode.

Full-duplex mode, on the other hand, allows simultaneous transmission in both directions. The only requirement is that enough time has elapsed since the end of the last frame was sent. Sections 3.2.2 and 3.2.3 cover both half-duplex transmission and full-duplex transmission, respectively, in greater detail.

3.3.2   Half-Duplex Transmission

Because you should already be familiar with the CSMA/CD operational principles and transmission methods introduced in Chapter 1, you should also be familiar with collision domains and the need for carrier sense monitoring during the collision window (a critical time period at the beginning of a frame transmission).

3.3.2.1   Deference

If the link is busy when frame generation is complete (the *PLS_CARRIER.indication CARRIER_STATUS* parameter will indicate *CARRIER_ON*), the MAC will defer (wait) starting transmission until a short period has passed to allow interframe recovery time for the transmission media and other CSMA/CD sublayers. This time is known as the *interFrameGap* time, and it is measured from the time the *CARRIER_STATUS* changes from *CARRIER_ON* to *CARRIER_OFF*.

When the medium is not busy and the *interFrameGap* time has expired, the MAC initiates transmission by generating *PLS_DATA.requests* with the *OUTPUT_UNIT* parameter value of either *ZERO* or *ONE* to transfer the bits in the MAC frame to the physical layer. The end of frame transfer is signaled by the parameter value *DATA_COMPLETE*.

3.3.2.2   Gigabit Carrier Extension

At Gigabit operating speeds, transmission of a minimum length frame will be completed before the collision window expires, allowing the possibility of a collision being undetected by the transmitting MAC. Two possible solutions were originally considered: increasing the minimum frame length or adding non-data carrier-extension bits after the FCS. The latter alternative was chosen to maintain minimum-frame-length consistency with 10 Mbps and 100 Mbps versions Ethernet LANs.

Figure 3.12 shows the MAC frame format with the carrier-extension field and the timing factors that affect the extension field length. The *slotTime* must be greater than the physical layer maximum round-trip propagation time plus the maximum *jamTime*. The maximum length of the extension field is equal to (*slotTime − minFrameSize*).

Figure 3.12   MAC Frame with Carrier Extension

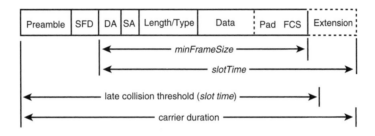

minFrameSize = the minimum length of an untagged frame
slotTime = the length of the collision window

The MAC generates the extension field bits by sending the physical layer a series of *PLS_DATA.request(OUTPUT_UNIT)* primitives with a parameter value of *EXTEND* immediately after the last bit of the FCS has been sent and before the *OUTPUT_UNIT* parameter value has been changed to *DATA_COMPLETE*. The physical layer, in turn, encodes the extension bits as reserved symbols that are readily distinguished from data symbols by the receiving entity, and that maintain the carrier during the extension period. Again, carrier extension is only required for MACs operating at 1,000 Mbps data rates and only when operating in half-duplex mode. Further, it is also not required after the second and subsequent frames in a frame burst, which is the next topic.

3.3.2.3   Gigabit Frame Bursting

The Gigabit MAC includes a standard feature known as *frame bursting* that allows users to send a series of (presumably small) frames in half-duplex mode without relinquishing control of the network medium after each frame. The transmitting MAC is allowed to initiate additional frame transmissions after the first frame, until the *burstLimit* timeout is reached, as shown in Figure 3.13. Any frame transmission that is in progress when the *burstLimit* is reached will be allowed to continue without interruption.

Figure 3.13   A Gigabit Frame Burst Sequence

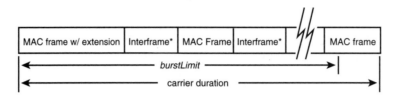

*Extension bits are sent during interframe gaps to ensure
an uninterrupted carrier during the entire burst sequence

If the frame size of the first frame is less than the *slotTime*, the first frame must contain an Extension field to allow detection of any late collision. Then, if no collision has occurred, the MAC continues the carrier by sending extension bits through each successive *interFrameGap* from the first to the last frame. Extension fields do not have to be added to any succeeding frames whose frame size is shorter than the *slotTime* bit length because the *interFrameGap* will be longer than the maximum Extension field length. Frame bursting is only defined for Gigabit MACs and is only used when the MAC is operating in half-duplex mode. The reason, as you'll see in Section 3.6, is that full-duplex mode transmission does not need to consider collision handling.

3.3.2.4   *Collision Handling*

The MAC monitors the collision detect signal from the physical layer during transmission for the existence of a collision (indicated by the *PLS_SIGNAL.indication* primitive whenever the *SIGNAL_STATUS* parameter changes from *NO_SIGNAL_ERROR* to *SIGNAL_ERROR*).

If a collision is detected, the MAC will continue transmitting until any additional bits as specified by *jamSize* (counting from when the collision was detected) have been sent.

The jam signal may be any fixed or variable pattern, but must not be equal to the FCS value of the partial frame transmitted prior to initiating the jam. Once the jam has been completed, the MAC enters the backoff and retransmission mode.

3.3.2.5 Backoff and Retransmission

If a transmission attempt must be terminated because of a collision, it is retried by the MAC until the transmission is successful or an *attemptLimit* has been reached. All attempts to send a given frame must be completed before an attempt is made to send a subsequent frame. Retransmission is scheduled by a random process known as a *truncated binary exponential backoff*.

The MAC enters a delay period after it has sent the last jam bit, where the delay is an integral multiple of *slotTime*. The number of *slotTime*s in the delay before the nth retransmission attempt is determined by a randomly chosen integer r from the evenly distributed range as expressed in Equation 3.1.

Equation 3.1

$$0 \leq r < 2^k$$

where:

$$k = \min(n, 10)$$

If the number of re-attempts reaches *attemptLimit* without a successful transmission, the event is reported to the MAC client as a transmission failure.

3.3.3 Full-Duplex Transmission (in Switched-Based Networks)

Full-duplex transmission is functionally much simpler than half-duplex transmission (refer back to Figure 3.11). Full-duplex operation is restricted to individual link connections between two network entities (end stations, network servers, switch/bridge ports, and so forth), as shown in Figure 3.14.

Figure 3.14 A Typical Multispeed Network with Likely Full-Duplex Links Highlighted in Bold

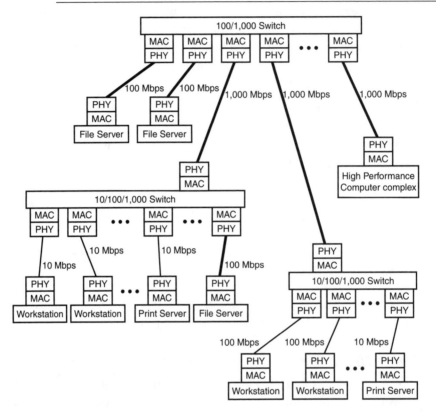

Both entities and the network medium must be capable of, and be configured for, two-way simultaneous frame transmission as shown in part (a) of Figure 3.15. Full-duplex transmission may not be used in repeater-based collision domains, unless the repeater has been equipped with full-duplex ports. We will discuss full-duplex operation in repeaters, bridges, and switches in Chapter 4 and will consider its system impact in Chapter 13.

Figure 3.15 Full-Duplex Operation

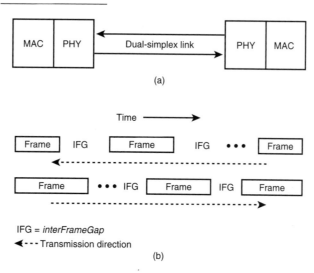

(a)

IFG = *interFrameGap*
◄ - - - Transmission direction

(b)

Because each transmission path supports simplex transmission (single direction only), and because there can be only two MACs for each full-duplex portion of the network, there can be no media contention. This means that there will be no collisions, no need to send a jam signal, no need for Extension bits at the end of a short frame, and no need to schedule retransmissions. Transmission on each simplex link is asynchronous, as shown in part (b) of Figure 3.15, and can begin whenever the frame is ready and the *interFrameGap* time has expired. Each transmitted frame must be at least *minFrameSize* octets in length.

3.3.4   Transmission of MAC Control Frames

MAC Control frames are MAC client data frames that are distinguished from LLC data frames by their particular type identifier. Transmission is essentially the same as for basic MAC frames, except that the transmission is initiated by receipt of a *MAC_CONTROL.request* primitive rather than an *MA_UNITDATA.request* (see Figure 3.16).

Figure 3.16   MAC Data and Control Communication Paths, MAC Control Implemented

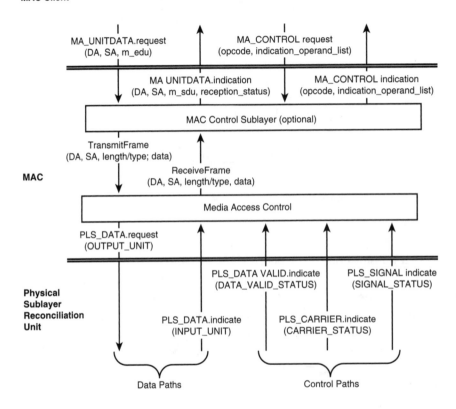

MAC Control frames are given transmission precedence over MAC client data frames, and MAC Control PAUSE frames can only be sent over a full-duplex link.

3.3.5 Transmission of VLAN-Tagged Frames

VLAN-tagged frames are also MAC client data frames that are distinguished from LLC data frames by their particular type identifier. Transmission is initiated and controlled in the same manner as a basic MAC frame. VLAN-tagged frames may be sent over either half- or full-duplex links.

3.4 Frame Reception

Frame reception is not just the opposite of frame transmission. Frame reception consists of the following sequence of operations, as illustrated in Figure 3.17.

1. Address recognition

2. Framing

3. FCS validation

4. Frame type determination

5. Frame disassembly and forwarding

Figure 3.17   Gigabit Ethernet Frame Reception

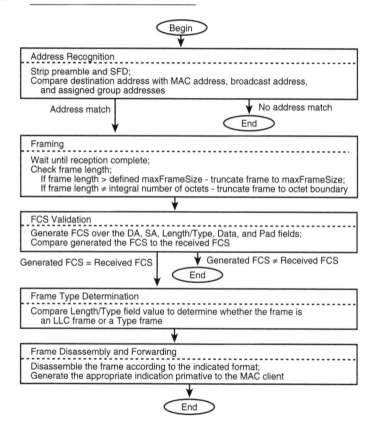

Frame reception is triggered by the receipt of a *PLS_DATA_VALID.indicate* primitive with a *DATA_VALID_STATUS* parameter value of *DATA_VALID* and begins with the detection of the SFD. The MAC presumes that it is the possible destination of all frames crossing the network and does an address recognition check as soon as the DA has been received.

3.4.1 Address Recognition

The destination addresses of all incoming frames are matched against the receiving station's address list (its individual address plus all of its assigned group addresses and the broadcast address) to determine whether the frames may be destined for the receiving station. Whether or not the frame is further processed and forwarded by the MAC is determined by the following rules:

- Any frame with a destination address equal to the receiving station's individual MAC address is accepted and processed.

- Any frame with a destination address equal to any currently active group address that has been specified for the receiving station by a network management or a higher layer is accepted and processed.

- Any frame with a destination address equal to the broadcast address is accepted and processed.

Incoming frames with destination addresses not matching any of the preceding criteria are discarded as part of normal operation.

3.4.2 Framing

Incoming frames are checked for two possible types of framing errors: the frame is too long, or the frame length is not an integral number of octets. The MAC is not required to enforce the frame size limit; however:

- If the MAC does not support VLAN tagging, it may truncate frames with octet counts that exceed *maxUntaggedFrameSize*.

- If the MAC supports VLAN tagging, it may truncate frames with octet counts that exceed (*maxUntaggedFrameSize* + 4).

- If the frame does not contain an integral multiple of 8 bits, the frame is truncated to the nearest octet boundary.

3.4.3 FCS Validation

The frame is checked for transmission errors by generating a new FCS value over the bits in the incoming frame (except for the FCS field) and by comparing the newly generated FCS value with the transmitted FCS value. If an exact match is not obtained, a transmission error has occurred and the frame is identified as being invalid.

3.4.4 Frame Type Determination

The value of the Length/Type field defines the type of frame being received:

- If the value ≤ 1,500, the frame is an LLC data frame.

- If the value = 34,824 (88-08 hexadecimal), the frame is a MAC Control frame.

- If the value = 33,024 (81-00 hexadecimal), the frame is a VLAN-tagged frame.

- If the value is none of the above, the frame may be a private-use Type-Frame. Private-use frames are not defined by the standard, and it typically implies a non-standard proprietary function.

Earlier versions of the standard allowed frames with Length/Type field values > 1,500 to be ignored, discarded, or used in a private manner. This provision has recently been deleted from the frame format definition section of the standard and replaced with a note indicating that the Registration Authority of the IEEE Standards Department now administers Type field assignments. We interpret this as continuing to allow private type field designators, so long as they are properly registered.

3.4.5 Frame Disassembly and Forwarding

If the incoming frame passes all error checks, it is then disassembled according to the format indicated by the Length/Type field and forwarded as indicated in sections 3.4.5.1 through 3.4.5.3.

3.4.5.1 LLC Data Frames

If the Length/Type value indicates that the frame is an LLC data frame, the pad is stripped from the Data field, and the DA, SA, and LLC data octets are forwarded to the MAC client as parameters in an *MA_UNITDATA.indication* primitive.

3.4.5.2 MAC Control Frames

If the MAC is implemented with MAC Control capability, and if the Length/Type value indicates that the frame is a MAC Control frame, the reserved octets are stripped from the MAC Control parameters field, and the DA, SA, MAC Control Opcode, and the opcode parameters are forwarded to the MAC client as parameters in a *MAC_CONTROL.indication* primitive.

Otherwise, the frame is treated as a type frame, and the contents of the Data and Pad fields are presumed to be correct. The DA, SA, type field indicator, and the entire contents of the Data and Pad fields are forwarded to the MAC client as parameters in an *MA_UNITDATA.indication* primitive.

3.4.5.3 VLAN-Tagged Frames

VLAN-tagged frames are treated the same as data frames. The octet sequence in the Tag Control Information field, the MAC client Length/Type field, the MAC client Data field, and the Pad fields are treated as the Data+Pad field in a basic MAC frame. The DA, SA, type field indicator, and the entire contents of the Data+Pad fields are forwarded to the MAC client as parameters in an *MA_UNITDATA.indication* primitive.

3.4.6 Collision Filtering

While collision monitoring is part of the transmission control process, collisions cannot be monitored, per se, during frame reception. Collision detect is generated only during transmit operations and is never valid during frame reception.

If the octet count < *minFrameSize*, the received frame is presumed to be a fragment resulting from a collision. The frame is discarded and, since collisions are a normal occurrence in CSMA/CD operation, the discarded fragment is not reported to the MAC client as an error.

3.4.7 Invalid MAC frames

Frames can be designated as invalid for any one of the following three conditions:

- The frame length is inconsistent with the length value specified in the Length/Type field, except when the value is a predefined type value (for example, for MAC Control, VLAN tagging, or registered private use).

- The frame length is not an integral number of octets.

- The frame is determined to contain an FCS error.

Invalid frames are not passed on to the LLC or MAC Control sublayers. However, invalid frames may be passed on to other types of MAC client sublayers to be used in a private manner.

3.4.8 Error Recovery

The MAC provides error detection, but not error recovery. Error recovery (requesting retransmission of frames received with detected transmission errors) is typically a function of layer 4 in the OSI model.

3.5 Idle Mode

Even though the MAC may not be transmitting a frame, waiting to transmit a frame, or receiving a frame, it is never completely idle. The MAC starts the *interFrameGap* timer when the last bit of the outgoing (or incoming) frame has been sent (or received) and continues to monitor the network for the presence of a carrier, which would indicate an incoming frame.

3.6 Summary

So what really are the differences between the various MACs? Are they just issues or do they result in compatibility problems?

3.6.1 Speed-Related Differences

As stated earlier, with the exception of speed differences, all pre-1997 MACs were functionally equal. Table 3.1 lists the implementation-dependent parameters for 10 Mbps, 100 Mbps, and 1,000 Mbps data transmission rates and shows a high level of operational consistency. Speed is not a compatibility problem. You'll see in Chapter 4 that speed differences are easily handled by bridges and switches.

Table 3.1   Implementation-Dependent MAC Parameters

Parameters	Values for 10 Mbps MACs	Values for 100 Mbps MACs	Values for 1,000 Mbps MACs
slotTime	512 bit times	512 bit times	4,096 bit times
interFrameGap	9.6 µs	0.96 µs	0.096 µs
AttemptLimit	16	16	16
backOffLimit	10	10	10
jamSize	32 bits	32 bits	32 bits
maxUntaggedFrameSize	1,518 octets	1,518 octets	1,518 octets
minFrameSize	64 octets	64 octets	64 octets
burstLimit	n/a	n/a	8,192 bits

3.6.2 Operational Mode Differences

The standard requires that network entities be capable of operating in half-duplex mode, full-duplex mode, or both. It also requires that at any given time all directly connected devices (such as end stations or switch ports at each end of a link) be configured to use the same mode, either half-duplex or full-duplex, but not both modes at the same time. There are two possibilities:

- End stations and intermediate network devices connected in a single collision domain must always operate in half-duplex mode.

- End stations and intermediate network devices that are connected to each other with a single link segment may operate in either half- or full-duplex mode, so long as both are configured to use the same mode.

This standard restriction is not really much of a restriction. It does not preclude the use of both half- and full-duplex stations in the same network. It just means that the central element in the star topology needs to be a device (repeater or switch) with ports that are capable of supporting the operational mode of the attached station.

The half- versus full-duplex issue should not be a concern for Gigabit Ethernet. Because the full-duplex standard was approved more than a year before Gigabit Ethernet, market pressure will probably force most, if not all, Gigabit Ethernet network devices to be compatible with both operational modes.

Chapter 13 discusses network configuration of multispeed networks with both half- and full-duplex stations, repeaters, and switches in greater detail.

3.6.3 Frame Format-Related Differences

Section 3.4 showed that the basic MAC frame format required one speed-related and two option-related changes.

3.6.3.1 The Carrier-Extension Field

The Carrier-Extension field is a format modification that is only required for Gigabit Ethernet operating in half-duplex mode. However, the Carrier-Extension field is appended to the end of the FCS field and is discarded by the receiving station before frame disassembly. You will see in Chapter 4 that multispeed bridges and switches will automatically handle short frames and will add or discard extension fields as required by the data rate. The Carrier-Extension field is not a compatibility issue.

3.6.3.2 MAC Control

While the MAC Control option includes the framework for the addition of future control opcodes and opcode parameters, the only currently defined control function is the PAUSE operation, which:

- Provides point-to-point flow control over a *single* full-duplex link

- Prevents potential memory overrun at a receiving device (such as a switch port, a lower speed user station, and so forth) that cannot process the frames as fast as the transmitting device (such as a high-speed server or another switch port) can send them

Because the PAUSE operation requires a specific action (cease frame transmission for an indicated period of time), both stations must be implemented with MAC Control capability.

The use of the PAUSE operation for flow control will be discussed in greater detail in section 4.4.2 of Chapter 4 with respect to its use in full-duplex repeater and switch port configurations, in section 8.4.5 of Chapter 8, "Physical Coding, Physical Medium Attachment, and Auto-Negotiation for 1000BASE-X," with respect to how it is enabled.

3.6.3.3 VLAN Tagging

While VLAN tagging was designed to aid routing and network management in an extended network, its real potential may be in a different application area. Earlier Ethernet networks were never intended for operating environments requiring real-time communications and frame-delivery guarantees. Because each local network is assigned a default VLAN identifier, VLAN tagging will allow frames to be assigned transmission priorities, and allow Ethernet networks to support time-sensitive applications (such as real-time process control, multimedia, and so forth). Chapter 13 revisits VLAN tagging and the use of transmission priorities.

3.6.3.4 The Gigabit Ethernet Impact

Table 3.2 shows the relationship and co-requirements (Std. MAC, MAC Control, VLAN tagging, full-duplex) for each of the currently defined MAC configurations.

Table 3.2   Gigabit MAC Configuration Co-Requirements

Installed MAC Options	Std MAC	MAC Control	VLAN tagging	Full-duplex	Comment
No options	req.	N/A	N/A	N/A	Fully backward compatible
MAC Control	req.	req.	N/A	req.	Currently allows single link flow control.[a] Additional control functions may be added in the future
VLAN tagging	req.	N/A	req.	N/A	Allows both routing designation and priority ority transmission, subsequently expanding application coverage
Full-duplex	req.	N/A	N/A	req.	More than doubles the effective link transfer rate. May not be used in repeater-based collision domains

[a]The MAC Control PAUSE operates on a single link basis only, and only in conjunction with full-duplex operation. The PAUSE operation provides a momentary recovery period for a switch port or end station approaching saturation from continuous or nearly continuous data flow across the connected link. It should not be confused with end-to-end flow control (for example, with reception acknowledgment and sliding-window transmission control), which must be provided by higher layers in the protocol.

So which options should be included in a Gigabit Ethernet MAC? The answer depends on the incremental cost and expected return for each option, plus the present and likely future application mix of the network. For example:

- Full-duplex is likely to be a very low-cost option because it only involves providing independent control and buffering for the already existing data transmission and reception paths in the MAC. The Gigabit physical layers are all defined for full-duplex transmission and the return on investment is more than twice the effective link transmission rate.

- MAC Control is a companion option to full-duplex operation, because it provides a way to control data flow across a full-duplex link and prevent loss of frames due to memory overflow. The full-duplex and MAC Control options can both be implemented on a link-by-link basis without affecting other parts of the network.

- VLAN tagging offers two powerful upgrade possibilities by allowing both extended network routing designation and transmission priorities to be included in the transmitted frame.

  - Network management of location changes should be easier because end station addresses can be associated with a VLAN rather than a station port number.

  - The network can be used for applications requiring time-dependent delivery guarantees even if the network is not part of a VLAN complex (each network has a default VLAN ID).

Unlike MAC Control and full-duplex, however, VLAN tagging cannot be implemented on a link-by-link basis. The affected end stations and all intermediate network entities must be VLAN-compliant to allow priority transmission. Implementation cost will also include the cost of new Ethernet cards and software drivers for each of the affected existing stations and switches. Priority designation cannot be used in repeater-based networks.

Gigabit Repeaters, Bridges, Routers, and Switches

A review of the various IEEE 802.3 and other supporting IEEE 802 standards will show that these documents specifically define only two intermediate network devices (bridges and repeaters) for use with Ethernet LANs, and that the repeater definition covers only half-duplex operation. However, Chapter 1, "Ethernet Development: The Need for Speed," stated that Ethernet LANs can also include routers and switches; Chapter 3, "Media Access Control," showed that end stations can be implemented with full-duplex capability; and in this chapter, you will see that repeaters can also be designed for full-duplex operation. Full-duplex repeaters are extensions of half-duplex repeaters, switches are extensions of bridges, and bridges have some of the operational features that are common to routers.

One purpose of this chapter is to round out the introduction of upper layer architectural concepts before beginning discussion of the physical sublayers. A second purpose of the chapter is to provide you with an insight into the structure of repeaters, bridges, routers, and network switches in sufficient depth to enable you to make reasoned decisions during the discussion of the system aspects configuring or upgrading a network. This chapter builds on the material covered in Chapter 2, "The OSI and Gigabit Ethernet Standard Reference Models," as well as the material covered in Chapter 3. This chapter also includes coverage of the following issues:

- **The logical structure and responsibilities of half-duplex Ethernet repeaters**. Because half-duplex repeaters do not contain a MAC, they are essentially physical layer (OSI layer 1) devices.

- **Extensions that allow repeaters to operate in full-duplex mode.** Full-duplex repeaters can probably be considered as layer 1 1/2 devices. They require some, but not nearly all, of the data link layer (OSI layer 2) capabilities normally included in a MAC.

- **The logical structure and responsibilities of bridges.** The bridge entity was originally on the same architectural level as the LLC in an end station, but as now defined in the standard, bridges also provide for the inclusion of higher layer entities.

- **Bridge extensions to allow operation as a router.** Routers are typically network layer (OSI layer 3) devices and may implement some transport layer (OSI layer 4) capabilities.

- **The structure and responsibilities of a switch.** Because switches are essentially multi-port bridges and may also include router capabilities, switches may be OSI layer 2, 3, or 4 devices.

- **Flow control and use of the MAC Control PAUSE function.** Flow control is important in full-duplex operation because it provides a way to prevent frame loss during periods of high traffic volume.

- **VLAN tagging and the implementation of priority-based frame transfer in switches and repeaters.** VLAN tagging provides two capabilities that have long been missing from the Ethernet protocol: the capability to assign priority levels that indicate the relative importance during frame selection-for-transmission at intermediate nodes along a network transmission path, and the capability to separate users based on logical relationships as well as their physical location.

4.1 Repeaters

Repeaters (sometimes called hubs) are the least complex, and hence lowest cost, intermediate network device in an Ethernet LAN. However, because they are still part of a collision domain, they are also the most performance-restricting of all the possible intermediate network devices.

A repeater is essentially a signal regenerator. Its primary purpose is to detect incoming signals received on one port, to restore these signals to their original shape and amplitude, and then to retransmit (repeat) the retimed and restored signals with minimal delay to all ports except the port where the signal is being received. Repeater operation is *transparent* to the attached end stations in that two end stations communicating with each other do not know whether they are connected directly together or whether they are communicating through one or more repeaters.

Figure 4.1 shows the logical reference model for Gigabit Ethernet repeaters. The physical layers are the same as the physical layers in an end station, and Ethernet repeaters support interoperability between independently developed electrical and optical Physical Medium Dependent Sublayers (PMDs) as long as all connected devices are operating at the same transmission rate.

Figure 4.1 A Logical Reference Model for Gigabit Ethernet Repeaters

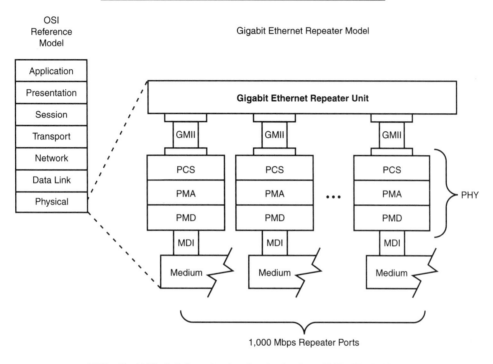

GMII = Gigabit Media Independent Interface (optional)   PHY = Physical Layer Device
MDI = Medium Dependent Interface   PMA = Physical Medium Attachment
PCS = Physical Coding Sublayer   PMD = Physical Medium Dependent Sublayer

The definition of flow control and full-duplex operation has also allowed development of full-duplex repeaters to complement the CSMA/CD half-duplex repeaters that are still common in many existing Ethernet LANs, or a lower-cost upgrade for networks that may need Gigabit capability at only the top level in the network hierarchy.

4.1.1 Half-Duplex Repeaters

Half-duplex repeaters operate in a shared-media carrier sense multiple access collision detect (CSMA/CD) environment where the shared media is contained within the repeater itself. Figure 4.2 is a conceptual depiction of a Gigabit Ethernet half-duplex repeater show-ing an incoming data stream being repeated (retransmitted) to all other *active* ports. Active ports are ports that are connected through a stable link to an active end station (such as a powered-up end station).

Figure 4.2   A Conceptual Diagram of a Half-Duplex Repeater

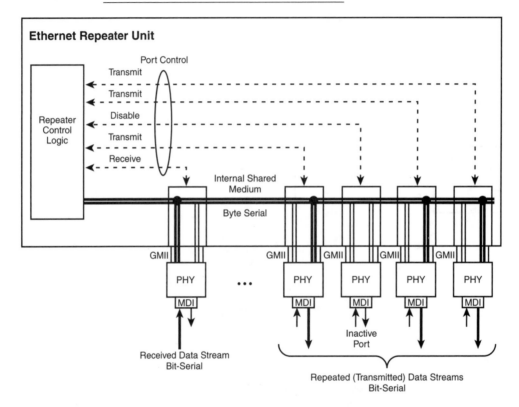

The repeater control logic monitors the control signals passed through the Gigabit Media Independent Interface (GMII) at each port in essentially the same manner as a MAC in an end station looks for the following conditions:

• **Collision-Free Retransmission**. If the network is quiet and a carrier is sensed at a port, the repeater control logic retransmits the incoming byte stream, including any received errors, to each port except the port receiving the incoming signal. Half-duplex repeaters are not equipped with frame buffers and typically exhibit port-to-port delays on the order of 20 bit times. The maximum allowable delay is 976 bit times.

Signal processing in a half-duplex repeater is the primary task of the physical layer:

- The incoming serial bit stream is detected, decoded, and translated into a serial byte stream by the Physical Layer Device (PHY) receive function in the receiving port.

  - Restoration of the outgoing signal to the correct amplitude, shape, and timing is performed by the PHY transmit function in each transmitting port.

- **Collision Detection**. Because the only shared medium is internal to the repeater, the repeater control logic is also responsible for detecting collisions. If carrier sense is detected at multiple ports, or if carrier sense is detected at any port other than the receiving port during frame retransmission, the repeater control logic generates a jam signal that is sent to all ports. The actual backoff and frame rescheduling is done by the MAC in each affected end station, as discussed in section 3.2.2 of Chapter 3.

- **Faulty Link Detection**. The repeater monitors each port to ensure that transient fault conditions on a single link (such as end-station power-up and power-down, cable disconnects, and so forth) do not cause the network to fail. If the repeater receives signals (*false carriers*) that do not meet the criteria for valid transmission, the port is disabled until the link is again stable. No frames can be sent or received while a link is unstable.

- **Jabbering End Station Detection**. The repeater also monitors incoming frames to prevent them from propagating through the network and blocking other frame transmissions. If an end-station fault causes a continuous transmission to occur (the end station is said to be *jabbering*), frame retransmission by the repeater will be stopped when the reception time exceeds a preset *jabber_timer* value. The port receiving the illegally long frame will be disabled until either power-up reset has occurred or there is no detectable carrier at that port.

Saturation can become an early problem in repeater-based networks. It is a condition where the utilization of a network collision domain is near or at the carrying capacity for that domain. In a half-duplex repeater-based network, the onset of saturation is a function of the frame-length mix (short frames requiring carrier extension are counted as minimum-length frames), frame burst usage, *interframe gap time* (IFG), and the collision frequency pattern. Chapter 13, "Upgrading Ethernet LANs: System and Topology Considerations," considers ways to keep a network out of saturation.

4.1.2 *Full-Duplex Buffered Repeaters*

Because all Gigabit Ethernet PHYs are already capable of full-duplex operation, all that is required to allow full-duplex operation in Gigabit Ethernet repeaters is transmit and receive buffers and buffer control for each port plus repeater-wide arbitration logic to schedule frame retransmissions (see Figure 4.3). The port buffer control is typically implemented with a separate MAC for each port, and port arbitration can be either by round robin sequencing or by order of frame reception.

Figure 4.3   Conceptual Diagram of a Full-Duplex Repeater

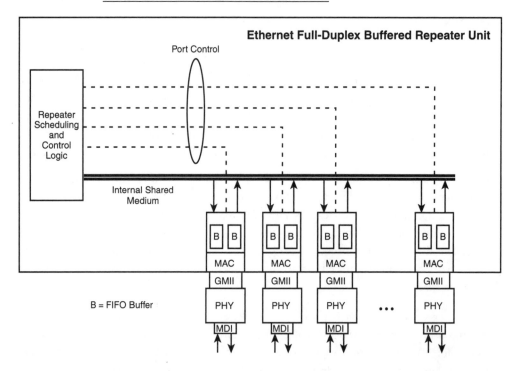

Full-duplex operation in a repeater may seem a little inconsistent in light of everything stated in Chapter 1 about repeater-based networks, but it is really not. Full-duplex repeaters provide a low-cost operational improvement over half-duplex repeaters, particularly during high-contention periods, such as:

- Full-duplex operation allows end stations to send and receive frames at the same time.

- Receive buffers in each port smooth the overall network flow by allowing the repeater to receive and temporarily store frames from several end stations at the same time it is sending frames from the transmit buffers in each port.

- The combination of individual port buffers and internal arbitration eliminates collisions in the shared media. Further, because collisions are eliminated, carrier extensions are also never needed. Frames can be transmitted from both repeater ports and end stations when ready and need only to be separated by the designated interframe gap.

Because transmission is collision-free, network saturation levels in a buffered repeater are a function of only the frame-length mix and the interframe gap. The result is increased network bandwidth and a transfer rate approaching 1,000 Mbps for a buffered Gigabit repeater.

However, buffers also create a potential problem. Transmissions from end stations are typically bursty, and if the network traffic level is already high, a port's receive buffer can fill faster than the repeater can empty it. If a receive buffer is already full and the attached end station sends another frame, that frame will be lost.

One obvious solution to the bursty transmission problem is to increase the size of the buffer space in each port. This leads to two questions. How much additional space will be needed, and how much will it increase the cost? The cost question is rather easily answered, once the buffer space is defined. However, predicting how much additional space is needed to prevent all frame loss under high traffic conditions is risky, at best. A large file transfer from a single high-speed workstation, for example, could consume the entire network bandwidth. If other end stations are also sending during the same period, at least some frames will be lost.

Figure 4.4 shows another possible solution to bursty transmission. If a port's receive buffer begins to fill up, the port buffer flow control logic issues a MAC Control PAUSE frame to stop transmission from the end station long enough to allow the buffer to be at least partially emptied.

Figure 4.4 A Conceptual Diagram of a Full-Duplex Buffered Repeater Port

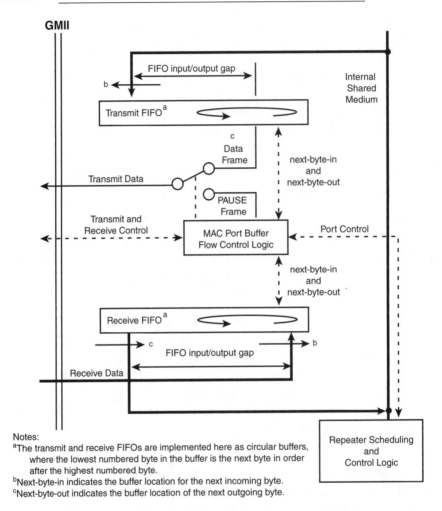

Notes:
[a]The transmit and receive FIFOs are implemented here as circular buffers, where the lowest numbered byte in the buffer is the next byte in order after the highest numbered byte.
[b]Next-byte-in indicates the buffer location for the next incoming byte.
[c]Next-byte-out indicates the buffer location of the next outgoing byte.

If the port buffers empty faster than expected, a second MAC Control PAUSE frame with the pause value set to zero can be used to resume transmission from the end station.

Note

A second PAUSE frame canceling the first may not be able to reach the end station before that entity has resumed sending frames. In this case, it would be better not to send the second PAUSE frame because it would interrupt the transmit stream.

The port buffer flow control unit in Figure 4.4 maintains a set of pointers and a frame queue for both the transmit and receive buffers, as shown in Figure 4.5.

Figure 4.5 Example Buffered Repeater Control Pointers and Queues

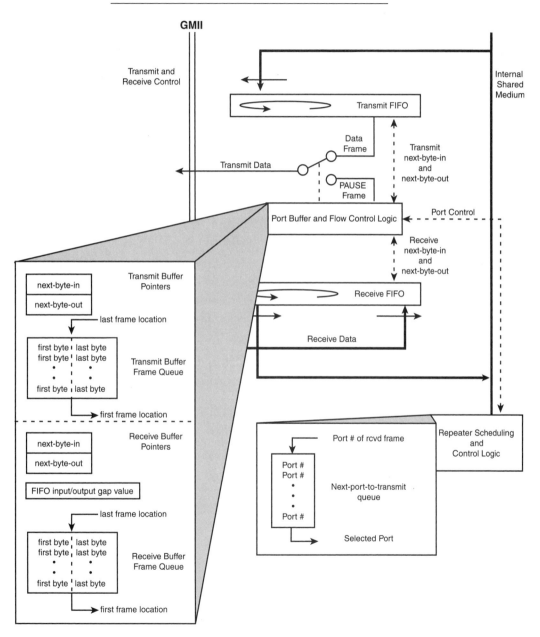

The next-byte-in pointer indicates where the next byte in the incoming frame is to be placed in the associated buffer and the next-byte-out pointer indicates the location of the next byte to be removed from the buffer. A first-in, first-out (FIFO) frame queue contains pointers to the beginning and end of each frame currently in the buffer. The *FIFO input/output gap* value (distance between the next-byte-in pointer and the next-byte-out pointer) indicates the buffer space currently available in the receive buffer. And finally, a master next-port-to-transmit queue in the repeater scheduling and control logic tracks the port frame-reception order and controls port selection for the next frame to be transmitted.

Port buffer sizes are typically limited to keep repeater costs down, but sufficient space must be available in the receive buffer to allow the port to continue receiving frames while the end station is notified of, and has had time to act upon, the PAUSE request.

The sequence shown in Figure 4.6 depicts a worst-case condition. The end station is in the middle of a long file transfer. It has been sending a series of maximum-length frames and:

- The FIFO input/output gap in the port receive buffer drops below the minimum allowable threshold value just as the port begins downloading a maximum-length data frame on the outbound half of the link. The port must finish sending this frame before it can send the PAUSE frame (a frame transmission in progress is never interrupted for MAC Control frames).

- By the time the end station has received, checked, and decoded the PAUSE frame, the end station port has just begun transmitting another maximum-length frame to the repeater.

- During the same period, several other ports occupy higher positions in the repeater control logic's next-port-to-transmit queue, and the repeater is not able to remove any of the frames currently in this port's receive buffer.

Figure 4.6 Receive Buffer Minimum Space Margin for Flow Control

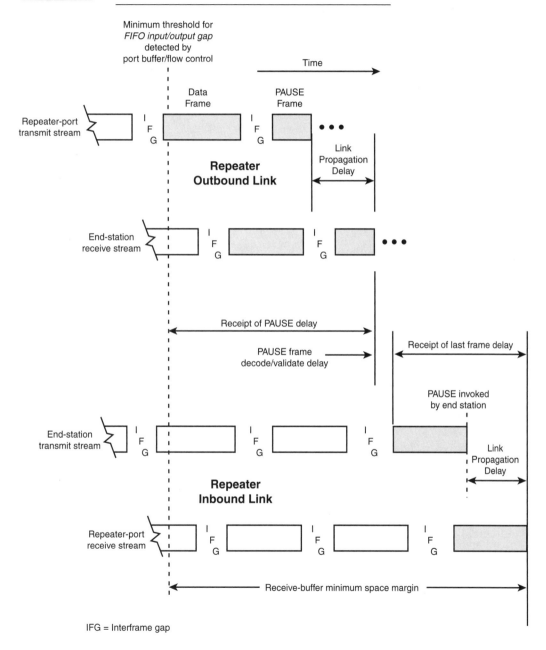

IFG = Interframe gap

The critical times are depicted by the shaded transmission sequence in Figure 4.6. The receive buffer in the repeater port must allow space for all frames that will have been sent between the time the minimum threshold was detected by the repeater port and the PAUSE frame has been received and acted upon by the end station.

The actual space margin required for the receive buffer in any specific network is dependent on the transmission rate, the link lengths, the propagation time for the installed cable, and the MAC Control decode time of the end station. If the scaling were correct in Figure 4.6 (which it isn't), you would need a space margin for slightly more than three maximum-length frames to avoid frame loss. However, you would probably want space for at least six or seven maximum-length frames to avoid having to invoke frequent pauses.

Note

MAC Control frames are subject to the same types of transmission errors as data frames. If an error occurred during transmission of the PAUSE frame, the end station would continue sending data frames and some would be lost. The extremely low bit error rate (BER—typically less than 10^{-10}) makes transmission errors in Ethernet networks extremely rare. Also, MAC Control frames are much shorter (88 bytes) than maximum-length data frames (12,208 bytes) so it is not much of a gamble to assume that PAUSE frames will be correctly received.

However, there are a couple of ways to mitigate the possibility of transmission error in MAC Control PAUSE frames. One is to send multiple PAUSE frames (two are probably enough). Another is to increase the minimum buffer margin. The trade-off is a one-time buffer cost versus a long-term decrease (very small) in available bandwidth each time a pause was invoked (the effective total PAUSE-frame length for two PAUSE frames would be 176 bytes plus two IFGs versus 88 bytes and one IFG if only one PAUSE frame is sent).

Transmit buffer sizes, on the other hand, can be smaller than receive buffer sizes for two reasons:

- The only time a port is required to stop transmitting data frames from the transmit buffer is when the port buffer/flow control logic requires the port to send a PAUSE frame. Data frame transmission can resume as soon as the PAUSE frame has been sent.

- Any time lost sending the PAUSE frame is automatically recovered the next time the repeater scheduling and control logic selects this port for frame retransmission (data frames received by a port are not retransmitted by that port).

Section 4.4.2 later in the chapter shows that these concepts also apply to port buffer configuration and flow control in switches. The Chapter 13 discussion on network topology and system considerations also revisits these topics and provides numerical values for the various dependent factors.

4.1.3 Managed Repeaters

Before moving on to bridges, routers, and switches, you need to become familiar with a topic that has been purposely ignored up to now: network management. While it is entirely possible to configure and successfully operate a small network with bare-bones repeaters (or switches) as intermediate network devices, the only indicators that something is not operating correctly or that the network is becoming overloaded are user complaints. Unfortunately, user complaints are often not very helpful in determining the cause or extent of the problem, and they seldom provide much lead time for a solution.

Management of larger interconnected networks, however, needs more than just anecdotal information about how the network is performing, what may be intermittently or continuously malfunctioning, or where a bottleneck is occurring. Repeaters (as well as bridges, routers, and switches) may be equipped with an optional network management capability that allows the network manager to monitor performance and load factors, to isolate faults, and to control network devices by setting the value of selected variables. Figure 4.7 shows a conceptual diagram of a managed repeater.

Figure 4.7   Conceptual Diagram of a Managed Repeater

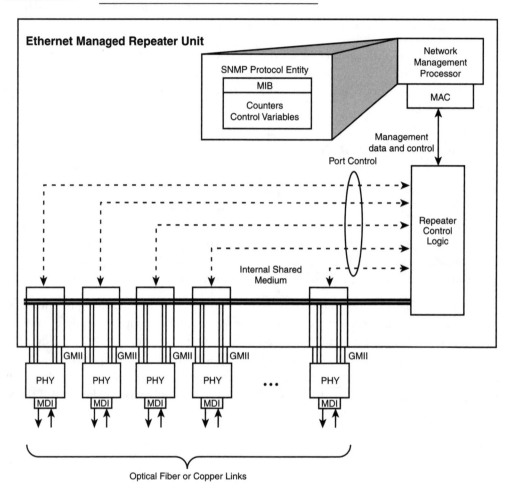

MIB = Management Information Base
SNMP = Simple Network Mangagement Protocol

The internal management processor is essentially equivalent to an end station. It utilizes the Simple Network Management Protocol (SNMP) developed by the Internet Engineering Task Force (IETF) and maintains a Management Information Base (MIB) that contains managed objects (counters, control variables, and so forth) relating to the performance and control of the repeater. Specific definitions of the managed objects in the MIB are contained in the IEEE 802.3 standards documents and in IETF Requests For Comment (RFCs).

Additional information on the IETF and its various RFCs pertaining to Ethernet managed objects may be found on the Internet at the IETF Web page (www.ietf.org) and at the Stanford Linear Accelerator Network Reference Information Web page (www.slac.stanford.edu/comp/net/reference.html).

4.2 Bridges

When bridges first appeared in the early 1980s, they were specifically designed to interconnect local networks that were operating under the same protocol. Individual LANs had begun to grow, and that started to be a problem. The maximum number of stations in an Ethernet collision domain is 1,024, but if you think about it, that is a rather ridiculous number. Imagine trying to gain access to a network with that many possible contenders. They certainly wouldn't all be trying to transmit at the same time, but there could still be a high probability of collisions at most times during the workday.

Clearly, something had to be done. The reasoning was that since an estimated 80 percent of the network traffic was localized to individual workgroups, partitioning networks into smaller network segments (subnets) would not only increase the average effective bandwidth available for each user, it would also greatly lower the probability of a collision during transmission.

The premise was correct, and bridges provided the means to allow an end station in one subnet to communicate with an end station in another. Furthermore, since bridges could be made to identify which traffic was local and which wasn't, they would only have to carry about 20 percent of the total network load (depending on how many subnets were involved in a network and how they were interconnected, the actual traffic on individual bridges could be considerably less than 20 percent).

Bridges were developed as layer 2 (data link) devices to provide both protocol and speed translation for frames originating in one LAN that needed to be sent to a station in another LAN. The following capabilities were to be included:

- Incoming frames were to be checked for transmission errors and were to be forwarded only if they were error free.

- If both LANs on either side of the bridge operated under the same protocol, format translation would not be required, and the bridge would be allowed to transfer the entire frame, as received, without having to append a new FCS.

- If the bridged LANs operated under different protocols, the bridge would translate the incoming frame into the appropriate format for the other LAN's protocol and append a new FCS before it was retransmitted on the other LAN.

- If the bridged LANs operated at different transmission rates, bridge buffers would provide speed conversion to match the transmission rate requirements of both LANs.

- Bridges would be able to be configured with the individual and/or group addresses associated with each of the connected LANs and would forward only those frames addressed to stations or groups known to be associated with the output port.

However, bridges did not keep up with advances in network technology (such as high-speed switches, routers, and routing switches) or with changing traffic patterns brought on by the development of the Internet and large corporate networks. As a result, bridges, per se, have essentially disappeared from the marketplace.

Note

Bridges have not actually disappeared from the marketplace, but their name has. Bridges are now commonly known as layer 2 switches. The name change may have originally been marketing hype—the need to differentiate the new devices from the bridges that were available at that time and to call attention to the fact that they were faster and had greater port capacity. Whatever the reason, however, the name has now become generic throughout the industry.

That being the case, you might question the need to discuss bridge architectures at all. Why not go immediately to discussions of routers and switches? There are several reasons not to do so:

- Bridges provide the architectural basis of both switches and routers.

- The current standards define bridges but not switches or routers [IEEE 802.1P and IEEE 802.1Q]. IEEE 802 openly accepts that switches are multiport bridges. However, definitions for new capabilities will continue to build on the well-established bridging architectural models and terminology.

- More and more, routers are becoming integrated with switches (sometimes called routing switches), making the differences between bridges, routers, and switches only an issue of how many layers are implemented in the particular device.

- And finally, some existing networks that will likely become candidates for upgrade may still contain intermediate network devices that are actually called bridges.

Two examples of added bridge capability that were developed after it became apparent that switches, rather than bridges, would become the dominant technology are the definitions for VLAN tagging and for learning bridges (a learning bridge has the capability to monitor packet addresses to learn the addresses of stations associated with each port, rather than requiring them to be entered manually).

Figure 4.8 shows the logical reference model for a bridge. It consists of a MAC and an LLC for each port, a bridge protocol entity, and a MAC relay unit. The MAC relay unit provides frame transfers (relays) that can be accomplished at the MAC level (such as frame transfer between two Ethernet LANs). The bridge protocol entity provides frame relays that must be accomplished at higher than MAC levels (between Ethernet and Token Ring, for example).

Figure 4.8 Bridge Reference Model

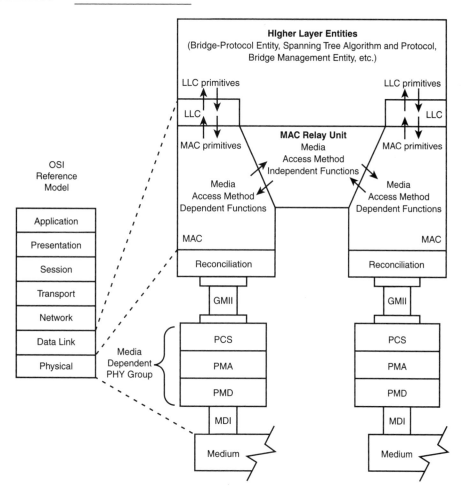

Bridges may have two or more ports, and the MAC and LLC layers for each port are essentially the same as a MAC and LLC layers in an end station. The physical layers in each port are also the same as the physical layers in an end station. Each port will have its own MAC address, and bridges, like repeaters, are transparent to network end stations.

Figure 4.9 shows the two data paths in a bridge through the MAC relay unit and through the bridge protocol entity. The decision as to which path a frame will take is based on the destination address of the frame:

- If the destination address of the received frame is different from the port's MAC address, the frame is sent to the MAC relay unit for processing.

- If the destination address of the received frame is the same as the port's MAC address, the frame is sent to the LLC for processing.

Figure 4.9   Bridge Data Paths

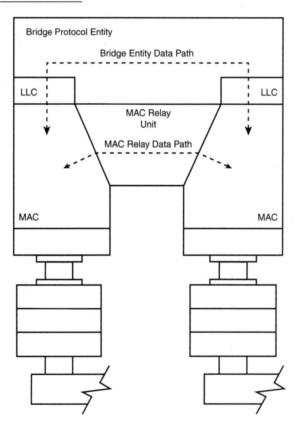

4.2.1 MAC Relay Frame Transfer

The MAC relay unit in a bridge contains two major information entities, a filtering database and a port state information register for each port, as shown in Figure 4.10.

Figure 4.10   The MAC Relay Unit

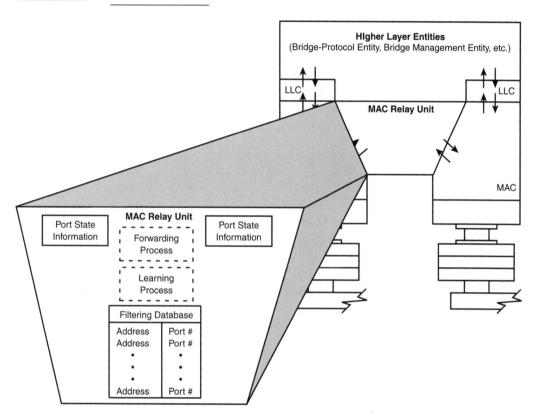

The following list explains the different components of the MAC relay unit.

- The *port state information* registers identify the protocol of the LAN attached to that port and contain the current operational state of each port. The primary port states are as follows:

  - **Blocking**. The port is not allowed to participate in an active frame relay. Frames received on a blocked port are discarded to prevent duplicate frames from circulating on the network. The port will be considered in Spanning Tree active topology calculations (see section 4.2.3 later in this chapter).

- **Forwarding**. The port is part of the active topology and is allowed to participate in an active frame relay.

- **Disabled**. The port has been disabled by network management and will not be considered in the Spanning Tree active topology calculation.

- The *filtering database* contains both individual and group addresses associated with each port. The addresses may be physical MAC addresses of network end stations and bridge ports, or logical IDs. Addresses may be inserted into, or deleted from, the filtering database by the learning process or by network management.

- The *learning process* monitors the source address of every frame received on each port and conditionally updates the filtering database port address list depending on the state of the port.

- The *forwarding process* compares the destination address of the received frames to the addresses in the filtering database, and if a match is found, conditionally forwards the frames to the indicated port(s).

When incoming frames are received by the MAC in a bridge port, they are decoded and checked for transmission errors in the same manner as in an end station. If the destination address of the frame is different from the MAC address of the receiving port, and if no errors are found, the MAC issues an *M_UNITDATA.indication* primitive transferring the frame to the forwarding process in the MAC relay unit (see Figure 4.11). Frames received with detected errors are discarded.

Figure 4.11   MAC Relay Frame Transfer

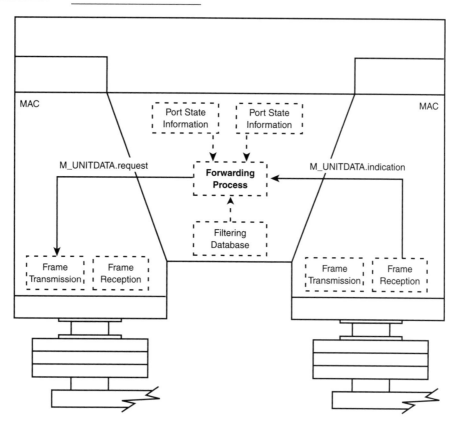

The basic concepts of the bridge relay operation can be seen by following the path of a received frame through the states of the forwarding process shown in Figure 4.12.

Figure 4.12   MAC Relay Unit Forwarding Process

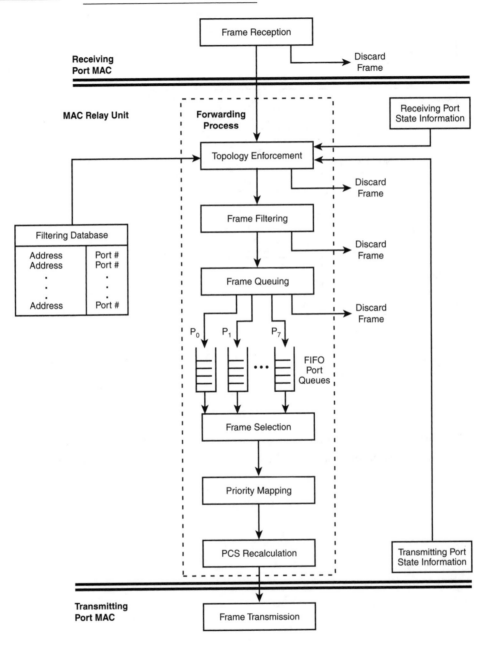

The following list details the steps of the MAC relay unit forwarding process in greater depth.

1. **Topology Enforcement.** If the state of the port where the frame was received is "forwarding," the received frame will be considered for potential retransmission (relaying). All ports in the "forwarding" state (other than the port receiving the frame) will be considered as potential destination ports so long as the data length in the received frame does not exceed the allowed data length of the protocol associated with the potential destination port. If no port meets these criteria, the frame is discarded.

2. **Frame Filtering.** The destination address of the received frame is matched against the MAC addresses associated with each potential destination port identified by topology enforcement. A copy of the frame is sent for queuing at each port where an address match is found.

3. **Frame Queuing.** Filtered frames are checked for priority and placed in the indicated output queues for each valid destination port as shown in Figure 4.12.

4. **Frame Selection.** Within each port, frames are selected for transmission based on priority level and order of receipt. Frames in highest priority queues are sent before frames in lower priority queues. Within a given priority queue, frames are sent in the same order that they were received (FIFO).

5. **FCS Recalculation.** A new frame check sequence (FCS) value will have to be calculated if the frame is being forwarded between two MAC entities (bridge ports) that operate under different protocols (Ethernet and Token Ring, for example) where the content of one or more fields within the format's FCS coverage has been converted to a different format representation. Frames being forwarded between two MAC entities with the same protocol (for example, both are Ethernet) may use the FCS value of the received frame.

4.2.2 Bridge Protocol Entity Frame Transfer

Frames that require higher level protocol actions are addressed to the receiving port's MAC, which forwards them through the LLC to the appropriate higher layer protocol entity for processing. Frames in this category may be forwarded to an output port as shown in Figure 4.13, or may be acted upon within the bridge itself (for SNMP queries and control actions, for example).

Figure 4.13   Network and Transport Layer Frame Relay

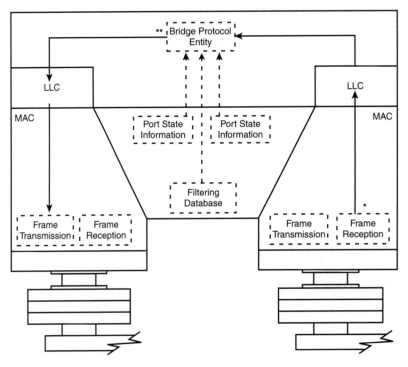

* Received frame destination address = port MAC address

** The address of next hop MAC has been inserted into the frame's destination address

The higher layer entity extracts the network destination address from the network level header (which is contained in the frame's data field) to determine whether the frame needs forwarding or whether it is a frame (such as SNMP) that can be acted upon within the bridge. If the frame needs forwarding, the protocol entity compares the frame's destination address to the addresses in the filtering database to determine the appropriate port for the next hop, and the frame is forwarded to that port for transmission.

4.2.3   Network Configuration and Reconfiguration

Another important bridge capability deals with network configuration on power-up and reconfiguration after faults. Consider the physical network shown in part (a) of Figure 4.14. Three bridges interconnect three LANs, providing two possible network paths between each pair of LANs. The alternate paths provide increased network reliability, since a failure of any one bridge would not disrupt network connectability, but they also present a problem. Multiple paths could mean multiple copies of the same frame being received by an end station, and that would violate one of the goals of the Ethernet protocol.

Figure 4.14   An Example Bridge-Connected-Network Topology Configuration

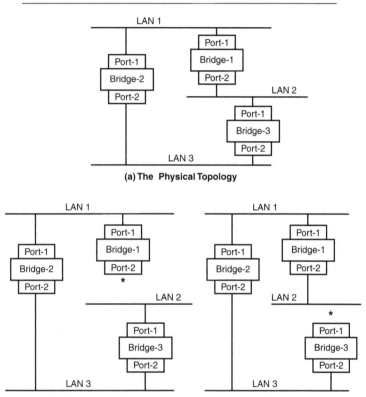

(a) The Physical Topology

* The Spanning Tree Algorithm and Protocol has blocked the indicated ports

(b) Alternate Active Topologies

IEEE 802 bridges utilize the IEEE Spanning Tree Algorithm and Protocol that monitors, evaluates, and configures (or reconfigures) the network topology to ensure that there will be only one active network path at any time between any pair of end stations. The particular configuration is typically selected based on segment traffic loads, accumulated *path costs* that reflect the speed of the segments to which the ports are connected, and so forth. The Spanning Tree Protocol enables or disables a bridge port by sending a configuration frame containing a port ID and a new port state value to the designated bridge. Part (b) of Figure 4.14 contains the two alternate single-path configurations for the example network.

4.2.4 *Bridge Buffer Control and Transit Delay*

Input buffers in bridge ports are subject to the same buffer overflow problems and can use the same control procedures that occur in full-duplex repeaters. The same cannot be said about the port transmit buffers.

Transmit buffers in full-duplex repeaters can always catch up with the traffic stream on the internal shared media after being interrupted to send a PAUSE frame because frames received by that port are never retransmitted by that port (frames received on a bridge port are also never retransmitted on that port). But, multiport bridges can receive and forward traffic streams from several ports at the same time, and several of these streams can have frames destined for the same output port, causing the total buffer input rate to be greater than the transmission rate of the port. Since ports in the same bridge entity cannot send PAUSE frames to each other, bridges are typically equipped with large output buffers, and frames that overflow the buffers are discarded.

Because of their capability to buffer data, bridges are less likely to lose data during short bursts. However, buffering, along with address filtering and priority queuing, does introduce transit delay in the bridge that can be much larger than the transit delay of a repeater. The defined maximum allowable delay for a bridge is four seconds, with a recommended value of one second. Frames delayed longer than the set maximum are discarded.

4.3 *Routers*

At first look, it could appear that routers and bridges serve the same function. However, bridges are designed to interconnect different segments of a LAN. Routers, on the other hand, are designed to interconnect different LANs. Bridges and routers also react differently when they do not have a next hop address:

- If bridges don't know the appropriate next destination node, they send the frame out all active ports except the port on which the frame was received (this process known as *flooding*).

- If routers don't know the route to the destination address, they drop the packet and send an error message back to the originating node.

Note
There is a terminology difference here that is sometimes confusing. Bridges, within an Ethernet for example, forward MAC *frames*. Routers, since they deal with a higher layer in the protocol stack, forward IP *packets*.

Routers also provide security firewalls to prevent unauthorized access to corporate networking sites, and they filter destination addresses in higher level protocol headers to prevent packets from being incorrectly sent to a WAN where access to telecom links are subject to change.

Because of their expanded capabilities, routers require more sophisticated software (protocols that determine and control packet routing) and expanded filtering databases than the ones considered in the discussion of bridges.

4.3.1 *Routing Protocols*

The fundamental role of the router is to forward packets to the appropriate subnets that are interconnected by one or more networks. It does this by using routines known as *network protocols* or *routing protocols*, which typically operate at layer 3 in the protocol stack.

A network protocol is a protocol that contains addressing and control information to allow packets to be routed (network protocols are also called routed protocols). Network protocols are routed through an internetwork by routing protocols. IP is an example of a network protocol. Some other network protocols that might be familiar are AppleTalk, DECnet, and Novell NetWare.

A routing protocol is a protocol that accomplishes routing through implementation of a *routing algorithm*. Routing algorithms are used to initialize and periodically update the information in the *routing tables* and to do the actual path selection. Routing tables, in turn, are used to store various information about the network that will aid in selecting a route through the network. [Ford et al, 1997]

Entries in routing tables may be either static or dynamic. Static routing table entries are set up and maintained by a network manager. They typically contain predefined route definitions to destination subnets and may only be changed on specific action by the network manager.

Dynamic routing table entries, on the other hand, are established by the routing protocol based on network topologies and conditions of the moment (such as link lengths, transmission rates, and traffic loads). Dynamic table entries are periodically updated by the associated protocol without human intervention. Border Gateway Protocol (BGP) and Routing Information Protocol (RIP) are examples of routing protocols from the Internet Protocol suite.

Two proprietary routing protocols that are widely used in IP are the Interior Gateway Routing Protocol (IGRP) and the Enhanced Interior Gateway Routing Protocol (EIGRP).

4.3.1.1 Layer 3 Routing

Internet Protocol (IP) is the layer 3 network (routed) protocol of the Internet Protocol Suite. Its primary functions are to provide the following:

- Transport layer (TSDU) packet disassembly and reassembly (as discussed in section 2.1.3 of Chapter 2).

- Connectionless, best-effort datagram delivery service through the Internet (as discussed in section 2.1.1 of Chapter 2).

> **Note**
>
> Best-effort delivery means that the network will do its best to deliver the packet to its ultimate destination, but that it is still possible for the packet to get lost along the way. Best-effort service does not guarantee delivery or make use of acknowledgment of packet receipt responses and it also does not guarantee that a sequence of datagrams will be received in the same order as they were sent. These are all functions that must be accomplished higher layer protocols (such as TCP).

Figure 4.15 shows the format IP packet header that is transferred from the LLC to the MAC as part of the *m_sdu* parameter in the *MA_UNITDATA.request* primitive (see section 3.2.1 of Chapter 3).

Figure 4.15   Network Service Data Unit—IP Packet Format

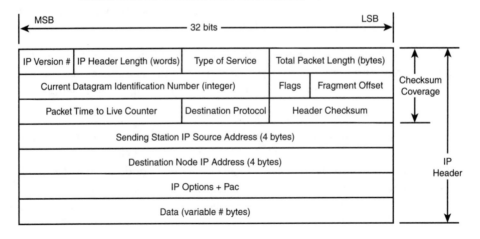

Several of the fields are somewhat self-explanatory. However, the following need a little more detail:

- **IP Header Length**. Used to define the beginning of the data fragment contained in this packet.

- **Type of Service**. Indicates a transmission priority level (see sidebar "Quality of Service" in section 13.2 of Chapter 13).

- **Total Packet Length**. Indicates the total length of this IP packet. Since the *m_sdu* must fit into the Data+Pad field of the MAC frame format, the total length of the IP packet transferred over Ethernet LANs must be ≤1,500 bytes.

- **Flags**. Indicates whether the packet can be fragmented and whether or not the packet is the last packet in a series of fragmented packets.

- **Fragment Offset**. Indicates the position of the data in this IP packet with respect to the beginning of the *m_sdu*. The Fragment Offset and the Datagram ID number are used to reconstruct the original *m_sdu* after all fragments have been received by the destination station.

- **Time to Live**. A counter that is decremented by each intermediate node to prevent the packet from endlessly circulating (looping) throughout the network. If and when the Time-to-Live counter becomes zero, the packet is discarded.

- **Destination Protocol**. The protocol for which the packet is intended.

Addressing in a TCP/IP network is different than what you have seen thus far in Ethernet LANs. Each end station and router port is assigned a unique logical address that identifies it and its connected network.

The IP address is a 32-bit address that is broken up into four octets in a "dotted decimal" format, with each octet representing a decimal number between 0 and 255 as shown in Figure 4.16. The dotted decimal format is strictly for human convenience—the routers see only a 32-bit binary number and the decimals are obviously not included. On shared data networks, the network portion (or prefix) of the address is the same for all connected devices, but the host portion is unique for each device.

Figure 4.16   IP Address Format

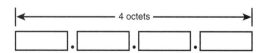

Note: The periods between the octets are the location of the
understood decimal points in the dotted decimal notation.

The first octet represents a network, and the succeeding octets of the address can represent either additional networks or hosts/subnets within a local organization. Network address assignments are controlled by the Internet Network Information Center (InterNIC), and local subnet assignments are controlled by a local administrator. Splitting the assignment responsibility for networks and subnets is part of the bottom-up control environment previously indicated for the Internet. It also ensures that the local organization's internal structure remains hidden from outside Internet users.

The IP address domain is divided into five separate address classes that differentiate the type of organization and/or the purpose of the class (see Table 4.1).

Table 4.1   IP Address Classes

IP Address Class	Format	Purpose	High-Order Bit(s)	Address Range	No. Bits Network/ Host	Max. Hosts
A	N.H.H.H[a]	Few large organizations	0	1.0.0.0 to 126.0.0.0	7/24	2^{24}-2[b]
B	N.N.H.H	Medium-size organizations	1,0	128.255.255.255 to 191.255.255.255	14/16	2^{16}-2
C	N.N.N.H	Relatively small organizations	1,1,0	192.0.0.0 to 223.255.255.255	22/8	2^{8}-2
D	N/A	Multicast groups (RFC 1112)	1,1,1,0	224.0.0.0 to 239.255.255.255	N/A (not for commercial use)	N/A
E	N/A	Experimental	1,1,1,1	240.0.0.0 to 254.255.255.255	N/A	N/A

[a]N = Network number, H = Host number.
[b]One address is reserved for the broadcast address, and one address is reserved for the network.

Packet forwarding is done on a hop-by-hop basis, where the address of the next node on the route is determined as part of the forwarding process by the network node that has just received the incoming packet. The forwarding process in a router is similar to the forwarding process described for bridges, except that the routing tables are based on the network portion of IP addresses (which by definition are logical addresses) rather than physical MAC addresses.

When a network service data unit needs to be sent across the Internet, the sending station needs to know the IP address of the intended receiver. It can be obtained either by accessing a list of frequently used addresses maintained by that station, or by requesting the Internet suite's Domain Name System (DNS) to determine the intended receiver's IP address. Once the IP address is known, the IP protocol uses it as the IP destination address, not only for this packet but also for all other packets going to the same destination address (for example, a packet stream that is transferring a data file that is too large to fit into only one packet).

When an IP packet arrives at a router port, the router extracts the network portion of the destination IP address from the IP header. This address is then matched with the network addresses in the router's routing table to determine the output port that is associated with the next hop.

Some routers also interrogate the Flags field to determine whether the packet is the first of a fragmented stream, and if so, to store the calculated route information so that the next packet can be sent immediately to the correct output port for retransmission. This procedure takes advantage of the fact that it requires less time to forward a packet if the routing information is already known than it does if the route has to be calculated for each packet in the fragmented IP stream. The procedure is becoming common in routing switches and is known as *route once, switch many.*

4.3.1.2 Layer 4 Routing

The Internet suite provides the following layer 4 protocols:

- The Transport Control Protocol (TCP) is a connection-oriented protocol that provides reliable data stream transfer with end-to-end flow control, error checking and recovery (including from errored, lost, delayed, or duplicated packets), packet resequencing (if needed), and full-duplex operation between communicating stations. File Transfer Protocol (FTP) is an application protocol that is often associated with TCP.

Note

Recent TCP flow control schemes (Slow-start) are designed to reach an equilibrium within several round-trip intervals, settling on a rate that matches the available bandwidth. Because most traffic is off-LAN (on a WAN) and most WAN end-to-end paths are much slower than LAN paths, flow rates for end stations will generally be low relative to LAN and LAN device capacity.

- The User Datagram Protocol (UDP) is a datagram-oriented (connectionless) protocol that provides a simpler transport layer service than TCP. UDP is appropriate where end-to-end flow control and error recovery is not required or is provided by a higher layer in the protocol stack (which is not provided by UDP). UDP is the transport level support protocol that is used for the Domain Name System (DNS), the Simple Mail Transfer Protocol (electronic mail—SMTP), and the Trivial File Transfer Protocol (TFTP).

Chapters 13 and 14 will revisit these and other layer 3 and layer 4 protocols. In the meantime, we need to discuss the technology that has been and currently is replacing both bridges and routers—switches that operate at layer 2, layer 3, or layer 4.

4.4   Switches

As stated earlier in the chapter, switches and routing switches are essentially just multiport bridges, but many modern switches also include router capabilities (switches with routing capabilities are often called routing switches). Switches are commonly designated by their protocol capability level:

- L2 indicates a switch with layer 2 capabilities. An L2 switch transfers frames using the transfer processes described for bridges in sections 4.2.1 and 4.2.2 of this chapter.

- L3 indicates a switch with layer 2 capability plus the layer 3 router capabilities that were discussed in section 4.3.1.1.

Some currently available L3 switches are able to distinguish the beginning of a fragmented IP stream, remember the route information established for that packet, and then switch the remainder of the fragmented IP stream across the same path as soon as each packet is identified as belonging to the fragmented stream. Since packet identification is located in the packet header, retransmission can begin before the entire packet has been received. This decreases the switch delay (latency) that would be required if each packet had to be processed independently. A switch with this capability is known as a *cut-through switch*. It embodies a *route once, switch many* operational philosophy.

Note

As with the name change where bridges became switches, the term "Layer 3 switch" is also marketing-hype to these new switches from conventional routers and to emphasize that this switch is faster. From a networking standpoint, there is no functional difference between a layer 3 switch and a router.

- L4 indicates a switch with layer 2, 3, and 4 capabilities.

- L3 indicates a switch with layer 2 capability plus the layer 3 router capabilities that were discussed in section 4.3.1.1.

  Some currently available L3 switches are able to distinguish the beginning of a fragmented IP stream, remember the route information established for that packet, and then switch the remainder of the fragmented IP stream across the same path as soon as each packet is identified as belonging to the fragmented stream. Since packet identification is located in the packet header, retransmission can begin before the entire packet has been received. This decreases the switch delay (latency) that would be required if each packet had to be processed independently. A switch with this capability is known as a *cut-through switch*. It embodies a *route once, switch many* operational philosophy.

- L4 indicates a switch with layer 2, 3, and 4 capabilities.

Chapters 13 and 14 discuss the system aspects of switching. Before then, we need to have a short discussion about switch architectures.

4.4.1   Switch Architectures

Switch architectures have changed over the years as the technology has evolved. There have been a number of switch architectures proposed, but because this is not a book on switch architecture or switch design, the discussion will be limited to only two basic structures that will help illuminate the concept—the cross-point switch, which is an adaptation of the telephone PBX, and the bus-based switch, which is an adaptation of an I/O bus in a processor.

4.4.1.1   Cross-Point Switches

Figure 4.17 shows a conceptual diagram of a cross-point switch. From one perspective, it could be viewed as an improved buffered repeater, although the cross-point switch has been around longer than the buffered repeater. Both have port buffers, both use bit-serial data paths to transfer frames between ports, and both use MAC Control PAUSE frames to prevent buffer overrun and frame loss.

Figure 4.17   A Conceptual Cross-Point Switch Architecture

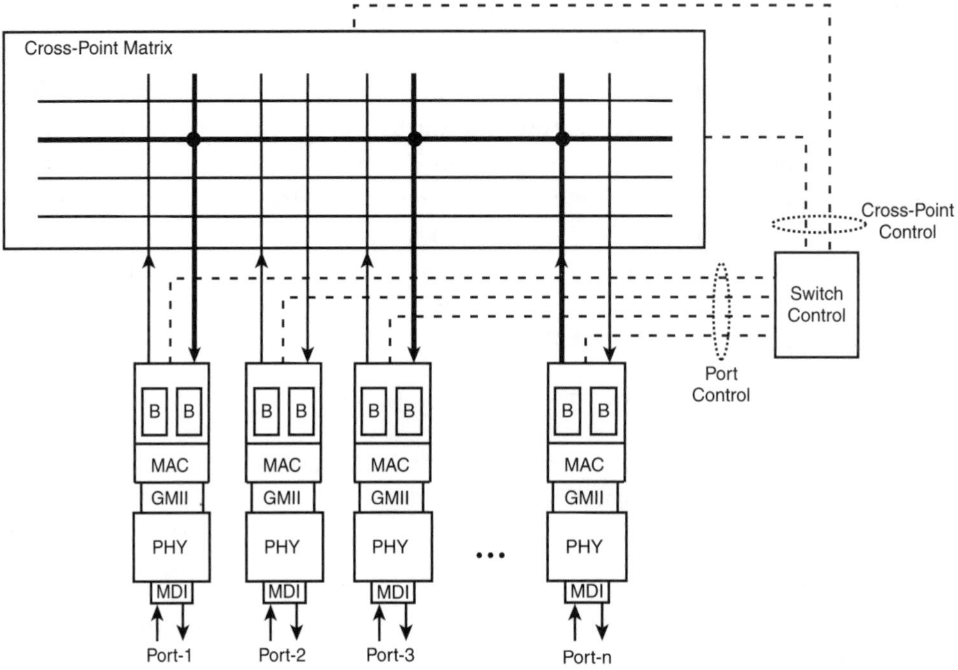

But that is where the similarity ends. Because switches also include bridging capabilities, frames are sent only to ports associated with the frame's destination address (repeaters send each frame to all ports other than the port on which it was received). Also, while repeaters have only one internal data path (the shared media), cross-point switches have several.

The primary function of the switch controller is to transfer next-in-line frames at the port input-buffer queues to the appropriate output port(s). At a conceptual level, the transfer sequence requires the controller to take the following steps:

1. Interrogate the destination address of the next-in-line frames at each port input-buffer queue to determine the appropriate output port(s).

2. Select an input-output frame set where the output port(s) are not currently busy (an output port may be transmitting a frame, but the switch is not loading another frame into its output buffer).

3. Select a non-busy cross link and enable the appropriate port connections.

4. Transfer the frame from the input buffer queue to the connected output buffer(s). Figure 4.17 shows a frame transfer between port-n and ports 1 and 3.

Obviously, the transfer procedure is not quite that simple. The selection of which frames to transfer next must take into consideration any designated frame priority levels, the length of time the frame has been waiting at the top of the queue, whether the frame needs to be sent to an individual port or several ports on the switch, and so on.

The maximum throughput of a serial cross-point switch is dependent on the source/ destination address mix of the incoming frames and the number of cross links implemented in the switch. Since the maximum transfer capacity of a single cross link in a Gigabit Ethernet switch would be approximately 1,000 Mbps, the capacity of the switch would appear to be approximately $n \times 1,000$ Mbps, where n is the number of cross links.

However, the increased capacity may not be sufficient to keep up with all arriving frames. Port output buffers cannot accept transfers from more than one source at a time, and several ports may be sending frames at the same time to the same destination address (such as a file server).

Obviously, output traffic at the destination port of a single-rate switch will run at capacity, but several of the input ports may have to invoke PAUSEs to avoid frame loss. When this occurs, the switch is said to be *blocked*. It cannot handle the traffic load and destination mix of its connected nodes.

4.4.1.2 Bus-Based Switches

One way to increase the internal transfer rate is to increase the internal clock frequency. Another way is to use a wide-format internal shared bus like that shown in Figure 4.18. Instead of transferring one bit at a time, the internal bus can transfer several bytes at a time. The result is increased bandwidth.

Figure 4.18   A Bus-Based Switch Architecture

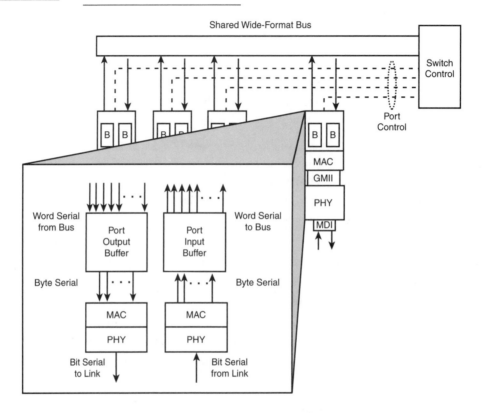

In bus-based switches, transfer capacity is a function of the bus width and the internal clock rate. However, because of the logic involved in bus control, internal bus transfer rates are typically less than the transfer rate of Gigabit Ethernet links. Therefore, the bandwidth of a Gigabit switch with a 32-bit bus, for example, would not be 32 Mbps.

4.4.1.3   Non-Blocking Switches

Full-duplex Gigabit Ethernet links can actually operate at a data rate of 2,000 Mbps, 1,000 Mbps in each direction. This means that the aggregate data capacity of an *n*-port switch is $2n \times 1{,}000$ Mbps. For a switch to be *non-blocking*, it must be able to transfer the aggregate load from all ports running at *wire rate*. Wire rate is the actual transmission rate of the link. As you will see in the next chapter, for Gigabit links, wire rate is actually 1,250 Mbps because each data byte is transmitted as a 10-bit code group.

An obvious solution to the blocking problem is to use a switch with an interconnection architecture (called the *switch fabric*) that combines the wide format and bandwidth of buses with the multiple paths and interconnectivity of some sort of matrix. Non-blocking switches are commercially available, but as we said earlier, their architectures are beyond the scope of this book.

> **Note**
>
> If you wish to delve further into alternative switch structures, we suggest you begin your search with the following matrix types: Banyan, Batcher-Banyan, and sort-merge.

Now that you are familiar with the different switch types, turn your attention to the next section—switch port buffer size and how switches handle flow control.

4.4.2 Flow Control and Port Buffer Structure

Flow control initiated by a switch port is the same as flow control initiated by full-duplex repeaters and bridges. However, flow control initiated by a switch is not the same as flow control initiated by an L4 protocol. MAC Control PAUSE frames only provide flow control between the link partners, and only for a very short time (the allowable PAUSE delay may be from 0.5 µs to 33.5 µs).

That said, the question of port buffer size and switch load capacity still needs to be addressed. There is no general answer that will fit all network situations, but the following list makes some observations that Chapter 13 expands upon:

- Frequent invocation of PAUSEs will lower the effective link transfer rate, but that might only mean that a background file transfer just takes a little longer.

- Port input and output buffers should be large enough to weather periodic frame bursts.

- Because there are more sources for output frames than input frames (input frames can only be received from the link, while output frames can come from all other ports on the switch), the output buffer should probably be larger than the input buffer.

- Switches can stand momentary periods of saturation so long as they don't perceptibly and frequently affect overall network performance.

4.4.3 Port Speed Handling

The discussion on switch topologies in Chapter 1 indicated that multispeed switches were very useful in multispeed network connections. All that is required to make a single-speed port into a multispeed port is a speed exchange buffer like those shown conceptually in Figure 4.19.

Figure 4.19 A Multispeed Port Input Buffer

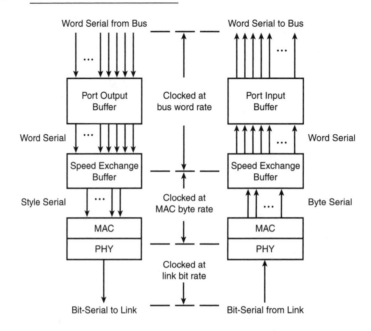

The speed exchange buffer isolates the lower-speed transfers to and from the link from the higher-speed transfers to and from the bus. Two clocks are required. The received byte stream is clocked in by the MAC clock rate, and the frame is transferred to the port buffer by the bus clock.

The port output buffer structure is the same as the input buffer structure except that the byte and word flow is obviously reversed. Each speed exchange buffer needs to be only large enough to store and forward one frame, and the port buffer/flow control unit controls the exchange buffer-to-port buffer transfer to ensure that incoming (or outgoing) frames do not overwrite the exchange buffer before it has been emptied.

4.5 VLAN Tagging and Priority-Based Frame Transfer

The introduction of VLAN tagging in Chapter 3 stated that it had two important characteristics that were formerly not available in Ethernet networks—priority-based frame transfer and extended network routing. Switches in VLAN networks must be VLAN compatible and must be able to recognize and decode VLAN tag fields (see section 3.1.3 in Chapter 3).

VLAN routing reduces the number of address table entries for intermediate network nodes since VLAN uses logical addressing rather than MAC addressing. VLAN IDs are treated as a group address, and the intermediate nodes only need to know which ports are associated with the VLAN indicated in the VLAN ID field. Address filtering is done by the receiving end station.

Priority-based frame transfer is the same as the priority transfer previously discussed in the forwarding process of the MAC relay unit in bridges. Port buffers must be configured to support eight priority levels (0–7, where 0 indicates lowest priority and 7 indicates the highest priority).

Network management is reduced because, unlike physical addresses that are associated with a particular port on a particular switch, once a user's end station has been identified as part of a VLAN, the VLAN ID becomes a logical address for the end station.

4.6 *Summary*

By this time, you should have a reasonable working knowledge of the network entities—the end stations, repeaters, bridges, routers, and switches that are on each end of the link. You should also have a reasonable understanding of their structure, how they work, and what their limitations are.

You should not be disappointed, however, if you do not yet feel qualified to set up or manage a network. You still have a lot of material to go over before launching into coverage of actual network design. The next few chapters introduce concepts of the physical layers and information transfer across the link.

You can find an excellent summary of the IP suite, as well as of a number of proprietary protocols in the *Internetworking Technologies Handbook*, published by Cisco Press [Ford et al, 1997].

PART III

Transmission Fundamentals

The two chapters in this part of the book cover transmission fundamentals of both optical fiber and shielded twisted pair copper cable. The material is presented in diagrammatic rather than mathematical form to accommodate a wider spectrum of readers. The information and concepts in both of these chapters are prerequisite to understanding the material in Parts IV and V.

Chapter 5: Fundamentals of Baseband Transmission

Chapter 6: Fundamentals of Fiber Optic Communication

5

Fundamentals of Baseband Transmission

Now that you have a working understanding of the data link layer, it is time to move down the protocol stack and introduce you to the physical layer. However, there are a few fundamental concepts that you need to know before you tackle the specifics of the various sublayers that comprise the Gigabit Ethernet implementation of the OSI physical layer. These include:

- Simplex, half-duplex, and full-duplex transmission

- Baseband transmission characteristics and functions

- Baseband reception characteristics and functions

- The relationship between the probability of error and the signal-to-noise ratio (SNR)

- Eye diagrams and the concept of an eye mask

- The relationship between the frequency content of a pulse and the pulse shape in time

- The effect of filtering and equalization on pulse shape and frequency content

- Coding to combat non-ideal channel response, to aid in clock recovery, and to ensure robust error detection

Comprehension of these topics is vital for providing a basis of understanding for the rest of the chapters of the book.

Figure 5.1 illustrates the fundamental elements of any digital communication system.

Figure 5.1   Digital Communication System Block Diagram

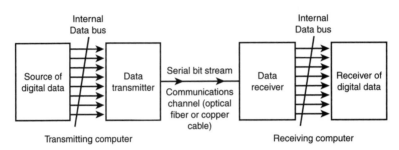

The elements of the digital communication system and the various hardware or software components associated with them are defined as follows:

- **Source of Digital Data**. This usually consists of a computer and its application software.

- **Data Transmitter**. This consists of network interface hardware and driver software.

- **Communications Channel**. This consists of optical fiber or copper cable that makes up the physical link. Sometimes portions of the transmit and receive electronics are also considered part of the channel.

- **Data Receiver**. This consists of network interface hardware and driver software.

- **Receiver of Digital Data**. This usually consists of a computer and its application software.

Data is normally transferred in parallel fashion over internal data buses within the transmitting and receiving computers; however, in the channel between the data transmitter and the data receiver, communication is bit-serial.

This chapter is essentially a non-mathematical introduction to baseband digital transmission, a method where the coded bit stream is coupled directly into the communications channel (a copper or fiber optic cable) without first being modulated onto a high-frequency carrier. All key concepts required to understand the underlying thinking, design procedures, and trade-offs that led to the final specifications for the 1000BASE-X Gigabit Ethernet physical layers are covered.

Note

Because 1000BASE-T is still in the development stage and is not likely to be an approved standard before mid-1999, we do not include the concepts utilized by 1000BASE-T for multilevel transmission over twisted pair. 1000BASE-T will be discussed in Chapter 15, "The Future: Gigabit Ethernet and Beyond," as an ongoing Ethernet development direction.

5.1 Simplex, Half-Duplex, and Full-Duplex Transmission

The remainder of this chapter assumes that the Gigabit Ethernet MAC has formatted the data and control signals for transmission by the physical layer. Based on this assumption, one Gigabit Ethernet MAC is the digital data source and another Gigabit Ethernet MAC is the digital data receiver. This means that you only need to consider the following elements:

- The data transmitter

- The communications channel

- The data receiver

While Gigabit Ethernet uses either half-duplex (see Figure 5.2) or full-duplex (see Figure 5.3) transmission, all 1000BASE-X physical layers are capable of full-duplex operation. The switch at each end of the link in Figure 5.2 is not real and is shown for functional illustration only. The MAC actually selects the direction for the half-duplex transmission through primitive generation as part of its media access control function.

Figure 5.2   Block Diagram of an Ethernet Communication System Using Half-Duplex Transmission

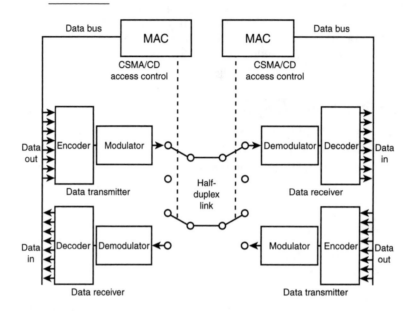

Figure 5.3   Block Diagram of an Ethernet Communication System Using Full-Duplex Transmission

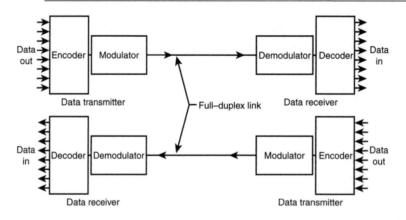

The next section focuses more closely on the transmit and receive functions (the encoder, modulator, demodulator, and decoder of Figures 5.2 and 5.3) of the baseband transmission system shown in Figures 5.4 and 5.5. Formal terms such as encoder, decoder, modulator, and demodulator are used because they are the terms that are generally used in textbooks on baseband transmission. In actual implementations of Gigabit Ethernet 1000BASE-X links, the encoder and decoder functions are typically carried out within a single application-specific integrated circuit (ASIC). Also, a *transceiver* (transmitter/receiver) generally carries out all modulator and demodulator functions with the exception of pulse regeneration for copper links and retiming for both copper and optical links.

Figure 5.4   The Functions and Key Waveforms of a Generic Simplex Baseband Link

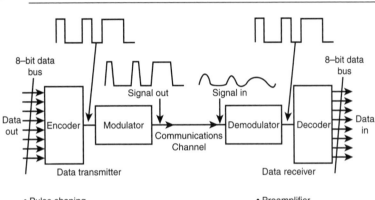

- Pulse shaping
- Control transition density
- Control DC content
- Multiplex code–groups into a single bit stream
- Unique code–groups for data and control signals
- Code to enable error detection

- Preamplifier
- Equalizer
- Pulse regenerator
- Retiming unit
- Demultiplexer
- Decoder

Figure 5.5 Waveforms in a Gigabit Ethernet Baseband System

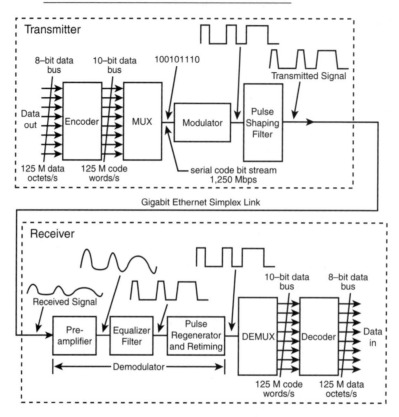

Figure 5.5 shows the major functional blocks of the transmitter and receiver. You should keep in mind their location in the transmission path as you go through the rest of sections 5.2 and 5.3.

5.2 Transmitter Characteristics and Functions

The transmitter, which consists of the encoder, multiplexer, modulator, and pulse-shaping filter (all of which are described in the sections that follow) must perform all signal processing required to prepare the signal for reliable transmission over the analog channel. The transmitter must also couple the signal onto the channel.

5.2.1 Encoder

The encoder accepts data bytes from the MAC and translates (encodes) each byte into an *n*-bit code word that has been specifically developed to gain reliable transmission. In binary systems, this is commonly achieved by converting each 8-bit data byte into an *n*-bit code word where *n* is greater than 8 (*n* = 10 in Gigabit Ethernet). The additional bits add transmission overhead, but since there are more *n*-bit code characters than 8-bit data characters, they provide a degree of transmission redundancy. This redundancy can be used to make error detection more reliable, to provide separate data and control words, and to combat poor channel characteristics.

5.2.2 *Multiplexer (MUX)*

After the data bytes are encoded as *n*-bit transmission characters, the character stream is multiplexed into a sequential bit stream according to the transmission sequence defined by the protocol before it is passed to the modulator (in Ethernet, the character transmission sequence is low order bit first). This is illustrated in Figure 5.5, which shows that the digital signal passed from the encoder to the modulator is essentially a perfect digital waveform.

5.2.3 *Modulator*

The modulator is the functional block that performs the digital-to-analog conversion, including any required pulse shaping for transmission over the channel. In 1000BASE-CX copper transmission systems, the modulator consists of the electrical line drivers, transmit filters, transformers, and connectors. In 1000BASE-X optical systems, the modulator consists of the laser driver electronics, the laser light source, the coupling optics, and optical connectors. The modulator may also convert a differential input electrical signal to a single-ended electrical or optical signal.

Figure 5.5 shows the modulator separately from the pulse-shaping filter to emphasize the difference between the essentially perfect waveform at the output of the modulator and the output waveform that is coupled to the communications channel.

Note

The transmission path in Figure 5.5 shows several transfer rates, beginning with 125 M data octets/s (where an octet is an 8-bit code group, also commonly called a *byte*) at the input to the encoder in the transmitter, to 1,250 M code bits/s at the output of the multiplexer. Further, the Gigabit Ethernet link transmission rate is interchangeably referred to as being either 1,250 Mbps or 1,250 Mbaud. In every case, we are actually referring to the transfer of bits, but all "bits" are not the same, and to avoid confusion, it is necessary to understand the context of the bit's location in the transmission path (see the sidebar, "A Bit Is a Bit Is a Bit").

A Bit Is a Bit Is a Bit

The widely understood purpose of a communications network is to transfer data bits between pairs (or groups) of network users or between users and network servers. However, as illustrated in Figure 2.4 in Chapter 2, "The OSI and Gigabit Ethernet Standard Reference Models," the user's data is passed through multiple levels in the architecture before it is actually transferred across the communication link.

Each layer treats all the information passed to it by the next higher layer as "data" and this sometimes leads to confusion about what is meant by "data bits". Each layer adds its own header (identification and control) information to the received "data" and then passes that "data" plus its own header information to the next lower layer as just "data." The result is that at any one level, the term "data bits" refers to the user's data plus all the headers that have been added by all the higher layers (see Chapter 2, Figure 2.4).

The data is passed to the Gigabit Ethernet physical layer as 8-bit "data octets" that are then encoded (translated) into 10-bit code words that are transmitted in bit-serial fashion over the link.

The encoding of 8-bit data octets into 10-bit transmission code words results in the two transmission rates of 1,000 Mbps and 1,250 Mbps that are defined for Gigabit Ethernet. Both are correct, but both must be taken in context. 1,250 Mbps refers to the *instantaneous transmission rate* for encoded MAC data. 1,000 Mbps refers to the instantaneous transmission rate for raw MAC data.

The instantaneous transmission rate is the rate that bits (of any kind) are transferred across the link *when the link is being used to transfer bits.* The rate is zero, otherwise. The instantaneous transmission rate for actual user data (the rate that user data is transferred) is:

$$\text{transmission rate}_{\text{user data}} = \frac{n_{\text{data}}}{n_{\text{total}}} \times (1{,}000 \text{ Mbps})$$

where n_{data} represents the number of user data bits transferred and n_{total} represents the total number of bits required to transfer the user data.

The effective transmission rate$_{\text{user data}}$ is the quotient of the number of *valid user data bits* transferred during an extended period (say one hour) divided by the number of seconds in the period. User data bits that were received in error or that were lost due to packet collisions do not count as valid user data bits, even though some may have been transferred over the link.

5.2.4   Pulse-Shaping Filter

The output pulse shape from the pulse-shaping filter will generally be different from the input pulse shape. For example, the filter may slow the rise- and falltimes of the digital pulses to limit electromagnetic emissions, or it may boost or attenuate the signal magnitude at different frequencies in the transmitted pulses to overcome frequency-dependent losses in the channel (see the pulse train diagrams before and after the pulse-shaping filter in Figure 5.5).

5.3   Receiver Characteristics and Functions

The receiver must recover the digital data from a distorted analog signal received at the input to the preamplifier in the receiver in Figure 5.5. The sections that follow describe the demodulator, demultiplexer, and decoder components of the receiver.

5.3.1   Demodulator

The demodulator is the functional block that performs the analog-to-digital conversion, including signal detection, signal preamplification, pulse equalization, and the pulse regeneration/retiming. In Gigabit Ethernet copper systems, the demodulator includes connectors, transformers, receive filters, electrical preamplifiers, and the pulse regeneration/retiming electronics. In Gigabit Ethernet optical systems, the demodulator consists of the optical connector, coupling optics, optical detector (a photodiode), electrical preamplifier, and the pulse regeneration and clock recovery electronics. The signal passed between the demodulator and the demultiplexer is a cleaned-up version of the received signal, as indicated in Figure 5.5. Depending on the actual implementation, it may or may not be completely retimed at this point.

5.3.2   Demultiplexer (DEMUX) and Decoder

The demultiplexer function demultiplexes the incoming bit stream into 10-bit transmission code words, which are decoded and translated into data bytes or control signals by the decoder, before being passed on to the MAC. The decoder may complete the retiming process or it may even do all of the retiming, depending on the particular implementation. For the Gigabit Ethernet 1000BASE-X links, both the decoder and encoder functions are generally carried out within a single ASIC.

5.4   Noise, Signal-to-Noise Ratio (SNR), and Bit Errors

Most of today's communications systems use digital regeneration of the received signal (all Gigabit Ethernet receivers regenerate the received signal). The most important aspect of a digital transmission system is that once the *signal-to-noise ratio (SNR)* is above a certain threshold, the bit error rate falls very rapidly with further increases in the SNR (see Figure 5.6).

The *SNR* is the ratio of the average power in the transmitted signal and the rms noise power in the communications channel at the point of measurement. SNR measurements are normally taken at the input to the receiver and are usually expressed in dB.

The *bit error rate (BER)* is the number of bits received with errors compared to the total number of bits received. A BER of 10^{-10}, for example, means that only one bit out of a total of 10^{10} bits can contain an error.

Figure 5.6   Relationship of Probability of Error to SNR for an On-Off, Binary-Pulse-Code Modulation (PCM) Transmission System

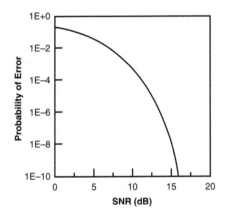

For the binary-pulse-code modulation used by Gigabit Ethernet, the threshold level is about 15 dB. Since digital transmission systems regenerate the data after every hop (link), error rates can be held to extremely low values if the SNR is greater than about 17 dB for each link.

Another important feature of digital regeneration that has led to its popularity is that the error rate increases linearly with the number of hops. This is different from analog transmission systems where the error rate rises in a very non-linear manner, because each repeater degrades the SNR by adding noise. As long as the SNR on each individual link can be kept above a certain, usually modest, threshold level (about 15 dB), digital regeneration will enable longer link lengths having lower error rates compared to analog-repeated systems. In digitally regenerated systems, the worst-case error rate performance is primarily determined by the worst individual link in the series of repeated links.

5.5   Eye Diagrams

An analytical tool that is commonly used to estimate the performance of a digital transmission system is the *eye diagram*. This section uses a series of drawings and associated text to explain the following:

- How an eye diagram is formed

- How the eye diagram can be used to assess system performance

- The general concept of an eye mask

Gigabit Ethernet 1000BASE-X systems use non-return-to-zero (NRZ), two-level (binary) modulation with a transmission code-bit period (baud period) of 0.8 ns. This simply means that the transmit waveform remains at one of the two binary levels for the duration of the bit-period. The waveform can only change levels at the boundary between bit-periods, and the waveform does not return to zero during strings of successive ones.

For the moment, to simplify discussions of eye diagrams, we will only consider signal degradation due to the limited bandwidth of the channel and component electronics. We will also assume perfect clocking and perfect transmit pulse widths. You will see later in this section that noise, clock frequency drift, and pulse width distortion will also degrade the eye, but first you need to define the eye diagram.

5.5.1   Transmit Eye Diagrams

Figure 5.7 shows plots of the following series of waveforms:

(a)   An example NRZ transmit waveform and bit stream

(b)   The equivalent components of a received waveform (equivalent unit pulses)

(c)   The resulting distorted received waveform (the sum of the individual equivalent unit pulses)

The transmitted bit sequence is printed above each waveform as a reference.

Figure 5.7   An Example Transmitted Bit Sequence and Received Waveform

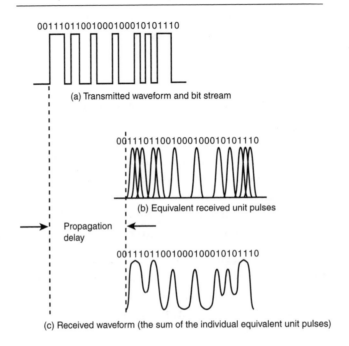

Figure 5.7 assumes that the individual unit transmit NRZ waveforms are distorted by the bandwidth limitations of the channel and the receive electronics to form an equivalent stream of received unit pulses. As should be expected, the received waveforms are delayed with respect to the transmit waveform, and the delay is the propagation time of the cable linking the transmitter and the receiver.

The received waveform is equal to the summation of the equivalent received unit pulse waveforms. Clearly, the example channel and receiver electronics have severely distorted the transmit waveform; however, the distortion is actually quite realistic because we have chosen the level of distortion to be roughly equivalent to a worst-case received optical waveform for 1000BASE-X.

The transmitter will generally produce a very good waveform, as shown in Figure 5.8a.

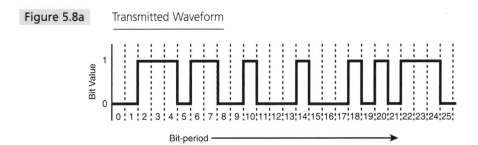

Figure 5.8a   Transmitted Waveform

The bit-periods have been delimited by dotted lines, and each bit-period has been numbered. The sequence of sampling intervals and superimposed waveforms of Figure 5.9 illustrate how the transmit eye diagram in Figure 5.8b is formed. The sampling intervals have a duration of two bit-periods centered on each bit-period.

Figure 5.8b   Transmit Eye Diagram Plotted in the Interval (–T,T) About the Eye Center

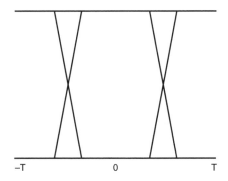

Note

The example transmit eye diagram in Figure 5.8b is an almost-perfect eye diagram. The eye is good because there is maximum separation between levels for most of the bit-period, and the transitions between levels occur within very short time periods centered on the bit-period boundaries.

The signal is measured (or calculated) and replotted on the interval (-T, T), where T is the bit-period. Figure 5.9 shows how superposition of the individual segments eventually forms the eye diagram shown in Figure 5.8b. This can be experimentally achieved by capturing the waveform using an oscilloscope in infinite persistence mode and continuously triggering the oscilloscope by the bit clock of the transmit-pattern generator. The time base of the oscilloscope can be adjusted to display a single eye diagram or multiple eye diagrams. We have chosen the plotting interval (–T, T) for the eye diagrams shown in this book. If larger intervals are used, multiple eye diagrams would be formed; however, repeated eye diagrams provide no additional information.

Figure 5.9   Formation of the Transmit Eye Diagram

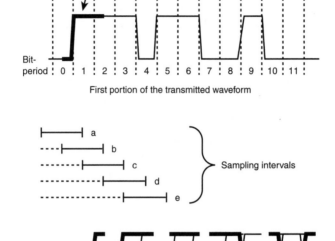

5.5.2   *Receive Eye Diagrams*

A receive eye diagram is formed in an analogous manner to the transmit eye diagram; however, the receive eye diagram is degraded compared to the transmit eye diagram due to the signal interaction with the channel during transmission. To understand why the receive eye looks different from the transmit eye and how it is degraded, we must revisit the received waveform of Figure 5.7 where you saw that the received waveform is equal to the summation of the received unit waveforms. We have replotted this receive waveform using an expanded scale in Figure 5.10.

Figure 5.10   Received Waveform (Sum of Received Unit Pulses)

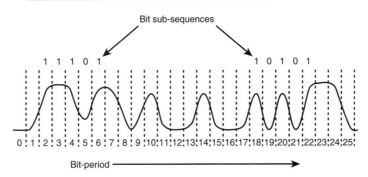

The severe distortion of the transmit waveform caused by the channel and the receiver electronics is very clear. The increased pulse rise- and falltimes have spread the received pulses into neighboring bit times. In addition, the waveform does not always reach the maximum or minimum value as shown by the 10101 and 111011 sub-sequences in our example.

As with the transmit diagram, the bit-periods of our received waveform are delimited by dotted lines, and each bit-period is numbered. Figure 5.11 uses the first few bit-periods of Figure 5.10 to illustrate how the receive eye diagram is formed. Here again, all segments of the waveform are two bit-periods' duration centered on each bit-period, and are measured (or calculated) and then replotted on the interval $(-T, T)$, where T is the bit-period.

Figure 5.11   Formation of the Receive Eye Diagram

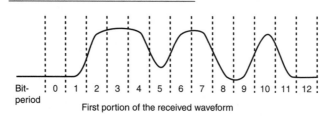

Bit-period   0   1   2   3   4   5   6   7   8   9   10   11   12

First portion of the received waveform

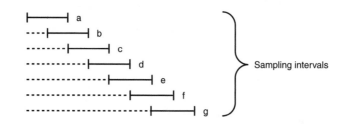

Sampling intervals

Superimposed waveform segments, last segment shown in bold

Figure 5.12 shows the resulting eye diagram.

Figure 5.12   Completed Receive Eye Diagram Plotted in the Interval (–T,T) About the Eye Center

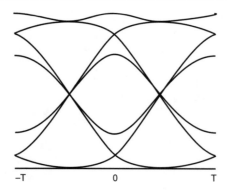

The effect of the distortion on the receive eye diagram of Figure 5.12 is obvious. Compared to the almost ideal transmit eye diagram of Figure 5.8b, the transition regions are much longer and the eye does not reach the binary limits in all cases. The eye is generally narrower both in amplitude (or height) and time. The receive eye is said to be more *closed* than the transmit eye. Because we have chosen the level of distortion to be roughly equivalent to a worst-case optical received waveform for 1000BASE-X, the eye in Figure 5.12 is roughly a worst-case 1000BASE-X optical eye.

5.5.3 *Eye Diagram Analysis*

The eye opening defines the boundary within which no waveforms exist for any code pattern. Thus, eye diagrams are useful for estimating worst-case system performance. Figures 5.13a and 5.13b show a receive eye diagram and an associated unit receive pulse waveform (bit 14 in Figure 5.10).

Figure 5.13a   Binary On-Off Modulation: Receive Eye Diagram with the Pulse Peaking in Period 14 Highlighted

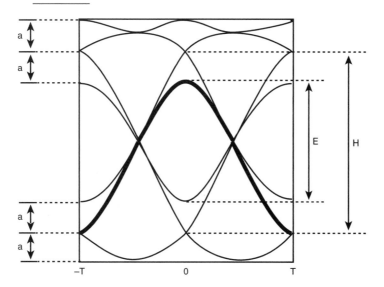

Figure 5.13b   Binary On-Off Modulation: Isolated Received Waveform Peaking in Period 14 of the Example in Figure 5.12

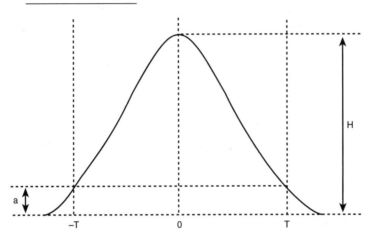

For the simple case of a symmetrical unit receive pulse with peak height, H, and height value of, a, at times -T and T (see Figure 5.13b), and height zero for all times, t, such that $|t| > |T|$, the eye opening E (in Figure 5.13a) is simply:

Equation 5.1

$$E = H - 2a$$

The second term (2a) in Equation 5.1 is called inter-symbol interference (ISI). The ISI clearly reduces the eye opening by a factor of (H/E). In other words, to maintain the eye opening, and hence the bit error rate, the signal must be increased by a factor of (H/E). Increasing the signal obviously means increasing the transmit power. For this reason, you can normally say that the ISI has caused a power penalty. The power penalty is just the factor, (H/E), which is usually expressed in dB units. Chapter 6, "Fundamentals of Fiber Optic Communication," discusses power penalties in more detail.

This reasoning clearly leads to a conservative design because the eye opening represents the worst-case transmit pattern, and by doing so, the analysis is assuming the worst-case pattern is continuously transmitted. However, for tightly constrained codes, like the 8B10B code used by Gigabit Ethernet, the design margin introduced by this approach is not excessive.

5.5.4 *Eye Masks*

Until now, we have not considered the effect of pulse width distortion, timing jitter, pulse height distortion, or other non-ideal behaviors. Figure 5.14 illustrates how such effects might further distort the eye diagram.

Figure 5.14   Conceptual Worst-Case Receiver Eye Mask for Binary Modulation

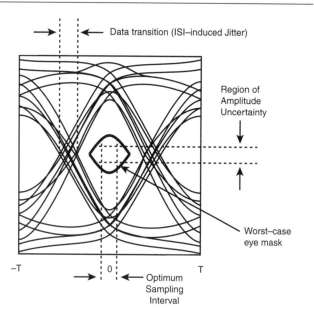

In contrast to Figure 5.13a, the eye of Figure 5.14 seems even more distorted and closed. In particular, the crossing points of the rising and falling edges at t = ±T are wider, as are the crossing points at t = 0.

To ensure that the specified bit error rate is not exceeded, the circuits in the regenerator must require that the sampled amplitude is greater than, or less than, the "zero" crossing point of the eye by some minimum value. Amplitude values that fall within the region of amplitude uncertainty in Figure 5.14 may not be correctly detected.

In addition, there will be an uncertainty in the phase of the regenerated bit clock that will dictate a minimum eye opening in time. This leads to the concept of the eye mask shown previously in Figure 5.14. The eye mask is defined so that if the measured eye is always wider than, or just equal to, the mask, and if the amplitude sample is taken within the period indicated by the eye mask, the data will be correctly recovered at the specified bit error rate. To ensure a performance safety margin and reliable bit recovery, the pulse regenerator's retiming circuit should be designed to ensure that the actual sampling occurs within the optimum sampling period shown in Figure 5.14.

Note

A note of caution is in order. Eye diagram measurements, by themselves, are insufficient to guarantee performance. Additional error rate tests must also be done if the specifications are to be thoroughly checked.

Figure 5.15, Figure 5.16a, and Figure 5.16b show examples of a severe distortion. Specifically:

- Figure 5.15 shows theoretical frequency response for a 10 m length of copper cable.

- Figure 5.16a plots the pulse response for various lengths of copper cable.

- Figure 5.16b plots the eye diagram for a 10 m length of copper cable.

Figure 5.15   Frequency Response for 10 m Length of Copper Cable

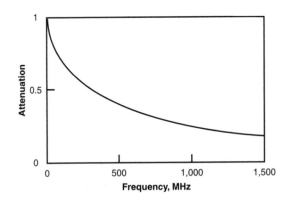

Figure 5.16a   Pulse Response for Various Lengths of Copper Cable

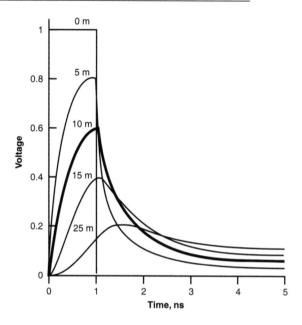

Figure 5.16b   Eye Diagram for a 10 m Length of Copper Cable Shown in Bold in Figure 5.16a

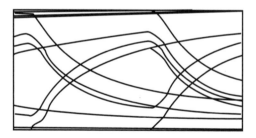

The high frequencies are clearly suppressed, and this distorts the pulse response as the length of the cable is increased. The eye diagram (Figure 5.16b) for a 10 m length of the cable is quite poor; however, it is roughly the worst-case eye that can be recovered by 1000BASE-CX. For copper systems, like this example, the main source of distortion is inter-symbol interference (ISI) caused by signal distortion in the cable. Because of this, the ISI is very deterministic and predictable. Eye masks are very useful in this situation, and as you will see in Chapter 11, "1000BASE-X: Optical Fiber and Copper PMDs," 1000BASE-CX has defined both the worst-case transmit and the worst-case receive eye masks. Clearly, if the cable illustrated in the three preceding figures were to be used as part of a 1000BASE-CX cable assembly, an equalizer would be needed to achieve the 25 m maximum distance.

In optical systems, noise effects become an additional consideration that combine with inter-symbol interference to make receive eye masks less useful. Nevertheless, worst-case transmit and worst-case receive eye masks have been defined for conformance tests in 1000BASE-LX and 1000BASE-SX systems.

5.6   *Pulse Distortion Due to Filtering Effects*

This section uses simple physical arguments and diagrams to analyze pulse distortion due to the filtering effects of link components. You will see how an *impulse* (a short pulse with a pulse width approaching zero) can be thought of as being made up of an infinite set of frequencies. In addition, you will see that a reduction in the frequency content of an impulse will cause it to spread and distort.

A pulse having a very short pulse duration must contain a very large set of frequencies. That fact may not seem obvious, but one way to deduce it is to realize that *the highest frequency of the pulse must be approximately equal to the inverse of its pulse width*. Another way to deduce it is to realize that a short pulse can be formed using a bank of signal generators, as shown in Figure 5.17. This might seem surprising, but it is in fact true. To form a short pulse, the signal generators must be phased so that at the time when a pulse is required to be generated, they are all in phase with each other.

Figure 5.17   Illustration of the Frequency Content of Short Pulses

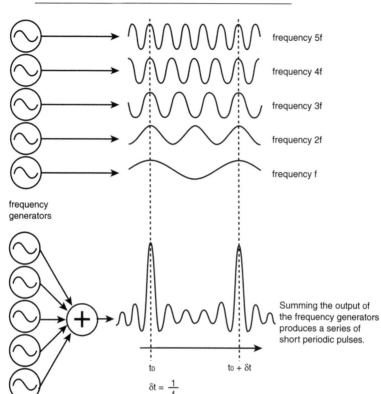

The example shown in Figure 5.17 assumes a constant frequency separation *f* between the frequency generators. The example also assumes that each generator produces equal output power. Therefore, the pulse-repetition rate will be *1/f* where *f* is the lowest frequency produced.

Clearly, an infinitely short pulse (an impulse) must have infinite frequency content. To generate such an impulse, you would need an infinite number of frequency generators where the lowest frequency generator would be set so close to zero that the universe would end long before the pulse would repeat! Although you clearly can't produce an impulse in this manner, it does give you a very simple way to visualize the frequency content of an impulse. This is illustrated in Figure 5.18a, which shows an impulse in the time domain and the equation for the impulse, and Figure 5.18b, which shows the equation for the impulse as well as a plot showing the frequency content of the impulse.

Figure 5.18a   An Impulse

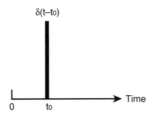

Figure 5.18b   The Frequency Spectrum of an Impulse

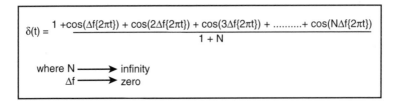

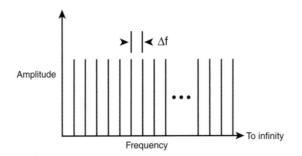

We now have a straightforward way to visualize the effect of filtering on the impulse. The series of figures 5.19a–5.19c illustrate the filtering of the frequency spectrum of an impulse by an ideal low pass filter. Specifically:

- Figure 5.19a shows the infinite frequency content of an impulse.

- Figure 5.19b shows the frequency response of an ideal low pass filter.

- Figure 5.19c shows the reduced frequency content of the impulse due to the low pass filter (an ideal low pass filter passes all frequencies up to the cut-off frequency and stops all frequencies above the cut-off frequency).

Because the frequency of the highest-frequency component has been reduced by the low pass filter, the width of the impulse (the inverse of the highest-frequency component) is increased.

Figure 5.19a   Frequency Spectrum of an Impulse

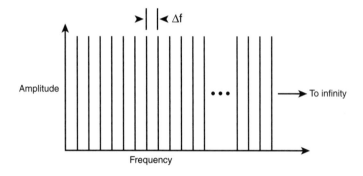

Figure 5.19b   Frequency Response of an Ideal Low Pass Filter Having a Bandwidth B

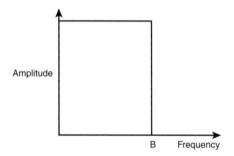

Figure 5.19c   Frequency Spectrum of Impulse after Filtering by the Ideal Low Pass Filter

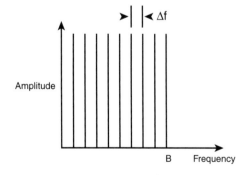

Figure 5.20 shows the broadening effect of an ideal low pass filter on an impulse in the time domain. The filtered impulse is at a maximum at time zero, and the pulse passes through the value zero at all times, $t = \pm nT$, where n is an integer greater than zero and $T = 1/(2B)$, where B is the cut-off frequency of the low pass filter. Therefore, B is the minimum bandwidth required to receive an eye diagram with zero ISI penalty at the optimum sampling time. Of course, ideal low pass filters are impossible to make, and a little extra bandwidth is always required in real systems if ISI is to be avoided. Nevertheless, it is common for the frequency response at $f = 1/(2T)$, the half-baud frequency, to be quoted for transmission system components. The reason is because $f = 1/(2T)$ is the theoretical minimum required bandwidth for ISI-free NRZ reception. This is why 1000BASE-CX specifies some of its cable parameters at the half-baud frequency of Gigabit Ethernet (625 MHz).

Figure 5.20   The Effect of an Ideal Low Pass Filter on an Impulse

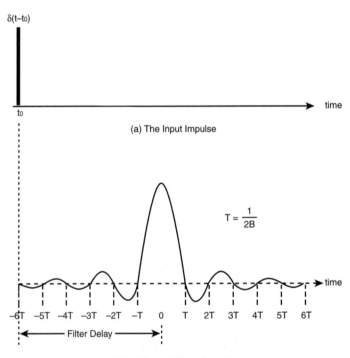

(a) The Input Impulse

$$T = \frac{1}{2B}$$

(b) The Output (Filtered) Impulse

As stated earlier, any pulse shape can be formed by a series of correctly timed impulses. The frequency content of any pulse shape can therefore be calculated as the sum of the outputs of the frequency generators required to produce each of the component frequencies. Because the component frequencies are slightly delayed with respect to each other, the phase of the generators for each frequency will be different.

Part (a) of Figure 5.21 shows an isolated NRZ unit pulse of duration T, where T is the bit-period. Use the frequency generator concept of Figure 5.20 to deduce the frequency spectrum of this pulse. First, you must realize that this pulse can be approximated by a large number of equally spaced (in time) impulses of height V within the interval $(-T/2, T/2)$. The approximation will get better as the number of impulses is increased and the spacing between them is decreased.

Figure 5.21   An Isolated Non-Return-to-Zero (NRZ) Transmit Pulse and its Amplitude Frequency Spectrum

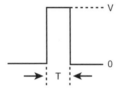

(a) Isolated non-return-to-zero (NRZ) transmit pulse

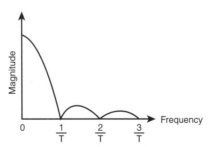

(b) Amplitude spectrum of isolated NRZ transmit pulse

At very high frequencies, the phase differences between the sets of generators (which generate the component impulses) will be large compared to the oscillation period. This will mean that each generator near a frequency f^{high} will have an essentially random phase compared to the other generators near f^{high}. Summation of the generator outputs at f_{high} will therefore result in an output close to zero.

At low frequencies, the phase differences between the sets of generators (which generate the component impulses) will be small compared to the oscillation period. This will mean that each generator near a frequency f^{low} will have essentially the same phase compared to the other generators having frequencies near f^{low}. Summation of the outputs at f^{low} will therefore result in a high output amplitude. Because phase is important, there may also be periodic nulls in the amplitude spectrum.

The amplitude spectrum in the frequency domain of the isolated NRZ pulse is shown in part (b) of Figure 5.21. This plot was calculated using a mathematical simulation of the frequency generator method discussed earlier in this section.

5.7 Equalization

You now have a simple, easily visualized method for analyzing the filtering effect of system components on transmitted NRZ pulses both in frequency and in time. This section uses this method to gain an understanding of the concepts and principles underlying equalizing filters (equalizers). Because it is easier to visualize the operation of an equalizer in the frequency domain, the frequency domain is used to discuss that type of filter.

The input to a digital communications channel is normally a series of isolated pulses, which taken together form the transmitted pulse stream. However, to understand equalization, it is only necessary to consider the transmission of one isolated pulse. The transmit spectrum of each pulse is shown at the input to the cable in Figure 5.22. The cable acts like a filter and attenuates the transmit frequency spectrum with a filter function C(f). Without correction for this filtering action, the receive pulses would be very distorted, as illustrated in Figure 5.16a for copper cable.

Figure 5.22   An Ideal Noiseless Equalization System

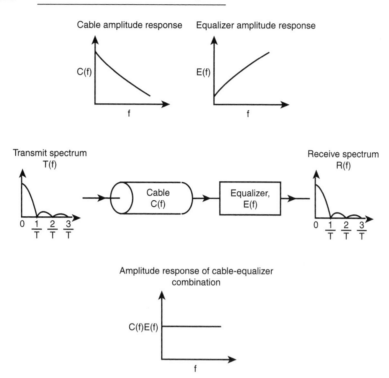

The basic function of an equalizer is to correct for the frequency response of the cable and/or other system components. In the example of Figure 5.22, the equalizer needs to boost the high frequencies by the function E(f) to compensate for the attenuation C(f) of the cable. In an ideal noiseless system, an equalizer exactly compensates for the distortion of the cable so that the combination of the cable and equalizer is a flat response. The receive pulse spectrum is then exactly the same as the transmit pulse spectrum.

The preceding discussion and figures arbitrarily place the equalizer at the receive end of the link. However, an equalizer can be placed anywhere in the system. Some systems use transmit equalizers (10BASE-T uses a form of transmit equalization), but transmit equalizers are usually relatively expensive because this is a high power point in the system. Equalizers can also be implemented within the receiver (as for 100BASE-T and 100VG-AnyLAN) or be part of the cable plant (as for 1000BASE-CX).

5.7.1 Bandwidth Limited Equalization and Receive Pulse Shapes

Real systems are exposed to both internal and external noise sources. The noise will generally be spread over the entire operational bandwidth of the receiver. However, broader receiver bandwidths imply more noise and lower SNRs, and lower SNR values imply more bit errors. This means that you must limit the bandwidth of the equalizer if you are to maximize the SNR and, hence, minimize the number of bit errors. Unfortunately, if the bandwidth is restricted too much, ISI will be increased! This means that the designer must make a trade-off between limiting the amount of ISI and the amount of noise.

One very common method for making this trade-off is to limit the bandwidth such that at the ideal sampling time, the ISI value is forced to zero. This has the effect of reducing the noise, because the bandwidth has been limited, while maintaining the signal height at the optimum sampling time. Pulse shapes that do this are called *Nyquist class 1 pulses.*

Nyquist class 1 pulses must obey the following frequency domain rules. Given that the normalized response at $f = 0$ is unity, and T is the bit-period, then:

- At $f = (1/(2T))$, the response must equal 0.5.

- At $f = (1/T)$, the response must equal zero.

- For $f > (1/T)$, the response must equal zero.

- In the region, $0 < f < (1/T)$ the response must be anti-symmetric about the point $f = (1/2T)$.

Many pulse spectra obey the Nyquist class 1 criteria; however, the minimum bandwidth pulse meeting Nyquist class 1 conditions is unique and is, in fact, the pulse produced by filtering an impulse with an ideal low pass filter as shown in Figure 5.19c. One family of pulses that fits the Nyquist class 1 criteria is the trapezoidal pulse family.

Figure 5.23a shows the frequency responses of the trapezoidal family. The frequency scale has been normalized to units of bandwidth of size B, where $B = 1/2T$, and T is the bit duration for the system of interest. The trapezoidal pulse family is defined by a parameter x, sometimes called the excess bandwidth factor, where $x = ((f_{max} - B)/(B))$ in normalized units.

Figure 5.23a Trapezoidal Filter Responses

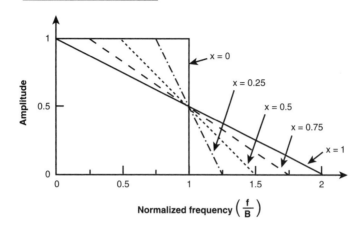

Figure 5.23b shows the time response of the trapezoidal pulse family as a function of the excess bandwidth factor, x. Clearly, the greater the excess bandwidth, the shorter the duration of the ISI. However, for all values of x, the ISI is zero at all times and t = ±nT where n is an integer. This means that at the optimum sampling time, there is no ISI penalty.

Figure 5.23b Impulse Response for Trapezoidal Filters

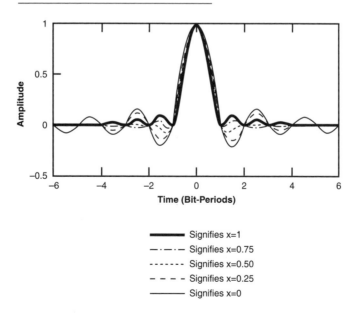

Eye diagrams illustrating minimum ISI at the optimum sampling time are shown in Figure 5.24a for x = 0.75 and in Figure 5.24b for x = 0.25.

Figure 5.24a   Eye Diagram for a Trapezoidal Response with x = 0.75

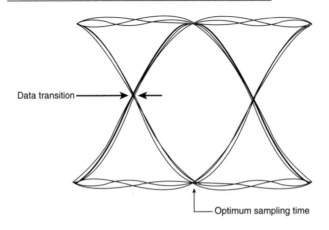

Figure 5.24b   Eye Diagram for a Trapezoidal Response with x = 0.25

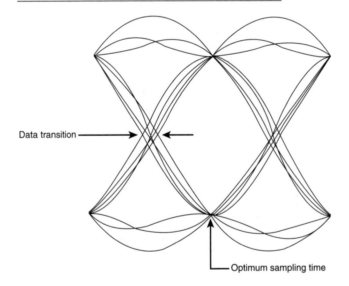

The eyes in both Figure 5.24a and Figure 5.24b clearly have the same vertical opening at the optimum sampling time; however, the slope of the inner eye is much steeper for x = 0.25 which, as illustrated in Figure 5.23a, also has less excess bandwidth. This means that as the excess bandwidth is reduced, timing accuracy becomes more critical. In addition, the eye with less excess bandwidth also has wider crossing points of the rising and falling transitions within the eye. This indicates that at times other than t = ±nT, ISI is producing deterministic jitter in the timing of the signal crossing points of the horizontal eye opening. The deterministic jitter grows as the excess bandwidth is reduced.

Additional jitter can affect the accuracy of the clock recovery process and make it more difficult to maintain sampling at the optimum sampling point. In general, as much excess bandwidth as possible should be allocated. However, there is little point in going beyond x = 1 because the little extra reduction of the ISI would be accompanied by an increase in noise.

5.8 Line Coding

A correctly designed transmission symbol set and transmission encoding procedure can compensate for non-ideal channel response, aid in clock recovery, and ensure robust error detection. Figure 5.25 shows three common alternative binary codes, non-return-to-zero (NRZ), return-to-zero (RZ), and Manchester, that can be used for baseband encoding prior to transmission. NRZ and RZ are level-based (the bit value is represented by the signal level), and Manchester is transition-based (the bit value is represented by the transition direction). The three look similar but present different frequency characteristics after they have been through the transmitter's modulator and pulse-shaping filter.

Figure 5.25   Alternative Binary Line Codes

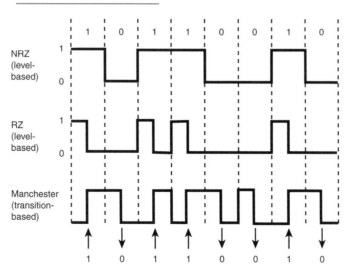

5.8.1 *Transmit Pulse Encoding*

A common channel problem is the lack of a DC (zero frequency) transmission path. This occurs because the transceivers are usually AC coupled with capacitors or transformers. The transmit pulses are distorted by a droop effect caused by the AC coupling's inability to maintain voltage levels for very long. This leads to an effect called *baseline wander,* as shown in the output NRZ bit stream in Figure 5.26. In the extreme case, where a long string of ones or zeros is transmitted, the droop is so severe that it passes right through the decision threshold and errors result.

Figure 5.26 Concept Example of Baseline Wander

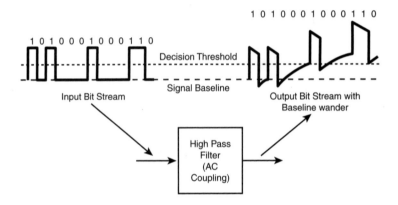

Line coding can significantly reduce the effect of baseline wander by removing the DC content from the transmit spectrum. Depending on the form of line coding used, other benefits, in addition to zero DC content, can also result, including:

- Increased transition density to aid clock recovery

- Separate code words for data and control signaling

- Error detection due to coding violations

The simplest form of line coding is to choose a transmit pulse shape to reduce the DC content of each transmitted pulse. Depending on which pulse shape is chosen, some of the other benefits previously listed may also be achieved.

Figures 5.27a and 5.27b show idealized transmitted pulse shapes and frequency spectra, respectively, for the NRZ, RZ, and Manchester line codes. The frequency content of each of these pulse shapes was calculated using the method outlined in section 5.6.

Figure 5.27a   Idealized Transmitted Pulse Shapes for NRZ, RZ, and Manchester Line Codes

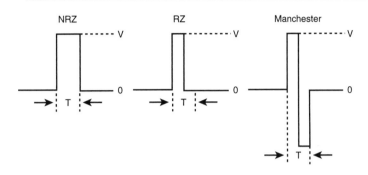

Figure 5.27b   Normalized Pulse Power Spectra for NRZ, RZ, and Manchester Line Codes

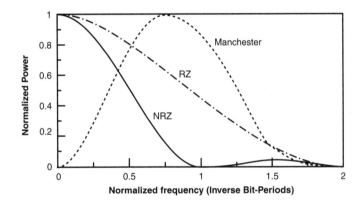

Clearly, because they never fall below zero, the NRZ and RZ pulses both have a large DC content. In addition, you can deduce if NRZ or RZ transmit pulses are used without any additional coding technique, long strings of zeros will produce no output. Therefore, with NRZ or RZ format there is no guarantee of level transitions, which are required for accurate clock recovery. The reason is that both RZ and NRZ formats represent, zero as a constant low (zero) level for the entire bit-period. NRZ also represents adjacent ones as a constant high (one) level. That said, it may be a shock to discover that both NRZ and RZ formats are extensively used in telecommunication systems. However, they are usually employed in conjunction with some form of statistical multiplexing, a rigid framing structure, and data scrambling to greatly reduce the probability of clock loss and/or baseline wander-induced errors.

The Manchester pulse shown in Figure 5.27a represents one. A zero would be represented by the inverse version of the plotted pulse. The Manchester pulse format (sometimes called bi-phase) is clearly excellent for removing DC content because it is symmetrical about the 0-level. The guaranteed level transition in each Manchester bit-period enhances clock recovery, and code violations can also be detected because the pulse must not remain at the same level for an entire bit-period. Unfortunately, both Manchester and RZ coding require twice the system bandwidth compared to NRZ because their minimum pulse width is half the width of the minimum NRZ pulse.

5.8.2   Block Coding

Manchester coding can be viewed as a simple block code. In block coding, the data bits are grouped into data words of length n. A set of code words having m bits where $m > n$ is then chosen, and the data words are mapped to the code words (called code-groups in Gigabit Ethernet). The choice of code words can be used to combat poor channel response, to provide transitions for clock recovery, and to aid error detection. The performance of DC-free codes is usually measured in terms of the following important parameters:

- **Run Length**. The maximum number of consecutive code bits having the same value.

- **Running Digital Sum (RDS)**. The running sum of the code bits where one is represented as 1 and zero as −1.

- **Digital Sum Variation**. The difference between the maximum and minimum values of the RDS.

- **Running Disparity**. The sign of the RDS value.

- **Transition Density**. The number of times the stream of code bits changes its value in a given number of bit-periods.

Block coding is not new to LANs or to Ethernet. Fibre Channel's 8B10B code was designed by IBM in the mid-1980s, the Manchester (1B/2B) code was included in the original Ethernet specification, and most 100 Mbps LANs use block codes.

Gigabit Ethernet elected to use the 8B10B block code because it is much more efficient than Manchester encoding and requires less transmission bandwidth. The 8B10B code has been widely implemented in Fibre Channel networks and has been proven to be very effective. Its properties (particularly high transition density, low RDS, and limited run length) ease the jitter budget requirements, especially for laser-based systems. Some features of the 8B10B code include:

- High transition density of 3 to 8 transitions per 10-bit code group

- DC balance; maximum run length of 5; maximum running digital sum (RDS) of 3

- Separate code words for data and control signaling

- Excellent error detection capabilities, especially with CRC-32, the error detection procedure used for the frame check sequence in the MAC frame format

Figure 5.28 shows the frequency spectra of the Gigabit Ethernet 8B10B block code, the 1B/2B (Manchester) code, and the NRZ code. The NRZ encoding uses the least bandwidth but has the largest DC content, the Manchester (1B/2B) encoding has the least DC content but uses the most bandwidth, and the 8B10B code falls in between, making it an excellent trade-off candidate for Gigabit Ethernet 1000BASE-X physical layers.

Figure 5.28   Normalized Code Spectra for NRZ, 8B10B, and Manchester (1B/2B) Codes

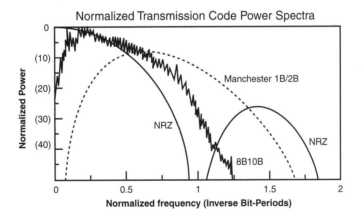

5.9 *Summary*

This chapter introduced all the key concepts of baseband digital transmission required to understand the underlying thinking, design procedures, and the trade-offs that led to the final specifications for the 1000BASE-X Gigabit Ethernet physical layers. You should now be familiar with the following concepts:

- Simplex, half-duplex, and full-duplex transmission

- Baseband transmit and receive characteristics and functions

- The relationship between the probability of error and the SNR

- Eye diagrams and eye masks

- The connection between the frequency content of a pulse and the pulse shape in time

- The effect of filtering on pulse shape and frequency content

- Equalization

- Coding to combat non-ideal channel response, to aid clock recovery, and to ensure robust error detection

These concepts and methods will be used in the analysis and discussions of the Gigabit Ethernet physical layer specifications in Chapters 9, 10, and 11.

CHAPTER

6

Fundamentals of Fiber Optic Communication

> Optical carrier frequency . . . yields far greater potential transmission bandwidth than metallic cable systems. [John M. Senor, 1992]

While it is possible to describe the 1000BASE-X optical physical media dependent sublayers (PMDs) without considering the physics and technology on which they are based, you will gain a better understanding if you first review the fundamentals of digital communications using optical fibers.

This chapter is a self-contained, essentially non-mathematical tutorial that introduces the basic optical fiber definitions, concepts, components, and technology relevant to Gigabit Ethernet. It places Gigabit Ethernet in an historical context compared to recent optical fiber technology and discusses some new issues surrounding multimode fiber links that were encountered during development of Gigabit Ethernet. After finishing with this chapter, you should be familiar with the following concepts:

- The elements that compose the Gigabit Ethernet optical path

- The concepts of power budgets and power penalties

- Basic properties of both single- and multimode optical fiber

- Optical fiber modes and rays

- Noise and signal distortion in Gigabit Ethernet links

- Optical transceivers

6.1 Gigabit Ethernet Optical Links

Figure 6.1 shows the optical elements for linking two Gigabit Ethernet stations or intermediate network devices (repeaters, bridges, routers, or switches). The link may be used to interconnect two Gigabit Ethernet stations, a station and a network device, or two network devices. Each physical layer dependent (PMD) link combination contains two simplex (unidirectional) optical links and is capable of operating in either half-duplex or full-duplex mode.

Figure 6.1   The Gigabit Ethernet Optical PMD/Link

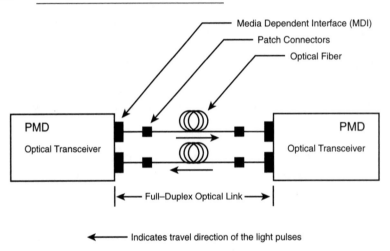

For simplicity, Figure 6.2 shows only one of the two simplex optical links from a full-duplex Gigabit Ethernet PMD/link (see Figure 6.1). The optical transmitter converts the binary bits in the outgoing electrical bit stream into pulses of light that are coupled (focused) onto the end of the fiber core. The optical receiver, in turn, detects the incoming pulses of light and converts them back into a bit stream for processing by the physical layer electronics. The critical requirement is to ensure that the received pulses are of appropriate shape and of sufficient intensity to be correctly detected. The challenge is to do so at Gigabit per second data rates.

Figure 6.2   The Elements of the Simplex Optical Link

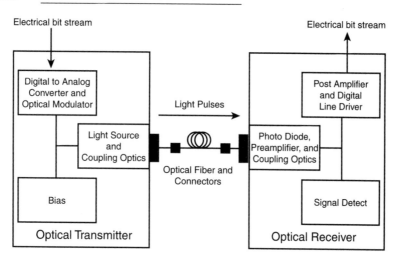

6.2   *Fundamental Design Constraints and Considerations*

Gigabit Ethernet was designed to operate over existing fiber optic cable plants for two primary reasons:

- The cost of upgrading existing networks can be significantly lower if most of the existing fibers can be reused.

- The characteristics of these fibers are already defined by existing international standards.

Commonly proposed advantages of optical fiber are its very high bandwidth, its immunity to electromagnetic interference (EMI) and its immunity to crosstalk. This might lead you to suppose that it is a trivial task to specify and design the optical PMD portions of Gigabit Ethernet. In fact, nothing could be further from the truth! Four major design considerations make it very difficult:

- A limited optical power budget

- Potential implementation costs

- The requirement for inter-operability in a multivendor (multisupplier) environment

- The restricted bandwidth of multimode fiber

6.2.1 *The Optical Power Budget*

The primary analysis tool used for the specification of the Gigabit Ethernet optical PMD is based on the following simple power transfer relation in Equation 6.1.

Equation 6.1

power-out = power-in − losses

In the Ethernet optical path, the power-in is the optical power inserted at the transmit end of the fiber; the power-out is the power delivered to the receiver at the output end of the fiber. In practice, however, the preceding power transfer relation is typically modified to provide some level of design margin, as shown in Figure 6.3.

Figure 6.3 The Conceptual Optical Power Budget

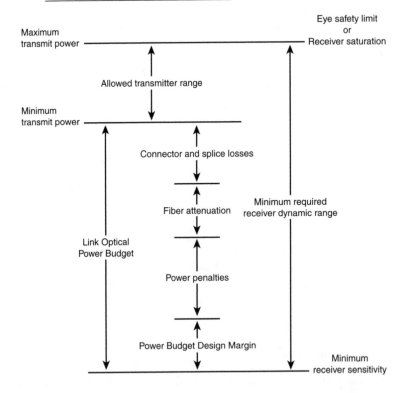

The maximum transmit power is set by either regulatory eye safety limits or the receiver saturation level, whichever is lower. The transmitter power must be approximately constant and be in the range between the maximum and minimum allowed transmit power. The minimum required receiver dynamic range is the difference between the maximum transmit power and the minimum receiver sensitivity. Typical values for the maximum transmit power, minimum receive power, and receiver dynamic range for a Gbps optical link would be approximately –3 dBm, –19 dBm, and 15 dB, respectively. Chapter 9, "The Gigabit Ethernet Optical Link Model," provides the actual specified values for Gigabit Ethernet.

The difference between the minimum transmit power (the minimum power launched into the fiber) and the minimum receiver sensitivity (the minimum power out of the fiber that is needed for reliable data recovery) is known as the link's *optical power budget*. The power budget is the sum of the link losses plus a safety margin (all of the factors in the optical power budget will be discussed later in this chapter). The task for the Gigabit Ethernet design team was to:

- Identify and determine the magnitude of all link losses and power penalties. *Link losses* represent power that is lost due to attenuation in the fiber, fiber splices, and optical connectors. *Power penalties* represent the additional power that must be added to the transmitted signal to counteract increases in error rates due to noise and interference.

- Determine a reasonable minimum sensitivity level for acceptable cost optical receivers.

- Set the minimum transmit power at a level that leaves a reasonable range for the transmitter design and still allows for all link losses and power penalties, plus a safety margin in the optical power budget.

6.2.2 Cost Considerations

Cost is a major consideration in local area network technology. If it's not low cost, it's not likely to be widely accepted by the market. The desire to limit costs means that relatively simple optical transmitters and receivers (compared to more complex, state-of-the-art telecommunications transceivers) have to be used. This, in turn, requires that the magnitudes of the received pulses be significantly greater than the lowest-level signals that can be received by the more costly telecommunications receivers.

6.2.3 Inter-Operability Considerations

The multivendor inter-operation requirement further increased the pressure on the optical power budget. For example, manufacturers can use a variety of technologies with differing receiver sensitivities and bandwidths. However, for inter-operation to be achieved, any arbitrary mixture of standard-compliant optical transmitters and receivers must be able to operate correctly over the longest specified link. This can be a problem for manufacturers with higher performing (and often higher cost) technology because the standard is set for the performance level of the lowest acceptable common denominator.

6.2.4 *Optical Fiber Considerations*

Field surveys in both the U.S. and Europe identified two types of optical fibers in use, single-mode and multimode. The multimode fiber was further split into two core diameters, 50 μm and 62.5 μm, with 62.5 μm being the predominant core diameter for link lengths under 2 km. Within local area networks, it was found that about 50 percent of the multimode fiber had link lengths less than 500 m. Single-mode fiber was typically used for wide area connections requiring link lengths greater than 2 km.

The goal of supporting existing fiber cable plants means that Gigabit Ethernet will be required to operate with three different kinds of optical fibers, each with different sets of physical characteristics. The final specification for the Gigabit Ethernet optical link was obviously the result of a series of trade-offs among all of the previous factors. Gigabit Ethernet uses two different transmission wavelengths: a short wavelength (850 nm) for short reach, low cost links; and long wavelength (1,300 nm) for long reach, slightly higher cost links. There is a different optical power budget and a different optical transceiver specification for each type of fiber and transmission wavelength.

Because the fibers are the only "constant" in the mix, you need to understand light transmission through fiber media before considering the other elements in the optical path.

6.3 *Light Transmission Through Optical Fibers*

An optical fiber is essentially an optical waveguide that has a transparent cylindrical inner *core* surrounded by a transparent *cladding*, as shown in Figure 6.4a.

Figure 6.4a   Optical Fiber

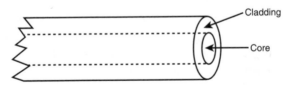

Cladding Outside Diameter = 125 μm (typical for Ethernet fibers)
Core Diameters:
    Single-Mode Fiber = 10 μm
    Multimode Fiber = 50 or 62.5 μm

The core and the cladding are made of essentially the same transparent material, either glass or plastic, and the fiber is typically covered with a protective covering. The key difference between the core and the cladding is the value of their respective indexes of refraction. While the following discussion of light transmission through an optical fiber can apply to both plastic and glass fibers, the current state of plastic optical fiber technology is not as advanced as glass fiber technology. Hence, the Gigabit Ethernet standard does not provide operational specifications based on plastic optical fibers.

The *index of refraction n* (also known as the refractive index) of a transparent medium is the ratio of the velocity of light in a vacuum, *c*, to the velocity of light in that medium, *v*, as in Equation 6.2.

Equation 6.2

$$n = \frac{c}{v}$$

The value of the index of refraction of the cladding is always less than the index of refraction of the core. The two basic refractive index profiles for optical fiber cores are known as step-index and graded-index (see Figure 6.4b).

Figure 6.4b   Typical Refractive Index Profiles for Step-Index Single-Mode Fiber, Step-Index Multimode Fiber, and Graded-Index Multimode Fiber

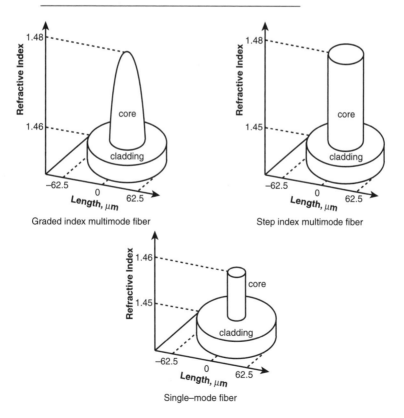

Step-index and graded-index optical fiber cores are defined as follows:

- In *step-index fiber*, the refractive index of the core is constant across the diameter (the refractive index of the core appears as a step up when compared to the refractive index of the cladding). Step-index fibers may be either single-mode or multimode.

- In *graded-index fiber*, the refractive index varies with the radius of the core.

The difference between single-mode and multimode fiber is described later in this chapter in section 6.3.5.1. You will also see that step-index multimode fibers are not appropriate for Gigabit Ethernet use; however, first you need to understand how light is actually transmitted through a fiber. The first step is to understand transmission through step-index fibers.

6.3.1 *Light Rays and Beams*

If a light ray is incident at an angle θ_i to the normal at the interface between two media with different refractive indices, part of the ray is transmitted into the second medium m_2, and part of it is reflected back into the first medium m_1, as shown in Figure 6.5a.

Note

The *normal* is an imaginary line perpendicular to the interface. Refer to the dotted line in Figure 6.5a for an example.

Figure 6.5a   Refraction and Reflection of a Single Light Ray

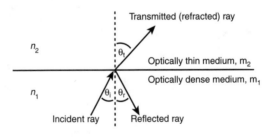

The Index of Refraction $n_1 > n_2$

If refractive index n_2 is less than refractive index n_1, the angle of the refracted ray θ_t will be greater than the angle of the incident ray θ_i. The angle θ_r of the reflected ray is always equal to the incident angle θ_i. The term *optically thin medium* denotes the medium with the lower refractive index (usually n_2). The term *optical dense medium* denotes the medium with the higher refractive index (usually n_1).

This section provides a straightforward explanation for the refraction and reflection of light at an optical media interface. Light travels more slowly in an optically dense medium than in an optically thin medium. This means that in any given period of time, the ratio of the distance light travels in an optically dense medium, L_1, to the distance light travels in an optically thin medium, L_2, is given by Equation 6.3.

Equation 6.3

$$\frac{L_1}{L_2} = \frac{n_2}{n_1}$$

Figure 6.5b shows a beam of light exiting from an optically dense medium, m_1, into an optically thin medium, m_2 (to avoid confusion, the reflected beam is not shown).

Figure 6.5b   Refraction of a Plane Wave Beam, Reflected Beam Not Shown

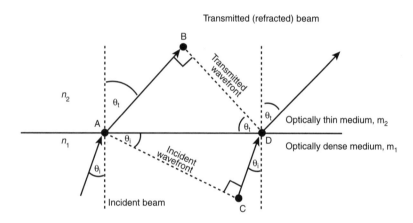

The Index of Refraction $n_1 > n_2$

The incident beam is a plane wave beam having straight wavefronts perpendicular to the path of the beam; it remains a plane wave beam after it crosses the interface as shown in the drawing. The angle of incidence in the optically dense medium is θ_i and the transmitted angle is θ_t. We will now show that since n_2 is less than n_1, the transmitted (refracted) beam is turned through a greater angle from the normal to the interface compared to the angle of incidence.

Let the length of any line connecting two points denoted by X and Y be XY. Then the incident plane of constant phase, AC, just before the beam exits the dense medium, must become the plane of constant phase, BD, just after the beam exits the dense medium. Therefore, the left extreme ray AB travels a distance AB in the same time that the right extreme ray CD travels a distance *CD*. From Equation 6.3, you can see that Equation 6.4 is true.

Equation 6.4

$$\frac{AB}{CD} = \frac{n_1}{n_2}$$

However, because $AB = AD \sin(\theta_t)$ and $CD = AD \sin(\theta_i)$, substituting for *AB* and *CD* results in Equation 6.5.

Equation 6.5

$$\frac{\sin(\theta_t)}{\sin(\theta_i)} = \frac{n_1}{n_2}$$

Alternately, Equation 6.6 can be used.

Equation 6.6

$$n_1 \cdot \sin(\theta_i) = n_2 \cdot \sin(\theta_t)$$

Equations 6.5 and 6.6 are known as *Snell's Law*.

Because the index of refraction n_1 of the core is greater than the index of refraction n_2 of the cladding, the angle of refraction θ_t will always be greater than the incidence angle θ_i. If the incidence angle continually increases, at some point the refraction angle will equal 90° and the refracted ray will be parallel to the interface between the two media, as shown in Figure 6.6.

Figure 6.6   Refraction When the Incident Angle θ_i = Critical Angle θ_c

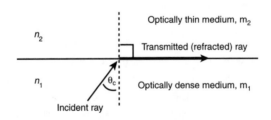

Because $\theta_t = 90°$ and $\sin(\theta_t = 0)$, substituting in Equation 6.2 results in Equation 6.7.

Equation 6.7

$$sin\left(\theta_i\right) = \frac{n_2}{n_1}$$

Equation 6.7 leads to Equation 6.8

Equation 6.8

$$\theta_i = \theta_c = sin^{-1}\left(\frac{n_2}{n_1}\right)$$

The value of the incidence angle θ_c is known as the *critical angle* because all incident angle values greater than θ_c will result in *total internal reflection* as shown in Figure 6.7.

Figure 6.7   Refraction When the Incident Angle θ_i > Critical Angle θ_c

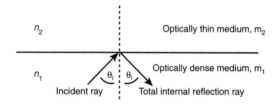

When light is to be transmitted through an optical fiber, the light rays must be launched into (aimed at) the end of the fiber. The critical angle can be used to determine the maximum acceptance or launch angle for the air-to-fiber interface (see Figure 6.8). Light rays that are incident on the air-to-fiber interface at angles less than θ_a will be transmitted through the fiber core by total internal reflection with little attenuation. Light rays that are incident at angles greater than θ_a will be refracted into both the core and the cladding, but will be only partially reflected into the core (and will diminish with each successive reflection).

Figure 6.8   The Maximum Cone of Acceptance for Light Ray Launch

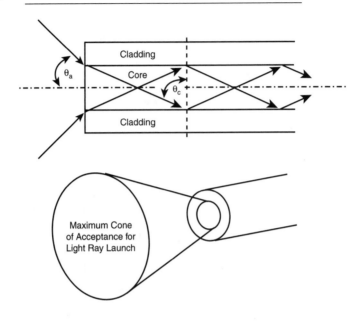

θ_a = Maximum angle of acceptance
θ_c = Critical angle

While the output of an optical transmitter may be allowed to impinge upon the entire face of the core, it is usually launched into the fiber using a lens. The lens focuses all the light power on a relatively small region of the core, typically coincident with the axis of the core, as shown in Figure 6.9. (You'll see later that this is not always the case for Gigabit Ethernet, which sometimes uses an off-axis launch [see section 6.3.5.1], but it is, nonetheless, appropriate for the following discussion.)

Figure 6.9   Typical Transmitter-to-Fiber Optical Coupling

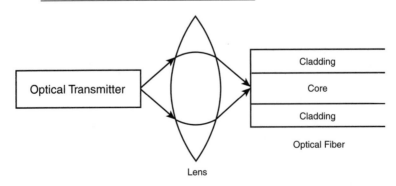

Up to this point, we have only considered light ray transmission in step-index fibers. We now need to extend the discussion to include light ray transmission in fibers with a parabolic refractive index profile.

Consider the conceptual multistep refractive index profile shown in Figure 6.10a.

Figure 6.10a   A Conceptual Graded-Index Core with a Multistep Refractive Index Profile

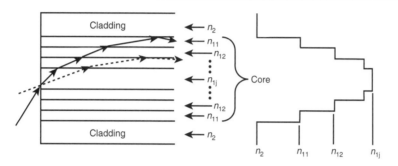

The core consists of a series of concentric cylinders with separate refractive indexes as shown in the profile. Light rays will be reflected at each interface between adjacent steps and, depending on the original launch angle, may even be reflected back towards the center of the core by one of the intermediate refractive index steps.

If we allow the thickness of each of the different "cylinders" in the core to approach zero, and we control the rate of change in the refractive index from cylinder to cylinder, in the limit, the number of cylinders will approach infinity, and the refractive index profile can take on the parabolic shape shown in Figure 6.10b.

Figure 6.10b   A Graded-Index Core with a Parabolic Refractive Index Profile

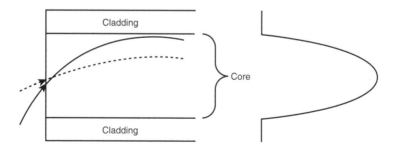

As the number of segments in the profile of Figure 6.10a tends to infinity, the length of each straight line ray segment will approach zero and the set of light rays will appear as a continuous curve, as shown in Figure 6.10b.

6.3.2   *The Three Basic Types of Light Rays*

Up to this point in the discussion on light rays and beams, the focus has been on the basics of light ray refraction and reflection, and you have only seen ray paths that are confined to a plane through the axis of the core. Figures 6.11 and 6.12 show that there are actually three basic ray types, as follows:

- **Meridional Rays**. These are rays launched into and confined within an axial plane of the core (the launch angle is parallel to a plane perpendicular to the axis of the fiber core).

  - In step-index fibers, meridional rays follow zigzag paths that pass through the axis of the fiber, as shown in part (a) of Figure 6.11.

  - In parabolic profile graded-index fibers, meridional rays follow curved paths that pass through the axis of the fiber, as shown in part (a) of Figure 6.12.

- **Axial Rays**. These are special meridional rays, launched along the axis of the fiber core, as shown in part (b) of Figure 6.11 and Figure 6.12.

- **Skew Rays**. These rays are launched into the fiber at angles to both the x- and y-axial planes of the fiber.

  - In step-index fibers, skew rays follow spiral-like point-to-point paths around the inside of the cylinder that is the core/cladding interface, as shown in Figure 6.11c. Each point-to-point path segment is a straight line whose length is determined by the original launch angle. Steeper launch angles result in shorter point-to-point segments; shallower launch angles result in longer point-to-point segments.

  - In parabolic profile graded-index fibers, skew rays follow continuous spiral paths around the axis of the core, as shown in Figure 6.12c. In these fibers, the launch angle determines the radius and pitch of the spiral. Steeper launch angles result in shorter spiral pitches and larger spiral radii; shallower launch angles result in longer spiral pitches and smaller spiral radii.

Figure 6.11 Meridional, Axial, and Skew Ray Paths in the Core of a Step-Index Fiber

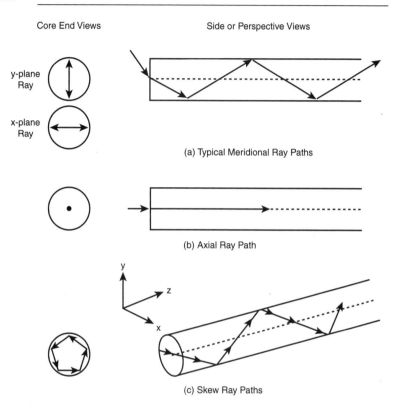

Core End Views

Side or Perspective Views

y-plane
Ray

x-plane
Ray

(a) Typical Meridional Ray Paths

(b) Axial Ray Path

(c) Skew Ray Paths

Figure 6.12 Meridional, Axial, and Skew Ray Paths in the Core of a Graded-Index (Parabolic Profile) Fiber

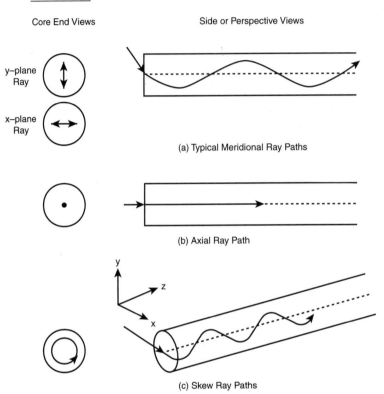

Core End Views   Side or Perspective Views

y–plane Ray

x–plane Ray

(a) Typical Meridional Ray Paths

(b) Axial Ray Path

(c) Skew Ray Paths

6.3.3 Rays and Modes

Each direct and reflected ray has an electric field wavefront perpendicular to the ray path, as shown in Figure 6.13a. The direct ray wavefront can have any phase value when the ray reaches the point of reflection, because at that point, the ray will have traveled an arbitrary path length from the light source.

Figure 6.13a   Electrical Field Wavefronts in Direct and Reflected Rays

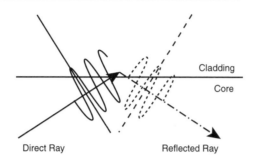

The reflected ray wavefront suffers a phase shift at the core/cladding interface. The value of the shift depends on the ratio of the core and cladding refractive indices and on the angle of incidence. Since it is very complicated to explain the magnitude of the phase shift without a lot of physics and some associated mathematics, we will simply note that Figure 6.13a is essentially correct. The phase shift is equivalent to moving the point of reflection a little into the cladding, allowing the light ray to actually penetrate the cladding, just a bit, before it turns back into the core.

Figure 6.13b illustrates wavefronts that could result from two rays being simultaneously launched into the fiber with the same angle of incidence.

Figure 6.13b   Electrical Field Wavefronts in Co-Directional Optical Fiber Direct and Reflected Rays

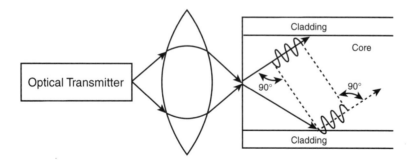

The wavefronts associated with upward-traveling direct and upward-traveling reflected rays are known as *co-directional wavefronts*. There are three important phase relationships for the co-directional wavefronts, which are as follows:

- If the co-directional wavefronts are in-phase as shown in the left-hand portion of Figure 6.13c, they will reinforce each other, the fiber will be excited, a light beam will form, and the light beam will be guided along the core.

- If the co-directional wavefronts are in anti-phase as shown in the right-hand portion of Figure 6.13c, they will cancel each other, the fiber will not be excited, and no light will be propagated.

- If the co-directional wavefronts are in an in-between phase, they will interfere as they reflect down the guide and the light beam will die away (a beam formed from wavefronts close to anti-phase will extinguish sooner than a beam formed from wavefronts close to in-phase).

Figure 6.13c   Beam Formation from In-Phase and Anti-Phase Wavefronts

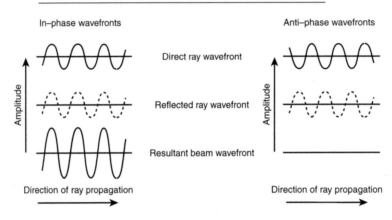

The three conditions listed for co-directional wavefronts allow us to state the only boundary condition for the core/cladding interface: A guided plane wave beam can form only if the co-directional direct and reflected wavefronts are in phase.

In-phase wavefronts will always reinforce each other and will suffer no loss due to optical interference.

Consider the interacting wavefronts shown in Figure 6.14a and Figure 6.14b. The downward-traveling direct ray and the downward-traveling reflected ray form a downward-traveling beam of light as shown in Figure 6.14a, and the upward-traveling direct ray and the upward-traveling reflected ray form a different, upward-traveling beam of light as shown in Figure 6.14b.

Figure 6.14a   Mode Formation in a Step-Index Optical Fiber: Downward-Traveling Beam and Wavefronts

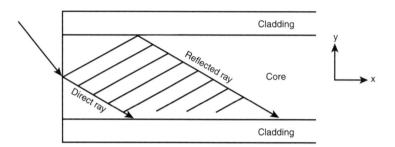

Figure 6.14b   Mode Formation in a Step-Index Optical Fiber: Upward-Traveling Beam and Wavefronts

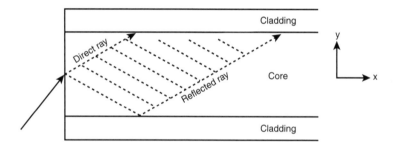

The wavefronts of the upward-traveling beam and the downward-traveling beam interfere with each other to form a standing-wave modal-field pattern perpendicular to the z axis of the fiber (illustrated, for example, by the dotted line from P to Q in Figure 6.14c). This standing wave pattern is called a *fiber mode*.

Figure 6.14c   Mode Formation in a Step-Index Optical Fiber: Standing Waves (Modal Fields) Form Perpendicular to the Z Axis

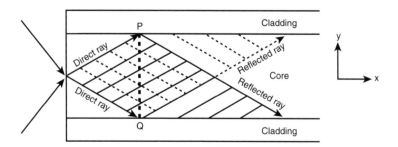

Since the light is confined to the core of the fiber, there is essentially no light in the cladding beyond points P and Q in Figure 6.14c. Therefore, the wavefronts of the upward-traveling beam and the downward-traveling beam must cancel (be in anti-phase) at P and Q, and there must be nulls in the modal field patterns at P and Q. Because there is always an upward-traveling wavefront and a downward-traveling wavefront to interfere at *every* position along the core/cladding interface, all points along the core/cladding interface are also points where nulls occur.

Figure 6.15a and Figure 6.15b show the geometry of mode formation in a step-index fiber. The direct ray wavefronts RQ and PT in Figure 6.15a are in-phase because they have experienced the same path delay (we assume that the path length from the source of the two rays impinging on the entrance facet of the fiber is the same, and within the fiber core, the path lengths are the same, as can be seen in the figure). Also, the two reflected wavefronts, PW and QS, are in phase with each other because they have also experienced the same delay from their respective points of reflection. But at point Q there is a null (electric field and light intensity equal zero) so wavefront RQ and wavefront QS must cancel at point Q. Therefore, the wavefronts RQ and QS are in anti-phase to each other. Since the direct ray wavefronts PW and QS are in-phase with each other, and wavefronts RQ and QS are in anti-phase to each other, the wavefronts RQ and PW must be in anti-phase to each other. This means that the path difference between wavefront RQ and PW must be an integer number of half wavelengths.

Figure 6.15a   Mode Formation in a Step-Index Optical Fiber: The Relationship of Phase to Allowed Ray Angles

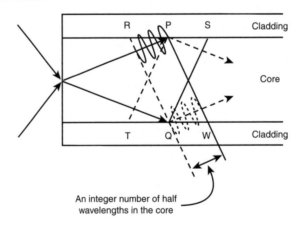

Now consider Figure 6.15b.

Figure 6.15b   Mode Formation in a Step-Index Optical Fiber: The Geometry of Allowed Ray Angles

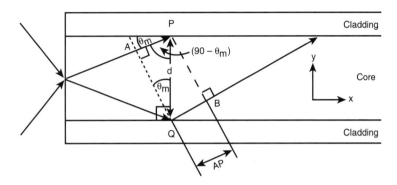

The direct ray is at an angle θ_m with the core/cladding interface and at an angle $(90 - \theta_m)$ with the line PQ (which is perpendicular to the axis of the core). The line AQ is at an angle θ_m to the line PQ, and the line AQ is parallel to the line PB. If d is the diameter of the core, then the length AP is equal to d $\sin(\theta_m)$. But, we have already seen in Figure 6.15a that the phase difference between wavefronts AQ and PB must be an integer number of half wavelengths.

Taking all of this into account, we can hold Equation 6.9 to be true.

Equation 6.9

$$AP = d \cdot \sin\left(\theta_m\right) = m \cdot \frac{\lambda}{2}$$

where:

    m = an integer

    λ = an optical wavelength in the core

This means that only specific ray angles will result in guided modes in an optical fiber. These ray angles are called *allowed ray angles* because they result in the excitation of a fiber mode. The measurement designation "half wavelength in the core" in Figure 6.15a and Equation 6.9 reflects the difference in the velocity of light in the core compared to light in a vacuum, and the resultant difference in wavelength of light in the core compared to that in a vacuum.

6.3.4 Modes: Electric Field and Intensity Patterns

Figure 6.16a shows the electric field amplitudes and Figure 6.16b shows the mode intensities for the first four modes associated with x-plane meridional rays in the core of a step-index fiber. Because in each section of the fiber the fields associated with each allowed upward-traveling beam and downward-traveling beam are in anti-phase at the plane of reflection (approximately the core/cladding interface), the electric field associated with the mode will tend to zero at, or just beyond, the core/cladding interface. This is just another way of saying that the majority of the light will be contained within the fiber core.

Figure 6.16a Electric Field Amplitudes for the First Four Modes, Associated with Meridional Rays, in a Step-Index Fiber

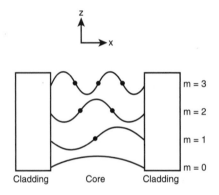

The electric field can also have other nulls (zeros) not located at the core/cladding interfaces. These non–core/cladding-interface nulls are marked with dots in Figure 6.15a. Low order modes have the fewest nulls; higher order modes, the most. If we let a be the number of non-core/cladding interface nulls, we can assign an identification number to each mode, m, such that Equation 6.10 is true.

Equation 6.10

$$m = a$$

Now it can be shown that the light intensity at each point in the field distribution is proportional to the square of the magnitude of the electric field at the same point—the light is brightest when the magnitude of the field is highest and dimmest where the electric field magnitude is lowest. Electric field nulls correspond to darkness in the mode intensity plot. Again, within the fiber core, the dark nulls of the mode intensity plot for the four modes are marked by the dots in Figure 6.16b. Figure 6.16b reveals that the number of bright peaks in a mode is equal to (m + 1), the mode number plus one.

Figure 6.16b   The Mode Intensities (Brightness) for the First Four Modes, Associated with Meridional Rays, in a Step-Index Fiber

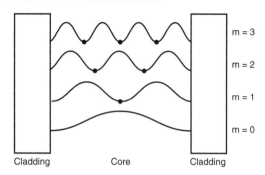

Figure 6.17a and Figure 6.17b allow us to compare the electric field amplitude and mode intensities for the first four fiber modes, associated with meridional rays, of a graded-index fiber with those of a step-index fiber, and to begin to see some differences. In graded-index fibers, the peak intensities of the lower order modes are confined to a region well within the core of the fiber instead of being spread uniformly across the entire core.

Figure 6.17a   Electric Field Amplitudes for the Low Order Modes in a Fiber with a Parabolic Index Profile

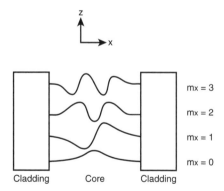

Figure 6.17b Mode Intensities (Brightness) for the Low Order Modes in a Fiber with a Parabolic Index Profile

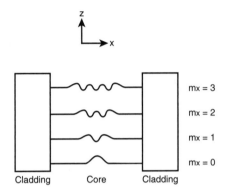

6.3.5 *Optical Fiber Bandwidth and Attenuation*

A launch that excites all modes of the fiber with approximately equal power is called an *overfilled launch* (*OFL*). To achieve an OFL, the fiber must be excited with an optical source that launches all ray angles at all points on the surface of the core. This can most easily be achieved with incoherent (that is, non-laser) sources like Light Emitting Diodes (LEDs). This is because each point on the surface of a non-coherent source emits light in all directions. OFL launches excite all three fiber ray types: axial, meridional, and skew.

As you will see in this section, typical laser transmitters directly excite axial and meridional rays, but very few skew rays, for the following reasons:

- The laser light is usually focused onto a small region of the core (to increase the power coupled into the fiber).

- The laser field is coherent over the focal region, and only a relatively small number of ray angles are contained within the focused laser beam.

Figure 6.18 shows a laser beam focused onto the center of the fiber core. Because the cone of light is made up of a number of rays having a number of different ray angles and paths, as shown in Figure 6.18, this launch excites many modes of the fiber. If an incident ray path is close to the angle that corresponds to a guided mode of the fiber, the light in that path will excite the mode. Each allowed-angle ray pair excites a different mode. This center laser launch condition is known as *radially overfilled launch* (*ROFL*). This is because the fiber is "overfilled" with rays that tend to excite modes having a bright spot at the center of the core. For this launch, the excited modes are associated with meridional rays. Therefore, ROFL-type launches only excite the axial and meridional fiber rays.

Figure 6.18   Radial Overfilled Launch (ROFL) into a Step-Index Fiber

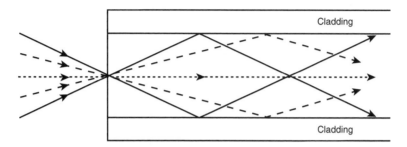

If the laser launch spot is offset from the center of the fiber core, skew rays and meridional ray are excited. Simply offsetting the launch spot can greatly increase the number of modes excited by a laser. For this reason, offset launch is a better simulation of OFL than ROFL.

6.3.5.1   *Intermodal Dispersion in Single-Mode and Multimode Fibers*

At the beginning of this chapter, we said that the critical requirement for an optical fiber link is to ensure that the received pulses are of appropriate shape and of sufficient intensity to be correctly detected by the optical receiver at Gigabit data rates. A little later we said that the fiber characteristics are fixed and cannot be changed, and that the fiber would be the constraining element in the optical design. The comparisons that follow of step-index multimode fiber and graded-index multimode fiber with step-index single-mode fiber enable us to begin evaluating the magnitude of that constraint. Each of the Figures 6.19a–c will illustrate the following items:

• The refractive index profile of the fiber

• A short impulse of light launched into the fiber

• The intensity profiles for the first few fiber modes

• The ray paths for the first few fiber rays

• The impulse of light output by the fiber

Figures 6.19a–6.19b offer a comparison of the impulse responses of step-index and graded-index multimode fibers. It is clear that they are decidedly different from each other, and they are also different from the impulse response of single-mode fiber shown in Figure 6.19c.

In the case of step-index multimode fiber, because all reflections take place in a region near the core/cladding interface, all the modal fields and the ray paths extend from the center of the core to the cladding. This may seem to be good, but it is actually a problem. Transmission delay is directly related to ray path length, and as you saw in Figure 6.18, the path lengths for each set of allowed ray angles are different. Because the ray velocity is constant across the core, the different modes have very different delay times. This is sometimes termed differential modal delay (DMD), and it is due to the different path lengths of the different modes. The DMD causes a spreading of the output pulse waveform, as shown in Figure 6.19a. The pulse spreading effect is called *intermodal dispersion*, and the amount of pulse spreading increases with fiber length. Unfortunately, at high data rates and long fiber lengths, the difference in modal delays can result in an overlapping of output waveforms for adjacent pulses, to the point that the output data stream becomes unrecoverable. This susceptibility to interpulse interference and the resultant significant decrease in bandwidth makes step-index multimode fiber unacceptable for Gigabit Ethernet.

Figure 6.19a   Typical Impulse Response Due to Intermodal Dispersion for Step-Index Multimode Fiber

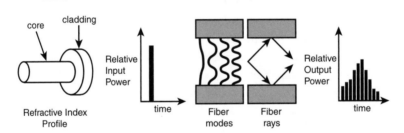

In the case of graded-index multimode fiber with a parabolic refractive index profile, the modal fields, modal intensities, and rays are confined near the core, and the modes have nearly equal delay times. Two factors are at work:

- The modes are primarily confined to the region of the core (as shown in Figure 6.19b).

- The ray velocity is highest near the core/cladding interface and slowest near the center of the core.

In a core with a parabolic refractive index profile, the area of the mode power increases with increasing mode number at approximately the same rate as the refractive index is reduced due to the refractive index profile shape. This means that skew rays, with paths near the cladding, appear to travel at the same velocity along the fiber as the rays whose paths are near the center of the core (axial and meridional rays). Modal delay is essentially equalized and pulse spreading is held to a minimum, as shown in Figure 6.19b.

Figure 6.19b   Typical Impulse Response Due to Intermodal Dispersion for Graded-Index (Parabolic Profile) Multimode Fiber

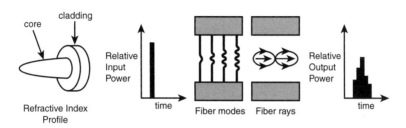

Given the pulse spreading problems with step-index multimode fiber, you might also conclude that step-index single-mode fiber is not appropriate for Gigabit Ethernet, but there is one major difference. Recall from the discussion surrounding Figure 6.15a and Figure 6.15b that the number of allowed modes in a fiber is related to the diameter of the core. The small core diameter of a single-mode fiber allows it to support only axial ray transmission, which means that all of the output power is contained in a single mode, pulse spreading is essentially non-existent, and bandwidth remains very high (see Figure 6.19c). Because of this, it will support transmission over much longer distances than graded-index multimode fiber. Single-mode fiber is not only appropriate for Gigabit Ethernet, but it is also widely used for long distance telecommunications applications.

Figure 6.19c   Typical Impulse Response Due to Intermodal Dispersion for Step-Index Single-Mode Fiber

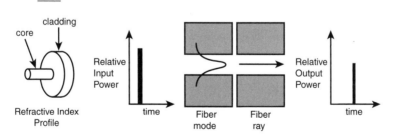

We now know why step-index multimode fiber cannot be used for Gigabit Ethernet—its DMD is too large. However, we still need to amplify our discussion of ray transmission through graded-index multimode fibers. Consider the two ray-launch conditions shown in Figure 6.20. Two x-plane rays have been launched into the fiber, R_0 on the axis of the core and R_1, parallel to, but offset from, the axis of the core. Both launch conditions could be achieved with a laser source (a coherent, thin light beam with parallel rays).

Figure 6.20   Center and Offset Ray Launch into a Graded-Index Fiber

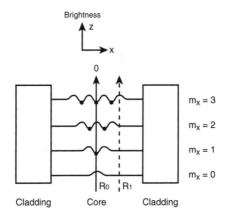

Ro = axial ray
R1 = x–plane ray offset from, but parallel to, the axis of the core

The intensity distribution of each of the first four x-plane modes (associated with meridian rays) are shown in Figure 6.20. The dots in the intensity plot for each mode represent no-light (darkness), and the flat portions of the intensity plot represent regions of low or no light. We shall state without proof that the optical power of each ray launched into the fiber is distributed among the fiber modes in proportion to the normalized mode intensity at the (x,y) launch position of the ray. Therefore, R_0 excites $m_x = 0$ and 2, but not $m_x = 1$ or 3, and ray R_1 excites some of $m_x = 2$, a lot of $m_x = 3$, almost none of $m_x = 0$, and only a little of $m_x = 1$.

Figure 6.21 is a plot of the relative power launched into each of the fiber modes by the two launches (R_0 and R_1). It can be seen that ray R_0 deposits a percentage of its power in the fiber modes as follows: 67% in mode $m_x = 0$, 0% in mode $m_x = 1$, 33% in mode $m_x = 2$, and 0% in mode $m_x = 3$. Also, R_1 deposits a percentage of its power in the fiber modes as follows: 1% in mode $m_x = 0$, 7% in mode $m_x = 1$, 32% in mode $m_x = 2$, and 60% in mode $m_x = 3$. By contrast, because the fiber is excited by many rays having many different launch positions and angles, an overfilled launch excites all modes equally.

Figure 6.21   Mode Power Content Pattern for the Axial and Offset Rays of Figure 6.20

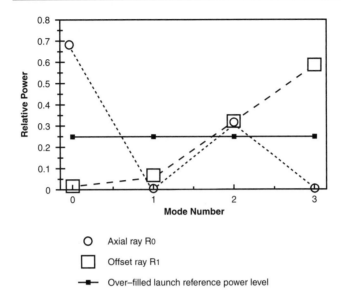

Note = The lines between the plotted points are for identification of mode–
power content patterns for each ray do not imply the existance
of mode power at intermediate positions between plotted points.

A similar analysis could be made of the y-plane, but in this case, only the axial ray R_0 would be present (because the y coordinates of both R_0 and R_1 are assumed to be zero).

Figures 6.22 and 6.23 show the calculated output intensity profiles and near field intensity patterns for the fiber supporting only four x and y modes when excited by the two rays of Figure 6.20 (the *near field* is the field localized at the output facet of the fiber). In each of the Figures 6.22–6.24, the core radius is normalized to 1.

Figure 6.22   Calculated Near Field Intensity Pattern for Launch R_0 of Figure 6.20

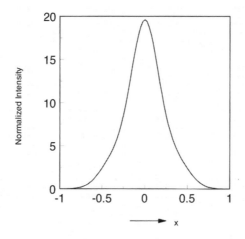

Calculated intensity profile at y=0

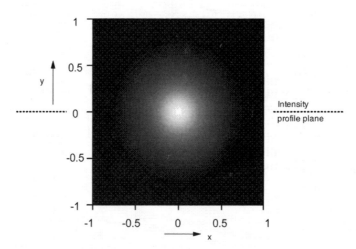

Calculated two dimensional intensity pattern at the output of the four moded fiber for launch R_0

Figure 6.23   Calculated Near Field Intensity Pattern for Launch R_1 of Figure 6.20

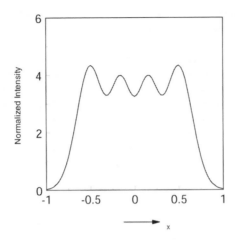

Calculated intensity profile at y=0

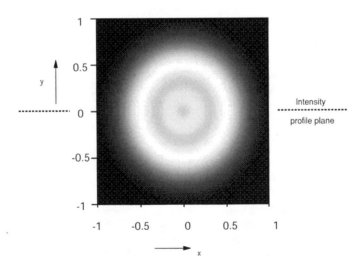

Calculated two dimensional intensity pattern at the output of the four moded fiber launch R_1

For fibers with approximately parabolic refractive index profiles, the near field amplitude at a point (x,y) is obtained by multiplication of the amplitude of the field at point x by the amplitude of the field at point y. The light intensity is then calculated by squaring the field amplitude at each point (x,y). The intensity profile and near field pattern for an overfilled launch of our simple fiber, having only four x and four y modes, are included for comparison in Figure 6.24.

Figure 6.24   Calculated Near Field Intensity Pattern for OFL Launch of Figure 6.20

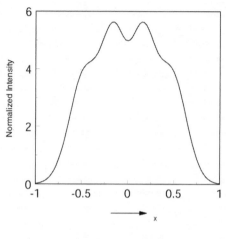

Calculated intensity profile = 0

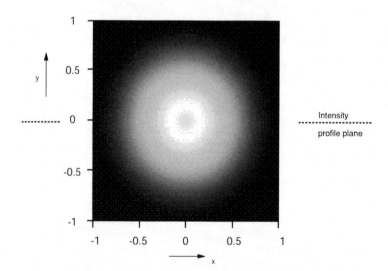

Calculated two dimensional intensity pattern at the output of the four moded fiber OFL launch.

Note the difference between the three launch conditions: center launch (R_0) concentrates the power in the central region of the core, whereas both OFL and offset launch (R_1) spread the power over the majority of the core.

The intensity profile resulting from the offset launch R_1 is important for Gigabit Ethernet. A small but significant percentage of the installed graded-index multimode fibers were found to have an abrupt change, either an increase or decrease, in the refractive index, at the center of the core. Figure 6.25a illustrates the case of a central depression in the refractive index profile.

Figure 6.25a Graded-Index Multimode Fiber with a Central Defect in its Refractive Index Profile

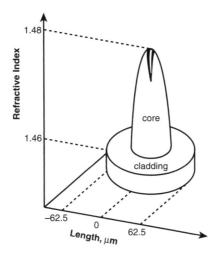

Unfortunately, for fibers with the central defect, the purpose of the parabolic refractive index profile is defeated because modal delays are no longer uniform across the diameter of the core. The effect of the defect is illustrated by Figure 6.25b.

Figure 6.25b Modal Delay in a Graded-Index Multimode Fiber with a Central Defect

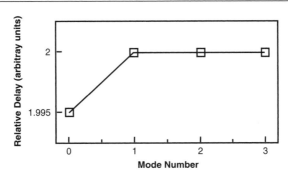

Mode m = 0 experiences less delay compared to the delay of the other modes. The percentage change in the delay is very small, but after propagation through many hundreds of meters of fiber, the delay difference is about a nanosecond or so.

Any restricted (that is, not OFL) launch condition that excites a set of modes having between 20 percent and 80 percent of the power in mode m = 0 is likely to be subject to pulse spreading somewhat like we saw in step-index multimode fiber. Figures 6.26a and 6.26b show the fiber impulse responses for the two different launch conditions, R_0 and R_1, respectively. The offset launch R_1 is positioned approximately halfway between the core center and the core cladding interface.

Figure 6.26a   Impulse Response for a Center-Launched Pulse Input to a Graded-Index Multimode Fiber Having a Central Defect

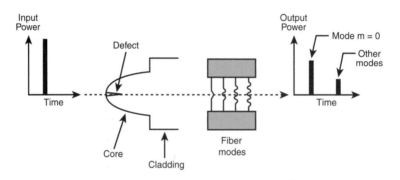

Figure 6.26b   Impulse Response for an Offset-Launched Pulse Input to a Graded-Index Multimode Fiber Having a Central Defect

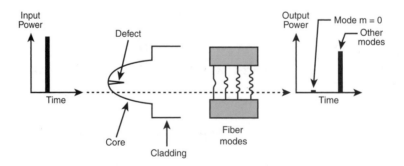

The response to the center-launched impulse R_0 suffers the maximum effect of the central defect. Pulse splitting occurs, and the resultant bandwidth is low. On the other hand, the impulse in the offset launch position R_1 misses the central defect, pulse splitting is avoided, and the bandwidth remains high.

The obvious solution to the central defect is to limit the launch conditions to those rays that do not result in different modal delay times. The following list offers some suggestions regarding axial, meridional, and skew rays.

- **Axial Rays.** Launch conditions that include mainly axial rays should be avoided.

- **Meridional Rays.** Because meridional rays pass through the center of the core, modes associated with meridional rays will experience the central refractive index defect and could cause differential delay problems.

- **Skew Rays.** Because skew rays don't pass through the center of the fiber, they are not affected by the central defect.

Clearly, launches (such as the offset launch) that excite mainly skew rays are preferred because they minimize DMD effects. The analysis and testing procedure that led up to the definition of offset launch as a way to correct for the central defect in graded-index multimode fibers is described in Chapter 10, "The Gigabit Ethernet Modal Bandwidth Investigation."

6.3.5.2 *Chromatic Dispersion in Single-Mode and Multimode Fibers*

Section 6.3.5.1 introduced intermodal dispersion—the dispersion due to the different path lengths of the modes. *Chromatic dispersion* is another source of dispersion that can be defined as the physical effect that allows a prism to separate the colors of white light and raindrops to form a rainbow. Chromatic dispersion results because the refractive index of a material changes with wavelength. This means that different wavelengths (different colors of light) experience different delays as their associated rays travel along the core of a fiber. The different delays, in turn, cause more or less spreading in the duration of the output pulse, depending on the wavelength span of the source and the length of the fiber. Chromatic dispersion causes pulse spreading within a mode, and because of this it is also sometimes called *intramodal dispersion*.

Figure 6.27 shows plots of the delay and dispersion as a function of wavelength for a 1 km length of typical 62.5 μm parabolic-profile multimode fiber.

Figure 6.27   Chromatic Dispersion in 1 km of Typical 62.5 μm Multimode Fiber

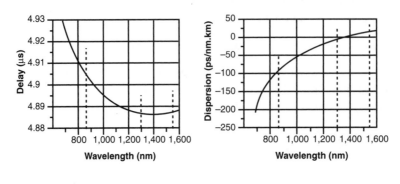

The three vertical dotted lines in Figure 6.27 identify the approximate wavelengths (850, 1,300, and 1,550 nm) of the most common operating ranges for optical fiber transmission systems. The dispersion curves for single-mode fiber would have the same shape as those shown in Figure 6.27 except that the zero dispersion point would be shifted to approximately 1,300 nm (instead of 1,365 nm for the multimode fiber shown in Figure 6.27).

6.3.5.3   *Attenuation in Optical Fibers*

The remaining fiber-related design constraint is attenuation. *Attenuation* is the decrease in optical power along the length of the fiber. Attenuation varies with wavelength and is typically defined as either a scalar ratio of the input magnitude to the output magnitude as shown in Equation 6.11, or as the decibel loss per kilometer of fiber length.

Equation 6.11

$$\text{number of decibels (dB)} = 10 \cdot log_{10} \left(\frac{P_i}{P_0} \right)$$

where:

P_i = optical power input to the fiber

P_0 = optical power output from the fiber

The attenuation for any length fiber then becomes the expression in Equation 6.12.

Equation 6.12

attenuation (dB) $= \alpha_{db} \cdot L$

where:

α_{db} = attenuation coefficient of fiber in dB/km

L = length of the fiber in km

Figure 6.28 shows the attenuation curves for both single-mode and multimode fiber for our range of interest. You can see that the short wavelength attenuation (around 850 nm) is more than three times the attenuation (in dB/km) at the two longer wavelengths (around 1,300 and 1,550 nm).

Figure 6.28   Attenuation in Single-Mode and Multimode Optical Fibers

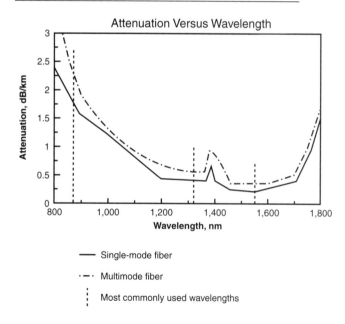

The summary at the end of the chapter discusses which of the three wavelengths are used for Gigabit Ethernet and the reasons for selecting them. You also still need to become familiar with the concept of modal noise, but before getting to that, you need to understand the characteristics of the light sources that are used in the Gigabit Ethernet optical transmitter.

6.4 *Transmitter Electronics and Light Sources*

The critical element in the optical transmitter is the light source, and there are several characteristics that it should have, including the following:

- The size and configuration of the light source must be compatible with optical fiber.

- The light output should be highly directional.

- The output pulse shape should accurately track the input signal so as to minimize noise and distortion.

- The wavelengths of the emitted light should match the wavelengths where fiber attenuation and dispersion are low.

- The average light output power should be stable over time and should be largely unaffected by changes in temperature.

- The average output power should be sufficient to account for the losses and power penalties in the power budget and still provide sufficient power to allow accurate bit detection and clock recovery.

- The optical source should be highly reliable and sufficiently low in cost to be competitive in the marketplace.

There are two possible semiconductor alternatives that exhibit all or most of these characteristics—Light Emitting Diodes (LEDs) and laser diodes.

Figure 6.29 illustrates the basic mechanism for generating light from a semiconductor. The electrons and atoms in the crystal lattice structure can exist in only discrete energy bands.

Figure 6.29   Semiconductor Energy State Diagrams

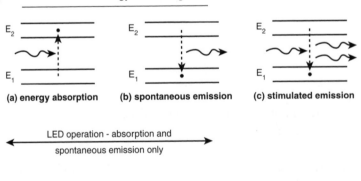

(a) energy absorption (b) spontaneous emission (c) stimulated emission

LED operation - absorption and
spontaneous emission only

Laser operation - absorption plus both spontaneous and stimulated emission

When the electrons and atoms are excited to higher energy states by an applied current, they absorb energy from the electrical power supply (see part (a) of Figure 6.29). However, excited atoms are unstable and they will *spontaneously* decay to lower energy states after a short but random period of time (see part (b) of Figure 6.29). During the spontaneous decay, the atomic structure releases its absorbed energy, usually as photons of light. The frequency of the spontaneously emitted light is a characteristic of the transition from the higher energy state to the lower energy state and is related to the difference in energy between the two states by Equation 6.13.

Equation 6.13

$$E = E_2 - E_1 = h \cdot f$$

where:

h = Plank's constant

f = the frequency of the emitted light

Light with a wavelength equal to the characteristic wavelength is called *resonance light.*

A beam of resonance light shining on atoms in unstable excited states can force, or *stimulate,* them to emit their resonance light by causing them to fall back to their lower states, as illustrated in part (c) of Figure 6.29. The stimulating light beam intensity is increased by the additional photons released through stimulated emission that, in turn, further increases the rate of stimulation.

The mechanism shown in Figure 6.29 applies to forward-biased *p-n* junctions in both lasers and LEDs. The amount of stimulated emission is proportional to the following:

- The difference in the number of excited state atoms compared to the number of lower state atoms

- The intensity of the resonance light shining on the active region of the semiconductor

6.4.1   *Light Emitting Diodes (LEDs)*

Light Emitting Diodes (LEDs) have been used as analog optical light sources in 10BASE-T and 100BASE-T optical PMDs, and for 622 Mbps, 500 m ATM links. However, the maximum power output from an LED is only on the order of –20 dBm (dBm is the power level referenced to 1 milliwatt). After we add –7.5 dB for link losses and power penalties, the required receiver sensitivity becomes –27.5 dBm. Unfortunately, reasonable cost optical receivers require input power levels in the –17 dBm to –20 dBm range. It is also difficult to manufacture LEDs with the fast rise- and falltimes required for Gigabit data rates. For these reasons, LEDs are not used for Gigabit Ethernet.

6.4.2 Diode Lasers

Semiconductor lasers are efficient and easily modulated at very high data rates, and their optical output is relatively easy to couple into optical fiber. Two fundamentally different types of laser are used for Gigabit Ethernet: edge-emitting lasers and vertical cavity surface emitting lasers (VCSELs).

6.4.2.1 Edge-Emitting Lasers

Edge-emitting lasers have been used for more than a decade by both the telecommunications and home entertainment industries. Because of this, the manufacturing process for edge-emitting lasers is very mature. They can be fabricated to produce optical outputs with wavelengths in either, but not both, the short or long wavelength regions.

Figure 6.30 shows the cross section of a simple, early edge-emitting laser. It is no longer used in any new applications, but it presents a model structure that will help to begin the discussion of laser operation. This type of laser was known as a *homojunction* Fabry-Perot laser because it has a single *p-n* junction and the structure of the laser acts like a Fabry-Perot resonator. It was a precursor to today's more complex lasers.

Figure 6.30   Schematic Representation of an Early Fabry-Perot Laser

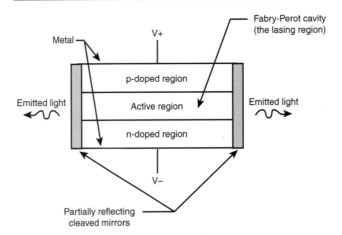

The operation of the laser can be explained as follows. A weak beam of resonance light is initially created within the laser by the spontaneous emission from excited atoms. The initial beam is reflected by the mirrors at each end of the laser that cause the resonance light to bounce back and forth, initiating stimulated emission. Then, if the mirrors have enough reflectivity, the light trapped between the mirrors increases the intensity of the resonance light, and this, in turn, increases the rate of stimulated emission.

If there are more atoms in excited states than in lower state, the resonance light will be amplified by the stimulated light that is produced. A medium that amplifies resonance light is said to have *optical gain*.

In semiconductor lasers, optical gain is created in the region of the diode's junction. The power source that maintains the gain is the electrical power supply. The higher the laser gain, the more light that is emitted by the laser. Mirrors can be the cleaved edges of the laser chip, or, for low gain lasers (which we will discuss a little further on), they can be specially fabricated for high reflectivity. The mirrors effectively trap the light in the cavity, which allows the light to interact with the gain medium over a relatively long period of time and which results in an increase in the overall gain.

Consider the ray diagram in Figure 6.31. The rays zigzag between the mirrors at a shallow angle. In real systems, the rays would have zero angle and their paths would actually overlap each other. However, introducing a small angle makes it simpler to see what is happening. The direct ray and reflected rays have plane wavefronts that are perpendicular to the ray paths. To form a beam of light that is resonant with the cavity, the wavefronts of all rays that travel to the right must be in phase with each other. At mirror 2, the wavefronts of the following rays must be in phase: direct, R2, R4, R6, and so forth.

Note

The *cavity* in a semiconductor laser is formed by the mirrors, at each end of the active region, by the active region of the laser, and any transparent material between the mirrors and the active region. In a basic laser, the mirrors are simply the cleaved end facets of the laser.

Figure 6.31   Light Ray Paths in a Laser Cavity

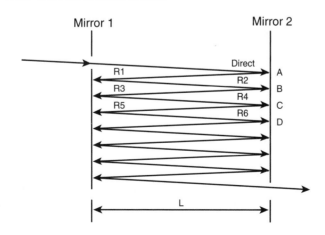

Similarly, the wavefronts of all rays that travel to the left must be in phase with each other. If the mirrors are nearly perpendicular, the distance the light travels between points A, B, C, D, and so on is 2L. To be in phase, the path length must be an integral number of wavelengths as shown in Equation 6.14.

Equation 6.14

$$2 \cdot n \cdot L = m \cdot \lambda$$

where:

> m = the mode number
>
> n = the refractive index of the optical amplifier
>
> λ = the wavelength of the mode frequency

and where the resonance condition L is given in Equation 6.15.

Equation 6.15

$$L = \frac{m \cdot \lambda}{2 \cdot n}$$

Good lasers require three basic things: a medium with optical gain, mirrors to feed some light back into a region of optical gain as shown in Figure 6.32, and a power source to maintain the optical gain (for clarity, the power source is not shown in the diagram).

Figure 6.32 The Basic Elements of a Laser

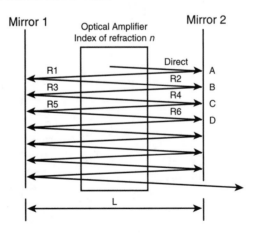

Modern edge-emitting lasers employ a *double heterojunction* structure (shown in Figure 6.33) that includes second *n*-doped and *p*-doped regions on either side of the active *p-n* junction to provide better optical confinement and to enhance optical gain and laser efficiency.

Figure 6.33 Edge-Emitting Gain-Guided Double-Heterojunction Fabry-Perot Laser

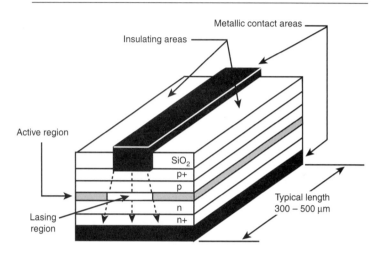

Front and rear end faces are cleaved mirrors.
Dotted arrows between metallic contacts indicate forward current flow.

Electrical current is concentrated or "pumped" into the active region below the metal contact to produce optical gain. The mirrors are cleaved edges of the laser chip.

The light rays bouncing back and forth in the cavity develop standing waves (modes), and from Equations 6.14 and 6.15, we know that the distance between the mirrors must be an integer multiple of half wavelengths.

The frequency of the standing wave is related to both the inter-mirror spacing and the refractive index of the material in the active region of the optical amplifier (the cavity) by Equation 6.16.

Equation 6.16

$$f = \frac{m \cdot c}{2 \cdot n \cdot L}$$

where:

m = mode number

c = the speed of light

n = index of refraction of the optical amplifier

L = separation distance between the mirrors

Substituting mode numbers into Equation 6.16 shows that the frequency difference, δf, between adjacent modes is given by Equation 6.17.

Equation 6.17

$$\delta f = \frac{c}{2 \cdot n \cdot L}$$

For higher mode numbers, the wavelength separation is expressed as in Equation 6.18.

Equation 6.18

$$\delta \lambda \approx \frac{2 \cdot n \cdot L}{m \cdot (m-1)}$$

While Equations 6.16–6.18 indicate that many modes can form in a laser cavity, the actual light emission is limited to the narrow spectrum of the gain curve of the optical amplifier, as shown in Figure 6.34a.

Figure 6.34a   Gain Curve of the Optical Amplifier

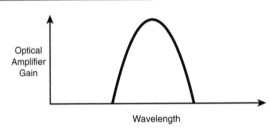

Figure 6.34b shows the expected wavelengths for the cavity modes of the Fabry-Perot cavity.

Figure 6.34b   Modes of the Fabry-Perot Cavity

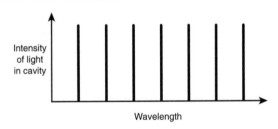

Figure 6.34c shows the output spectrum due to the combination of the gain curve of the optical amplifier and the cavity modes of the Fabry-Perot cavity. The figure includes only three cavity modes within the gain curve. Depending on the type of laser, more or fewer modes could be output.

 Laser Output Spectrum

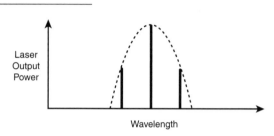

Figure 6.35a shows the measured output from an actual Fabry-Perot laser operating at a wavelength near 1,300 nm. Obviously, many cavity modes lie within the gain curve of the active region of the laser.

Figure 6.35a Measured Optical Spectrum for a Fabry-Perot Laser Operating at a Wavelength of 1,300 nm

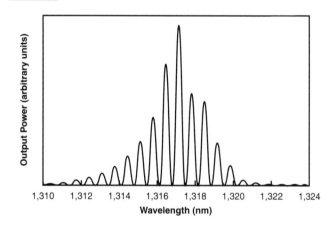

Figure 6.35b shows the light output versus input (bias) current for the laser used to obtain the results of Figure 6.35a. The laser starts lasing at a bias current of about 25 mA. Any current in excess of 25 mA produces large amounts of laser light.

Figure 6.35b Measured Light Output Power Versus Bias Current (L/I) for a Fabry-Perot Laser Operating at a Wavelength of 1,300 nm

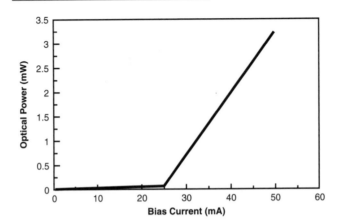

Before leaving this section, you should note that Equation 6.18 is only valid at higher mode numbers ($\delta\lambda$ would be indeterminate at m = 1). Figure 6.36 shows the mode number ranges for the Fabry-Perot lasers introduced in this section and also for the VCSELs discussed in the next section.

Figure 6.36 Laser Cavity Mode Number Ranges

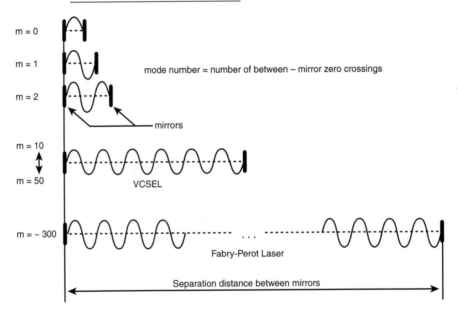

6.4.2.2 *Vertical Cavity Surface Emitting Lasers (VCSELs)*

VCSELs are a recently developed, new type of laser that are especially attractive for optical fiber applications for the following reasons:

- Fabrication of VCSELs is intrinsically a large-scale wafer deposition process, and the many thousand VCSELs on a single wafer will all have similar characteristics.

- VCSELs emit light perpendicular (vertical) to the surface of the wafer they are made on, making "on wafer" optical testing an easy process.

- The mirrors are created during deposition and do not need to be cleaved, avoiding a process that reduces the yield of edge-emitting lasers.

- VCSELs produce circular laser beams that couple very efficiently into optical fiber.

As Figure 6.37 illustrates, however, VCSELs have quite complicated structures compared to edge-emitting lasers. A VCSEL's mirrors are made from many thin dielectric or semiconducting layers, and sometimes with metal. The gain region consists of many even thinner layers of semiconductor material. VCSEL performance is critically dependent on the thickness of each of these layers.

Figure 6.37   Schematic Diagram of a Short Wavelength VCSEL

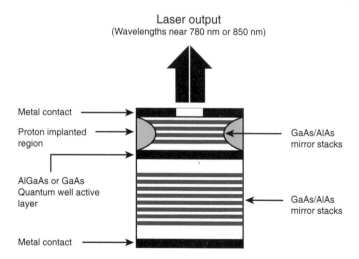

Figure 6.38a illustrates the cavity modes of the VCSEL; Figure 6.38b illustrates the gain curve of the VCSEL's active region; Figure 6.38c shows the resulting VCSEL optical output spectrum. This series of figures can be compared to Figures 6.34a–6.34c for the edge-emitting laser covered in the last section. Because VCSEL cavities are very short, only one

mode is usually contained within the gain curve of the VCSEL. Therefore, you can expect a VCSEL to have a much narrower optical spectrum compared to that of a Fabry-Perot laser.

Figure 6.38a Modes of the VCSEL's Fabry-Perot Cavity

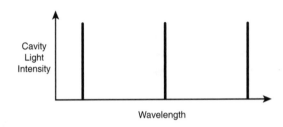

Figure 6.38b Gain Curve of the AlGaAs Quantum Well Active Layer

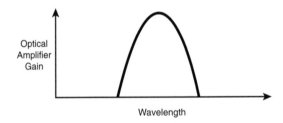

Figure 6.38c VCSEL Output Spectrum

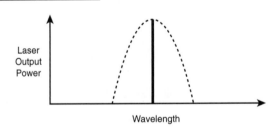

Figure 6.39a shows the measured optical output spectrum for a VCSEL operating near 850 nm wavelength. As expected, the output spectrum of the VCSEL is very narrow. The VCSEL spectrum is contained within a wavelength range of only 1 nm, whereas the Fabry-Perot laser spectrum extends over about 8 nm (refer to Figure 6.35a). Figure 6.39b shows the light output curve for the VCSEL. The curve is similar to that for the Fabry-Perot laser (refer to Figure 6.35b) except that the threshold for the VCSEL is only 5 mA.

Figure 6.39a Measured Optical Power Versus Output Wavelength for a Proton Implanted VCSEL Operating Near a Wavelength of 850 nm

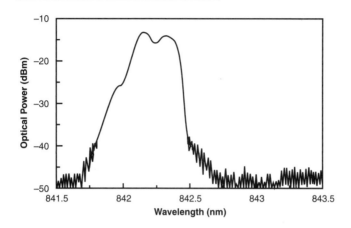

Figure 6.39b Measured Light Output Power Versus Bias Current (L/I) Curve for a Proton Implanted VCSEL Operating Near a Wavelength of 850 nm

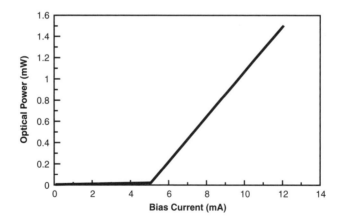

In contrast to edge-emitting lasers, VCSELs have only recently been introduced to the commercial marketplace. This is because the fabrication technology has taken longer to mature. Short wavelength VCSELs, near 850 nm, are now widely used for LAN and interconnect applications. However, it is very difficult to make VCSELs that operate at long wavelengths, and so it will be a few years before long wavelength VCSELs become available.

6.4.3 Mode Partitioning and Mode Partition Noise (MPN)

The discussion of chromatic dispersion in sections 6.3.5.1 and 6.3.5.2 did not consider how changes in the optical spectrum of the light source would affect the output of a fiber link. Figure 6.40 shows four output spectra of a CD laser, measured at one-minute intervals (CD lasers are the type of lasers used in compact disc drives). Clearly, the spectrum of the laser changes over relatively short periods of time. However, the total output power remained constant for all measurements.

Figure 6.40　Laser Spectra Variability—The Optical Spectra of a Fabry-Perot (CD-type) Laser Measured at One-Minute Intervals

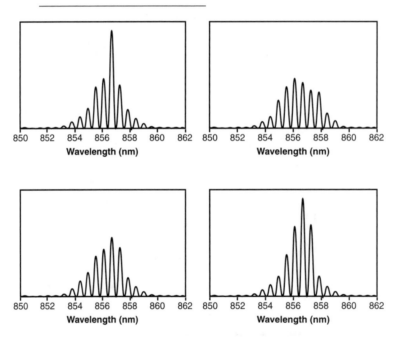

Note – Total optical output power remained constant for all spectra.

Figure 6.41 presents a more detailed view of the effect of laser mode partitioning where both the measured time waveforms of the complete laser power spectrum and the time waveforms due to individual modes are shown. You can see that the output power is partitioned between the different modes, with the power in some modes being reduced in favor of other modes.

Figure 6.41   Laser Mode Partitioning

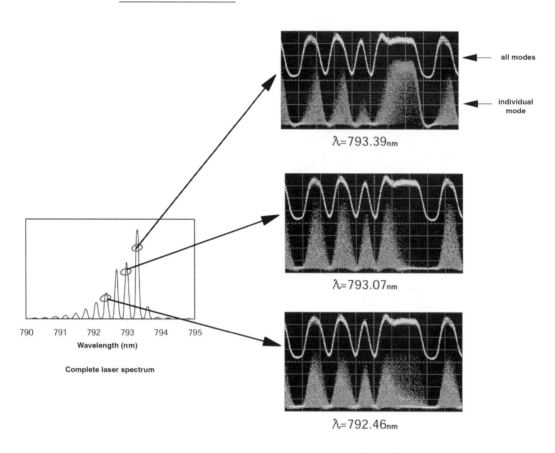

Individual Modes vs. all Modes

Partitioning of laser power between laser modes does not change the average total transmitted power and does not cause additional noise at the laser output. However, because the laser modes have different optical frequencies, and hence different colors, they travel at different velocities in the fiber. Therefore, partitioning of the power in the differently colored laser modes leads to fluctuations in the arrival time of the signal at the fiber output. These fluctuations broaden the received signal trace, as shown in Figure 6.42. This effect is known as *mode partition noise (MPN)*.

Mode partition noise affects *both* single-mode and multimode links by reducing the signal-to-noise ratio (SNR) and by degrading the eye diagram.

Figure 6.42   Mode Partition Noise (MPN)

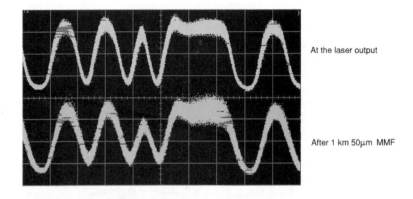

At the laser output

After 1 km 50μm MMF

Measured signals from a Fabry-Perot laser operating near 850 nm .

6.4.4   *Laser Transmit Electronics*

Gigabit Ethernet laser transmitters consist of the three basic functional blocks shown in Figure 6.43. The digital-to-analog converter and modulator converts the digital signal into an analog signal for modulation of the laser. The laser bias function adjusts the quiescent operating point of the laser. The light source is obviously the laser.

Figure 6.43   Optical Transmitter Block Diagram

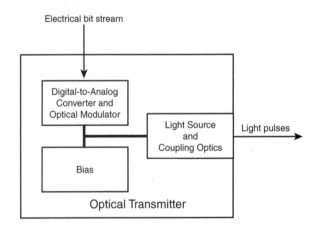

Figure 6.44 illustrates the primary electrical components of a Gigabit Ethernet laser transmitter in a little more detail. A small portion of the laser light is directed onto a monitor photodiode, and the output of the monitor photodiode is used as a feedback signal by the laser bias circuits to control the average output power of the laser.

Figure 6.44   Laser Driver Circuit with a Monitor Photodiode for Bias Control

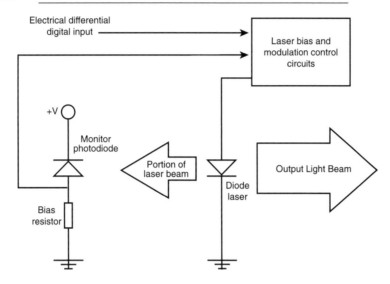

To avoid a time delay during transition through the spontaneous emission region at the start of a pulse, the bias current for the quiescent or "keep alive" operating point of the laser is usually set somewhat above the lower end of the stimulated emission region, as shown in Figure 6.45a.

Figure 6.45a   Laser Diode Modulation: The Light Output Versus Input Current (L/I) Curve for a Laser Diode

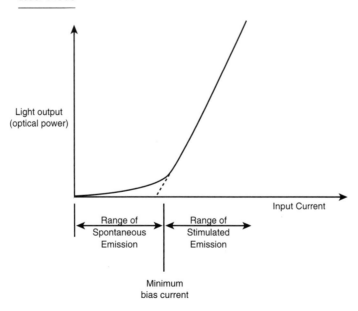

Laser modulation circuits convert the digital signal into an analog signal, which determines the forward current levels for both the high-pulse power and low-pulse power. The laser output is modulated by injecting current into the laser, as shown in Figure 6.45b.

Figure 6.45b   Laser Diode Modulation: Laser Light Output Versus Modulated Input Current

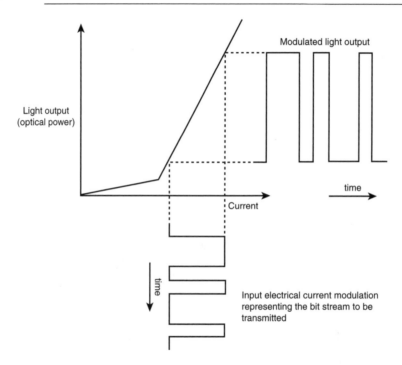

6.5   *Optical Fiber Splices and Connectors*

Figure 6.46 illustrates the principle of the operation of SC connectors. An alignment sleeve is used to guide the two ferrules, which contain the optical fibers, into physical contact so that the cores of the fibers are aligned. The alignment of the fiber core is precise enough to ensure typical loss values of about 0.3dB. The ends of the ferrules are polished and, when the connector is mated, there is sufficient pressure to deform the fiber to produce a flat physical contact. The quality of both the polish and the physical contact ensures low reflectivity (return loss), typically much better than 26 dB.

Figure 6.46   Physical-Contacting Butt-Coupled Connector

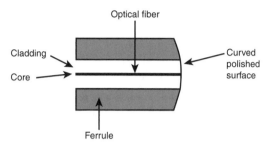

a) The ferrules are polished to form a slightly convex surface.

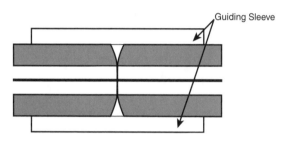

b) The sleeve guides the ferrules and the force of the contact is
large enough to deform and flatten the mating surface.

The duplex SC connector is specified as the Medium Dependent Interface (MDI) for both 1000BASE-SX and 1000BASE-LX. The MDI provides the connection between the active device (PMD) and the fiber optic cabling. However, other types of optical connections (fusion splices, mechanical splices, and other types of mechanical connectors) may also be used for fiber optic cabling, as long as they meet the optical fiber connection specifications of attenuation (forward loss) and back reflection (return loss) specified in the Gigabit Ethernet standard.

If you looked ahead, you may have wondered why we elected to discuss optical transmitters before considering fiber connectors and splices. The reason is that connectors and splices can be additional sources of noise.

6.5.1 *Modal Noise*

Section 6.4.3 introduced mode partition noise—noise caused by the interaction of the different modal frequencies (modes) in the laser output spectrum and the subsequent signal distortion due to the chromatic dispersion of the fiber. With that in mind, you need to become familiar with a different mode-related noise.

Imperfect connectors, splices, or optical couplers create mode selective loss. Mode selective loss combined with changes in the optical spectrum of a laser can create a form of noise known as *modal noise* (sometimes also called speckle noise). The amount of power lost in the mode selective element varies, due to the changing speckle pattern (shown in Figure 6.47) creating amplitude noise at the receiver, which degrades the bit error rate. This, in turn, means that the transmitter output power must be increased to compensate for the modal noise and to maintain the bit error rate (BER) at the level that would have been present without the modal noise. The amount of additional power is called the *modal noise power penalty.*

Figure 6.47   Modal Noise: The Speckle Pattern at a Point of Mode Selective Loss

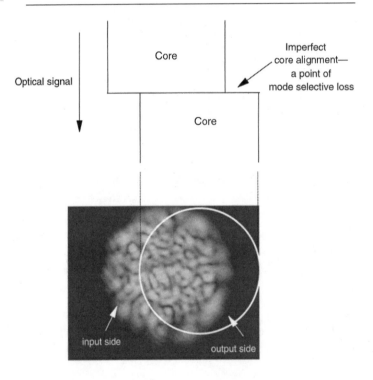

Three conditions must be present for modal noise to occur:

- There must be a speckle pattern (see Figure 6.47).

- The topology of the speckle pattern must change with time.

- There must be points of mode selective loss.

The use of multimode fiber and coherent lasers ensures that the first condition will be fulfilled and a speckle pattern will be produced. Variations in the speckle pattern are caused by small changes in the relative phase of the fiber modes at the point of mode selective loss. For example, the laser spectrum may change because of transient modulation effects (as shown in Figure 6.48), modal power partitioning, or slow variations in the optical spectra due to temperature changes. These small changes in the optical spectrum are sufficient to cause phase fluctuations of the fiber modes and, hence, speckle variation. Similarly, the length of the fiber could actually change due to mechanical vibration, mechanical stress, or expansion/contraction due to temperature changes.

Figure 6.48   CD Lasers: Theoretical Relaxation Oscillations and Optical Spectra

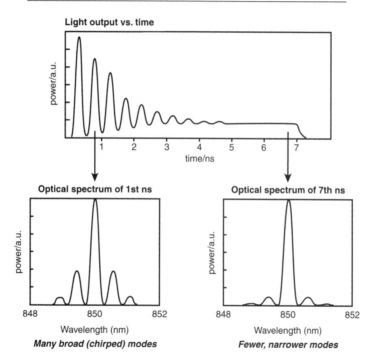

The intensity versus time graph and optical spectra in Figure 6.48 are simulations of a typical edge-emitting CD laser operating near 850 nm. In this simulation, a constant current pulse, having a duration of 7 ns, modulates the laser. The laser starts emitting light about 0.3 ns after the current pulse is injected. For the first few nanoseconds, the laser's output is oscillatory and the laser has a relatively broad spectrum. Near the end of the pulse, the oscillations disappear and the laser spectrum narrows.

6.6 *Optical Signal Detectors*

Section 5.3 in Chapter 5, "Fundamentals of Baseband Transmission," introduced receiver characteristics and functions, which showed the preamplifier as the first element of a Gigabit Ethernet receiver (refer to Figure 5.5). That section in Chapter 5 also alluded to the need for some sort of signal detection at the input to the receiver. In optical systems, the optical signal must first be detected and converted to an electrical signal before it can be processed by the receiver electronics. This is accomplished by focusing the light output of the fiber on the photodiode as shown in the simplified schematic of an optical receiver in Figure 6.49.

Figure 6.49   Schematic of an Optical Signal Detector and Preamplifier

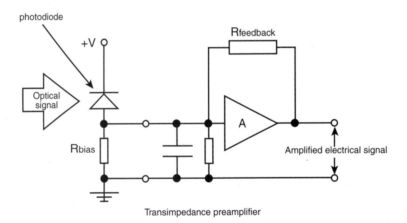

Figure 6.50 shows two types of semiconductor photodiodes commonly used in high data rate optical receivers. Both are called PIN photodiodes because their structures incorporate p-type, intrinsic (non-doped), and n-type semiconductor layers. Light passes through both the dielectric window and the p-type layer before it is absorbed within the intrinsic material. The absorbed light produces charge carriers that result in a photocurrent that is proportional to the light intensity. The photodiode is reverse-biased to minimize dark currents (the current that would result from the photodiode being in the dark) and to encourage the speedy movement of the photo-induced charge carriers through the intrinsic region of the diode.

Figure 6.50 Photodiode Structures for Operation Near Wavelengths of 850 nm and 1,300 nm

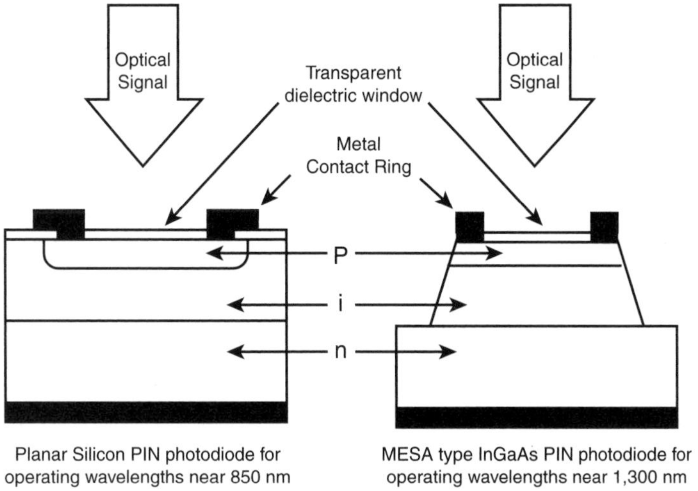

Planar Silicon PIN photodiode for
operating wavelengths near 850 nm

MESA type InGaAs PIN photodiode for
operating wavelengths near 1,300 nm

The type of base material determines the operational wavelengths of PIN photodiodes. Silicon absorbs light at short optical wavelengths and is appropriate for operation in the 850 nm region. InGaAs, on the other hand, absorbs light at long wavelengths, and is used for operation in the 1,300 nm region.

6.7   Summary

This chapter introduced the basic principles, concepts, components, and technology relevant to optical baseband transmission in Gigabit Ethernet, including the following:

• The elements that compose the Gigabit Ethernet optical link

• The concepts of power budgets and power penalties

• Basic properties of both single-mode and multimode optical fiber

• Optical fiber modes and rays

• Noise and signal distortion in Gigabit Ethernet links

• Optical transceivers

6.7.1   The 850 nm, 1,300 nm, and 1,550 nm Wavelength Trade-Off

As mentioned periodically throughout this chapter, there is a third low-loss window near 1,550 nm wavelength. By now, you are probably wondering why this wavelength was not specified for Gigabit Ethernet even though the telecommunications industry operates its long distance links at wavelengths near 1,550 nm. Some issues that discouraged the use of the 1,550 nm band for Gigabit Ethernet are as follows:

- The dispersion in the single-mode fiber specified for internal building use by ISO/IEC 11801 (generic cabling for customer premises) is greater at wavelengths near 1,550 nm than the dispersion at wavelengths near 1,300 nm. This additional dispersion would lead to larger mode-partition penalties if Fabry-Perot lasers were used.

- The additional mode-partition noise and chromatic dispersion can be effectively eliminated with the use of single frequency lasers operating at wavelengths near 1,550 nm. However, long wavelength single frequency lasers operating near 1,300 nm or 1,550 nm are much more expensive than Fabry-Perot lasers.

- Multimode fiber supports many fewer modes at wavelengths near 1,550 nm compared to the number of modes supported at 1,300 nm, which could lead to increased modal noise and modal bandwidth penalties.

6.7.2 *Optical Fiber Performance Comparison*

This chapter concludes with two graphs indicating the performance limitations of single-mode and multimode optical fiber links. Figure 6.51 shows the performance of single-mode systems based on the use of long wavelength (1,300 nm) Fabry-Perot, edge-emitting lasers. The graph indicates the theoretical limits, due to optical attenuation at transmission rates below about 0.6 Gbps, and to mode partition noise at transmission rates above about 1.0 Gbps.

Figure 6.51   Link Length Versus Signaling Rate for Single-Mode Fiber, Fabry-Perot Laser-Based Systems Operating at Wavelengths Near 1,300 nm

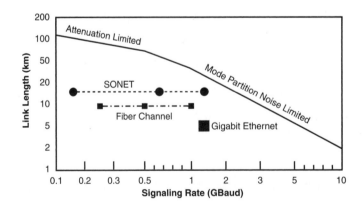

Figure 6.51 also shows the performance range specified by SONET, Fibre Channel, and Gigabit Ethernet. Obviously, the dual need for network inter-operation in a multivendor (multisupplier and multimanufacturer) environment and for low cost has reduced the link length of the standards-based systems compared to the theoretical limits.

The second graph, Figure 6.52, shows the performance of 62.5 µm multimode fiber links for various types of optical transmitters with overfilled launch conditions. It is easy to see that short wavelength optical sources cannot support the link lengths that are possible with long wavelength sources. However, short wavelength VCSELs are still very attractive because of their extremely low cost.

Figure 6.52   Link Length Versus Signaling Rate for Various Laser and LED-Based Multimode Fiber Systems

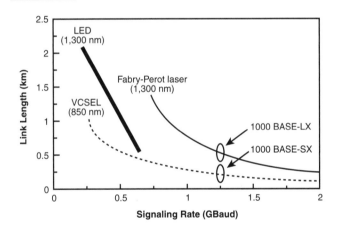

Figure 6.52 also shows the actual distances specified for 1000BASE-LX and 1000BASE-SX operation over multimode fiber. The 1000BASE-LX link length was chosen to be 550 m to match the building backbone requirement. However, the power budget margin for 1000BASE-LX can allow link lengths of 700 m to be easily supported over worst-case fiber.

PART IV

The Common 1000BASE-X Physical Layers

This part of the book covers the physical sublayers that are common to more than one Gigabit Ethernet implementation. Chapter 7 is applicable to all 1000BASE-T and 1000BASE-X implementations. Chapter 8 is applicable to only 1000BASE-X because it uses a different transmission coding procedure than is used in 1000BASE-T.

Chapter 7: The Common Physical Sublayers: Reconciliation and the GMII

Chapter 8: Physical Coding, Physical Medium Attachment, and Auto-Negotiation for 1000BASE-X

The Common Physical Sublayers: Reconciliation and the GMII

The Gigabit Media Independent Interface (GMII) was developed by IEEE 802.3 to provide physical sublayer independence so that a common media access controller could be used with any of the 1000BASE-X implementations and, eventually, with the 1000BASE-T physical layer implementations. During the specification of the GMII, it was assumed that the interface would be implemented as a chip-to-chip (integrated circuit to integrated circuit) interface with interconnecting traces on a printed circuit board. However, it was not the intention of the working group to preclude motherboard-to-daughterboard implementations.

The Reconciliation Sublayer and Gigabit Media Independent Interface lie between the MAC layer and the various Gigabit Ethernet physical layers. Figure 7.1 shows the relationship of the Reconciliation Sublayer and GMII to the OSI and IEEE 802 reference models.

Figure 7.1   Gigabit Ethernet Reference Model and Media Options

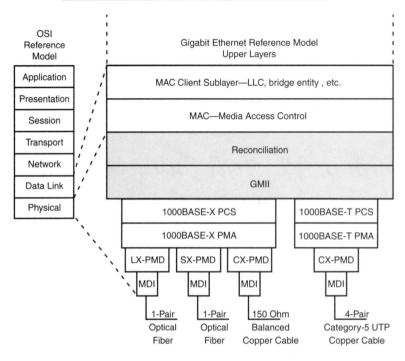

GMII = Gigabit Media Independent Interface (optional)   LX = 1000BASE-X Long Wavelength
MDI = Medium Dependent Interface   SX = 1000BASE-X Short Wavelength
PCS = Physical Coding Sublayer   CX = 1000BASE-X Copper
PMA = Physical Medium Attachment   T = 1000BASE-T Category-5 or better UTP

The interface to the network management entity is not shown in Figure 7.1, but is included in Figure 7.2. The Reconciliation Sublayer maps the PLS service primitives, provided by and for the MAC sublayers, to GMII signals. Figure 7.2 illustrates this process, and Table 7.1 relates the GMII signals to the Physical Layer Signaling (PLS) primitives shown in Figure 7.2.

Figure 7.2   MAC/Reconciliation Sublayer Service Primitives and Primitive-to-GMII Signal Mapping

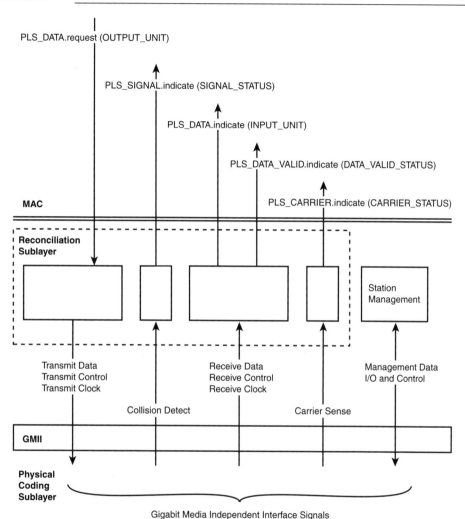

Gigabit Media Independent Interface Signals

Table 7.1   MAC/Reconciliation Sublayer Primitives Mapped to GMII Signals and Signal Descriptions

Primitive	GMII Signal	Signal Description (see Figure 7.2)
PLS/GMII Transmit		
PLS_DATA.request (OUTPUT_UNIT)	TXD<7:0>	Transmit Data (one byte— MAC data for transmission)
	TX_EN	Transmit Control (Transmit Enable)
	TX_ER	Transmit Control (Transmit Error)
	GTX_CLK	Transmit Clock (125 MHz)
PLS/GMII Receive		
PLS_DATA.indicate (INPUT_UNIT)	RXD<7:0>	Receive Data (one byte— received MAC data)
PLS_DATA_VALID	RX_DV	Receive Control (Data Valid)
	RX_ER	Receive Control (Receive Error)
	RX_CLK	Receive Clock (~125 MHz)
PLS (CSMA/CD) Status		
PLS_SIGNAL.indicate (*SIGNAL_STATUS*)	COL[a]	Collision Detect
PLS_CARRIER.indicate (*CARRIER_STATUS*)	CRS[a]	Carrier Sense
Network Management		
N/A[b]	MDC	Management Data Clock
N/A[b]	MDIO	Management Data Input-Output

[a]The behavior of COL and CRS are unspecified for full-duplex operation.
[b]No MAC/PLS interface primitives are specified for MDC and MDIO.

As Table 7.1 illustrates, there are four different signal groups passed through the GMII. Three groups are associated with Physical Layer Signaling (PLS) service primitives and information transfer to and from the MAC. The fourth group is associated with the transfer of messages to and from the network management entity.

7.1 PLS/GMII Transmit Signal Group

As you will see in Chapter 8, "Physical Coding, Physical Medium Attachment, and Auto-Negotiation for 1000BASE-X," MAC data plus intra- and interframe control signals must all be encapsulated into physical layer packets. The MAC/Reconciliation Sublayers use combinations of the GMII signals TX_EN, TX_ER, and TXD<7:0> to indicate to the Physical Coding Sublayer (PCS) how to encode the MAC data and frame control signals for transmission (see Table 7.2). The Reconciliation Sublayer also provides the transmit clock (GTX_CLK), which has a nominal frequency of 125 MHz.

Table 7.2   TX_EN, TX_ER, and TXD<7:0> Encodings (set by MAC/RS)

Description	TX_EN	TX_ER	TXD<7:0>
Normal Frame	1	0	00–FF
Normal Interframe	0	0	00–FF
Carrier Extend	0	1	0F
Carrier Extend Error	0	1	1F
Error propagation	1	1	00–FF
Reserved	0	1	00–0E
Reserved	0	1	10–1E
Reserved	0	1	20–FF

In half-duplex (CSMA/CD) mode, Carrier Extend is used both to extend minimum size packets and to ensure carrier continuation during frame bursting. Error propagation is used by repeaters operating in half-duplex CSMA/CD mode to signal all of its ports that the current frame has a detected error.

7.2 PLS/GMII Receive Signal Group

The PCS encodes combinations of the GMII signals RXD<7:0>, RX_DV, and RX_ER to indicate to the Reconciliation Sublayer whether MAC data or frame control signals are being presented to the GMII (see Table 7.3). The Reconciliation Sublayer converts these signals into the form expected by the MAC. The physical layer of Gigabit Ethernet is capable of detecting errors that may be undetectable by the Ethernet frame check sequence (FCS).

Should such errors be detected, the PCS uses RX_DV and RX_ER to indicate an error. An important function of the Reconciliation Sublayer then is to ensure that frames containing such errors will be detected as errored frames by the MAC. The PCS provides the receive clock (RX_CLK), which has a nominal frequency of 125 MHz.

Note

The MAC's FCS error check process will detect at least two errors anywhere within an Ethernet frame—even after 8B10B encoding. If more than three errors occur anywhere in the frame, there is a very, very slight chance that the frame may appear to the FCS as being correct. However, the Gigabit Ethernet 8B10B decoder also checks to ensure that each received code word is a valid code word (see Section 8.7 in Chapter 8, "Physical Coding, Physical Medium Attachment, and Auto-Negotiation for 1000BASE-X"). Therefore, if an error pattern is not capable of being detected by the MAC's FCS error check process, but due to the transmission errors, the coding rules have been broken (a likely possibility), the decoder will detect this otherwise undetectable error.

Table 7.3   RX_DV, RX_ER, and RXD<7:0> Encodings (set by PCS)

Description	RX_DV	RX_ER	RXD<7:0>
Normal Frame	1	0	00 through FF
Normal Interframe	0	0	00 through FF
Normal Interframe	0	1	00
False Carrier Indication	0	0	0E
Carrier Extend	0	1	0F
Carrier Extend Error	0	1	1F
Data Reception Error	1	1	00 through FF
Reserved	0	1	00 through 0D
Reserved	0	1	10 through 1E
Reserved	0	1	20 through FF

7.3   PLS (CSMA/CD) Status Signal Group

The CSMA/CD (carrier sense multiple access collision detect) access method requires each station on a CSMA/CD LAN to do a number of things.

Each station must continually monitor signals received from the LAN to detect the transmissions of other stations. In the original broadcast versions of Ethernet this was done by simply detecting the presence of a carrier signal. This is the carrier sense of CSMA/CD.

If no transmissions have been detected for a minimum period of time (the inter-packet gap time) and if a station needs to send a message, it may then transmit one packet. However, it is possible that two stations on different parts of the LAN have detected no transmissions and have each started to send a packet. In this case (which is a normal event in Ethernet LANs), the packets will collide. The collision will corrupt both packets. For this reason, each station must also monitor signals received from the LAN to detect collisions. This is the collision detect of CSMA/CD.

After detection of a collision, a station must continue to transmit its packet to ensure that all stations on the LAN detect the collision event and stop transmitting packet data. The station must then wait for a random period of time before attempting to transmit using the stated rules.

To enable Gigabit operation, the CSMA/CD access method was slightly modified to allow a transmitter to extend its carrier (see section 3.2.2.2 in Chapter 3, "Media Access Control") and to allow multiple packets to be transmitted in a burst (see section 3.2.2.3 in Chapter 3). Therefore, Gigabit Ethernet operation in half-duplex CSMA/CD mode requires the presence of carrier or collision events to be signaled to the CSMA/CD MAC. In full-duplex mode (switched-based operation) the CSMA/CD MAC is not used, and so carrier sense and collision detect are not required. Sections 7.3.1 and 7.3.2 summarize the operation of the Carrier Sense and Carrier Detect functions in Gigabit Ethernet.

7.3.1   Carrier Sense

Carrier Sense is a PCS function. The behavior of CRS is unspecified for full-duplex operation.

In a repeater, the physical layer asserts CRS when the receive medium is not idle and de-asserts CRS when the receive medium is idle.

In an end station operating in half-duplex mode, the physical layer (PCS) asserts CRS when either the transmit or receive medium is not idle and de-asserts CRS when both the transmit and receive media are idle. The physical layer (PCS) ensures that CRS remains asserted throughout the duration of a collision.

7.3.2 Collision Detect (COL)

Collision Detect is also a PCS function and is asserted upon detection of a collision on the medium. It remains asserted while the collision condition persists.

The behavior of the COL signal is unspecified for full-duplex operation.

7.4 GMII Network Management Signals and Associated Registers

The network management interface consists of two serial signals, the Management Data Clock (MDC) and the Management Data Input-Output (MDIO). The MDC and MDIO are part of the MII defined in the 100 Mbps Fast Ethernet standard (IEEE 802.3u). The network management registers can be written to and read from by the management entity (implemented in software in a repeater, switch, or NIC). The Gigabit Ethernet network management entity contains all the management registers specified for Fast Ethernet plus several additional registers needed for Gigabit operation.

Two types of GMII network management registers are specified:

- Basic—Register addresses (0, 1, 15)

- Extended—Register addresses (2–14 and 16–31)

IEEE 802.3z requires the basic register set to be implemented; the extended register set is optional.

7.4.1 Basic Register Functions

The contents of the control register (address 0) can be set in either of two ways: manually or by the auto-negotiation process. The control register is used for the following operations:

- Resetting the physical layer

- Placing the physical layer in loop-back mode

- Enabling auto-negotiation

- Powering down the physical layer

- Electrically isolating the data paths of the physical layer from the GMII

- Selecting the mode for duplex operation (half or full)

- Testing the COL (Collision Detect) signal at the GMII

The status register (register address 1) was introduced as part of the MII specification for 100 Mbps Fast Ethernet. It indicates the operational modes of the physical layer.

The extended status register (register 15) was introduced by Gigabit Ethernet and is used to indicate that the physical layer is one of the following types:

- 1000BASE-X full-duplex

- 1000BASE-X half-duplex

- 1000BASE-T full-duplex

- 1000BASE-T half-duplex

7.4.2 Extended Register Functions

The extended register set is used for the following functions:

- Physical layer identification (registers 2 and 3)

- Auto-Negotiation Advertisement (register 4)

- Auto-Negotiation Link Partner Base Page Ability (register 5)

- Auto-Negotiation Expansion (register 6)

- Auto-Negotiation Next Page Transmit (register 7)

- Auto-Negotiation Link Partner Received Next Page (register 8)

- 100BASE-T2 Control Register (register 9)

- 100BASE-T2 Status Register (register 10)

- Reserved Registers (registers 11–14)

- Vendor-Specific Registers (registers 16–31)

7.5 Summary

This chapter introduced the Reconciliation Sublayer and GMII.

The functions of the Reconciliation Sublayer are as follows:

- It converts MAC service primitives into GMII signals.

- It guarantees frames containing errors that were detected by the physical layer are recognized as errored frames by the MAC.

This chapter also showed that the purpose of the GMII is to provide a simple, inexpensive, and easy-to-implement interconnection between the MAC and physical layers, and between physical layers and the network management entity.

- It provides a common interface enabling a common controller to be used with any type of Gigabit physical layer.

- It was defined on the basis of a chip-to-chip implementation, but does not exclude other implementations.

- It provides independent byte-wide transmit and receive data paths.

- It provides two CSMA/CD status signals, COL and CRS, to indicate a collision or the presence of carrier.

- The GMII management interface is used to control the physical layer and to gather information regarding the physical layer.

Finally, remember that there is no requirement to implement the GMII. A major reason for the definition of the GMII (and the definition of the Reconciliation Sublayer) was to define an architectural reference model and method to translate MAC service primitives into signals used by the PCS of the physical layer. Implementers are always free to define interfaces within their product as they choose—so long as the behavior of the system is equivalent to that of the reference model.

Chapter 8 discusses how the PCS generates the GMII receive and status signals based on information received from the physical media. Chapter 8 will also discuss how the PCS translates GMII transmit data bytes into code-bits for transmission over the physical media.

Physical Coding, Physical Medium Attachment, and Auto-Negotiation for 1000BASE-X

The purpose of this chapter is to introduce you to the concepts and operational fundamentals of the Physical Coding Sublayer (PCS), Physical Medium Attachment Sublayer (PMA), and Auto-Negotiation unit that are common to all 1000BASE-X systems. PCS, PMA, and Auto-Negotiation form the upper part of the physical layer in a 1000BASE-X system.

Note

IEEE 802.3ab (1000BASE-T Gigabit Ethernet) will define new PCS, PMA, and Auto-Negotiation sublayers and functions that are different from the PCS, PMA, and Auto-Negotiation sublayers for 1000BASE-X. The 1000BASE-T will be covered in Chapter 15, "The Future: Gigabit Ethernet and Beyond." Its physical layer will not be discussed in this chapter.

This chapter begins with an overview of the 1000BASE-X physical layer that will include an implementation example of a network interface card (NIC), its relationship to the LAN architectural model, and a block diagram of the Gigabit Ethernet 1000BASE-X physical layer functions and interfaces. The chapter then investigates the detailed operation of the Physical Medium Attachment Sublayer (PMA) and the Physical Coding Sublayer (PCS), including the Auto-Negotiation function that is used to establish the operational configuration of the link. The chapter works from the bottom up, from the serial interface at the bottom of the PMA to the GMII parallel interface below the Reconciliation Sublayer, as shown in shaded areas of Figure 8.1.

Figure 8.1 1000BASE-X Ethernet Reference Model and Media Options

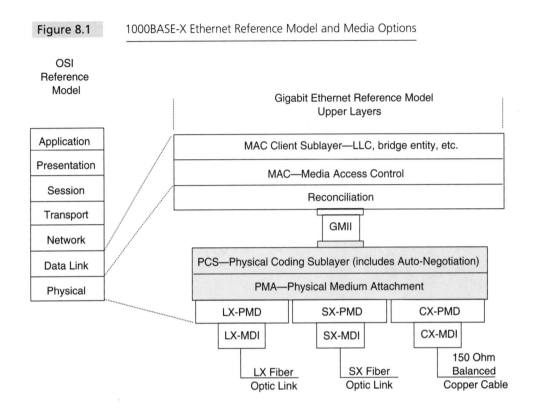

GMII = Gigabit Media Independent Interface (optional)

MDI = Medium Dependent Interface

LX = 1000BASE-X Long Wavelength

SX = 1000BASE-X Short Wavelength

CX = 1000BASE-X Copper

The description will include block diagrams of the primary functions and simplified state diagrams. The chapter also introduces the concept of 10b code-groups, *ordered_sets*, and their naming in order to describe the encapsulation of MAC frames into PCS frames for transmission by the physical layer.

A detailed description of the Gigabit Ethernet 8B10B code will be given at the end of the chapter and will include its design, structure, and capability to encode and decode MAC data and control signals. This encoding, plus careful physical layer design, allows 1000BASE-X Gigabit Ethernet networks to operate at a very low bit error ratio of 10^{-12}.

8.1 Physical Layer Overview

All 1000BASE-X Gigabit Ethernet physical layers and their associated links are designed to support both half- and full-duplex point-to-point communication, as shown in Figures 8.2a and 8.2b, respectively.

Figure 8.2a   Gigabit Ethernet Half-Duplex Transmission

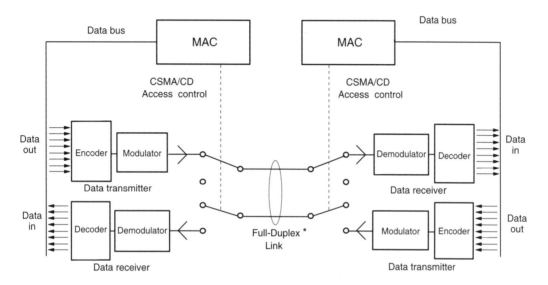

* The half-duplex transmission mode is invoked by the MAC access control function.

Figure 8.2b   Gigabit Ethernet Full-Duplex Transmission

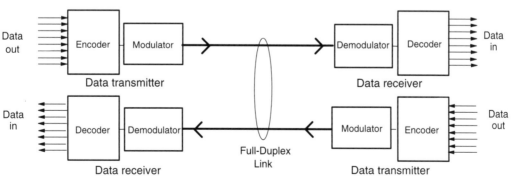

Each link and its associated physical layers must be properly configured before the link can be used to transmit Ethernet packets. The Auto-Negotiation functions in the network entities at each end of the link (the link partners) operate in concert to perform the following tasks:

- Ensure the link is operational (see note).

- Negotiate whether the link will be operated in half-duplex (CSMA/CD) or full-duplex mode. Both link partners must be capable of operating in the same mode, either half- or full-duplex.

- Negotiate whether and how flow control will be used. Flow control is not allowed with half-duplex links, and if asymmetrical flow control is desired, there must be agreement on which link partner will be allowed to initiate PAUSE requests. Chapter 13, "Upgrading Ethernet LANs: System and Topology Considerations," shows that there are topological constraints on which link partners should be allowed to initiate PAUSE requests and how these constraints can be mitigated.

If these negotiations fail, the link partners are incompatible and communication will not be allowed.

Note

Gigabit Ethernet 1000BASE-CX cable and connectors are fundamentally incompatible with either 1000BASE-SX or 1000BASE-LX cable and connectors. However, both single-mode and multimode 1000BASE-X optical cables and transceivers use the same connectors. It is therefore physically possible to connect incompatible combinations of optical transceivers (short wavelength to long wavelength) and cables (single-mode to multimode). Auto-Negotiation will fail under these circumstances.

8.1.1 *The Gigabit Ethernet Simplex Link*

Gigabit Ethernet full-duplex links are made up using two contra-transmitting simplex links. Chapter 5, "Fundamentals of Baseband Transmission," introduced the basic functional elements of a simplex link, related these functional elements to typical waveforms at key places in the signal path, and discussed the fundamentals of baseband transmission. The Gigabit Ethernet physical layer designers had to decide how to specify and partition these functions so that real inter-operable implementations could be manufactured. Figure 8.3 revisits Figure 5.5 and shows where the design team chose to partition the PCS, PMA, and PMD sublayers.

Figure 8.3   Gigabit Ethernet Physical Sublayer Assignment

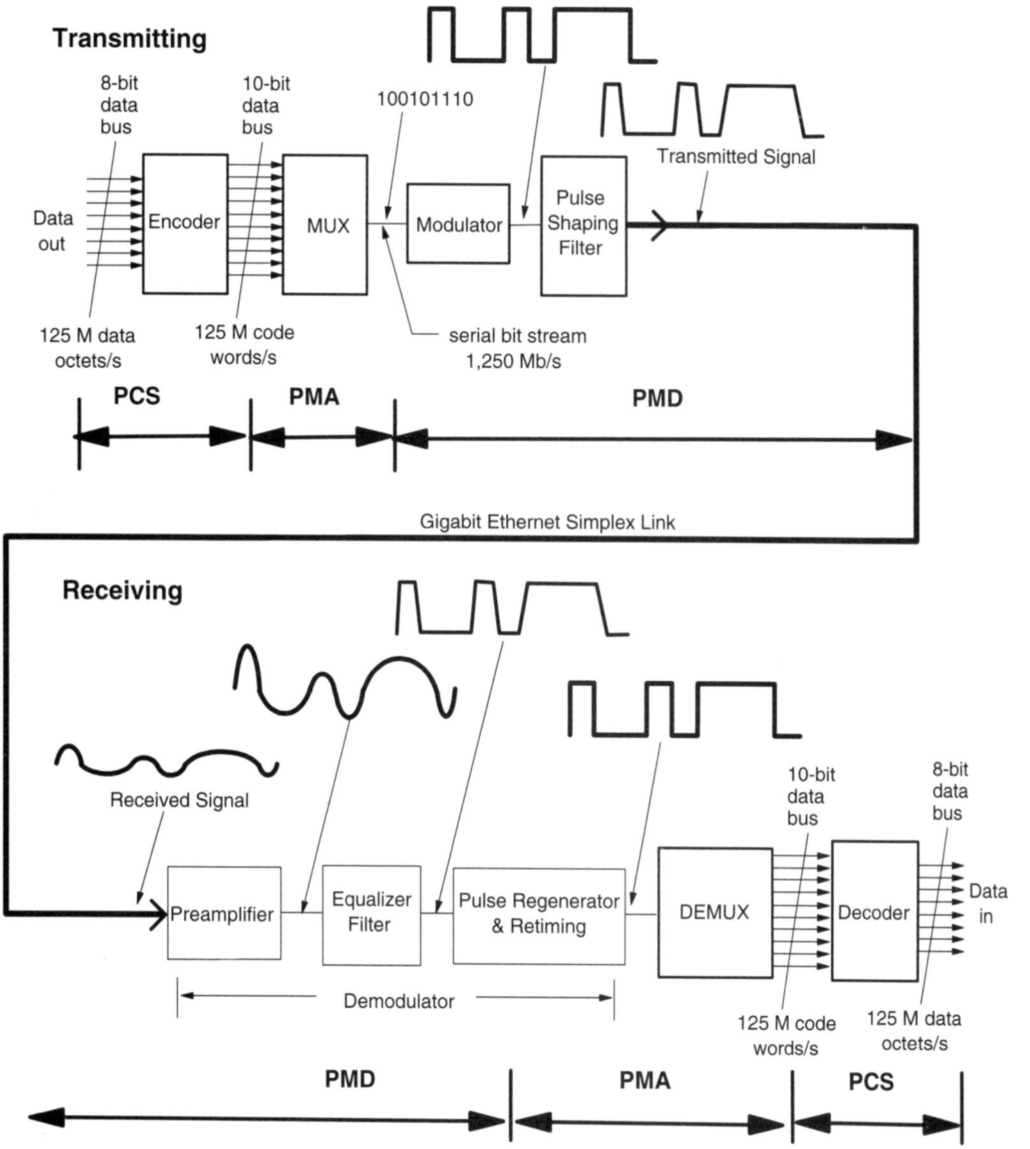

The physical layer transmitter consists of the encoder, multiplexer (MUX), modulator, and pulse shaping filter. These modules must perform all signal processing required for reliable transmission over the analog channel, including coupling the signal onto the channel.

The Gigabit Ethernet working group evaluated different coding options and decided to use the 8B10B code developed by IBM in the mid-1980s because it had been widely implemented and shown to be successful for Fibre Channel applications. The 8B10B encoder is the basic element in the Gigabit Ethernet PCS transmit function.

After the data bytes are encoded as 10-bit (10b) transmission code-groups, the code-group bit stream is multiplexed into a sequential serial bit stream for transmission. Later in the chapter, you will see that the PMA transmit function is basically a 10-to-1 multiplexer (although it should be noted that Gigabit Ethernet does not actually require all implementations to be based on 10:1 multiplexing). The PMA also includes a selectable data loopback function for diagnostic tests.

The PCS and PMA receive functions are essentially the reverse of the PCS and PMA transmit functions. The difference is in clocking and synchronization. The PMA must first recover the clock from the received pulse train and then adjust the alignment of the incoming code-groups so that the frame can be properly decoded. Transmit streams, on the other hand, are already correctly aligned in code-groups and synchronized by the internal clock.

The modulator is basically the PMD transmitter and is media dependent. The 1000BASE-X fiber-optic–based PMDs and the copper-based PMD will be discussed in Chapter 11, "1000BASE-X: Optical Fiber and Copper PMDs."

8.1.2 An Implementation Example: The Network Interface Card

Up to this point, the discussion has been somewhat abstract. You have seen the architectural model of the network adaptors that connect end stations, bridges, repeaters, and switches to network links, but you do not know anything about their size and physical layout. Figure 8.4 illustrates a network interface card (NIC), including illustrations of the important parts along with their relationship to the Gigabit Ethernet physical layer architecture.

Figure 8.4   Network Interface Card (NIC) and Its Relationship to the LAN Architectural Model

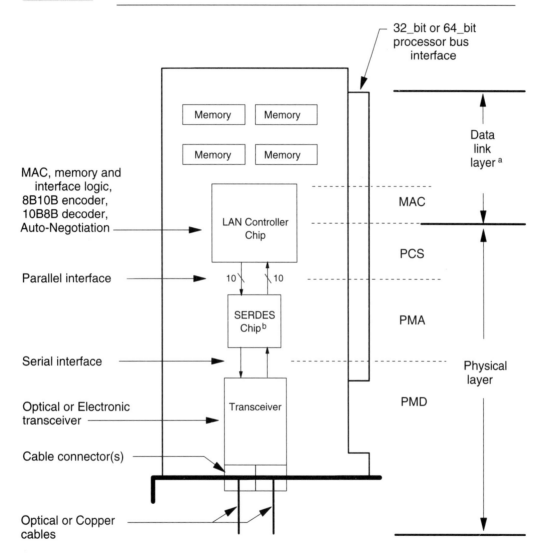

---

[a]The data link layer includes device driver software.

[b]SERDES means serializer/deserializer. This is the commercial designation for the optional PMA implementation defined in IEEE 802.3z as the Ten-Bit Interface (TBI).

Figure 8.4 reflects current (1999) implementations with separate chips for the MAC, PCS, and Auto-Negotiation functions (the LAN controller) and for the PMA (the SERDES chip).

8.1.3 *Physical Layer Functions and Interfaces*

The block diagram in Figure 8.5 shows the various functions and interfaces of the 1000BASE-X Gigabit Ethernet physical layer.

Figure 8.5   Functional Block Diagram of the Gigabit Ethernet Physical Layer

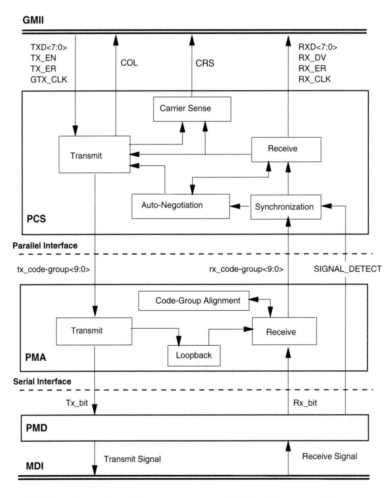

```
TXD<7:0>  = Transmit Data Bytes        RXD<7:0> = Reveive Data Bytes
TX_EN = Transmit Enable                RX_DV = Receive Data Vaild
TX_ER = Transmit Error                 RX_ER = Receive Error
GTX_CLK = GMII Transmit Clock          RX_CLK = GMII Receive Clock
COL = Collision                        CRS = Carrier Sense
```

Sections 8.2–8.4 describe the purpose and operation of the functions and interfaces of the 1000BASE-X Gigabit Ethernet physical layer, starting with the PMA sublayer and its interfaces.

8.2   The Physical Media Attachment Sublayer

As illustrated in Figure 8.5, the Physical Media Attachment Sublayer (PMA) has four basic functions: Transmit, Receive, Loopback, and Code-Group Alignment.

The PMA Transmit function is responsible for accepting code-groups from the physical coding sublayer and multiplexing them into a serial bit stream that is then passed to the physical media-dependent sublayer for transmission. The bits in the 10b code-groups transferred from the PCS to the PMA are labeled 0–9 and the Transmit function multiplexes these into a serial bit stream having the following bit order: 0, 1, 2, 3, 4, 5, 6, 7, 8, 9 (the bits are transmitted in ascending bit position order).

The Receive function performs the inverse operation of the Transmit function. However, before the PMA receive function can pass code-groups to the PCS, it must correctly align the code-group boundaries.

A special 7-bit pattern called a *comma sequence* is used during code-group alignment. A valid comma sequence is 0011111 in bit positions 0–6 of a 10-bit code-group:

```
Bit Position  0  1  2  3  4  5  6  7  8  9
Binary Value  0  0  1  1  1  1  1  x  x  x
```

The bits in bit positions 7–9 may be either 0 or 1.

This property is used by the Code-Group Alignment function. The PMA is allowed to delete or modify at most four received code-groups during code-group alignment. The process is called *code-group slipping*. Typically, Code-Group Alignment and code-group slipping will occur during Auto-Negotiation at link startup.

The Loopback function disables the PMA transmit path to the PMD and enables an alternate connection to the PMA receive path. How this is implemented (that is, at the parallel interface or serial interface level) is not specified by the standard, but the function is mandatory and enables self-testing.

8.3   Ten-Bit Interface

Initial Gigabit Ethernet implementations showed that the PCS/PMA interface is a natural position for a chip-to-chip interface. Because of this, IEEE 802.3z includes an optional definition for the PMA that is known in the standard as the *Ten-Bit Interface* (TBI). The reason for the name is unknown, but it probably came about because the data paths at the top of the TBI are both 10-bits. However, do not make the mistake of believing that the TBI is just an interface. The block diagram in Figure 8.6 shows that the TBI is the *entire PMA sublayer* with not one, but two interfaces, parallel at the top and serial at the bottom.

Figure 8.6   Functional Block Diagram of the Ten-Bit Interface—An Optional PMA Sublayer

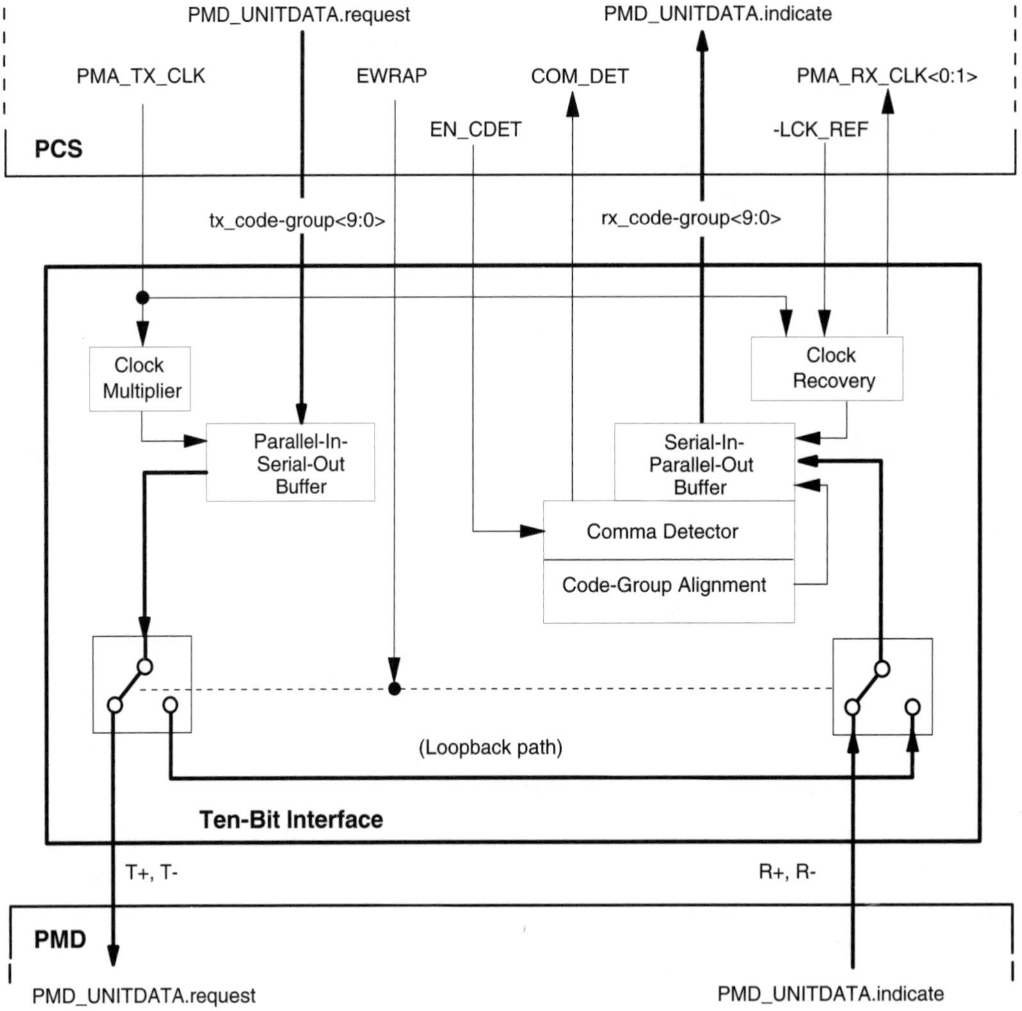

EWRAP = Enable Wrap (loopback)
EN_CDET = Enable Comma Detect
-LCK_REF = Lock to Reference Clock

While it is not required that partitioning of the PCS and PMA be implemented or exposed, the TBI definition has ensured commercial availability of interoperable LAN controller and SERDES chipsets and the network interface cards shown in Figure 8.4. The SERDES chip is the TBI.

8.3.1 TBI Transmitter

The TBI transmitter has the following major blocks:

- **Parallel-In-Serial-Out Buffer**. This is the code-group bit multiplexer.

- **Clock Multiplier**. Multiplies the 125 MHz PMA_TX_CLK (PMA transmit clock) by a factor of 10 to provide a bit clock of 1,250 MHz for serial transmission.

- **Loopback Switching Function**. If EWRAP (enable wrap-loopback) is enabled, the output of the TBI transmitter function will be connected to the input of the TBI receiver function via the loopback path. Otherwise, the transmitter will pass the bit stream out of the serial interface to the PMD.

8.3.2 TBI Receiver

The TBI receiver has the following major functions:

- **Serial-In-Parallel-Out Buffer**. This is the received code-bit demultiplexer.

- **Clock Recovery Unit**. Recovers a clock with a frequency of 1,250 MHz from the received serial code bit stream to provide a bit-clock for the demultiplexer.

  The clock recovery unit also provides the PMA_RX_CLK<0:1> signals to the PCS. The two 62.5 MHz receive clocks are used by the PCS to latch alternate code-groups (termed odd and even) in the received stream. PMA_RX_CLK<0> and PMA_RX_CLK<1> are in anti-phase with each other. Within 500 μs of receiving the signal, -LCK_REF = TRUE, the TBI clock recovery unit will lock onto the PMA_TX_CLK. This input is not used by the Gigabit Ethernet PCS, but is useful for testing TBI products.

- **Comma Detector Unit**. Detects comma patterns in the received serial bit stream.

  The signal, COM_DET = High, indicates that the code-group associated with PMA_RX_CLK<1> contains a valid comma. The PCS does not require this signal, but it is useful for TBI testing.

- **Code-Group Alignment**. Aligns demultiplexed code-group boundaries based on the detected comma patterns.

- **Loopback Switching Function**. If EWRAP = High, the input to the TBI receiver function will be connected to the output of the TBI transmitter function via the loopback path. Otherwise the receiver will pass the data through the serial-in-parallel-out buffer to the PCS.

Finally, although the 1000BASE-X PMD transceivers provide a SIGNAL_DETECT signal, it is not required that the TBI pass this signal to the PCS.

8.4 *The Physical Coding Sublayer*

The Physical Coding Sublayer (PCS) has five major functions—Carrier Sense, Transmit, Synchronization, Receive, and Auto-Negotiation—plus two interfaces—the PMA service interface and the GMII, as shown in Figure 8.7.

Figure 8.7   Functional Block Diagram of the PCS Sublayer

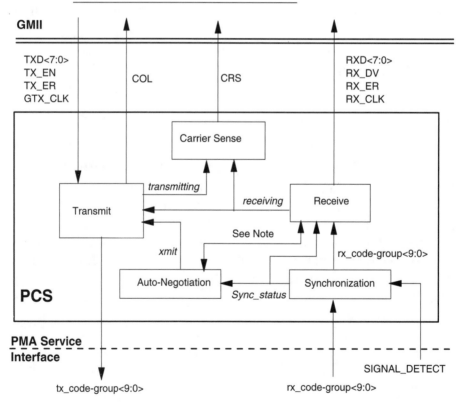

> **Note**
>
> The Receive function directs decoded data to the GMII and, when required, the Auto-Negotiation function. When the Auto-Negotiation *xmit* flag indicates CONFIGURATION or IDLE, the Receive function will direct CONFIGURATION ordered_sets, IDLE ordered_sets, and the contents of the Receive configuration register to the Auto-Negotiation function. CONFIGURATION, IDLE, and INVALID ordered_sets are sent only to the Auto-Negotiation process and not the GMII.
>
> During reconfiguration, the Transmit function will ignore the GMII and will transmit CONFIGURATION ordered_sets as directed by the Auto-Negotiation process.

8.4.1 PCS Carrier Sense

The Carrier Sense function monitors the *receiving* flag generated by the Receive function and the *transmitting* flag generated by the Transmit function and sets CRS = TRUE under the following conditions:

- Full-duplex mode allows transmission and reception to occur continuously and simultaneously—CRS will always be signaled in this case.

- In half-duplex mode, the CRS signal is interpreted differently by different network devices, as follows:

  - CRS = FALSE when *transmitting* and *receiving* are both inactive.

  - For CSMA/CD repeaters, CRS = TRUE only if a carrier is sensed by the PCS Receive function. Because half-duplex repeaters simultaneously retransmit received frames to all ports except the port on which the frame is being received, the *transmitting* flag may not be used as a condition to set CRS to TRUE. As noted in Chapter 4, "Gigabit Repeaters, Bridges, Routers, and Switches," half-duplex repeaters monitor the CRS signal from all ports, and if they detect multiple CRS = TRUE flags, a collision has occurred.

  - For all other CSMA/CD network entities, CRS = TRUE if either *transmitting* or *receiving* are TRUE.

Figure 8.8 shows the state diagram for the PCS Carrier Sense function.

Figure 8.8   Simplified PCS Carrier Sense State Diagram

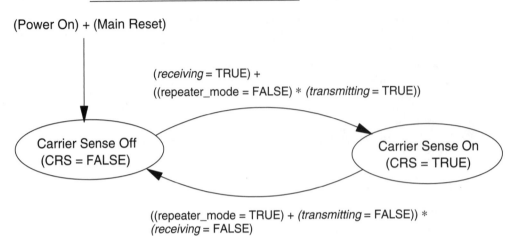

* Indicates logical AND
+ Indicates logical OR

In half-duplex repeaters: repeater_mode is set to TRUE and CRS will be TRUE only if *receiving*=TRUE.
In full-duplex repeaters and all other network devices, repeater_mode is set to FALSE and CRS will be TRUE if
either *receiving*=TRUE or *transmitting*=TRUE.

8.4.2   PCS Transmit

Figure 8.9 shows the block diagram of the PCS Transmit function.

Figure 8.9   Block Diagram of the PCS Transmit Function

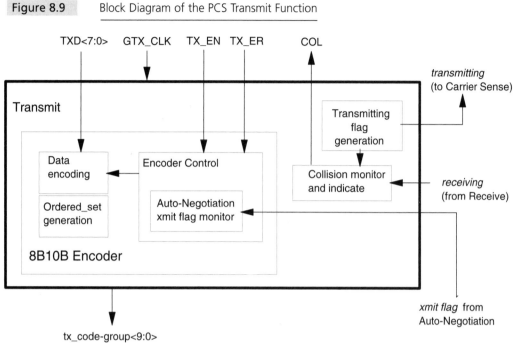

The core of the Transmit function is the 8B10B encoder, which is responsible for encoding the MAC output data bytes (TXD<7:0>) into 10b code-groups (tx_code-group<9:0>) and for generating other predefined special non-data code-groups (also known as *special* code-groups).

Sets of these special code-groups, sometimes combined with data code-groups, can be used to construct control signals (such as packet delimiters) or to exchange non-packet data for link configuration. These sets of special code-groups are known as *ordered_sets*. The encoder and its associated logic must be able to generate these ordered_sets when required.

The encoder control block monitors the xmit flag from the Auto-Negotiation function and both TX_EN and TX_ER from the GMII. Based on these signals, the encoder controller will force the encoder to pass the following code-groups or ordered_sets to the PMA:

- **Carrier_Extend**. The de-assertion of TX_EN and simultaneous assertion of TX_ER causes the PCS to transmit Carrier_Extend (with a two code-group delay to give PCS time to complete its EPD). One Carrier_Extend code-group is emitted per GMII GTX_CLK period while the GMII signals Carrier_Extend.

- **Configuration ordered_sets**. These are used to configure the link during the Auto-Negotiation process.

- **Data**. 10b encoded code-groups (tx_code-group<0:9>) corresponding to the MAC octets (TXD<7:0>).

- **End_of_Packet Delimiter (EPD)**. When the GMII signals end-of-packet (deassertion of TX_EN), an EPD is generated.

- **Error_Propagation**. The normal use of Error_Propagation is for repeaters to propagate received errors. The GMII indicates the error condition to the PCS by activating both TX_EN and TX_ER.

- **IDLE ordered_sets**. These ordered_sets are transmitted when the GMII is idle. The IDLE ordered_sets are used as *keepalive signals* for both the clock recovery electronics and the electro-optics of a link.

- **Start_of_Packet Delimiter (SPD)**. An SPD is generated when the GMII indicates start-of-frame (fresh assertion of TX_EN).

Ordered sets will be discussed in more detail later in this chapter in section 8.5, "Encapsulation of a MAC Frame into a Code-Group Stream."

The Transmit function also generates the *transmitting* flag for the PCS Carrier Sense function and monitors the *receiving* flag from the Receive function. If a collision has occurred, the Transmit function sets the COL flag to TRUE.

The primary activity for the PCS Transmit function is the generation of ordered_sets for transmission over the link. Figures 8.10 and 8.11 are simplified state diagrams for ordered_set and code-group transmission. These have been simplified from the state diagrams in IEEE 802.3z by grouping some states together and by removing or simplifying transition conditions. The intention here was to make it easier to follow the transmission process.

Figure 8.10   Simplified PCS Transmit ordered_set State Diagram

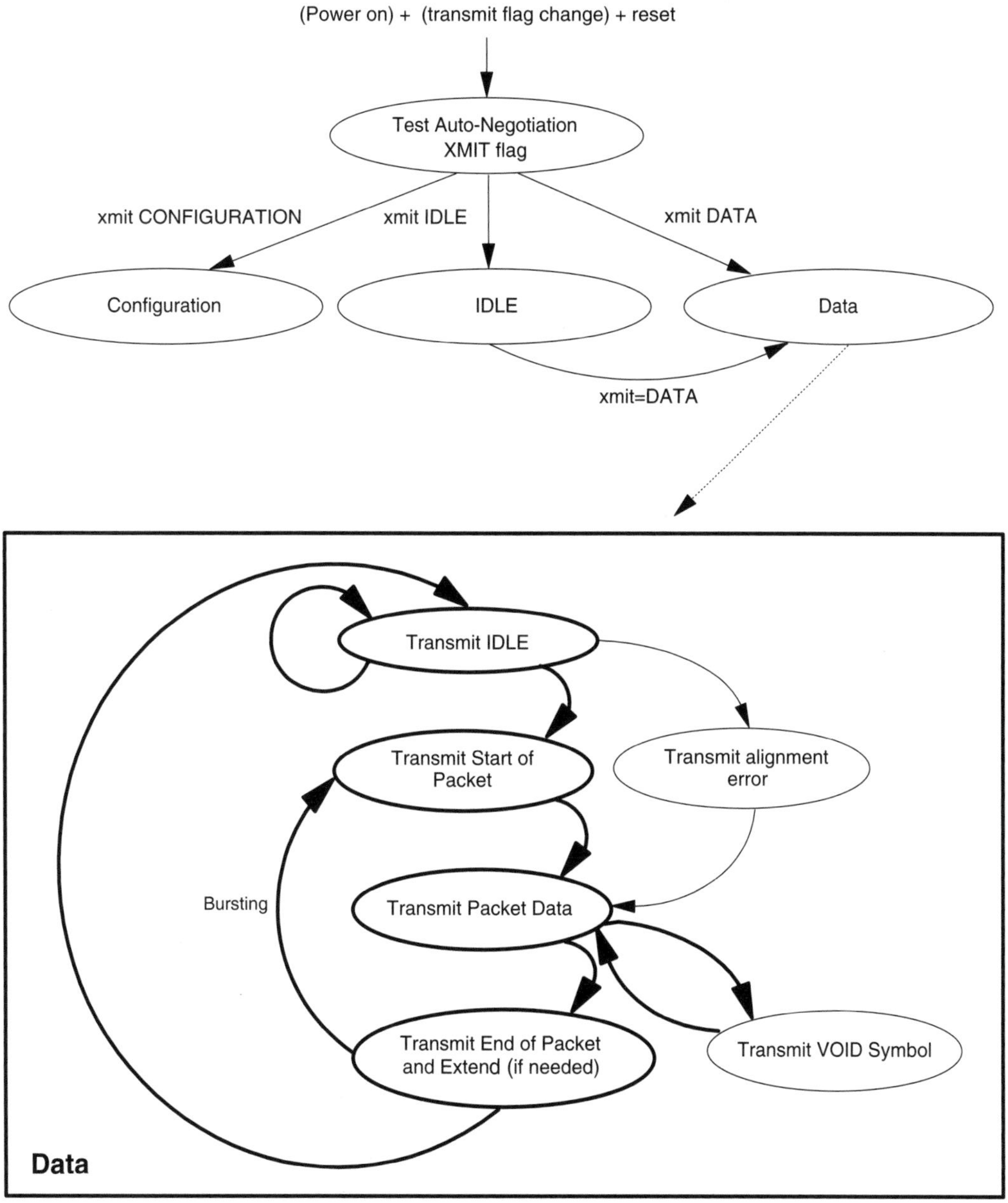

(Power on) + (transmit flag change) + reset

Test Auto-Negotiation
XMIT flag

xmit CONFIGURATION

xmit IDLE

xmit DATA

Configuration

IDLE

Data

xmit=DATA

Transmit IDLE

Transmit Start of
Packet

Transmit alignment
error

Bursting

Transmit Packet Data

Transmit End of Packet
and Extend (if needed)

Transmit VOID Symbol

Data

The xmit flag, which is used by the PCS Transmit and Receive functions, is set by Auto-Negotiation.

Figure 8.11   Simplified PCS Transmit Code-Group State Diagram

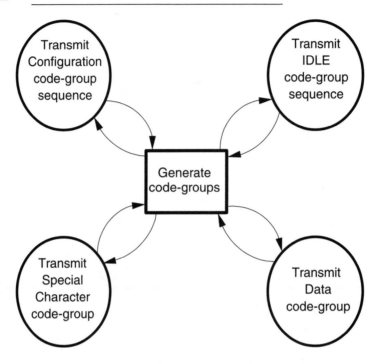

The PCS transmit ordered_set process can be in one of three states: transmitting configuration, transmitting IDLE, or transmitting data (see Figure 8.10). Once the process is in the transmitting data state, packets are transmitted according to the Data state diagram portion of Figure 8.10. The normal path between states for half-duplex mode (in the absence of errors) is indicated by the bold transition paths. The transmit VOID state would be a normal state for repeaters because they are required to retransmit all received frames, including errors. As such, a *void* code-group is inserted in the output frame wherever an invalid code-group has been received. The PCS Transmit code-group process generates the actual code-group sequences as required by the transmit ordered_set process and passes them to the PMA.

There are four types of code-group sequences that the PCS transmit code-group process may generate: Configuration, Special Character code-groups, IDLE, and Data (see Figure 8.11).

8.4.3 PCS Synchronization Function

The primary purpose of the PCS Synchronization function is to check that the PMA is passing correctly aligned code-groups to the PCS. Synchronization passes a sync_status flag to the Auto-Negotiation function and, once it is sure that the code-group boundaries are correct, it also passes code-groups to the PCS Receive function (refer back to Figure 8.7). Figure 8.12 is a simplified state diagram of the PCS Synchronization function. The normal states are circled in bold.

Figure 8.12   Simplified PCS Synchronization State Diagram

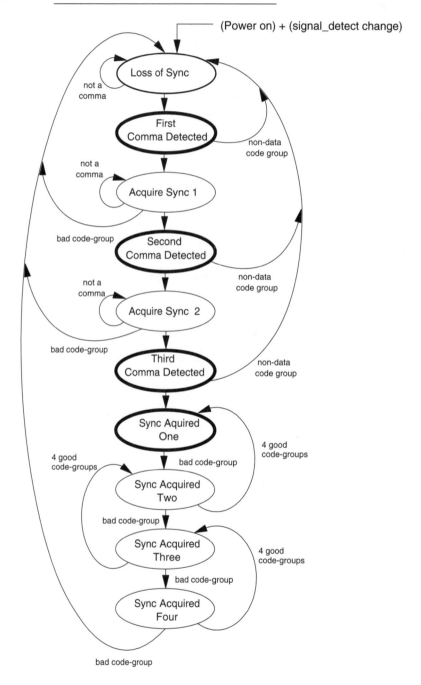

The Synchronization function is tolerant to a few errors in the received code-group stream. However, long error bursts will cause the Synchronization function to stop passing code-groups to the Receive function and to recheck code-group boundaries. At startup, and at any time the PCS has been unsynchronized for 10 ms or more, Auto-Negotiation will reconfigure the link.

The Synchronization function will enter the Loss of Sync state at power-up or on a change in the signal_detect indication from the PMD. Before it can transition to the Sync Acquired One state, the Synchronization function must detect three unerrored commas with no errored (invalid) code-groups in the code-group stream between the commas.

There are actually four Sync Acquired states, and code-groups will be passed to the Receive function while the Synchronization function is in any of these states. Receipt of a single errored code-group will cause a transition from the Sync Acquired n state to the Sync Acquired $n+1$ state. The Synchronization function requires the receipt of four consecutive unerrored code-groups to transition from the Sync Acquired n state back to the Sync Acquired n-1 state.

After the Synchronization function is in the Sync Acquired Four state, the reception of only one errored code-group will cause a transition to the Loss of Sync state. This hysteresis between the four Sync Acquired states allows the Synchronization function to be tolerant to a few (at least four) bit errors in the received data.

8.4.4 PCS Receive Function

Figure 8.13 is a block diagram of the PCS Receive function. Like in the Transmit function, the core of the Receive function is the 8B10B decoder. The Receive function directs decoded data to the GMII and, when required, to the Auto-Negotiation function.

Figure 8.13   Block Diagram of the PCS Receive Function

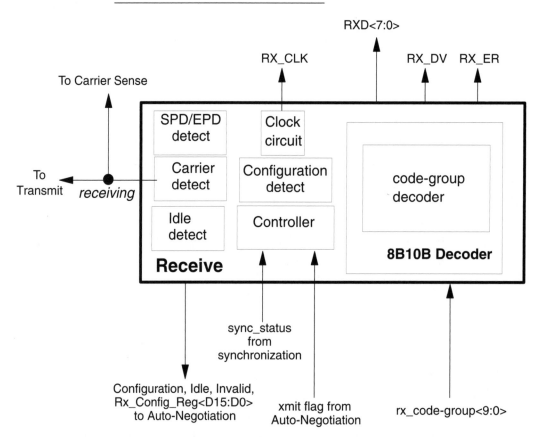

When the Auto-Negotiation xmit flag indicates CONFIGURATION or IDLE, the Receive function will direct CONFIGURATION ordered_sets, IDLE ordered_sets, and the contents of the Receive configuration register to the Auto-Negotiation function. CONFIGURATION, IDLE, and INVALID ordered_sets are only sent to the Auto-Negotiation process and not the GMII. During Auto-Negotiation, the Transmit function will not accept input from the GMII, but will transmit configuration ordered_sets as directed by the Auto-Negotiation process.

The Receive controller monitors the xmit flag and the code-groups being received for the following conditions:

- Auto-Negotiation xmit flag detect

- Carrier detect

- Carrier_Extend detect

- Code-group detect (Valid decode)

- End_of_Packet detect

- Error_Propagation detect

- Special_character detect (IDLE, Configuration)

- Start_of_Packet detect

The Receive function also sets the RX_DV and RX_ER outputs to the GMII to indicate when the data and/or a packet delimiter sequence is valid or errored (packet delimiters are part of the MAC frame encapsulation protocol). The Carrier detect unit generates the signal *receiving* and passes it to both the Transmit and Carrier Sense functions. The Receive clock (RX_CLK) synchronizes the data byte transfer (RXD<7:0>) to the GMII.

A simplified state diagram for the PCS Receive function is given in Figure 8.14. As in the previous state diagrams, the normal operation states are shown in bold.

Figure 8.14 Simplified PCS Receive State Diagram

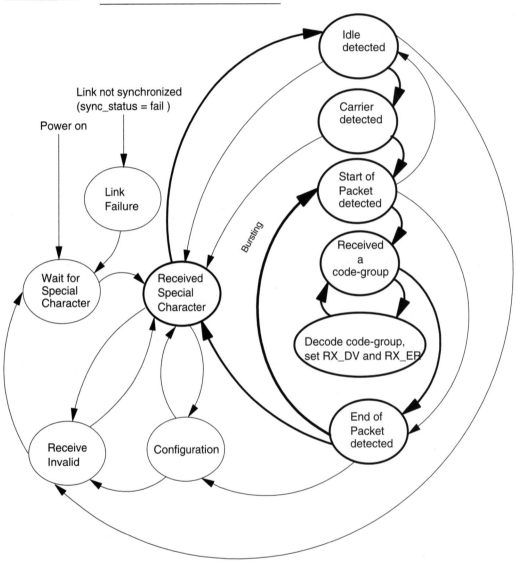

Note: The sync_status flag is set by the Synchronization function.

During Auto-Negotiation, the Receive function will enter the Configuration state where it will detect, decode, and pass the configuration codes and the contents of the Receive configuration register to Auto-Negotiation until the link is configured.

The transition from the Carrier detected state to Received a Special Character state is caused by a false Carrier detect. When this happens, the Receive function outputs the value 0000 1110 on RXD<7:0> and sets RX_ER to TRUE.

8.4.5   PCS Auto-Negotiation Function

As noted early in the physical layer overview (section 8.1), Auto-Negotiation must be completed before a link can be used to transmit Ethernet packets. The Auto-Negotiation function tests that the link is ready for operation, negotiates whether the link will be operated in half- or full-duplex mode, and also negotiates whether and how flow control will be used.

Figures 8.15 and 8.16 and Tables 8.1 and 8.2 explain the Auto-Negotiation process. Figure 8.15 is a simplified state diagram for Auto-Negotiation, Figure 8.16 shows the Configuration register encoding, Table 8.1 provides the encoding for the PAUSE capability alternatives, and Table 8.2 contains the flow control configurations that can result.

Figure 8.15 Simplified PCS Auto-Negotiation State Diagram

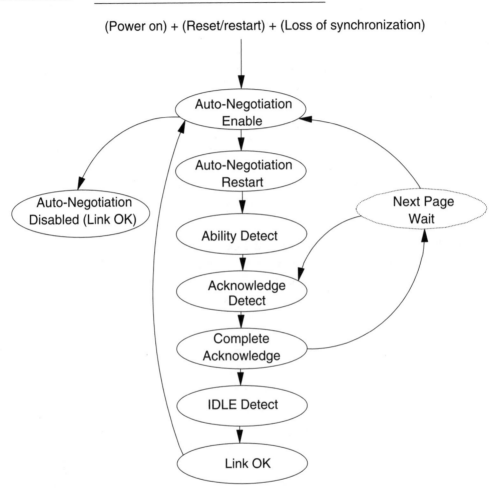

Note: The xmit flag which is used by the PCS transmit and receive functions is set by auto-negotiation

Figure 8.16 Configuration Register Base Page Encoding Format

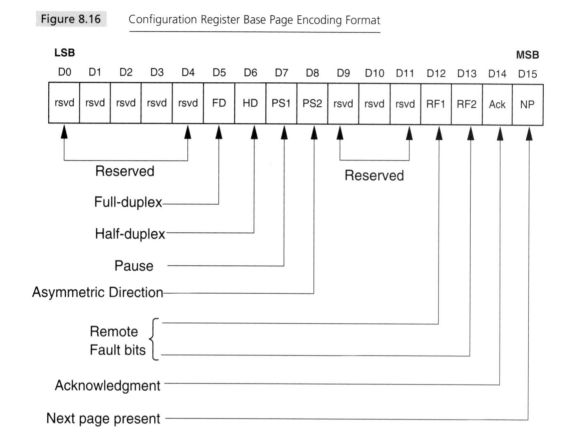

Table 8.1 Pause Encoding

PAUSE (D7)	ASM_DIR(D8)[a]	Capability
0	0	No PAUSE
0	1	Asymmetric PAUSE toward link partner
1	0	Symmetric PAUSE
1	1	Both Symmetric PAUSE and Asymmetric PAUSE toward local device

[a]ASM_DIR + Asymmetric direction

Table 8.2   Flow Control Resolution

Local Device: Pause (P1)	Local Device: Direction (P2)	Remote Device: Pause (P1)	Remote Device: Direction (P2)	Resolution
1	Any value	1	Any value	Full symmetric flow control
0	1	1	1	Asymmetric flow control to partner
1	1	0	1	Asymmetric flow control from partner
0	0	Any value	Any value	No flow control
0	1	0	Any value	No flow control
0	1	1	0	No flow control
1	0	0	Any value	No flow control
1	1	0	0	No flow control

The goal of Auto-Negotiation is to configure the link in a manner that results in maximum use of the link partners' mutual capabilities and then to transition to the Link_OK state. Each link partner uses the knowledge of its own capabilities and those obtained from the remote link partner to resolve the mode of operation using the priority resolution rules. Because Auto-Negotiation ensures that the devices on both ends of the link have the same information, they will choose the same mode of operation. The following actions are involved:

- **Transmitting the local entity's configuration register**. This occurs in the Auto-Negotiation and Auto-Negotiation restart states for a fixed period of time (about 10 ms). The local entity's capabilities (the operational modes it can support) are encoded in a 16-bit configuration register known as the *base page* according to the format in Figure 8.16 and the encoding definitions in Table 8.1.

- **Receiving configuration register of the remote link partner**. This takes place during the Ability Detect state.

- **Acknowledging the detection of the link partner's abilities**. This happens in the Acknowledge Detect state. If the remote entity's configuration register is successfully received and decoded, the value of the acknowledge bit in the local entity's configuration register is changed from 0 to 1.

- **Detecting an acknowledgment from the link partner**. This occurs in the Complete Acknowledge state. An acknowledgement bit value of 1 in the Received configuration register indicates that the remote partner has successfully received and decoded the local entity's configuration information.

- **Resolving the mode of operation: half-duplex or full-duplex**. This happens in the IDLE detect and Link OK states. If both entities can support full-duplex mode, the operational mode will be full-duplex. If neither or only one entity can support full-duplex mode, the operational mode will be half-duplex.

- **Resolving the flow control operation by deciding pause control mode**. This happens in the IDLE detect and Link OK states. If the operational mode is half-duplex, no flow control will be allowed. If the operational mode is full-duplex, flow control initiation will be allowed according to the indicated resolution matrix in Table 8.2.

8.4.5.1 Transmission of Configuration ordered_sets (Alternating C1 and C2)

The base page of the configuration information is encapsulated in the last two code-groups of the following four code-group sequences:

```
Configuration 1 = /C1/ = /K28.5/D21.5/Config_Reg
Configuration 2 = /C2/ = /K28.5/D22.2/Config_Reg
```

where:

    /K28.5/D21.5/ and */K28.5/D22.2/* are predefined ordered_sets

    Config_Reg are the two configuration code-groups

Two configuration codes are defined to enable the encoder to tightly control the *running disparity* (RD) of the code-group stream (see Chapter 5, section 5.8.2). Both link partners transmit their configuration base page register to each other as a continuous code-group stream, alternating between C1 and C2 ordered_set sequences. Both C1 and C2 contain comma sequences that are used by the PMA comma detect process.

Sensing and reporting faults via the remote fault bits is optional. If a device does not sense or report its own faults and doesn't make use of received remote fault bits, it sets RF1 and RF2 to zero, the default setting.

8.5 Encapsulation of a MAC Frame into a Code-Group Stream

The major function of the PCS after startup is the encapsulation of MAC frames into code-group streams for transmission by the PMA and the PMD. Figure 8.17 diagrams the encapsulation process. The PCS reception process is essentially the reverse of the transmission process.

Figure 8.17   PCS Encapsulation of a MAC frame

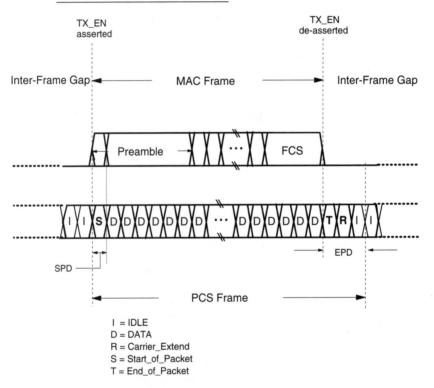

I = IDLE
D = DATA
R = Carrier_Extend
S = Start_of_Packet
T = End_of_Packet

Earlier in the chapter, you were introduced to the names of a number of different code-groups and ordered_sets. The following sections describe them in detail in relation to and to help explain the encapsulation/decapsulation process.

8.5.1   IDLE ordered_sets (I)

The IDLE ordered_sets are transmitted when there is no MAC traffic. There are two IDLE ordered_sets (I1 and I2), each consisting of two code-groups. The two versions of IDLE are used to control the running disparity of the code-bit stream. IDLE I1 changes the RD, while I2 maintains the disparity. IDLEs are transmitted to ensure that the disparity is negative.

Because I2 maintains the RD of the code-group stream, I2s can be inserted or removed from the IDLE stream without causing transmission problems. This can be useful for repeaters or switches that need to compensate for slight transmit (locally generated) and receive (remotely generated) clock mismatches.

Transmission of IDLE ordered_sets also keeps the receive electronics and optics "alive" between packets. For example:

- The clock recovery unit in the receiver needs periodic transitions to maintain synchronization of the receive clock.

- The optical transceivers used by Gigabit Ethernet have not been designed to recover signals after a very long period of no light. If nothing (no light) was transmitted during inter-packet gaps, the optical transmitter might not perform properly.

- If no light was transmitted between packets, the Signal_Detect function would indicate a link failure and the Synchronization and Auto-Negotiation functions would start up!

8.5.2   Start_of_Packet ordered_sets

Start_of_Packet (S or SPD) is an ordered_set containing one code-group that indicates the start of the PCS data transmission. TX_EN is asserted with the first octet of preamble and will remain asserted for the whole of the MAC frame. When the PCS detects that TX_EN has been asserted, it will replace the current octet of preamble with the Start_of_Packet ordered_set S (see Figure 8.17). On reception, the PCS will decode S with the value of the first octet of preamble. The S ordered_set follows I for an isolated packet or the first packet in a burst of packets, but follows R (you will see why later) for all other packets in a burst.

8.5.3   End_of_Packet ordered_sets

The End_of_Packet (T) is always the first ordered_set (a single code-group long) that indicates the end of the PCS data transmission. TX_EN is deasserted at the end of the frame check sequence (FCS) of the MAC frame being transmitted, and then the T ordered_set is transmitted (see Figure 8.17).

8.5.4 *Carrier_Extend ordered_sets*

The Carrier_Extend (R) ordered_set is a single code-group that has three purposes:

- It forms part of the End_of_Packet delimiter, which separates packets within a burst of packets.

- It is used by the MAC to extend the carrier event during frame extension.

- An R ordered_set is sometimes used to ensure the correct code-group alignment of the first IDLE (I) after packet transmission.

8.5.5 *Error_Propagation ordered_sets*

The Error_Propagation (V) ordered_set is a single code-group that is used to indicate errors in a code-group stream that is being repeated onto another link by a CSMA/CD repeater (see section 8.4.2, "PCS Transmit"). Figure 8.18 depicts encapsulation of frames with errors.

Figure 8.18   Propagating Errors in the PCS Frame

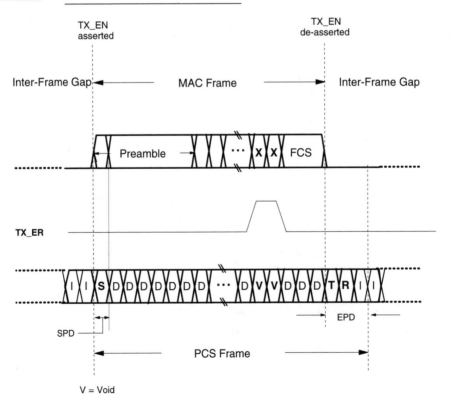

8.5.6 TX_EN, TX_ER, RX_EN, and RX_ER Signals

The TX_EN (transmit enable), TX_ER (transmit coding error), RX_EN (receive enable), and RX_ER (receive error) signals play an important part in the encapsulation and de-encapsulation of MAC frames (see section 8.5, "Encapsulation of a MAC Frame into a Code-Group Stream" and Figures 8.17 and 8.18). This is because these signals, along with TXD<7:0> or RXD<7:0>, are used to indicate the state of the MAC—for example, whether the MAC is transmitting a normal data frame or a control signal such as Carrier_Extend (see Tables 8.3 and 8.4).

Table 8.3   TX_EN, TX_ER, and TXD<7:0> Encodings (Set by MAC)

TX_EN	TX_ER	TXD<7:0>	Description
1	0	00–FF	Normal Frame
0	0	00–FF	Normal Inter-frame
0	1	0F	Carrier Extend
0	1	1F	Carrier Extend Error
1	1	00–FF	Error propagation
0	1	00–0E	Reserved
0	1	10–1E	Reserved
0	1	20–FF	Reserved

Table 8.4   RX_EN, RX_ER, and RXD<7:0> Encodings (Set by PCS)

RX_EN	TX_ER	TXD<7:0>	Description
1	0	00–FF	Normal Frame
0	0	00–FF	Normal Inter-Frame
0	1	00	Normal Inter-Frame
0	1	0F	Carrier Extend
0	1	1F	Carrier Extend Error
1	1	00–FF	Data Reception Error
0	1	00–0D	Reserved
0	1	10–1E	Reserved
0	1	20–FF	Reserved

8.6   The 8B10B Code

Chapter 5, "Fundamentals of Baseband Transmission," introduced the concept of block coding. The Gigabit Ethernet encoder accepts data bytes from the MAC via the GMII and translates (encodes) each byte into 10-bit code-groups that have been specifically chosen for reliable transmission. The additional bits add transmission overhead, but because there are more 10-bit code-groups than 8-bit data words, they provide a degree of transmission redundancy. This redundancy is used for the following: to make error detection more reliable, to separate code-groups for data and control, to provide sufficient transition density for clock recovery, to allow simple code-group synchronization, and to combat poor channel characteristics.

Some features of the Gigabit Ethernet 8B10B code are as follows:

- High transition density of 3–8 transitions per 10-bit code-group

- DC balance; maximum run length of 5; maximum running digital sum (RDS) of 3 (also see Figure 5.27)

- Separate code-groups for data and control signaling

- A comma for code-group synchronization

- Excellent error detection capabilities, especially with CRC 32, the frame check sequence in the MAC frame format

The high transition density and excellent DC balance of this code also make it almost ideal for use with low-cost laser transceivers. This is because the high transition density causes the laser's optical spectrum to broaden slightly (in Chapter 6, see section 6.4.2, "Diode Lasers" and Figure 6.48) and, as a result, modal noise in multimode fiber links is reduced (see section 6.5.1, "Modal Noise").

Also, the DC balance reduces data-dependent heating effects in the laser and enables simpler AC coupled receiver designs to be used.

Section 8.7 provides a detailed looked at the 8B10B code and its design. The Gigabit Ethernet code is the same code used by Fibre Channel and, with slight modifications, IEEE 1394b (commercially known as Firewire). The code was originally designed by IBM research laboratories, and it is based on a special combination of a 5B6B and a 3B4B code.

8.7 Code-Group Encoding and Decoding

Appendix B, "8B10B Code Table," contains a complete listing of the valid code-groups for the 256 possible bit combinations in an 8-bit octet. One possible encoding procedure would be to use that table to encode octets into 8B10B code-groups during frame transmission and to decode 8B10B code-groups back into octets during frame reception. Another way is to break the octet into a 3b and 5b that are then encoded/decoded, in a coordinated manner, so that the resulting 8B10B encodings/decodings are the same as those in Appendix B.

Tables 8.5–8.8 show the 5B6B and 3B4B codes from which the 8B10B code is constructed. Because the combined size of these two tables is much smaller than the single large table shown in Appendix B and because combinatorial logic can be used to simplify the coding tables still further, implementations based on the split 5B6B and 3B4B tables can be very hardware-efficient.

Table 8.5   5B6B Coding for Data

Data Label	Data Bits EDCBA	Encoded Bits Current RD (–) abcdei	Encoded Bits Current RD (+) abcdei
D0	00000	100111	011000
D1	00001	011101	100010
D2	00010	101101	010010
D3	00011	110001	110001
D4	00100	110101	001010
D5	00101	101001	101001
D6	00110	011001	011001
D7	00111	111000	000111
D8	01000	111001	000110
D9	01001	100101	100101
D10	01010	010101	010101
D11	01011	110100	110100
D12	01100	001101	001101
D13	01101	101100	101100
D14	01110	011100	011100
D15	01111	010111	101000
D16	10000	011011	100100
D17	10001	100011	100011

continues

Table 8.5   Continued

Data Label	Data Bits EDCBA	Encoded Bits Current RD (–) abcdei	Encoded Bits Current RD (+) abcdei
D18	10010	010011	010011
D19	10011	110010	110010
D20	10100	001011	001011
D21	10101	101010	101010
D22	10110	011010	011010
D23	10111	111010	000101
D24	11000	110011	001100
D25	11001	100110	100110
D26	11010	010110	010110
D27	11011	110110	001001
D28	11100	001110	001110
D29	11101	101110	010001
D30	11110	011110	100001
D31	11111	101011	010100

Table 8.6   3B4B Coding for Data

Data Label	Data Bits HGF	Encoded Bits Current RD (–) fghj	Encoded Bits Current RD (+) fghj
.1	000	1011	0100
.1	001	1001	1001
.2	010	0101	0101
.3	011	1100	0011
.4	100	1101	0010
.5	101	1010	1010
.6	110	0110	0110
.7	111	1110 or 0111	0001 or 1000

Table 8.7	5B6B Coding for Special Groups		
Data Label	Data Bits EDCBA	Encoded Bits Current RD (−) abcdei	Encoded Bits Current RD (+) abcdei
K23	10111	111010	000101
K27	11011	110110	001001
K28	11100	001111	110000
K29	11101	101110	010001
K30	11110	011110	10000

Table 8.8	3B4B Coding for Special Groups		
Data Label	Data Bits HGF	Encoded Bits Current RD (−) fghj	Encoded Bits Current RD (+) fghj
.1	000	1011	0100
.1	001	1001	1001
.2	010	1010	0101
.3	011	1100	0011
.4	100	1101	0010
.5	101	0101	1010
.6	110	1001	0110
.7	111	0111	1000

The structure of the 5B6B and 3B4B code tables has also been used to develop convenient naming conventions for the 10-bit code-groups. The code can generate data code-groups for the transmission of normal data and also special code-groups for the transmission of control sequences (commas, ordered_sets, and so forth). The naming conventions for the 10-bit code-groups are as follows:

- Data code-groups are all given labels beginning with D (for data).

- Control code-groups are given labels beginning with K (for Control).

- The letter D or K is followed by the data label from the 5B code table—which is just the decimal value of the 5B input data bits (the bits to be encoded; see 5B tables).

- The data label corresponding to the 3B input bits from the 3B4B code table is added to complete the code-group label.

Examples of code-group labels are D20.1, D0.7, and K28.0. While all of the possible data code-groups named in this way are considered to be valid code-groups, only 12 of the control code-groups are defined as valid control code-groups.

Figure 8.19 shows the translation from input octet bits (TXD<7:0>) to input octet bit labels, to output code-group bit labels, to output code-group bits (tx_code-group<9:0>). The code-group bit_0 is the first bit transmitted, and code-group bit_9 is the last transmitted bit for each code-group.

Figure 8.19   Simplified PCS 8B10B Encoder Diagram and Notation

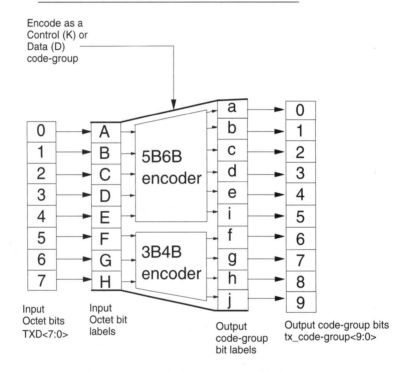

Note: Code bits <0:9> are transmitted serially on the physical media; code bit 0 is transmitted first and code bit 9 is transmitted last.

The 5B6B and 3B4B code tables have two encoded bit columns called current RD plus and current RD minus for the 6B and 4B sub-blocks, where the current RD refers to the state of the RD at the end of the last sub-block. The 8B10B code-groups are constructed from the split code tables as follows:

- The RD for a code-group is calculated on the basis of sub-blocks, where the first six bits (abcdei) form one sub-block and the second four bits (fghj) form the other sub-block.

  - The RD at the beginning of the 6-bit sub-block is the RD at the end of the last code-group.

  - The RD at the beginning of the 4-bit sub-block is the RD at the end of the 6-bit sub-block.

  - The RD at the end of the code-group is the RD at the end of the 4-bit sub-block.

- The RD for the sub-blocks is calculated as follows:

  - RD at the end of any sub-block is positive if the sub-block contains more ones than zeros. It is also positive at the end of the 6-bit sub-block if the 6-bit sub-block is 000111, and it is positive at the end of the 4-bit sub-block if the 4-bit sub-block is 0011.

  - RD at the end of any sub-block is negative if the sub-block contains more zeros than ones. It is also negative at the end of the 6-bit sub-block if the 6-bit sub-block is 111000, and it is negative at the end of the 4-bit sub-block if the 4-bit sub-block is 1100.

  - Otherwise, RD at the end of the sub-block is the same as at the beginning of the sub-block.

- To limit the run length of zeros or ones between sub-blocks, the 8B10B transmission code rules specify that:

  - Sub-blocks encoded as 000111 or 0011 are only generated when the RD at the beginning of the sub-block is positive; thus, RD at the end of these sub-blocks is also positive. Likewise, sub-blocks containing 111000 or 1100 are only generated when the RD at the beginning of the sub-block is negative; thus, RD at the end of these sub-blocks is also negative.

  - D11.7, D13.7, D14.7, D17.7, D18.7, and D20.7 must use the alternative 4B encoding.

These rules were used to generate the full 8B10B code tables that are included in Appendix B.

The transmitter will initially assume a negative RD and will then encode all data sent to it using the 8B10B code tables and rules. The receiver may assume either a negative or positive RD. The decoder will decode code-groups, determine if they are valid, and calculate the new RD. The RD can also be used to detect errors, as it must be either +1 or −1 exclusively.

Although there are 12 special code-groups (see Table 8.9), only six are used to construct ordered_sets for Gigabit Ethernet (see Table 8.10). The comma pattern 0011111xxx, used for code-group alignment by both the PMA and the PCS, occurs in special code-groups K28.1, K28.5, and K28.7. However, in normal operation, only the K28.5 comma is used. The K28.7 code-group may be used for testing, but it should be used with care because this code-group, in combination with some others, may generate a comma that is not code-group aligned!

Table 8.9   Gigabit Ethernet Special Code-Groups

Special Code-Group Name	RD (−) abcdei fghj Value	RD (+) abcdei fghj Value
K28.0	001111 0100	110000 1011
K28.1a	**001111 1001**	**110000 0110**
K28.2	001111 0101	110000 1010
K28.3	001111 0011	110000 1100
K28.4	001111 0010	110000 1101
K28.5a	**001111 1010**	**110000 0101**
K28.6	001111 0110	110000 1001
K28.7a,b	**001111 1000**	**110000 0111**
K23.7	111010 1000	000101 0111
K27.7	110110 1000	001001 0111
K29.7	101110 1000	010001 0111
K30.7	011110 1000	100001 0111

K28.1a, K28.5a, and K28.7a,b characters contain *comma* sequence for byte synchronization. K characters with the b subscript cannot be repeated without violating the *comma* sequence condition.

Table 8.10   Gigabit Ethernet Defined ordered_sets

Code	Ordered_Set	Number of Code-Group	Encodings
/C/	**Configuration**		**Alternating—/C1/ and /C2/**
/C1/	Configuration 1	4	/K28.5/D21.5/Config_Reg[a]
/C1/	Configuration 1	4	/K28.5/D2.2/Config_Reg[a]
/I/	**IDLE**		**Correcting /I1/, Preserving /I2/**
/I1/	IDLE 1	2	/K28.5/D5.6/
/I2/	IDLE 2	2	/K28.5/D16.2/
	Encapsulation		
/R/	Carrier_Extend	1	/K23.7/
/S/	Start_of_Packet	1	/K27.7/
/T/	End_of_Packet	1	/K29.7/
/V/	Error_Propagation	1	/K30.7/

[a]Two data code-groups representing the Config_Reg value

Ordered_sets consist of one, two, or four code-groups (see Table 8.10) and always start with a special code-group. The first code-group after power-up is considered even and code-groups that follow the first one alternate between odd and even.

Section 8.5 showed how these ordered_sets can be used for control sequences and to encapsulate MAC frames into a PCS frame. Now you have the actual code-group encodings for them, which completes the story.

8.8 *Summary*

This chapter reviewed the detailed operation of the upper portions of the Gigabit Ethernet 1000BASE-X physical layer. You should now understand how Auto-Negotiation configures a link for transmission and how MAC data bytes, control signals, and line states are encoded, first into 8B10B code-groups, and then into a serial code-bit stream.

The next few chapters will complete the physical layer story by defining the operation of the physical layer transceivers and cable plant.

PART V

The 1000BASE-X Media Dependent Layers

The purpose for this part of the book is to define the optical link model used for specifying 1000BASE-LX (long wavelength) and 1000BASE-SX (short wavelength) PMDs, to discuss the problems encountered with existing multimode fiber cables during development of Gigabit Ethernet and how they were solved, and to discuss in detail the short-haul copper and optical 1000BASE-X PMD specifications.

Note: 1000BASE-T was not yet fully defined when this part of the book was written, and as such, a description of the media dependent sublayers for that implementation was not included in this part of the book. We recommend that you read section 15.1 of Chapter 15 for a description of 1000BASE-T before going on to Chapters 12 and 13.

Chapter 9: The Gigabit Ethernet Optical Link Model

Chapter 10: The Gigabit Ethernet Modal Bandwidth Investigation

Chapter 11: 1000BASE-X: Optical Fiber and Copper PMDs

The Gigabit Ethernet Optical Link Model

As Chapter 6, "Fundamentals of Fiber Optic Communication," stated: "Commonly proposed advantages of optical fiber are its very high bandwidth, its immunity to electromagnetic interference (EMI), and its immunity to crosstalk." This might lead you to suppose that it is a trivial task to specify and design the optical PMD portions of Gigabit Ethernet. In fact, nothing could be further from the truth! Four major design considerations make specification and design very difficult:

- A limited optical power budget

- Potential implementation costs

- The requirement for inter-operation in multivendor environments

- The restricted bandwidth of multimode fiber

Obviously, these factors are not independent and various trade-offs are possible. It became clear during the Gigabit Ethernet standardization process that a common optical link model was required if agreement was to emerge. This chapter describes the Gigabit Ethernet link model that was used by the optical task force to understand potential trade-offs. The model also provided a common baseline for discussion of the optical link specification. Given that a whole 802.3z committee was to use the model, it had to be simple to understand, easy to use, and yet reasonably accurate.

The Gigabit Ethernet optical link model is based on the concept of power budgeting introduced in Chapter 6. The power budget model is essentially an extension of a spreadsheet model initially proposed by Hewlett-Packard (HP). HP had modified models for LED-based links to simulate laser-based links [Hanson, 1996; Smith and Personick, 1982; Brown, 1992; Gowar, 1983; Gimlett and Cheung, 1986]. Initially, jitter was not directly accounted for, but a contribution to the committee from IBM showed how to allocate a maximum amount of jitter within the model by slightly changing the input parameters.

This chapter departs from the essentially non-mathematical approach used in Chapter 6. While the link model described in this chapter is mathematical in nature, it is presented in a step-by-step development, backed up by graphical examples.

Also, during the writing of this book, one of the authors became aware of a previously reported laser link model very similar to the Gigabit Ethernet model [Laskey et al, 1995]. Where appropriate, the chapter provides a comparison of the power losses and penalties of the two models, and, since the Gigabit Ethernet model was experimentally tested as part of the standardization process, this chapter presents some of the important experimental results. Finally, this chapter indicates any known limitations of the Gigabit Ethernet model by comparing theoretical models followed by a discussion of experimental results.

9.1 Preliminaries: The IEEE 802.3 Worst-Case Design Philosophy

Ethernet is a very successful technology. A major reason for this has been IEEE 802.3's use of a *worst-case design philosophy,* which states the following: When all specified link parameters are at their worst-case values, the link should operate normally.

This is a very restrictive design philosophy, but over the years, it has proven its worth to customers (and suppliers) in the marketplace.

The Ethernet committee will rarely relax this design criteria, and then only to allow a small number of terms in a link specification not to be at their absolute worst-case values. Classic relaxation examples are the near-end crosstalk (NEXT) specifications for 10BASE-T and 100BASE-T. These were relaxed to the 99th percentile values. Because all other specification values remained at worst-case, the link design is still very conservative—as has been proven by the successful mass deployment of 10BASE-T in multivendor environments.

Note

Multivendor inter-operability means that products developed independently by different companies will work, as dictated by the standard, when interconnected at the standardized electrical or optical physical interfaces.

If the Ethernet committee is to allow a statistical specification of a parameter in a multivendor environment, then it expects full statistics of the behavior of that parameter to be disclosed. The committee also expects only to be asked to relax the parameter a little, that is, to something like the 99th percentile value. The more parameters to be relaxed, the higher the percentiles are likely to be. For example, if two parameters were to be relaxed, then the percentile might need to be 99.5 percent.

The worst-case philosophy caused great contention within the optical sub-taskforce for two reasons:

- Vendors felt that a worst-case link (worst-case in the sense that all parameters are at their worst-case value) would be extremely improbable in the field. They argued that specifications based on worst-case criteria would be artificial.

- Vendors were also not inclined to provide a worst-case analysis. They preferred instead to provide a typical case analysis. The problem was that when they were forced to do the worst-case analysis, they were very disappointed by the results compared to the typical case.

The Ethernet committee did not allow any Gigabit optical parameters to be statistically specified. The principal reason for this was the lack of good multivendor component statistics.

Since the optical specification is worst-case, you can expect excellent multivendor inter-operability at the specified link length limits. As with all previous Ethernet standards, even better performance is possible if a small subset of suppliers is exclusively used. However, in today's multivendor network environment, this is difficult to achieve because there is no single supplier of optical cable, optical transceivers, or optical connecting hardware. Additionally, network equipment manufacturers generally do not manufacture the computers and servers used on a network, and it is difficult to ensure that all end stations use the same transceivers. Even specifying the use of the same network interface card does not guarantee that all transceivers are the same. Obviously, an international standard cannot be based on one vendor's optimized specifications. The final result is always a trade-off, even though every supplier knows which specifications would particularly suit them, and they all try to slant the standard to their own benefit!

9.2 Introduction to the Optical Link Model

The Gigabit Ethernet optical link model is a power budget model based on the power conservation equation (Equation 9.1).

Equation 9.1

power-out = power-in − losses − link margin

The components of Equation 9.1 are defined as follows:

- *power-in* is the optical power launched into the fiber by the transmitter.

- *power-out* is the power delivered to the optical receiver.

- There are two types of *loss* that must be accounted for:

  - The loss of average optical power as measured with an optical power meter.

  - The loss of the modulated signal due to a system impairment as determined from an eye diagram. As covered in Chapter 6, the loss of modulated signal strength can be compensated for by increased optical power. This type of loss is called an *optical power penalty*.

- The *link margin* is an amount of power set aside for a safety margin.

The Gigabit Ethernet optical link model assumes that the laser and multimode fiber impulse responses are Gaussian in shape [Hanson, 1996 and Brown, 1992]. In addition, the model assumes that the optical receiver is essentially non-equalized and has a raised cosine response.

Expressions that convert the root-mean-square (rms) impulse widths of the laser, fiber, and optical receiver to risetimes, falltimes, and bandwidths are included in the model. The calculated risetimes, falltimes, and bandwidths are then used to determine the fiber and composite channel exit response time. The composite channel exit response time is then used to calculate the inter-symbol interference (ISI) penalty that is required for the link power budget analysis.

In the link model, power penalties are calculated to account for the following effects:

- Finite laser extinction ratio

- Inter-symbol interference (ISI)

- Minimum eye opening requirement at the receiver output

- Mode partition noise (MPN) [Agrawal et al, 1988]

- Laser relative intensity noise (RIN)

In addition, power loss or power penalty allocations are made for the following items:

- Fiber attenuation

- Connectors and splices

- Modal noise

- Duty cycle distortion

Note

Duty cycle distortion (DCD): The fraction of time the signal is on during a periodic waveform is called its duty cycle. Gigabit Ethernet has a nominal duty cycle of 50 percent so that the pulse width of an "on" pulse equals the pulse width of an "off" pulse. However, distortions in the performance of link components can cause the duty cycle to be reduced or increased during a measurement period. This is called duty cycle distortion.

9.3 Pulse Widths, Bandwidths, and Transition Times

It can be shown that the bandwidth of any positive pulse is inversely proportional to its rms pulse width, while its risetime is proportional to its rms pulse width [Smith and Personick, 1982; Brown, 1992; Gowar, 1983]. Now, let an optical system be built from a number of optical components where each component has an individual pulse width, σ_i, and a bandwidth, BW_i. Also, let the resulting system output pulse have an rms pulse width, σ_s, and a risetime, T_s. You can then write Equation 9.2 and Equation 9.3.

Equation 9.2

$$\sigma_i = \frac{a_i}{BW_i}$$

Equation 9.3

$$\sigma_s = \frac{T_s}{b_s}$$

where a_i and b_s are constants.

It has also been shown that the rms output pulse width, σ_s, of an optical system made from components having pulse widths, σ_i, is given by Equation 9.4 [Smith and Personick, 1982; Brown, 1992; Gowar, 1983]:

Equation 9.4

$$\sigma_s = \sqrt{\sum_i \left(\sigma_i\right)^2}$$

The well-known central limit theorem, from statistical analysis, has been used to show that the composite impulse response of a multimode fiber optic link, constructed from a number of components (laser, fiber, connectors, optical receivers), tends to a Gaussian impulse [Brown, 1992]. This is true even for a relatively small number of link components, say 3 or 4, if some of the individual component responses are close to Gaussian and no single term dominates. Substituting the expressions for σ_i and σ_s into Equation 9.4 leads to the relationship stated in Equation 9.5.

Equation 9.5

$$T_s = \sqrt{\sum_i \left(\frac{a_i \cdot b_s}{BW_i}\right)^2}$$

The constants, a_i and b_s, depend on how the bandwidth and risetimes are specified (see Table 9.1). Obviously, Equation 9.5 may be simplified to Equation 9.6.

Equation 9.6

$$T_s = \sqrt{\sum_i \left(\frac{C_i}{BW_i}\right)^2}$$

where C_i is a constant.

Table 9.1   Values for a and b for Various Impulse Responses

Impulse Shape	a (3 dB Optical)	a (3 dB Electrical)	b
Gaussian	0.1871	0.1323	2.564
Single pole low pass filter	0.2748	0.1588	2.197
Raised cosine	0.1776	0.1292	2.732

For the equations presented in this chapter, risetimes and falltimes are defined as the 10 percent to 90 percent transition time, fiber bandwidth components are the 3 dB optical bandwidths, and the bandwidth of the optical receiver is its 3 dB electrical bandwidth. Because of the current-to-light-to-current conversion of the laser and of the optical receiver, the 3 dB optical bandwidths are equivalent to 6 dB electrical bandwidths.

Note

The Gigabit Ethernet specification specifies 20 to 80 percent transition times, which can be converted to the 10 to 90 percent transition times required by the link model by multiplying each 20 to 80 percent transition time value by 1.52.

9.4 Fiber and Channel Transition Times

Equation 9.7 can be used to calculate the 10 to 90 percent transition time, T_e, at the fiber exit point:

Equation 9.7

$$T_e = \sqrt{(T_L)^2 + \left(\frac{0.48}{BW_m}\right)^2 + \left(\frac{0.48}{BW_{ch}}\right)^2}$$

where:

BW_m is the 3 dB optical modal bandwidth of the fiber link

BW_{ch} is the 3 dB optical chromatic bandwidth of the fiber link

T_L is the 10 to 90 percent transition time of the laser transmitter

Similarly, for a link using a raised cosine receiver response having a 3 dB electrical bandwidth, BW_r, the electrical transition time at the output of the analog portion of the optical receiver, due to the effect of the whole channel, can be calculated as shown in Equation 9.8.

Equation 9.8

$$T_c = \sqrt{(T_e)^2 + \left(\frac{0.35}{BW_r}\right)^2}$$

where T_c is known as the channel exit response time.

9.4.1 Multimode Fiber Modal Bandwidth

The fiber modal bandwidth is the worst-case 3 dB optical modal bandwidth specified for the type of optical cable to be used. Modal bandwidths for common multimode fibers are documented in Chapter 10, "The Gigabit Ethernet Modal Bandwidth Investigation." However, for convenience, Table 9.2 provides a subset of cable types and their modal bandwidths with various Gigabit Ethernet transceivers. The fiber bandwidths are quoted in units of MHz *times* km; to convert to bandwidth, these values should be *divided* by the length of the fiber used.

Table 9.2   Modal Bandwidth for Some Commonly Installed Cable and Laser Wavelength Combinations

Cable and Gigabit Ethernet Transceiver Combination	Modal Bandwidth, MHz.km
62.5 µm, 1000BASE-SX	160
62.5 µm, 1000BASE-LX	500
50 µm, 1000BASE-SX	400
50 µm, 1000BASE-LX	400

9.4.2   Fiber Chromatic Bandwidth

The chromatic bandwidth of the multimode fiber, in Hz, may be calculated using Equations 9.9–9.11 [Hanson, 1996; Brown, 1992].

Equation 9.9

$$BW_{ch} = \frac{0.187}{L \cdot \sigma_\lambda} \cdot \frac{10^{12}}{\sqrt{(D_1)^2 + (D_2)^2}}$$

Equation 9.10

$$D_1 = \frac{S_0}{4} \cdot \left[\lambda_c - \frac{(\lambda_0)^4}{(\lambda_c)^3} \right]$$

Equation 9.11

$$D_2 = 0.7 \cdot S_0 \cdot \sigma_\lambda$$

where:

L is the link length in km.

σ_λ is rms optical spectral width of the laser source in nm.

λ_0 is the wavelength of zero dispersion of the fiber in nm.

λ_c is the center wavelength of the laser in nm.

S_0 is the dispersion parameter of the fiber in ps/(km.nm^2).

At this point, it would be natural to calculate the eye opening penalty due to the finite transition time of the channel. However, you should refresh your memory regarding eye diagrams, eye openings, and optical power penalties with a simpler case first.

9.5 *The Extinction Ratio Power Penalty*

The power penalty associated with transmitting a non-zero power level for a zero code bit is called the *extinction ratio power penalty*, as illustrated in Figure 9.1.

Figure 9.1   Extinction Ratio Power Penalty

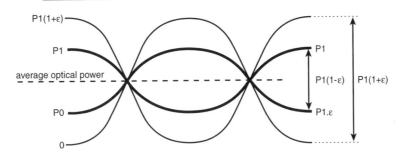

$$\text{Extinction Ratio Power Penalty} = \frac{1+\varepsilon}{1-\varepsilon}$$

Figure 9.1 shows the inner transitions of two transmit eye diagrams. The average optical power of both the transmitted signals shown in Figure 9.1 is the same, but the modulation depths of the two signals are different. The eye having a non-zero power level for "zeros" (the bold traces in Figure 9.1) has a smaller opening compared to the eye that has no optical power for "zeros" (the thin traces in Figure 9.1). The eye that transmits no optical power for "zeros" is referred to as the reference eye. The ratio of the reference eye maximum opening (in amplitude) to that of the eye having a non-zero power level for "zeros" is called the *extinction ratio power penalty*. In linear units, it is given by Equation 9.12 [Smith and Personick, 1982; Lasky et al, 1995; Kazovsky et al, 1996].

Equation 9.12

$$P_e = \frac{1 + \varepsilon}{1 - \varepsilon}$$

where P_e is the extinction ratio power penalty (in linear units) and ε is the laser extinction ratio, the ratio of the power on "zeros" to the power on "ones", as shown in Figure 9.1.

The finite extinction ratio is said to have caused an eye opening power penalty, because the opening of the impaired eye is equal to that of the reference signal attenuated by a factor equal to the extinction ratio power penalty.

9.6 Inter-Symbol Interference (ISI)

Since each component in the communications channel acts like a filter, the transmitted pulse will broaden as it traverses the optical link, as shown in Figure 9.2.

Figure 9.2   Broadening of the Transmit Pulse by the Link Components

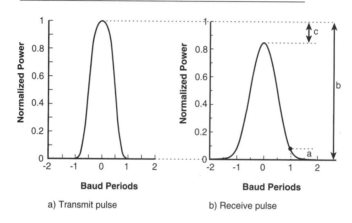

a) Transmit pulse   b) Receive pulse

As noted earlier, the Gigabit Ethernet model assumes that the channel impulse response is Gaussian in shape. In addition, Gigabit Ethernet uses a coded non-return-to-zero (NRZ) data format. The combination of NRZ data pulses and the Gaussian channel impulse response produces pulse shapes having an *error function (erf)* functional dependence. This means that the pulses transition faster than a Gaussian pulse having the same rms pulse width.

Figure 9.2 has been drawn to compensate for the link attenuation. This means that the power of both the transmit pulse and the receive pulse are equal. Also, the time scale of each graph is relative to the instant of peak power. Pulse broadening has caused the receive pulse to spread into the next transmission baud period. The value of the received pulse at times ± 1 baud period is *a*, the peak amplitude of the transmit pulse is *b*, and the peak amplitude of received pulse has been reduced to *(b – c)* as shown in the diagram.

To plot Figure 9.2, we assumed that an isolated "one" was transmitted. If instead an isolated "zero" were transmitted in an otherwise continuous stream of ones, the reduction in pulse amplitude of the received pulse would be the same. However, now the signal would take on its minimum value of *c* at times equal to zero, and at times equal to ± 1 baud period, the received signal would be *(b – a)*.

By plotting both cases, the isolated one and the isolated zero, on the same graph, we can show the inner eye diagrams for the system. Figure 9.3 shows the inner eye diagrams for both the transmitter (thin curves) and the receiver (bold curves). From the diagram it is clear that the received eye opening is *d*. Also, *d* is exactly equal to *(b – 2c)* or, because *c* is approximately *2a*, we can say that *d* approximately equals *(b – 4a)*. Obviously, so long as the received pulse has not spread so much that there is significant amplitude at ± 2 baud periods, this approximation is very good.

Figure 9.3   Transmit and Receive Eye Diagrams Due to ISI

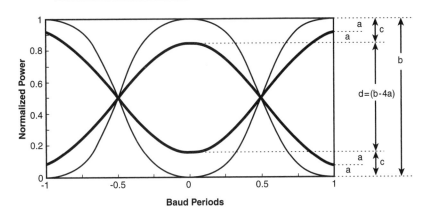

Figure 9.3 shows that the optical power penalty induced by the ISI is *(b/d)*. However, most spreadsheets do not regularly include the error functions required to calculate *d*. Therefore, for spreadsheet analysis, the exact equation for the ISI power penalty (as a linear ratio, not in dB) is approximated by Equation 9.13.

Equation 9.13

$$P_{isi} = \frac{1}{1 - 1.425 \cdot \exp\left[-1.28 \cdot \left(\frac{T}{T_c}\right)^2\right]}$$

where T is the baud period and T_c is the channel exit response time.

The graphical procedures of Figures 9.2 and 9.3 and the associated equations are valid for any symmetrical pulse shape. To illustrate how the pulse shape affects the magnitude of the ISI penalty, Figure 9.4 plots the ISI power penalty for various pulse shapes as solid lines. The labels refer to the shapes of the rising and falling edges of the pulses and the cases plotted are: erf (the exact version of the Gigabit Ethernet model), linear, and Gaussian transitions. In addition, the power penalties according to two other well-known models are plotted: a quadratic approximation to the ISI penalty [Lasky et al, 1995] and the original model for the ISI penalty used for Ethernet, FDDI, and ATM LED-based links [Hanson,

1996]. Interestingly, the original ISI penalty developed by Hanson is equivalent to the first order term, involving the factor *[b − 4a]*, of the exact version of the Gigabit Ethernet ISI model (see Figure 9.3). Finally, the results according to the spreadsheet approximation (Equation 9.13) used by the Gigabit Ethernet model are plotted as open circles on the graph.

Figure 9.4 ISI Power Penalty for Various Pulse Transition Shapes and Two Well-Known ISI Power Penalty Models

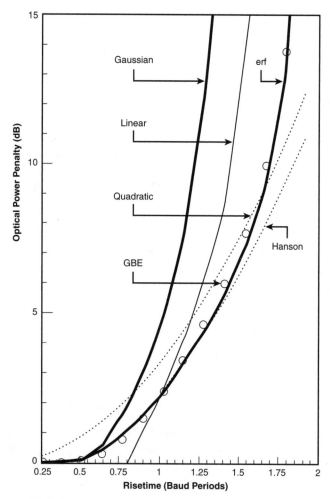

GBE = Gigabit Ethernet

The ISI penalty is critically dependent on the particular output pulse shape at the end of the link. That is, for the same transition time, the power penalty is very different for the different pulse shapes. Worse, there is a maximum risetime beyond which the data cannot be recovered, and the maximum risetime value is very pulse shape dependent. Clearly, the Gigabit Ethernet model is not the worst ISI power penalty model that could have been used. Both the linear and Gaussian transition time models produce significantly higher power penalties. This means that if there are any bandwidth anomalies in any of the link components that change the output pulse transition shape from erf-like toward linear- or Gaussian-like, then the power penalty increases significantly. As an example, Table 9.3 provides the calculated power penalties (rounded to the nearest 0.5 dB) for various pulse transition shapes, assuming the output pulse transition time is approximately 1.2 baud periods.

Table 9.3 Power Penalties for an Output Pulse Transition Time of 1.2 Baud Periods and Various Pulse Transition Shapes

Pulse Transition Shape	Power Penalty (dB)
erf	3.5
Linear	5
Gaussian	9

The power budget for Gigabit Ethernet multimode fiber links is only 7.5 dB and, for multimode fiber links, ISI will make the largest power penalty contribution. If this penalty changed from 3.5 to 5 dB, because, for example, an anomalous fiber bandwidth characteristic had forced the response toward linear transition shapes, then the link is likely to fail.

Because of this potentially catastrophic pulse shape dependence of the ISI power penalty, the Gigabit Ethernet committee realized it was very dangerous to increase the allowed ISI power penalty in order to gain link distance. The maximum ISI penalty allowed by Gigabit Ethernet was set at about 3.6 dB, *and even this concerned some committee members.* Although the committee was put under the most severe pressure to allow the ISI penalty to be increased beyond the self-imposed 3.6 dB limit (so that a 300 m link length could be supported with short-wavelength lasers on 62.5 multimode fiber (MMF) with a 160 MHz.km modal bandwidth), the committee refused on the grounds that the penalty was already dangerously high!

9.7 Cabled Fiber Attenuation

Cable attenuation is usually the second largest loss term after the ISI penalty. The worst-case value for the attenuation of *cabled* optical fiber is modeled by Equation 9.14.

Equation 9.14

$$A = L \cdot \frac{R_\lambda}{C_\lambda} \left[\frac{1.28}{\left(\lambda_c \cdot 10^{-3} \right)^4} + 1.05 \right]$$

where:

A is the cable attenuation in dB.

R_λ is the actual worst-case cable attenuation specified at the wavelength λ.

$R_{850\ nm}$ equals 3.5 dB/km.

$R_{1,300\ nm}$ equals 1.5 dB/km.

C_λ equals 3.5 for the short-wavelength 1000BASE-SX links.

C_λ equals the 1.5 for long-wavelength 1000BASE-SX links.

λ_c is the actual center wavelength, in nm, of the laser used.

L is the length, in km, of the link.

Equation 9.14 was proposed to the Gigabit Ethernet committee by Corning and Lucent. The equation is based on the worst-case attenuation specifications for multimode fiber, but can be applied to single-mode fiber (SMF) in the 1,310 nm region. However, it does not model the OH absorption peak near 1,400 nm. The constant C_λ is used as a scaling factor to model the attenuation versus wavelength curve around the two windows of operation relevant to Gigabit Ethernet. The original LED-based model used a slightly different equation which gave essentially the same attenuation values over the range of interest of Gigabit Ethernet. It should be noted that these worst-case attenuation values are for fiber that is already cabled and installed for use. The attenuation of uncabled fiber or uninstalled fiber can be significantly less than the values predicted by Equation 9.4.

Figure 9.5 shows plots of the worst-case cabled-fiber attenuation versus link length for 1000BASE-SX at a laser center wavelength of 830 nm, and for 1000BASE-LX at a laser center wavelength of 1,270 nm.

Figure 9.5   Worst-Case Cabled Fiber Attenuation Curves for 1000BASE-SX and 1000BASE-LX

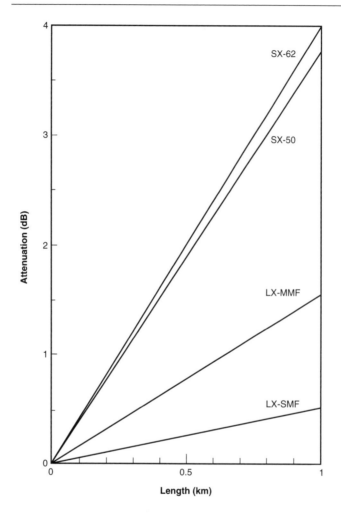

9.8   Connection Insertion Loss

The maximum link distances for multimode fiber are calculated based on a total allocation of 1.5 dB for connection and splice losses. For example, this allocation can support three connections with an average insertion loss equal to 0.5 dB (or less) per connection, or two connections with a maximum insertion loss of 0.75 dB. These loss values are for measurements made with a source that overfills the connectors and fiber.

At first glance, the multimode connector loss allocation might seem too small to be practical. However, two facts indicate that this allocation is more than sufficient:

- The connector loss values quoted are the loss values that would be measured with the connectors overfilled.

- It was shown during the standardization process that the laser transceivers used by Gigabit Ethernet significantly underfill the fiber.

Because lasers underfill the fiber and connectors, the actual loss experienced will be much less than that due to a test source that overfills the fiber and connectors. Although the connection losses given are strictly correct, in practice, an additional connector or two is unlikely to cause a loss problem in a Gigabit Ethernet link. Also, test equipment and associated procedures will eventually become available for qualifying the loss that would be experienced by laser sources. These will allow the link losses to be qualified in a manner more suited to Gigabit Ethernet.

The maximum link distances for single-mode fiber are calculated based on an allocation of 2.0 dB total connection and splice loss. This allocation supports four connections with an average insertion loss per connection of 0.5 dB.

9.9 Return Loss

The Gigabit Ethernet model does not explicitly include penalties due to the reflection of laser light from the receiver or connectors back into the laser. These reflections are usually called *back-reflections*. Rather, the maximum loss experienced by the reflected laser light (the return loss) from the link components is specified to allow the worst-case link to operate normally.

It is well-documented that back-reflections can severely degrade the performance of laser-based fiber optic links [Lasky et al, 1995; Hakki and Bosch, 1989; Kazovsky et al, 1996]. For example, for Gigabit transmission systems, it has been shown that a single point of back-reflection of approximately 12 dB can reduce the signal-to-noise ratio (SNR) of a link by more than 4 dB. However, for such a single strong back-reflection, the SNR would still be expected to be greater than about 15 dB, and a low bit error rate (BER) can still be achieved [Hakki and Bosch, 1989]. However, because the laser is the source of the noise, increasing the transmit power will not improve the bit error performance of a link that is limited by back-reflections.

The worst-case receiver back-reflection of Gigabit Ethernet is specified to be 12 dB. Thus in the worst case, the SNR of a Gigabit Ethernet link could be severely constrained by the back-reflection from the receiver.

Additional fiber connections have two effects. They will:

• Increase the total back-reflection and associated laser noise.

• Cause multiple reflections that will optically interfere and cause additional optical interference induced noise within the laser. This noise is usually called *interferometric noise* [Lasky et al, 1995].

Given that the SNR is already constrained by the worst-case 12 dB receiver reflection, there is very little room for these additional reflection effects. To keep interferometric noise penalties below 0.5 dB requires the connector return loss specifications to be as follows:

• The return loss for multimode connections must be greater than 20 dB.

• The return loss for single-mode connections must be greater than 26 dB.

The multimode return loss specification is relaxed, compared to the single-mode return loss specification, because generally less reflected light can couple back into the laser source from multimode fiber.

9.10   *Minimum Received Inner Eye Opening*

For the link to operate at its minimum specified BER, the eye at the output of the optical receiver must be open by a minimum amount for a sufficient fraction of the baud period. This is to ensure that the SNR delivered to the clock and data recovery circuit is acceptable, and that its duration is sufficient for the baud clock and data to be reliably recovered. An analytical relationship for the eye opening penalty was developed to specify the eye opening for the LED-based link standards, for example, 100BASE-FX, FDDI, 100VG-AnyLAN, and ATM Forum [Hanson, 1996]. The analytical model assumed that the received inner eye could be approximated by a raised cosine function. Figure 9.6 compares the received analog eye diagram due to the Gigabit Ethernet link model and the raised cosine approximation to it.

Figure 9.6   Inner Eye Diagram at the Receiver Due to Gigabit Ethernet Link Model and a Raised Cosine Approximation

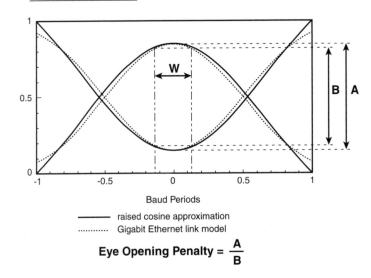

The dotted lines are the eye due to the Gigabit Ethernet link model, and the solid lines are the raised cosine approximation. The eye opening must be greater than *B* for a duration *W* for the clock and data to be regenerated. Since the eye has to remain open for a duration *W*, the SNR has been reduced by the ratio, *B/A*. All other penalties in the model were only calculated at time zero, the eye center. The eye opening penalty (compared to time equals zero) is therefore computed as the ratio, *A/B*, as shown in Figure 9.6. The analytical expression for the power penalty, based on the raised cosine approximation, is given in Equation 9.15 [Hanson, 1996]:

Equation 9.15

$$P_{eye} = -10 \cdot \log \left[\frac{2 \cdot \sin(\pi \cdot W)}{\pi \cdot W \cdot (1 - W^2)} - 1 \right]$$

where P_{eye} is the eye opening penalty in dB, and *W* is the duration of the eye opening as a fraction of the baud period.

9.11 Mode Partition Noise

Chapter 6, "Fundamentals of Fiber Optic Communication," introduced and explained mode partition noise (MPN). To recap, the various wavelength components of a laser output travel at slightly different speeds through an optical fiber due to chromatic dispersion.

The long-term time-averaged laser spectrum gives rise to an average chromatic bandwidth, BW_{ch}, per Equation 9.9. However, in a multimode laser, although the total power is constant, the power in each laser mode is not constant. As a result, the power fluctuations between laser modes lead to an additional chromatic dispersion induced ISI power penalty, P_{mpn}. This is mode partition noise and the mpn power penalty (in linear units, not dB) has been estimated as Equation 9.16 [Agrawal et al, 1988]:

Equation 9.16

$$P_{mpn} = \frac{1}{\sqrt{1 - \left(Q \cdot \sigma_{mpn}\right)^2}}$$

where the value of the digital SNR, Q, is determined from Equations 9.17 and 9.18.

Equation 9.17

$$BER = \frac{1}{Q \cdot \sqrt{2 \cdot \pi}} \cdot \exp\left(\frac{-Q^2}{2}\right)$$

Equation 9.18

$$\sigma_{mpn} = \frac{k}{\sqrt{2}} \cdot \left[1 - \exp\left[-\left(\frac{\pi \cdot D_1 \cdot L \cdot \sigma_\lambda}{T}\right)^2\right]\right]$$

For Equations 9.17 and 9.18:

BER is the minimum acceptable bit error rate for the link.

k is the mode partitioning factor (a number between 0 and 1).

σ_{mpn} is the is the rms value of the mpn.

T equals the baud period, in ps.

D_1 is defined in equation (10) and has units (ps/(nm.km)).

L is the link length, in km.

σ_λ is the rms width of the laser spectrum, in nm.

The MPN penalty was one of the terms that forced Gigabit Ethernet to change its laser linewidth specification compared to that of the Fibre Channel specification, which the Gigabit Ethernet committee was trying to reuse as much as possible.

Fibre Channel is a computer system interconnection standard rather than a LAN standard. Because of this, it does not have to operate over installed optical cables to distances specified by building wiring standards. In many cases Gigabit Ethernet will be a data rate upgrade for existing, installed, multimode fiber links with lengths up to 550 m in the building backbone, and existing, installed, single-mode fiber up to 5 km in the campus backbone. These distances cannot be supported with the Fibre Channel linewidth as demonstrated in Figure 9.7 and Figure 9.8.

Figure 9.7   Mode Partition Noise Limited Link Length for 1000BASE-SX Multimode Fiber

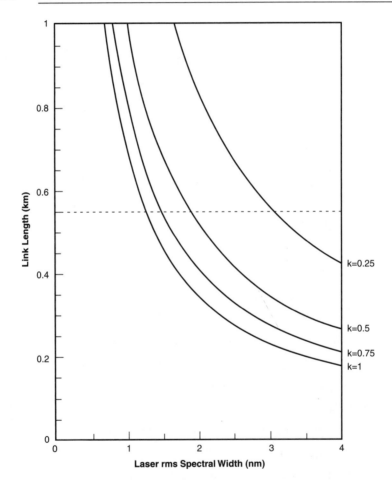

Figure 9.8   Mode Partition Noise Limited Link Length for 1000BASE-LX Single-Mode Fiber

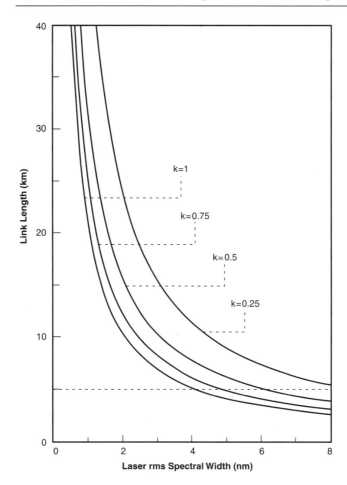

Figures 9.7 and 9.8 show contour plots of the maximum link length versus the laser rms spectral width for 1000BASE-SX and 1000BASE-LX systems, respectively. The definition of the maximum link length used to generate the plots is *the link length for which the power penalty is equal to 2 dB at a BER of 10^{-12}.*

The dotted horizontal line that traverses Figures 9.7 and 9.8 represents the target link length for Gigabit Ethernet. Power penalty contours for k equal 0.25, 0.5, 0.75, and 1 are shown. Typical lasers have k values in the range 0.25 to 0.6. However, you must be conservative when using Equation 9.18 because it is known that this equation *underestimates* the MPN [Lasky et al, 1995; Agrawal et al, 1988]. For this reason, the Gigabit Ethernet link model sets k equal to 0.8.

For 1000BASE-SX to achieve link lengths of 550 m, with an MPN power penalty much smaller than 2 dB, the laser rms spectral width must be well below 1.25 nm. The Fibre Channel linewidth specification of 4 nm rms would only have allowed a link length of about 200 m or so! Similarly, for 1000BASE-LX, to achieve link lengths of 5 km on single-mode fiber, the rms laser spectral width must be less than 4 nm; again, the original Fibre Channel specification was 6 nm rms, which would have only allowed link lengths of a few kilometers! The final Gigabit Ethernet laser linewidth specifications were 0.85 nm for 1000BASE-SX and 4 nm rms for 1000BASE-LX.

Many end-users are showing interest in extended link lengths beyond those currently specified in 1000BASE-LX. Such links are only possible with *selected laser transceiver modules* having laser linewidths guaranteed to be less than 4 nm rms (see Figure 9.8).

A final point worth making about MPN is that, although the theory discussed here is valid for Fabry-Perot lasers, it probably severely overestimates the MPN penalty for vertical cavity surface emitting lasers (VCSELs). This is because the optical spectrum is essentially clipped by the highly reflecting mirrors of the VCSEL. Hence, the total VCSEL spectrum is not as extended as that of a Fabry-Perot laser having the same rms spectral width. Since the VCSEL spectrum is clipped, the VCSEL output cannot partition to the extreme wavelength values that the Fabry-Perot laser could—therefore, the MPN *must* be less for a VCSEL.

9.12   Relative Intensity Noise

Fluctuations in the output intensity of a laser result in optical intensity noise, which is usually called relative intensity noise (RIN). RIN can be defined as the mean square intensity fluctuation divided by the square of the average intensity at the laser output. RIN is usually quoted in units of dB/Hz, and all lasers generate this type of noise. Back-reflections also strongly influence the RIN level [Hakki and Bosch, 1989].

The Gigabit Ethernet model uses Equation 9.19 in conjunction with Equation 9.20 to calculate the power penalty (in linear units, not dB) due to RIN:

Equation 9.19

$$P_{rin} = \frac{1}{\sqrt{1 - \left(Q \cdot \sigma_{rin}\right)^2}}$$

Equation 9.20

$$\sigma_{rin} = \sqrt{\alpha \cdot \frac{0.48}{T_c} \cdot 10^{\frac{RIN}{10}}}$$

where:

P_{rin} is the power penalty due to RIN.

σ_{rin} is the rms noise due to rin.

α equals 0.7 for 100BASE-LX.

α equals 0.6 for 1000BASE-SX.

T_c is the transition time of the channel, in Hz, from Equation 9.8.

RIN is the laser RIN in units of dB/Hz.

Equation 9.20 is very different from well-known expressions for the rms noise due to RIN. The differences are as follows:

- α is normally within the range 1 to 4 [Lasky et al, 1995; Kazovsky et al, 1996].

- Normally, only the risetime or bandwidth of the optical receiver would be used in the calculation.

The original equation proposed by Hewlett-Packard set α to its worst-case value of four. However, the Gigabit Ethernet committee thought this was too pessimistic. Therefore, Equation 9.20 was developed by the committee using the following arguments:

- In the usual equations for RIN, the receiver bandwidth response is assumed to be equal to one out to the 3 dB electrical bandwidth of the receiver, BW_r. For frequencies greater than BW_r the receiver bandwidth response is assumed to be zero.

- However, for multimode fiber links it was argued that the fiber modal bandwidth also acts as a filter for the RIN. This means that the bandwidth of both the fiber and the receiver should be taken into account in the calculation of the RIN power penalty.

- Also, the Gigabit Ethernet model assumes that the channel will have an approximately Gaussian frequency response. Therefore, the equation for the rms noise of the RIN should be corrected for the Gaussian shape of the channel.

These changes were implemented in the spreadsheet model by calculating the value of α, the correction for the Gaussian bandwidth response of the channel formed by the receiver and the modal bandwidth of the fiber, at the link length limits and modal bandwidth specifications of the 802.3z D3.1 draft standard. The correction was made only at the link length limit because it was argued that the only time RIN could have a significant effect on link length performance was near the link length limit, with all other terms at their maximum allowed values. The different values for α for 1000BASE-SX and 1000BASE-LX are due to the slightly different link bandwidths at the limits of the D3.1 specification. These values were never updated based on the final D5 specifications. If this update were done, the value of α would be increased by about 0.1 for both cases.

Inspection of Equation 9.20 shows that it was the total channel transition time, not just the transition time due to the optical receiver and the fiber modal bandwidth, that was included in the spreadsheet model. Arguments as to whether this should have been done continue to this day. For example, it is not clear how the laser transition time and the chromatic dispersion filter the RIN, and this may be revisited if the Gigabit Ethernet model is to be used as the baseline for developing new standards.

Although the original equation for the RIN penalty, proposed by Hewlett-Packard, might have been too pessimistic, the final version of the equation can now reasonably be viewed as being slightly optimistic.

9.13 *Modal Noise Power Penalty Allocation*

Concern over the amount of modal noise generated using lasers with multimode fiber has engendered much debate for many years. Expanding on the concept of modal noise introduced in Chapter 6, when coherent sources (lasers) are used with a multimode fiber link containing connectors, splices, or even photodiodes that don't collect all of the light, there may be an additional amount of intensity noise at the receiver. This additional noise is caused by the partial sampling of the fluctuating interference pattern of the laser light.

If all of the light traveling in the different fiber modes passing through the fiber and connectors is collected by the photodiode, then no additional noise arises. This is because the interference between the modes is spatially correlated such that the total power within the area of the fiber guiding the light must always average to the total transmitted power. However, if there is an area of the guided light that is not collected by the receiver, then because of the spatial correlation, the power collected by the receiver will not now always average to the same value as when all the light was collected. (Obviously, if you could average the power that was lost and the power that was collected, once again the average would be the transmitted power.) It is the incomplete collection of the spatially correlated interference pattern that causes modal noise.

There are various ways that the light can be lost and modal noise generated; for example, loss due to offsets at connectors or splices, or differential modal attenuation in the link components. Loss that selects only a portion of the interference pattern or that is different for different modes is called mode selective loss (MSL).

MSL alone is not enough for there to be modal noise. This is because, if the interference pattern is static, then although the spatial correlation is broken by the presence of MSL, the power in the collected area will still be constant—it just won't be equal to the same power value as when all the light was collected. However, if the frequency of the laser varies with time or if the laser light is traveling in different modes at different times, then the power detected after passing through a MSL will vary also. This variation would not occur if the loss was not MSL because the loss would affect all modes equally.

This means there are four conditions that must be satisfied for modal noise to be generated:

- A coherent light source (a laser) must be used.

- The fiber must be multimode.

- There must be MSL.

- The interference pattern produced by the laser must be varying in the fiber.

Various models exist for calculating the power penalty due to modal noise. A model that has been used extensively by the data communications industry was documented by Bates in 1995 [Bates et al, 1995]. This model was used by Gigabit Ethernet to calculate worst-case power penalty allocations for 1000BASE-SX and 1000BASE-LX. Figure 9.9 shows the results for 1000BASE-LX and 1000BASE-SX for 62.5 μm and 50 μm fiber, respectively.

Figure 9.9 Worst-Case Theoretical MPN Penalty for 1000BASE-SX with 50 μm Fiber and 1000BASE-LX with 62.5 μm Fiber

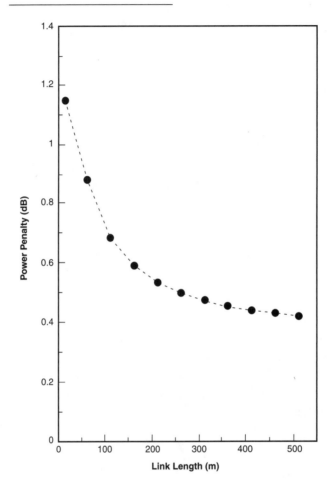

One graph covers both cases because the same number of modes propagate in 62.5 μm fiber at 1,300 nm and in 50 μm at 850 nm. The graph was calculated for the case where there are two points of MSL, each with approximately 1.5 dB of loss, as shown in Figure 9.10. It was also assumed that the transmitter and receiver were connected to the cable plant by 2 m patch cords. The link length in Figure 9.9 is the total length of fiber between the transmitter and the receiver.

Figure 9.10   Link Configuration for the Calculation of Figure 9.9

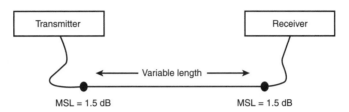

From Figure 9.9, you can see that the power penalty initially falls off quite rapidly with distance, only to reach a power penalty plateau of about 0.5 dB. The Gigabit Ethernet committee noted that modal noise will tend to have its worst effect on links near the link length limit with all other penalties and losses at their maximum values. For this reason, the value of the modal noise power penalty of interest is the penalty on the plateau region. However, the committee also made, presented, and discussed many measurements of modal noise in links of various types and configurations of interest to Gigabit Ethernet.

Happily, all measurements produced experimental power penalties significantly less than the penalties predicted by the worst-case theory: an example modal noise power penalty measurement is shown graphically in Figure 9.11. Remember, the total connector loss budget of a Gigabit Ethernet link is only 1.5 dB. For these reasons, and after much debate, the power penalty allocations for each link type were chosen to be as listed in Table 9.4.

Figure 9.11   Measured BER Curves for 1000BASE-LX with 50 μm Fiber for 3 dB MSL (Twice the Allowed Connector Loss), 12 m from the Laser

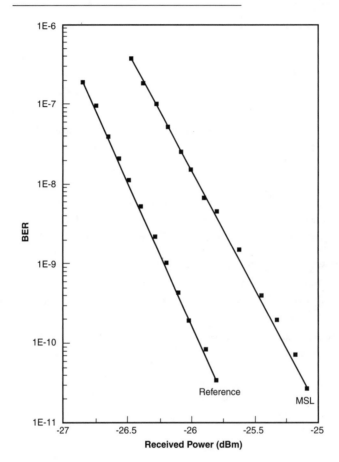

Table 9.4   Modal Noise Power Penalty Allocations for the Gigabit Ethernet Model

Link Type	Modal Noise Power Penalty Allocation
1000BASE-SX, 50 µm	0.3 dB
1000BASE-SX, 62.5 µm	0.15 dB
1000BASE-LX, 50 µm	1.0 dB
1000BASE-LX, 62.5 µm	0.5 dB

Generally, the 1000BASE-SX allocations were reduced, compared to the worst-case theoretical values, by much more than the 1000BASE-LX allocations. The 1000BASE-LX allocations were not reduced significantly because the LX links had plenty of margin in their power budgets and there was no particular need to reduce them.

9.14 Additional Experimental Results

The two most limiting power penalty terms are mode partition noise (MPN) and intersymbol interference (ISI). These terms had major effects on the final form of the Gigabit Ethernet specification. It is useful to show some of the experimental results obtained by the committee to confirm that the theory was valid.

Figure 9.12 shows experimental and theoretical results for short-wavelength, 780 nm, and long-wavelength, 1,300 nm, operation over various lengths of 62.5 µm fiber. All the lengths of fiber were from the same spool, and all the component input parameters required by the model were experimentally measured.

Figure 9.12   Power Penalty Versus Link Length, in 62.5 µm Multimode Fiber, for 780 nm and 1,300 nm Operation

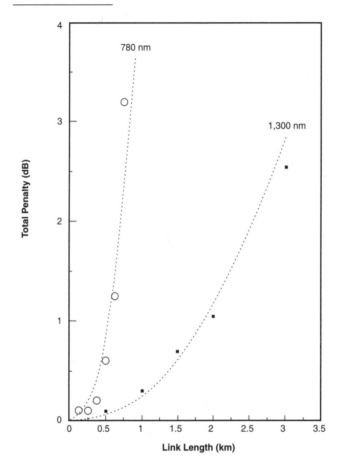

Obviously, readily available, typical components were used instead of the worst-case component/fiber scenario. No fitting has been used—the experimentally measured input parameters were just fed into the Gigabit Ethernet link model and the results plotted along with the experimental power penalties. Clearly there is very good agreement (see Figure 9.12).

During the Gigabit Ethernet standardization, it was discovered that there is an installed population of anomalous fibers that have differential modal delay (DMD) characteristics that can cause the overall channel impulse response to be non-Gaussian. For 1000BASE-LX, operating with such fibers, the impulse response is returned to near Gaussian using mode conditioning patch cords (see Chapter 10) and so the theory presented here is a reasonable model for worst-case 1000BASE-LX links. For 1000BASE-SX links, specification of the receiver upper bandwidth range is believed to control the overall impulse response sufficiently for the Gigabit Ethernet link model to be used as a worst-case model.

Figure 9.13 shows plots of some BER curves for a laser with a center wavelength of 780 nm and an rms spectral width of 2 to 3 nm (this is 2.4 to 3.5 times that allowed by the Gigabit Ethernet specification). The fiber used was very high bandwidth (>1 GHz.km), 50 μm fiber.

Figure 9.13   Measured BER Curves for a Laser Operating at 78 nm, with an rms Spectral Width of 2 to 3 nm (2.4 to 3.5 Times that Allowed by Gigabit Ethernet)

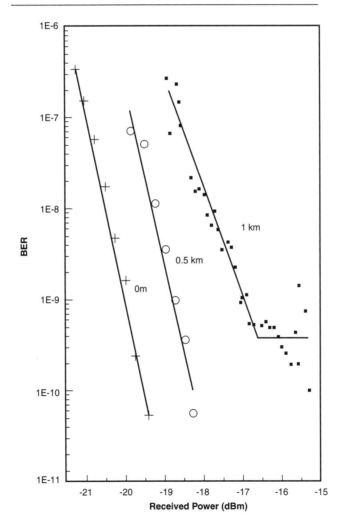

Measured eye diagrams at the output of each fiber length confirmed that the system was not limited by ISI. The curves shown in Figure 9.7 indicate that a large power penalty due to MPN should be observed for the link lengths of 500 m and 1,000 m. This is indeed what is observed (refer to Figure 9.13). In fact, for the 1 km link length case, the bit error ratio cannot be decreased below about 10^{-10} and a BER floor has occurred. This link fails the Gigabit Ethernet BER objective of 10^{-12}. However, such large MPN-induced power penalties will not occur for Gigabit Ethernet because the maximum rms linewidth has been specified as 0.85 nm (refer to Figure 9.7). The results, shown previously in Figures 9.7 and 9.13, powerfully illustrate why the Fibre Channel linewidth of 4 nm rms, for 1000BASE-SX, could not have been used by Gigabit Ethernet.

9.15   Deterministic Jitter Allocation

Near the end of the standardization process, it was realized that the eye closure due to duty cycle distortion (DCD) could be accounted for by the model. This is done by setting the effective baud period equal to the actual baud period minus the amount of duty cycle distortion for all calculations. The reasoning for this is that sometimes the DCD will shorten the baud period. By setting the effective baud period always equal to the actual baud period minus the DCD, all penalties associated with the baud period will be increased, which is obviously pessimistic.

9.16   Example Power Budget

This completes the description of the Gigabit Ethernet link model. All that remains to be done is to put it all together. The easiest way to do this is to use an example power budget. The following example assumes a worst-case link for 1000BASE-SX with 62.5 μm multimode fiber having a 160 MHz.km modal bandwidth. Table 9.5 provides the input parameters for this example power budget.

Table 9.5   Link Model Input Parameters for Power Budget Example

Input Parameter	Value
Link length	0.22 km
Transmit Parameters	
Transmit power	–9.5 dBm
Center wavelength	830 nm
Linewidth (rms)	0.85 nm
Extinction ratio	0.126 (equals –9 dB)

Input Parameter	Value
Risetime	0.26 ns
RIN	–117 dB/Hz
k	0.8
DCD allocation	80 ps
Receive Parameters	
Electrical bandwidth (3 dB)	1 GHz
GBE specified sensitivity (eye center) with degradation due to P_e included	–17 dB
Sensitivity; $P_e = 0$ (eye center)	–18 dBm
Fiber Parameters	
Wavelength of zero dispersion	1,365 nm
R_λ	3.75 dB/km
C_λ	3.5
S_0	0.093 $(ps/(nm^2.km))$
Modal bandwidth	160 MHz.km
Connector Parameters	
Total loss allocation	1.5 dB
Total modal noise allocation	0.15 dB

Table 9.6 tabulates some of the intermediate results of the link model calculation.

Table 9.6	Intermediate Results of the Link Model

Intermediate Parameter	Value
D1	–122 $(ps/(nm.km))$
BW_{ch}	8.2 GHz
BW_m	0.73 GHz
T_e	0.77 ns
T_c	0.85 ns
W	0.28

Table 9.7 provides the calculated power penalties and losses.

Table 9.7   Power Penalties and Losses

Calculated Parameter	Value
Connector loss	1.5 dB
Cable attenuation (A)	0.88 dB
P_{ISI}	3.6 dB
P_e	1.1 dB
P_{eye}	0.45 dB
P_{mn}	0.15 dB
P_{RIN}	0.07 dB
P_{mpn}	0.003 dB

Table 9.8 provides the calculated power budget, power penalties, losses, and margins.

Table 9.8   Calculated Power Budget, Power Penalties, Total Losses, and Link Margin

GBE budget	7.5 dB
Power penalties (excluding P_e)	4.28 dB
Total losses	2.37 dB
Link margin	0.84 dB

For the items in Table 9.8, the following is true:

- Link Margin = GBE Budget – Power Penalties – Total Losses

- GBE Budget = Min Transmit Power – GBE Rcvr Sensitivity

- GBE Rcvr Sensitivity = (Rcvr Sensitivity; $P_e = 0$) – P_e

The Gigabit Ethernet committee considered this link to be dispersion limited at 220 m; that is, there is a positive power margin, but it cannot be used to increase the link length any further because the ISI penalty is already dangerously large.

9.17   *Summary*

You should now be familiar with the following:

- The IEEE 802 worst-case design philosophy.

- The Gigabit Ethernet optical link model.

> **Note**
>
> The Gigabit Ethernet link model is only worst case when all its input parameters are set to their worst-case values—if typical values are used, the typical link performance will be modeled.

- Why Gigabit Ethernet changed some of the laser specifications relative to the Fibre Channel specification, which was the starting point for all Gigabit Ethernet discussions. In particular, this chapter showed theoretically and experimentally that, for 1000BASE-SX, the laser rms linewidth had to be reduced to 0.85 nm from Fibre Channels 4 nm value. This ensures that mode partition noise induced BER floors will not occur.

- With commonly installed multimode fiber the Gigabit Ethernet 1000BASE-SX worst-case link length (given in Table 9.5) is ISI limited. This means that although there is a power budget margin, the margin cannot be used to increase the worst-case link lengths.

> **Note**
>
> If the industry perfects conditioned launch techniques for 1000BASE-SX, it may be possible to reduce the ISI penalty and to increase the worst-case link lengths.
>
> New installations can benefit from new optical fiber types having higher modal bandwidth for use with lasers that are already available.

- The worst-case link length of 1000BASE-LX on single-mode fiber is limited by four issues: its rms linewidth, its relatively broad center wavelength range, its limited power budget, and its relatively poor back-reflection specifications. Extended link lengths can be achieved with specially selected 1000BASE-LX transceivers, but these are more costly than standard 1000BASE-LX transceivers. For example, links compliant with the Serial HIPPI standard can reliably achieve 10 km link lengths with a reduced laser linewidth (3 nm rms), a reduced center wavelength ranged (about half of the Gigabit Ethernet range) relatively expensive pigtailed lasers, excellent return-loss specifications (>40 dB from receiver and >30 dB from connectors), and better receiver sensitivity specifications (−22 dBm) compared to Gigabit Ethernet.

The Gigabit Ethernet optical link model is currently (1999) the state of the art as far as laser-based data communication standards are concerned. Most other standards are actively reviewing their specifications in light of it.

Chapter 11, "1000BASE-X: Optical Fiber and Copper PMDs," uses the link model to explain the Gigabit Ethernet optical PMD specifications. However, before we can consider the optical PMDs, you will need to go over Chapter 10, "The Gigabit Ethernet Modal Bandwidth Investigation," which fills out the background information that you will need to fully understand the optical PMD specifications and issues discussed in Chapter 11.

The Gigabit Ethernet Modal Bandwidth Investigation

The purpose of this chapter is to discuss the resolution of some long-standing and fundamental issues regarding laser-based multimode fiber transmission that were addressed by the Gigabit Ethernet PMD sub-task force, in collaboration with the Telecommunications Industry Association, Fiber Optic 2.2 standards committee (TIA FO 2.2).

Before the telecommunications industry decided to use single-mode fiber, it had seriously considered standardizing on multimode fiber. Multimode fiber was attractive because mechanical tolerances of link components (connectors, splices, laser-coupling optics) are greatly relaxed compared to the single-mode case. However, in the end, two basic technical problems made multimode fiber unsuitable for the telecommunications industry:

- Modal noise (see section 6.5.1 in Chapter 6, "Fundamentals of Fiber Optic Communication")

- Unpredictable bandwidth performance

The telecommunications industry had identified these problems, but it never developed solutions for them.

Chapter 9, "The Gigabit Ethernet Optical Link Model," discussed how the Gigabit Ethernet task force resolved the first issue. They were able to make a worst-case power penalty allocation for modal noise by using known worst-case models and extensive experimental testing. The ATM forum also uses this approach.

The basic reason this worst-case approach works for data communication links is that the total connection loss is relatively small. This made it straightforward for the Gigabit Ethernet committee to conduct experiments with mode selective loss much greater than is likely to be encountered in the field. A large proportion of the committee's work during the first 18 months of the Gigabit Ethernet standardization process was spent ensuring that modal noise would not be a problem.

However, during that period, little attention was paid to the second problem—unpredictable bandwidth. This was probably because the industry believed that any form of restricted-mode launch would produce higher bandwidth than the overfilled launch (OFL) bandwidth specified for multimode fiber (see Chapter 6, section 6.3.5 for descriptions of OFL and restricted launches). Therefore, the Gigabit Ethernet task force made the seemingly reasonable assumption that the worst-case bandwidth was the OFL bandwidth specification for each multimode fiber type of interest. In fact, many members of the Gigabit PMD sub-task force were also involved in an investigation led by TIA FO 2.2 regarding the launch dependence on the modal bandwidth of multimode fiber. It was believed that because all laser-based transceivers produce a restricted-mode launch, compared to OFL, all laser-based transceivers would perform much better than predictions based on the OFL bandwidth. It was also hoped that a particularly good (high bandwidth) set of restricted-mode launch types could be identified. These high bandwidth restricted launches could then be used by both transceiver and fiber manufacturers to specify much better performance.

The TIA FO 2.2 committee was conducting a round robin bandwidth evaluation during the initial stages of the Gigabit Ethernet specification. Everyone was confident that the results of the round robin would enable Gigabit Ethernet to specify longer link lengths.

Unfortunately, when the first results from the modal-bandwidth round robin began to be reported, it was clear that there was a major problem. Counter to all expectations, it was discovered that many of the laboratory-defined restricted launches produced lower bandwidth than an OFL. Worse, the effect also occurred with real laser-based transceivers, especially when operating at long wavelengths. Figure 10.1 shows measured bandwidth obtained with an unconditioned 1000BASE-LX transceiver launch and a selection of fibers.

The fibers have an OFL bandwidth spread representative of the range expected in commercial systems. The solid line on the graph represents the expected result for the case where the measured bandwidth equals the OFL bandwidth. The dotted line represents the specified worst-case (minimum) OFL bandwidth specification for operation in the long-wavelength region with the fiber type used.

Clearly, the majority of the bandwidths measured with the transceiver are well below the OFL bandwidth. Shockingly, for the Gigabit Ethernet committee, many results don't even achieve the worst-case (minimum) OFL bandwidth specifications for the fiber type used.

Figure 10.1   Measured Bandwidth Using a 1000BASE-LX Unconditioned Launch Transceiver

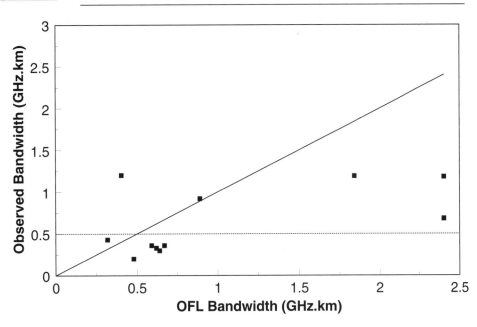

Note

Two of the fibers used for these tests have OFL bandwidths less than the 500 MHz.km specification. These are only included for completeness, and it is not expected that fibers with such low OFL bandwidth would be encountered by Gigabit Ethernet.

Although Figure 10.1 shows results for only long-wavelength operation, the effect was also observed for operation at short wavelengths. However, the effect was more dramatic with long-wavelength operation.

The initial TIA FO 2.2 results only became available during May 1997. At that time, it was planned to complete draft D3.1 at the July plenary meeting of IEEE 802.3 and to ballot draft D3.1 as the final Gigabit Ethernet specification. The expectation was that Gigabit Ethernet would become an IEEE standard by November 1997.

The rest of this chapter describes the process by which the Gigabit Ethernet committee resolved the bandwidth issue. Part of the solution was to introduce new receiver conformance tests and specifications for laser-based multimode fiber link design into the Gigabit Ethernet standard. Chapter 11, "1000BASE-X: Optical Fiber and Copper PMDs," provides the specifications and details of these new tests.

It is important to understand the committee process so that you can then understand the working environment and pressures that the committee was under. Developing solutions to the bandwidth issue was not conducted in a relaxed academic environment or to academic time scales. Rather, it was done in a standards environment, under public scrutiny, to commercial time scales. It is a great tribute to all concerned that such a difficult technical problem was understood and resolved in time to make Gigabit Ethernet the success it is.

10.1 The Effective Modal Bandwidth Investigation

The poor performance of laser-based multimode fiber links called the November 1997 completion date for Gigabit Ethernet into question. Obviously, between May and July 1997, the Gigabit Ethernet community put considerable pressure on the PMD sub-taskforce with a view to forcing a solution to the bandwidth issue. The response to this pressure was the formation of an ad hoc committee chaired by Dave Smith (Honeywell). It was known as the *Effective Modal Bandwidth Investigation (EMBI)*. Between May and July 1997, the EMBI met weekly (sometimes biweekly) by phone and also had several face-to-face meetings. The members of the EMBI performed many theoretical and experimental studies and then pooled their results so that a reasonable solution could be found by the July plenary meeting. The final results of the EMBI investigation were as follows:

- Less than 5 percent of fibers were observed to have bandwidth less than 160 MHz.km at short wavelengths with restricted-mode launch.

- As many as 30 percent of fibers were observed to have bandwidth less than 500 MHz.km for operation at long wavelength with restricted-mode launches.

Table 10.1 summarizes some key bandwidth results reported by the EMBI.

Table 10.1 Range of Modal Bandwidths Observed by the EMBI for 62.5 μm MMF

	Minimum Observed Bandwidth (MHz.km)	Mean Observed Bandwidth (MHz.km)	Maximum Observed Bandwidth (MHz.km)
SX	140	400	>2,400[a]
LX	250	800	>2,400[a]

[a]Limited by measurement capabilities

10.1.1 Gigabit Ethernet Link Model Worst-Case Operating Ranges

The EMBI also concluded that the Gigabit Ethernet link model (see Chapter 9), as it existed then, could be used to predict worst-case operating ranges. However, instead of using the OFL bandwidth specification for each fiber type, a new value based on the performance of restricted-mode launch should be used. Based on the measurements conducted by the EMBI, Gigabit Ethernet chose the worst-case modal bandwidth (WCMB) values for each link type shown in Table 10.2.

Note

Multimode fiber is abbreviated to MMF in tables and graphs throughout this chapter.

Table 10.2	Worst-Case Modal Bandwidth Values (MHz.km) Used for Draft D3.1	
	62.5 μm MMF	50 μm MMF
SX	160[a]	500[a]
LX	250	375

[a]Very few cases were observed to have bandwidth less than OFL bandwidth, so the OFL bandwidth was used.

Based on these worst-case effective modal bandwidths, the Gigabit Ethernet link model (with jitter due to duty cycle distortion [DCD] equal to zero) was used to calculate the operating ranges for D3.1 shown in Table 10.3.

Table 10.3	Operating Ranges of Draft D3.1	
	62.5 μm MMF	50 μm MMF
SX	260 m	550 m
LX	440 m	550 m

10.1.2 Gigabit Ethernet Jitter Budget Problems

At the July plenary meeting of IEEE 802.3, some members of the committee thought that the standard should *not* go to its final sponsor group (IEEE 802) ballot. They felt that Gigabit Ethernet had not met the objective of supporting the installed base of 62.5 μm MMF within the building backbone and proposed that more work should be done with the goal of achieving a 550 m operating distance on 62.5 μm MMF. In the end, it was decided that the ability to achieve 550 m on 50 μm MMF was sufficient, and draft D3.1 went to sponsor group (IEEE 802) ballot. The members of the Gigabit Ethernet PMD,

TIA FO 2.2, and the EMBI were greatly relieved that the panic was over and the standard was done. We all believed we had done the best job possible and that by reducing the bandwidth used to calculate operating distances, we had picked a "better safe than sorry" solution.

Between July and the September interim meeting of Gigabit Ethernet, lightning struck the PMD group again. Results of both laboratory and customer testing indicated that the D3.1 draft had not sufficiently solved the modal bandwidth problem!

Digital Equipment Corporation (DEC) reported at the September interim meeting that there was a jitter budget problem that D3.1 had not addressed. They reported that the additional jitter was due to excessive differential mode delay (DMD) (see Chapter 6, section 6.3.5.1) due to the restricted-mode launch of laser-based transceivers. Furthermore, it was pointed out that the Gigabit Ethernet link model does not take jitter into account. To illustrate their point, the contributors from DEC showed measured step responses similar to that of Figure 10.2.

Figure 10.2   Step Response for a 500 m Length of Fiber Exhibiting Severe DMD

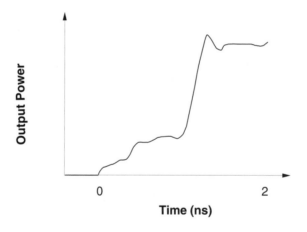

This step response was obtained using an unconditioned 1000BASE-LX transceiver and a 500 m length of fiber having severe DMD. Due to the DMD characteristics of the fiber, the unconditioned laser launch excites mainly two mode groups with a DMD of 1,800 ps/km. This bimodal DMD causes the step response to have two transition regions separated by a plateau. Jitter is very clearly a problem for this transceiver-fiber combination, as can be seen from the eye diagram in Figure 10.3.

Figure 10.3   Eye Diagram for a 500 m Length of Fiber Exhibiting Severe DMD

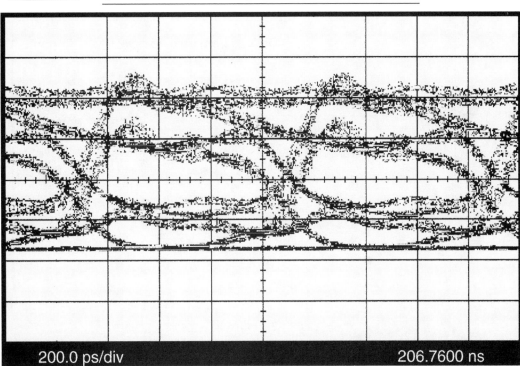

200.0 ps/div   206.7600 ns

During the London meeting, Hewlett-Packard presented a graph of lowest measured modal bandwidth, or worst-case modal bandwidth (WCMB), as it was known (see Figure 10.4). The WCMB estimated from the peak-to-peak DMD data clearly indicated a strong correlation between peak-to-peak DMD and WCMB.

Figure 10.4   Correlation between WCMB and Peak-to-Peak DMD Data

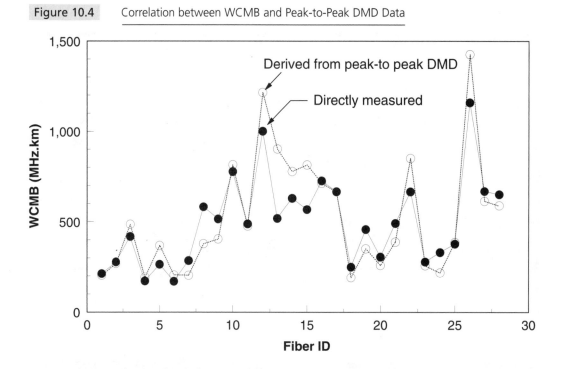

10.2   *The Modal Bandwidth Investigation*

Reluctantly, the Gigabit Ethernet committee accepted that the bandwidth performance and jitter consequences of the modal bandwidth had not been resolved. The PMD subtask force once again came under extreme pressure to investigate and solve this problem. Another ad hoc committee, called the *Modal Bandwidth Investigation (MBI)* group, was formed. One of the authors of this book (David Cunningham) was elected chair of the MBI. During the period between September 1997 and March 1998, the members of the MBI did a tremendous amount of work in the following areas: theoretical studies, laboratory testing, and field testing. The MBI met by phone once per week and face-to-face about once per month.

One of the first issues addressed by the MBI was whether the results presented by DEC would be a real world issue for installed Gigabit Ethernet links. Field tests were conducted to answer this question. These tests consisted of systems tests, where actual Gigabit Ethernet links were set up and their performance (bit error count, and so forth) was measured. Bandwidth tests were also conducted, where the fiber bandwidth was measured. Both the systems and the fiber bandwidth tests confirmed that the issues raised by DEC were real and occurred in the field.

Figures 10.5 and 10.6 show a selection of the modal bandwidth data obtained during field testing by Hewlett-Packard Laboratories. These figures also show results for radial over-filled launch (ROFL) (see section 10.2.1) and OFL testing with short-wavelength and long-wavelength lasers. The solid line indicates the expected result if the ROFL bandwidth equaled the OFL bandwidth.

Figure 10.5 MBI Field Tests for 62.5 μm MMF: ROFL Bandwidth Versus OFL Bandwidth for LX and SX Operation

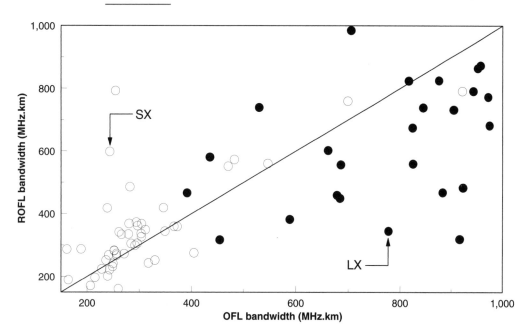

In 62.5 μm MMF (Figure 10.5), the majority of the LX results clearly have modal bandwidth much less than the OFL bandwidth. Some of the SX results also exhibit the same effect.

In 50 μm MMF (Figure 10.6), both LX and SX ROFL bandwidths are less than the OFL bandwidth with approximately the same occurrence rate. The group of results encountered near 400 MHz.km were due to installed fibers having a 400/400 MHz.km specification.

Figure 10.6   MBI Field Tests for 50 µm MMF: ROFL Bandwidth Versus OFL Bandwidth for LX and SX Operation

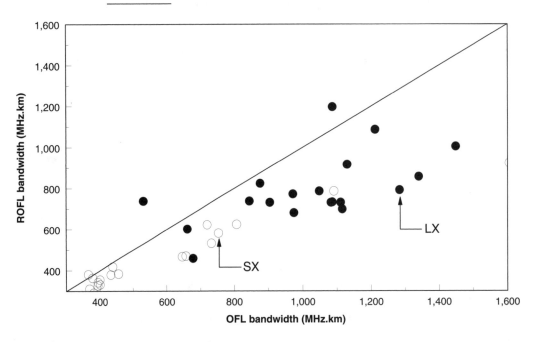

Note

Multimode fiber is specified for use with sources operating at short and long wavelengths. The modal bandwidth is therefore a dual specification: the first number being the bandwidth in the 850 nm region, and the second the bandwidth in the 1,300 nm region. A specification of 200/500 MHz.km means that the fiber modal bandwidth is 200 MHz.km for short-wavelength (850 nm) operation and 500 MHz.km for long-wavelength (1,300 nm) operation. The 400/400 MHz.km fiber specification means that the bandwidth for short-wavelength transmission is 400 MHz.km and the bandwidth for long-wavelength transmission is also 400 MHz.km.

The field tests also indicated that 400/400 MHz.km, 50 µm MMF is a very common fiber type in the installed base. This is why the final Gigabit Ethernet specification includes the 400/400 MHz.km, 50 µm MMF case. During systems field testing for Gigabit Ethernet, it was found that the maximum link length for normal Gigabit Ethernet operation was approximately 500 m on these 400/400 MHz.km, 50 µm MMF.

10.2.1   *Radial Overfilled Launch (ROFL)*

Early in the effective model bandwidth investigation, it was realized that a simple, reproducible, laser launch that approximated a worst-case launch was required. If available, such a launch would increase the reproducibility of measurements from laboratory-to-laboratory. Measurements with transceivers generally showed similar trends between laboratories, but because different transceivers produce different launches, reproducibility was a problem, especially between different laboratories. The ability to estimate the likely worst-case performance of a fiber due to unconditioned laser launch is obviously very useful.

After some initial experimental and theoretical work, ROFL was proposed by Dave Smith (Honeywell), Mark Nowell (Hewlett-Packard), and David Cunningham (Hewlett-Packard). Section 6.3.5 in Chapter 6 introduced the basic concept of ROFL launches. This section looks at the fine details. Figure 10.7 shows the geometry for ROFL.

Figure 10.7   Geometry of a Radial Overfilled Launch (ROFL)

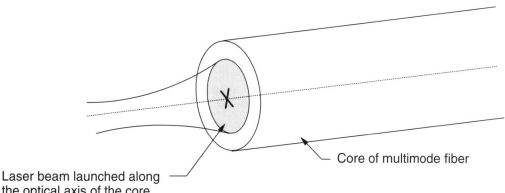

Laser beam launched along
the optical axis of the core

Core of multimode fiber

An approximately circularly symmetric single-mode laser beam illuminates a large portion of the core of a multimode fiber. The axis of the laser beam is approximately coincident with that of the fiber.

This arrangement ensures that the laser excites only modes that have a non-zero electric field at the center of the fiber. Consider Figure 10.8:

Figure 10.8   ROFL Preferentially Excites the Radially Symmetric Fiber Modes

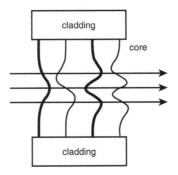

Because the laser field is spatially coherent, it may be considered as being formed by a series of in-phase light rays. Three rays are shown in Figure 10.8, a central ray and two rays near the extreme edges of the beam. The electric field of each ray will excite modes in proportion to the fiber's normalized modal electric field at the position of the ray. Figure 10.8 shows that the central ray can excite only the modes that have peaks or troughs at the core center (these are shown in bold). The edge rays can also excite these same modes. This is because, for these fiber modes, the edge rays always excite the modes that are in-phase with each other and with the central ray. However, each edge ray excites the other modes, shown as thinner lines, in anti-phase to the other edge ray. Therefore, the total mode excitation is small due to cancellation effects. Hence, ROFL excites modes with a large component (electric field or intensity) at the core center. This ensures that the lowest order mode and a selection of higher order modes are well excited by ROFL. Because of this, if the fiber has a large spread of DMDs, ROFL will produce a relatively low bandwidth launch.

For some fibers, ROFL is not worst-case. A small offset of about 5 μm would be worse. However, ROFL is simple to produce, as shown in Figure 10.9.

Because the single-mode fiber has a finite numerical aperture, the exiting beam will diverge slightly (see Figure 10.9), causing an increased illumination diameter on the end of the multimode fiber. And, because the coupling loss is related to the distance of the gap between the single-mode and multimode fibers, the desired coupling loss level can be attained by simply moving the two fibers closer together or farther apart.

Coupling losses of 0.5 dB, 1 dB, and 2 dB were usually used for the investigations of the EMBI and the MBI. Also noteworthy is that for some fibers, the OFL bandwidth is actually the worst-case bandwidth, even for laser launches. The EMBI and the MBI used the term "worst-case modal bandwidth" (WCMB) to mean the lowest measured value between ROFL (0.5 dB, 1 dB, and 2 dB) or OFL bandwidth measurements.

Figure 10.9   Simple Method for Producing a ROFL

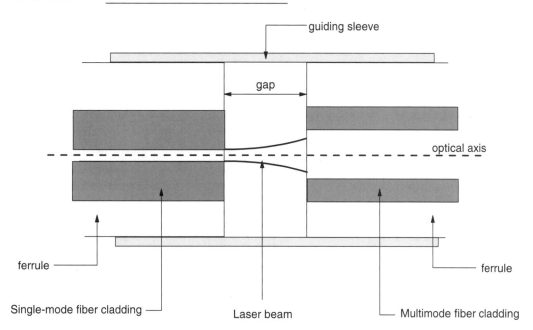

10.2.2 *Resolving the Gigabit Ethernet Jitter Budget Problem*

The jitter observed in Figure 10.3 is on the order of 200 ps peak-to-peak. A major portion of this jitter is obviously induced by the laser-fiber interaction, although some could also be due to the optical receiver characteristics. It turned out to be extremely difficult to decompose the jitter observed with restricted-mode launch into a part associated with the fiber and a part associated with the receiver. This difficulty occurs because Gigabit Ethernet does not specify the actual receiver implementation.

An initial proposed solution, discussed by the MBI, was to do the following:

- Assume that all the jitter is due to DMD

- Assume that the jitter scales linearly with fiber link length

- Calculate worst-case operation ranges based on these assumptions

The proposal allocated all the DMD jitter to the fiber. Unfortunately, DMD jitter is deterministic, and Gigabit Ethernet draft D3.1 had allocated zero deterministic jitter for the fiber! Rather, 96 ps of random jitter had been allocated to the fiber, which, if converted to deterministic jitter, would be equivalent to about 25 ps. Even if the 96 ps of random jitter were converted to a deterministic jitter allocation, the resulting multimode fiber link lengths would still have been very short—about 250 m for 1000BASE-LX and 150 m for 1000BASE-SX over 62.5 μm MMF.

The MBI rejected the proposal because it did not support customer requirements for a 550 m link length with multimode fiber. It was also generally felt that the assumptions and conclusions were too conservative.

However, the proposal did make the MBI realize that there were serious problems surrounding the jitter budget. Specifically, it was clear that a larger jitter allocation was required for the fiber. The MBI, in collaboration with the Gigabit Ethernet Alliance, renegotiated the jitter budget allocations for SERDES chips, optical transceivers, and the fiber to allow for this larger jitter allocation. This was a very painful process for all affected manufacturers because the jitter budget had been stable and essentially fixed for a very long time. In the end, however, an additional allocation of 40 ps for deterministic jitter was assigned to the fiber.

Another issue that came to light during laboratory and field testing was the realization that the optical receiver characteristics could magnify the DMD-induced jitter. It became clear that this was an important contribution in many cases. It was also shown that the DMD-induced jitter could be reduced by limiting the allowed range of receiver bandwidth and specifying the performance of receivers when subjected to test signals having controlled amounts of jitter.

The realization that the receiver design should be tested led to new receiver conformance tests for Gigabit Ethernet, which are described in detail in Chapter 11. Some members of the MBI believed that these modifications were sufficient, by themselves, to guarantee the link distances of the final Gigabit Ethernet standard.

However, good receiver design does not attack the fundamental source of DMD-induced jitter. The only way to do this is to control the DMD characteristics of the modes excited by the source. In order to achieve a more fundamental solution to the DMD issue, conditioned launches were investigated. The goal was to identify a range of testable launch conditions that reduce DMD to acceptable limits for both SX and LX cases. In the time available, the MBI only managed to specify launch conditioning for 1000BASE-LX. This means that while 1000BASE-LX benefits from both launch conditioning and improved receiver design, 1000BASE-SX only benefits from the improved receiver design. This is not as bad a situation as it might seem because the DMD problem was generally less of a problem for 1000BASE-SX when compared to 1000BASE-LX. Work is continuing within TIA FO 2.2 to develop testable conditioned launch techniques for 1000BASE-SX systems.

The rest of this chapter will describe the 1000BASE-LX launch conditioning method and its verification as a solution to the DMD problem for 1000BASE-LX systems. (Note: 1000BASE-LX mode conditioning patch cords must *NEVER* be used with 1000BASE-SX systems.)

Warning

The 1000BASE-LX offset launch mode conditioning patch cords will only condition the launch for 1000BASE-LX transceivers. They must *NEVER* be used with 1000BASE-SX transceivers. This is because 1000BASE-SX transceivers will not couple well into the single-mode fiber of the mode conditioner. Even if some power is coupled into the mode conditioner, the conditioner will not function properly for 1000BASE-SX.

10.3 Offset Launch

The OFL bandwidth specification method for multimode fiber has been extremely successful for LED-based systems. This is because LEDs excite a mode distribution very similar to the OFL distribution used to test the fiber. Obviously, if a laser-based launch method could be defined that in some sense simulates OFL, then predictable performance could be achieved, even with lasers.

The OFL test method tends to "put" a lot of power near radii in the range between (R/2) and R, where R is the core diameter of the fiber. Thus, the OFL launch test method ensures that the DMD of modes with high power in this region of the fiber is well controlled; these will be higher order fiber modes. From this argument, it should be clear that if a laser source is launched into a fiber at some radius beyond (R/2) and less than R (where R is the core radius), a subset of modes similar to those generated by OFL will be excited. Therefore, "offset launch" should have a performance similar to that of OFL and its link performance, in a worst-case sense, should be predictable.

Luckily, about one year before the formation of the MBI, experiments at the University of Bristol and at Hewlett-Packard Laboratories confirmed that "offset" laser launches controlled DMD effects and assured at least OFL bandwidth performance with lasers. This was the first laser launch that truly solved the unpredictable bandwidth problem of laser-based multimode fiber links. The collaboration between the University of Bristol and Hewlett-Packard Laboratories developed a detailed understanding of the offset launch method.

Hewlett-Packard and the University of Bristol made the MBI aware of one implementation of offset launch that seemed relevant to Gigabit Ethernet. Figure 10.10 provides the geometry of the proposed single-mode-offset launch.

Figure 10.10   Geometry of Single-Mode Offset Launch

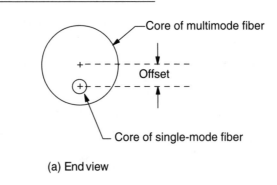

(a) End view

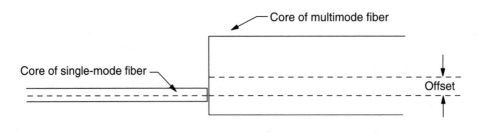

(b) Side view

A single-mode fiber is offset relative to a multimode fiber to form the offset launch. The initial proposed offset range was (18±4) µm. Connector experts confirmed that such tolerances could be met relatively easily. On this basis, Hewlett-Packard and the University of Bristol agreed to perform detailed simulations of near worst-case fiber to prove that OSL bandwidth ≥ OFL bandwidth specification, as well as to identify specification parameters.

A few connector companies, notably Siecor, agreed to provide prototype offset launch patch cords to the MBI for testing. Figure 10.11 shows the step response of the 500 m length of fiber used to obtain the results for Figures 10.2 and 10.3.

Figure 10.11 Step Response with Unconditioned Laser Launch (Dotted Line) and Single-Mode Offset Launch (Solid Line)

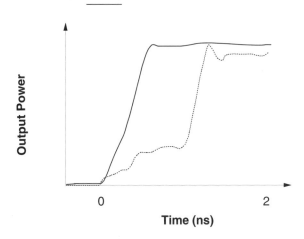

Step responses are plotted for both unconditioned launch and offset single-mode launch via a single-mode offset patch cord. The offset launch dramatically improved the step response of the link. Figure 10.12 shows the eye diagram of the same 500 m link with the offset launch. The eye is essentially fully open in both amplitude and time (no jitter impairment). The improvement compared to Figure 10.3 is dramatic.

Figure 10.12 Eye Diagram with Offset Launch Mode Conditioning

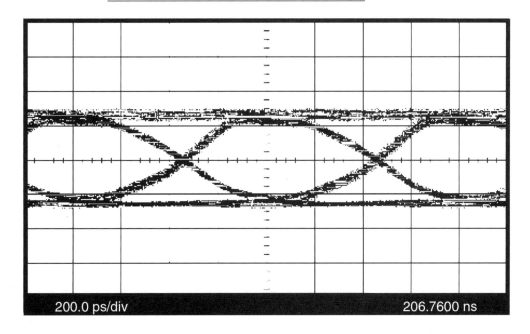

An issue addressed early on by the University of Bristol and Hewlett-Packard Laboratories was the effect of connections in a link employing offset launch. It was found, both experimentally and theoretically, that further offsets at connectors tended to iterate the offset launch bandwidth toward the overfilled launch bandwidth of the fiber. Additionally, in contrast to center launched systems, offset-launch systems are not adversely affected by mechanical agitation of the connectors, the fiber, or other link components.

10.3.1   Fiber DMD Values

The MBI next discussed how a reasonable statistically significant set of simulations of offset launch could be performed. Optical fiber cable manufacturers decided that the only common parameter available to them was DMD data. However, they were concerned that because each manufacturer used slightly different factory-based measurement setups there might be cross-calibration errors. In the end, the cable manufacturers provided estimates for the peak-to-peak value of the DMD at approximately the 2 sigma point of the statistical distribution of their DMD data. Table 10.4 provides the values.

Table 10.4   Peak-to Peak DMD Values Provided to MBI

	50 µm MMF (2 Sigma DMD Value)	62.5 µm MMF (2 Sigma DMD Value)
LX	2 ns/km[a]	2 ns/km
SX	2 ns/km[a]	4 ns/km[a]

[a]These values were provided informally. Only the 62.5 µm MMF, LX case was formally provided to the MBI and Gigabit Ethernet.

10.3.2   Fiber Refractive Index Distortions

It was also determined that common perturbations of the refractive index profile of real fibers could be simplified into one of the following categories:

- Central index distortions

- Mixed power law profiles

- Index distortions near the core-cladding interface

The University of Bristol had a simulation program that could accurately determine the modal delays of all modes within a fiber from its refractive index profile. This program was used to develop a set of theoretical "worst-case" fibers by assuming the three refractive index distortions shown in Figure 10.13 and described in the following bulleted list.

Figure 10.13   Index Perturbations for Worst-Case Simulations

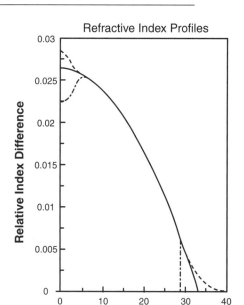

- **Central Distortion.** A Gaussian distortion having a full width half maximum (FWHM) value of 3 μm and relative index amplitude of +0.002, 0 or -0.004 (see Figure 10.10).

- **Mixed Power Law Distortion.** The refractive index profile was assumed to have a power law coefficient g_1 for $(0 >$ or $= (R/2))$ and g_2 for $R/2 < r \leq R$ where g_1 and g_2 could take one of the following values: 1.89, 1.97, or 2.05 for 62.5 μm MMF or 1.84, 1.98, or 2.12 for 50 μm MMF (r is radial parameter for the power law function and R is the nominal core radius).

- **Core-Cladding Distortion.** Three distortions were assumed as follows (for both 62.5 μm MMF and 50 μm MMF, these core/cladding distortions were introduced at $r = 0.88$ R):

  - No distortion—Power law coefficient g_2 continues until it reaches the cladding value.

  - Positive distortion—The power law is replaced by a negative exponential function.

  - Negative distortion—The refractive index is suddenly reduced to the cladding value.

10.3.3   Worst-Case Fiber Simulation

Eighty-one different fiber profiles can be constructed using all combinations of these distortions. The modal delays for each fiber were calculated and stored in a database, and DMD curves were calculated for each fiber. The OFL bandwidth was also calculated for each fiber. If the OFL bandwidth was less than 500 MHz.km, the minimum allowed according to ISO/IEC 11801, the fiber was ignored. Even though the perturbations were reasonably severe, the DMD of many of the fibers was well below the 2 ns/km value. Also, with offset single-mode launch, all fibers easily achieved the 500 MHz.km modal bandwidth target. This was a first indication of the robustness of the offset launch technique.

Next, the DMDs of all remaining fibers were scaled as follows:

Scale DMD to 2 ns/km and if OFL bandwidth of scaled fiber ≥ OFL bandwidth specification (500 MHz.km), include this scaled fiber in simulation.

Else:

Scale DMD to the value at which the OFL bandwidth equals 500 MHz.km.

This scaling process ensured that all fibers were at or beyond the 2 sigma of the statistical distribution. The worst-case performance could now be understood by studying the performance of single-mode offset launch with these worst-case fibers. The advantage of the simulation technique was that a wide range of very poor fibers could be investigated, a much wider range than was available for experimental investigation.

10.3.4   Offset Launch Simulation Results

Figure 10.14 summarizes the results of the theoretical simulations.

The three curves are the lower bandwidth limit, the average bandwidth, and the upper bandwidth limit from the simulations using the set of scaled worst-case fibers. Each curve is plotted as a function of the offset radius. For worst-case analysis, the lower bandwidth limit is the important curve. Four distinct performance regions are noticeable in Figure 10.14:

- A very high bandwidth region for offsets < 3 μm

- A very low bandwidth valley for offsets between 5 and 12 μm

- A medium bandwidth peak for offsets between 14 μm and 25 μm

- Another low bandwidth region for offsets > than 25 μm

Figure 10.14 Statistics of the Bandwidth Due to Single-Mode Offset Launch as a Function of the Offset Radius for 62.5 µm MMF

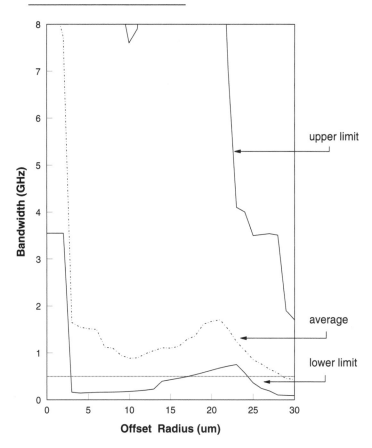

Clearly there are two regions where high bandwidth operation may be achieved: near center single-mode launch and offset single-mode launch for 17 µm ≤ offset radius ≤ 23 µm.

Why was center single-mode launch rejected? Some reasons for the rejection of center single-mode launch are as follows:

• The tolerances of multimode connectors are such that offsets between 3 µm and 5 µm are likely—this would cause the bandwidth to collapse into the valley region.

• Mechanical agitation or mechanical stressing of the fiber can cause mode coupling, which could also cause bandwidth collapse.

- The use of center single-mode launch would require multimode connector tolerances to be tightened (to single-mode tolerances) and even then, offsets between the center of the core and the center of the cladding might be sufficient to cause bandwidth collapse after a few connectors.

- Because it was a goal that Gigabit Ethernet should operate on installed ISO/IEC 11801 multimode cable plants, connector tolerances could not be changed.

Thus, the only viable operating region for single-mode offset launch was in the 20 μm offset region. For offsets between 18 μm and 23 μm, the modal bandwidth is greater than or equal to 500 MHz.km specification limit.

During the simulations, the effect of angular misalignment was also considered. There was little change in the lower limit bandwidth curve for angles up to one degree. However, focusing on the "worst-case" performance of single-mode offset launch doesn't do it justice. The simulated average bandwidth for offset launch using the set of scaled worst-case fibers for offsets in the range 17 μm to 23 μm is 1.3 GHz.km! In addition, for this offset range, 90 percent of worst-case fibers have bandwidth greater than approximately 700 MHz.km. For the (20±3 μm) offset range, the highest bandwidth of a worst-case cable (DMD = 2 ns/km) was over 10 GHz.km (off the scale of the graph in Figure 10.10)!

The Gigabit Ethernet committee remained concerned that single-mode offset launch (offset range 20±3 μm) might be susceptible to modal noise. This was because it was felt that the single-mode launches could only excite a few modes. This concern was removed by proving, contrary to intuition, that for offsets in the range of interest, greater than 40 percent of the fiber modes are excited. In fact, it is precisely because offset launch excites so many modes that it is robust to mechanical agitation of connectors, stressing of the fiber, and further offsets in link connections.

During the simulations of offset launch, it was also confirmed that the coupled-power ratio was strongly correlated with the worst-case link bandwidth of offset launch. This provided a simple, measurable parameter that could be specified to check conformance of offset launch mode conditioning patch cords.

It is worth noting that Corning Incorporated did extensive simulations of the performance of multimode fiber with a very wide range of launch mode power distributions. They performed the simulations for both SX and LX systems and discovered a reasonably wide range of mode power distributions that gave good bandwidth performance.

The simulations indicated that offset launch would perform well for the 1000BASE-LX case. In general, Corning felt that the University of Bristol simulations were too pessimistic. This was especially true for the 50 μm MMF, 1000BASE-LX case where Corning felt that the offset launch patch cord was not required to achieve the 550 m Gigabit Ethernet link length. To a large extent, the Bristol University simulations were in agreement with Corning's observations. However, the committee took a conservative view and specified the offset launch patch cord for 50 µm MMF, 1000BASE-LX also.

The University of Bristol extended their simulations to investigate a wider range of mode power distributions for both SX and LX systems. These simulations confirmed Corning's observations—that a reasonably wide range of mode power distributions exist that produce high bandwidth and low jitter. Work continues within TIA FO 2.2 to turn this conclusion into practical, commercial launch schemes and possibly higher bandwidth grades of multi-mode fiber.

10.3.5 *Experimental Verification of Offset Launch Operation*

The only remaining question is, "Did the offset launch method really work in practice?" Figure 10.15 plots the results for both unconditioned laser launch and conditioned 1000BASE-LX launch.

Figure 10.15   Measured Bandwidth Improvement with 100BASE-LX Conditioned Launch

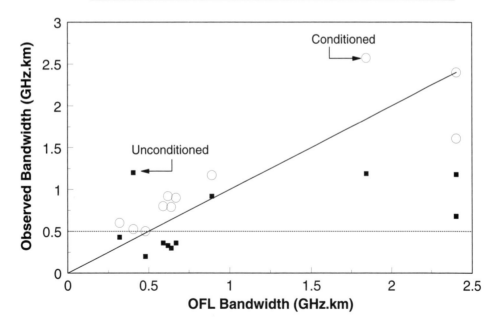

The dark squares are the results for unconditioned 1000BASE-LX transceiver launch (these are the results of Figure 10.1), and the results with the mode conditioning patch cord are plotted as open circles. The improvement is immediately obvious. Except for one case, results obtained with the mode conditioning are better than those without it. And as predicted, all mode-conditioned bandwidths are equal to or greater than the OFL specification limit of 500 MHz.km (shown as a dotted line in Figure 10.15).

In general, the fibers with the largest DMD problem (lowest unconditioned bandwidth) have been improved the most. Given that this sample of fibers contained some very DMD-challenged fibers, this is an excellent experimental verification of the effectiveness of the 1000BASE-LX mode-conditioning patch cord. Other members of the MBI tested the offset launch patch cords on various DMD-challenged fibers with similar results. In all cases, any DMD-related jitter was reduced to levels consistent with the Gigabit Ethernet jitter budget.

Warning

The 1000BASE-LX offset launch mode conditioning patch cords will only condition the launch for 1000BASE-LX transceivers. They must *NEVER* be used with 1000BASE-SX transceivers. This is because 1000BASE-SX transceivers will not couple well into the single-mode fiber of the mode conditioner. Even if some power is coupled into the mode conditioner, the conditioner will not function properly for 1000BASE-SX.

10.4   Summary

This chapter reviewed how the Gigabit Ethernet committee resolved the two fundamental problems that have plagued laser-based multimode fiber links for decades: modal noise and unpredictable bandwidth (or jitter) performance. This is a contribution that will be a great credit for Gigabit Ethernet.

Modal noise was resolved with the realization that, due to a limited power budget, connection losses are relatively small. This greatly reduces the amount of modal noise that could be generated. In addition, a worst-case power penalty was allocated to allow for modal noise in the Gigabit Ethernet link model.

Unpredictable link performance due to decreased bandwidth and increased jitter with unconditioned laser launch was more difficult to resolve. The solution has two parts:

- Receiver bandwidth and conformance tests to ensure a sufficiently good performance—this is enough to allow 1000BASE-SX links to operate over the range specified.

- Offset launch mode conditioning was proven theoretically and experimentally to reduce DMD-related jitter and guarantee bandwidth greater than or equal to 500 MHz.km for 1000BASE-LX links.

Because mode conditioning ensures an approximately monotonically decreasing bandwidth characteristic in the bandwidth range important for Gigabit Ethernet (0 to 1,500 MHz), the Gigabit Ethernet link model is valid for 1000BASE-LX. However, the committee also used the link model for 1000BASE-SX. With the improved receiver specifications, the link model was deemed adequate for the 1000BASE-SX case because only a small number of rogue laser-fiber combinations are expected to fall outside the link model.

Finally, within TIA FO 2.2, work continues to further understand how conditioned laser launches can be produced for 1000BASE-SX. It is expected that this work will quickly be translated into practical commercial products.

1000BASE-X: Optical Fiber and Copper PMDs

As noted in Chapter 3, "Media Access Control," there are two basic compatibility dimensions in an Ethernet network: access compatibility and link compatibility (see Figure 11.1). Access compatibility is MAC-driven and depends on the particular Media Access Control (MAC) option set. Link compatibility, on the other hand, involves all of the media dependent sublayers—Physical Coding Sublayer (PCS), Physical Medium Attachment (PMA), and Physical Medium Dependent Sublayer (PMD). Link compatibility only requires that the entities at *each end of the link* be compatible, both with the link media and with each other.

Figure 11.1 Ethernet Link Compatibility Dimensions

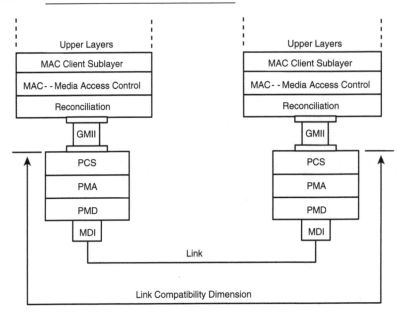

GMII = Gigabit Media Independent Interface (optional)
PCS = Physical Coding Sublayer
PMA = Physical Medium Attachment
PMD = Physical Medium Dependent Sublayer
MDI = Medium Dependent Interface

Link compatibility is determined on a link-by-link basis. There is no requirement that the entire network be configured with the same media or that the various subnets operate at the same transmission speeds.

Chapter 8, "Physical Coding, Physical Medium Attachment, and Auto-Negotiation for 1000BASE-X," discussed the upper portions of the physical layer—the PCS and the PMA. They are functionally the same for all 1000BASE-CX, 1000BASE-LX, and 1000BASE-SX implementations. This chapter concerns the operation of, and specifications for, the lowest sublayer of the Gigabit Ethernet baseband physical layer—the PMD sublayers and their associated Media Dependent Interfaces (MDIs). Figure 11.2 shows the PMD and its interfaces.

Figure 11.2   Functional Block Diagram of the Gigabit Ethernet Physical Layer

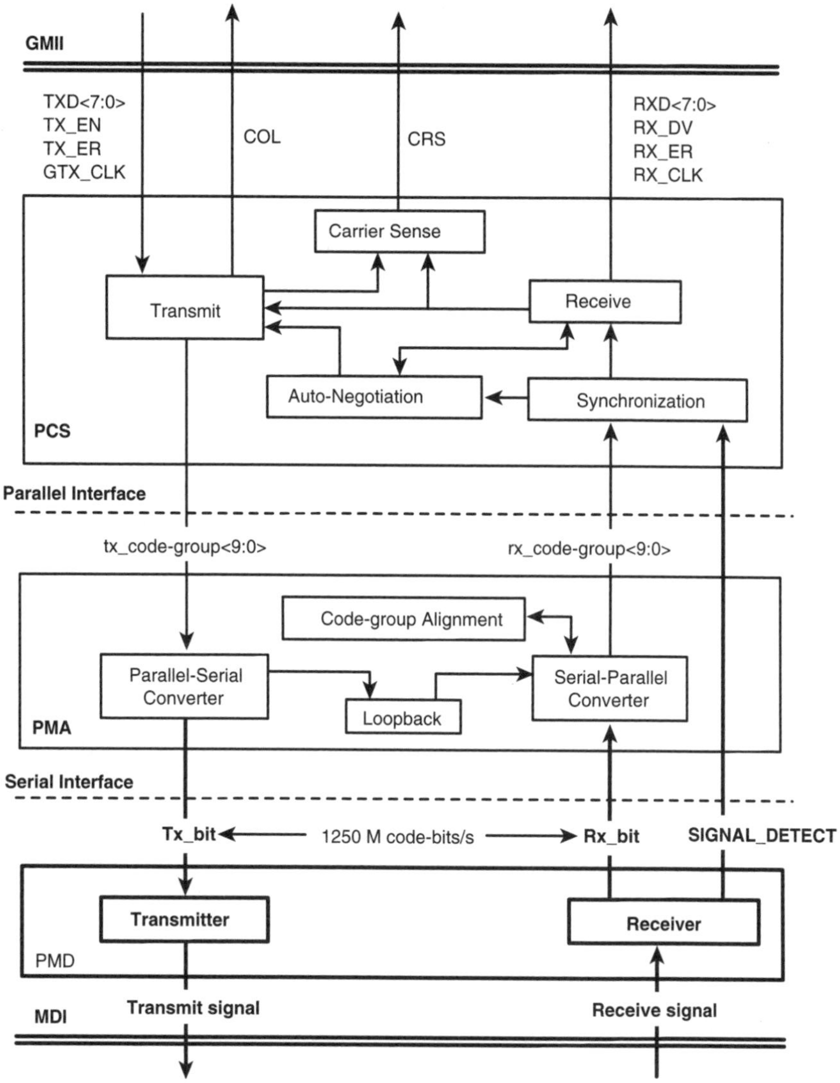

TXD<7:0> = Transmit Data bytes
TX_EN = Transmit Enable
TX_ER = Transmit Error
GTX_CLK = GMII Transmit Clock
COL = Collision

RXD<7:0> = Receive Data Bytes
RX_DV = Receive Data Valid
RX_ER = Receive Error
RX_CLK = GMII Receive Clock
CRS = Carrier Sense

Both the optical and copper PMDs consist of the same three elements: a transmitter, a receiver, and the signal detect function. The list that follows details the functionality of these elements.

- The PMD transmitter accepts code-bits from the PMA via the serial interface and then converts the code-bits into physical signals appropriate for transmission over the link. The physical signals are then output to the cable through the MDI.

- The PMD receiver performs the inverse of the Transmit function—it accepts physical signals from the cable through the MDI and converts these signals into code-bits.

- The PMD receiver also monitors the received signal quality and, if it is deemed good enough, SIGNAL_DETECT is generated and passed through the PMA to the PCS Synchronization function.

Although Gigabit Ethernet optical links each transfer optical signals, the links can be either single-mode or multimode. Furthermore, if they are multimode links, they can have a core diameter of either 50 μm or 62.5 μm and can operate at wavelengths of approximately 850 nm (short wavelength, 1000BASE-SX) or 1,300 nm (long wavelength, 1000BASE-LX). Keep in mind that the transmitted signal in copper-based links is an electrical, rather than optical, pulse train.

Because of these obvious link-level signal differences, this chapter separates the discussion of the optical- and copper-based PMDs. Also, because Chapter 9, "The Gigabit Ethernet Optical Link Model," and Chapter 10, "The Gigabit Ethernet Modal Bandwidth Investigation," concentrated on the optical link model and modal bandwidth, respectively, it seems reasonable to begin with the optical-based PMDs.

11.1 The Optical PMDs

The optical PMD sublayer has the following components:

- Optical-fiber link, which consists of the following components:
  - Cable and patch cords
  - Connectors
- Optical transmitter, which consists of the following components:
  - Laser light source
  - Laser-to-fiber coupling optics

- Laser-drive circuitry

- MDI connector receptacle

- Optical receiver, which consists of the following components:

  - MDI connector receptacle

  - Photodetector

  - Preamplifier and equalizer

  - Electrical pulse regenerator

The short wavelength (1000BASE-SX) optical transceivers are specified so that the same transceiver can operate with either 50 μm multimode fiber (MMF) or 62.5 μm MMF optical fiber (but it obviously can only be plugged into one cable type at any one time). This means that 1000BASE-SX optical transceivers must simultaneously satisfy the transmit and receive specifications for operation with both 50 μm MMF and 62.5 μm MMF optical fiber. Short wavelength transceivers are not compatible with the regular single-mode optical fiber used for long distance transmission.

Long wavelength (1000BASE-LX) optical transceivers are specified so that the same transceiver can operate with either single-mode fiber (SMF) or MMF optical fiber (and again, it obviously can be plugged into only one cable type at any one time). However, both the attenuation and bandwidth of multimode fiber are generally better at long wavelengths than at short wavelengths. Hence, with multimode fiber and mode conditioning, 1000BASE-LX generally allows operation over much longer link lengths than 1000BASE-SX.

For example, even in the worst case, 1000BASE-LX can transmit twice as far as 1000BASE-SX on 62.5 μm MMF cable. However, 1000BASE-LX transceivers are more costly than 1000BASE-SX transceivers and there is also the additional cost of the mode conditioning patch cord. Nevertheless, the capability of 1000BASE-LX to transmit over the full range of building backbone distances with multimode fiber and up to 5 km on single-mode fiber is very important. Figure 11.3 summarizes the Gigabit Ethernet-defined operating ranges for several common cable types.

Figure 11.3   Defined Gigabit Ethernet Operating Ranges for Common Fibers

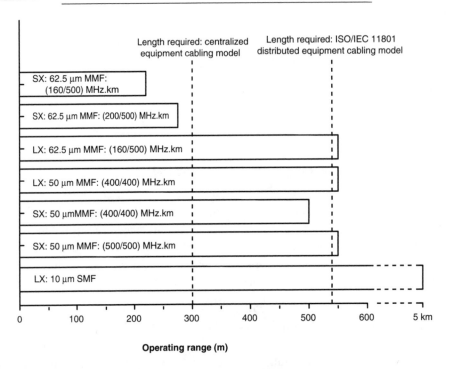

Operating range (m)

> **Note**
>
> The notation (160/500) MHz.km in the top bar of Figure 11.3 means that the fiber bandwidth is specified as 160 MHz.km for short-wavelength transmission and 500 MHz.km for long-wavelength transmission.

Figure 11.4 shows a block diagram of a simplex optical PMD link configured according to the Gigabit Ethernet cable model.

Figure 11.4 Gigabit Ethernet Optical PMD Link Cable Model

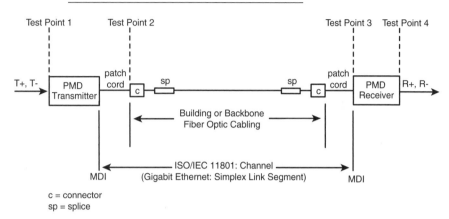

The PMD transmitter must be connected to the installed cable or to test equipment using a patch cord. Four test points are identified:

- Test Point 1 is at the input to the PMD transmitter. Although Gigabit Ethernet specifies that the PMD must accept code-bits for transmission via the serial interface, the physical signals at Test Point 1 are not specified because this interface is generally not exposed, but is buried within a product. However, many implementations use positive emitter coupled logic levels (PECL) at this interface.

- Test Point 2 is defined as the output of a short (2–5 m) patch cord that is connected to the PMD transmitter. All optical transmit parameters are measured at Test Point 2. For multimode operation with 1000BASE-LX, *a single-mode offset-launch patch cord mode conditioner must be used* for compliance testing. The patch cord is connected to the transmitter, and Test Point 2 is the output of the mode-conditioning patch cord.

- Test Point 3 is the output of the Gigabit Ethernet simplex optical link segment. This is the output that would be connected to the PMD optical receiver at the MDI.

- Test Point 4 is the serial output of the PMD. Again, although Gigabit Ethernet specifies that the PMD must output code-bits to the PMA via the serial interface, the physical signals at Test Point 4 are not specified. However, PECL is a common output format.

The Gigabit Ethernet cable model is based on the worst-case optical cable model defined in ISO/IEC 11801.

11.1.1 Cable Model and Component Specifications

The insertion loss of the individual connectors is not specified. Rather, a total connection insertion-loss budget is defined—1.5 dB for multimode fiber and 2 dB for single-mode fiber. The power budget of Gigabit Ethernet is quite low because Gigabit Ethernet assumes active regeneration after each link segment. As a result, the connection-loss allocations are unlikely to support passive cascading of horizontal and building backbone or building and campus backbone optical links. If this is attempted, the installer must ensure that the Gigabit Ethernet link power budget is met. Worst-case cable attenuation values are calculated using the cable attenuation Equation 9.14 in Chapter 9.

To limit reflection-induced laser noise (see Chapter 9, section 9.9), the connector return loss is specified as 20 dB for multimode fiber cables and 26 dB for single-mode fiber cables.

Both SX and LX full-duplex transceivers use the same MDI connector type—the SC connector. However, to increase the port density of switches and repeaters, new small-form-factor (SFF) transceivers are becoming popular (see Figure 11.5). Moving from right to left, Figure 11.5 shows the following: a full-duplex SFF MT-RJ transceiver, a full-duplex SC transceiver, and (for a size comparison) two ASICs having the dimensions 23 mm by 17 mm. As Figure 11.5 shows, the small-form-factor full-duplex MT-RJ transceiver is about half of the volume of the SC-based transceiver. This means that the SFF MT-RJ transceiver has a packing density similar to that of an RJ45 connector used for unshielded twisted pair (UTP) systems.

Figure 11.5   Small-Form-Factor MT-RJ and SC Transceiver Comparison

The 1000BASE-LX transceiver is connected to the multimode cable by a mode-conditioning offset-launch patch cord. Although it will still operate perfectly if it is *followed* by other patch cords, the mode-conditioning patch cord *must* be connected to the transceiver. Figure 11.6 shows a sketch of a mode-conditioning patch cord (see Chapter 10, section 10.2 for a complete explanation of the offset-launch mode-conditioner and its operation).

Figure 11.6   1000BASE-LX Single-Mode Fiber Offset-Launch Mode-Conditioning Patch Cord Assembly

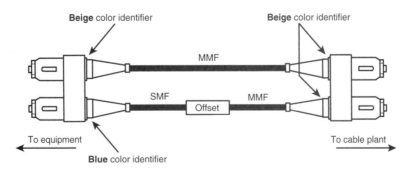

The patch cord is color-coded and labeled as shown in Figure 11.6 to reduce the risk of misconnection. The end that plugs into the Gigabit Ethernet equipment (switch, repeater, NIC) is labeled *To equipment;* the other end, which connects to the cable plant or following regular multimode patch cord, is labeled *To cable plant.*

> **Note**
>
> The preceding paragraph is strictly true to the IEEE 802.3z standard, however, the link will still operate correctly over shorter distances with a regular (non-offset) MMF patch cord. If a regular patch cord is used with 1000BASE-LX transceivers, the maximum operational length of the fiber is reduced to about 250 m.

The coupled-power-ratio (CPR) values quoted for 1000BASE-LX are the CPR values measured directly out of the mode conditioning patch cord. As discussed in Chapter 10, the 1000BASE-LX offset-launch mode-conditioning patch cord provides *almost perfect* mode conditioning. The mode-conditioning patch cords have a very low insertion loss of less than 0.5 dB. In addition, mode-conditioning patch cords have an internal SMF-to-MMF offset launch where the offset equals (20 ± 3) µm for 62.5 µm MMF fiber and (14 ± 2) µm for 50 µm MMF fiber, and where the angular offset is less than $1°$.

The CPR specification values are very useful because they can be used to confirm that the patch cord has been manufactured properly and is field testable. Some manufacturers even monitor the CPR using calibrated camera systems as the patch cord is being fabricated and use it in a feedback system to ensure specification compliance. Finally, the offset launch is an integral part of the patch cord, and the offset is not adjustable.

11.1.2 *Optical Transmit Parameters*

Table 11.1 summarizes the optical transmit parameters for the optical PMDs. All of these parameters can be measured with commonly available test equipment as follows:

- Wavelength and rms spectral width are standard functions for optical spectral analyzers.

- Rise and fall times and the optical extinction ratio are standard functions of most optical communications grade oscilloscopes that include optical inputs.

- Optical power is measured using optical power meters.

- Coupled power ratio is measured using an optical power meter, and a single-mode and a multimode patch cord.

Table 11.1   Optical Transmit Parameters

Fiber Core Diameter (μm)	SX: 50 μm MMF	SX: 62.5 μm MMF	LX: 10 μm SMF	LX: 50 μm MMF	LX: 62.5 μm MMF
Center Wavelength Range (nm)	770–830	> 830–860	1,270–1,355	1,270–1,355	1,270–1,355
Maximum Transition Time (ns)	0.21	0.26	0.26	0.26	0.26
Maximum RMS Spectral Width (nm)	0.85	0.85	4	4	4
Minimum Average Optical Launch Power (dBm)	–9.5	–9.5	–11.0	–11.5	–11.5
Minimum Extinction Ratio (dB)	9	9	9	9	9
Maximum RIN (dB/Hz)	–117	–117	–120	–120	–120
Minimum Coupled Power Ratio (dB)	9	9	NA	12–20	28–40

Note

For SX links, the maximum allowed transmit power is the lesser of the class 1 eye safety limit or the maximum allowed receive power as defined in section 11.1.3, Table 11.2. For LX links, the maximum allowed transmit power is –3 dBm.

Apart from the CPR values, Table 11.1 provides all the transmit input parameters required by the Gigabit Ethernet link model. In addition, the Gigabit Ethernet standard specifies that high optical power (highest light intensity) corresponds to a code-bit value of ONE, and low optical power to a code-bit value of ZERO. The transmit specifications are completed with the eye mask shown in Figure 11.7.

Figure 11.7   Gigabit Ethernet Transmit Eye Mask Measured at Test Point 2 (from Figure 11.4)

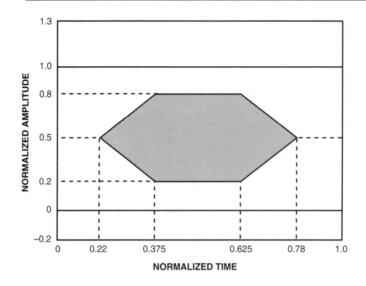

It should be obvious (hopefully) that the 1000BASE-LX operation with single-mode fiber needs no mode conditioning—this is why CPR is not applicable (N/A) for this case. The CPR values were added to ensure at least partial mode conditioning of the transmitter, which reduces differential mode delay (DMD) in multimode fiber links. The concept of DMD was introduced in Figures 6.25b and 6.26a in Chapter 6, "Fundamentals of Fiber Optic Communication," and was discussed in detail in Chapter 10 in sections 10.1 and 10.2. The basic problem is that lasers, especially when launched near the optical axis of a multimode fiber, can excite only a few mode groups. If the velocity matching of the graded index fiber is not good for these mode groups, possibly because of a slight index profile defect, the propagation delay between the excited mode groups can be very different. And because only a few mode groups have been excited, the bandwidth can be very different from the OFL bandwidth, in many cases less than the OFL specification.

For 1000BASE-SX, the CPR specification values are too low to guarantee significant mode conditioning—but they do help. For example, one class of launch that would meet the 1000BASE-SX CPR specification is the so-called radial overfilled launch (see section 10.2 in Chapter 10 for more information on ROFL)—but ROFL is almost the worst case in terms of generating large DMD values!

11.1.3 Optical Receive Parameters

Table 11.2 summarizes the optical receive parameters for the optical PMDs.

Table 11.2   Optical Receive Parameters

Fiber Core Diameter (μm)	SX: 50 μm MMF	SX: 62.5 μm MMF	LX: 10 μm SMF	LX: 50 μm MMF	LX: 62.5 μm MMF
Center Wavelength Range (nm)	770–860	770–860	1,270–1,355	1,270–1,355	1,270–1,355
Maximum Average Receive Power (dBm)	0	0	−3	−3	−3
Center of Eye Sensitivity (nm)	−17	−17	−19	−19	−19
Stressed Sensitivity (dBm)	−13.5	−12.5	−14.4	−14.4	−14.4
Maximum Return Loss (dB)	12	12	12	12	12
Maximum Electrical 3 dB Upper Bandwidth (MHz)	1,500	1,500	1,500	1,500	1,500

For 1000BASE-LX, the maximum receive power level is only −3 dBm. This level was chosen to avoid saturation of the electronics in commonly available optical receiver designs (those originally designed for use in SONET or ATM Forum links) for long-wavelength operation. The maximum receiver return loss is quite high, −12 dB. Thus, as discussed in Chapter 9, the signal-to-noise ratio (SNR) of the link will be severely reduced by worst-case reflections; hence, the need for reasonably good connector return loss specifications.

There are two sensitivity specifications that must be met by the optical PMD receiver:

• Center of received eye sensitivity

• Stressed receiver sensitivity

The center of eye sensitivity is the normal specification for receiver sensitivity that has been used in all optical link standards. This sensitivity would usually be obtained using a bit error rate (BER) tester to measure the BER as a function of received power, usually called the BER curve, for the optical receiver. Gigabit Ethernet has an average BER specification of less than 1 error in 10^{12} bits. The center of eye sensitivity is the minimum received optical power required to meet this BER specification. However, it would take a long time, many hours, to directly test for a BER of 1 in 10^{12}. For this reason, it is acceptable to deduce the center of eye sensitivity by extrapolation of the measured BER curve.

The Gigabit Ethernet task force introduced receiver conformance requirements and tests as part of its solution to the DMD problems of multimode fiber links (see Chapter 10, sections 10.1 and 10.2). These new requirements and tests are as follows:

- The stressed-receiver sensitivity specification

- A 3 dB upper frequency cut-off specification

- Test methods to confirm PMD conformance (see sidebar, "Receiver Stress Test Methodology")

Both Gigabit Ethernet sensitivity specifications assume that the test laser has an extinction ratio of 9 dB, and as such, include the worst-case extinction ratio power penalty (1.1 dB) of the laser.

Laser-fiber-launch-induced DMD effects can result in significant deterministic jitter at the output of the optical receiver. Unfortunately, poor receiver design can also exacerbate this problem. The goal of the 3 dB upper frequency cutoff specification is to ensure that a minimum amount of filtering is included in the receiver to partially alleviate DMD jitter.

The receiver stress sensitivity test and receiver-bandwidth conformance test are used to ensure that Gigabit Ethernet receivers have the required bandwidth and that they adequately control jitter. These tests are discussed in sections 11.1.3.1 and 11.3.1.2.

11.1.3.1   Receiver Stress Test Signal

The IEEE 802.3z standard recommends the following method for producing the stress test signal:

1. The test data pattern is first input to a length of coaxial cable.

2. The output of the coaxial cable is fed into a limiting amplifier.

3. The output of the limiting amplifier is fed into a Bessel-Thompson filter.

4. The output of the filter drives a linear laser source.

5. The laser output is connected to an optical attenuator.

6. The output of the optical attenuator is input to the receiver under test.

The coaxial cable introduces the required amount of DCD (at least 65 ps). It is up to the test implementer to determine experimentally the correct length of coaxial cable for this purpose. The coaxial cable also distorts the pulse transition shape of the transmitted code bits, and the limiting amplifier is used to restore fast rise and fall times. The Bessel-Thompson filter is selected to produce the required vertical eye closure for the test. The optical attenuator is used to control the optical power delivered to the receiver under test. The optical attenuator must be of a design that is known not to introduce mode selective loss.

Figure 11.8 defines the stress-test signal for Test Point 3 in Figure 11.4. Figure 11.8 shows the distorted eye diagram of the test signal as defined by IEEE 802.3z.

Figure 11.8   Required Characteristics of the Conformance Test Signal at Test Point 3 in Figure 11.4

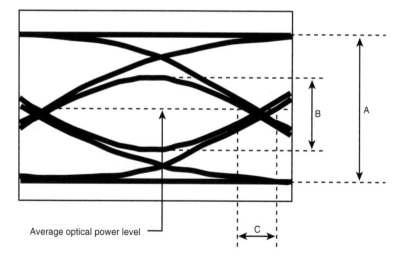

The three quantities marked A, B, and C define the stressed eye diagram. The ratio (A/B) is called the *vertical eye closure* and its value is 2.2 dB for 1000BASE-SX receivers for use with 50 μm MMF. For all other cases, the vertical eye closure is 2.6 dB. The horizontal eye closure, C in Figure 11.8, must have a high frequency duty cycle distortion (DCD) component with a minimum duration of 65 ps. The horizontal eye closure is measured at the level defined by the average optical power of the test signal, which, as shown in the figure, may not necessarily be at the crossing of the eye. The vertical and horizontal eye closures used for receiver conformance testing are verified using a fast photodetector and amplifier. It is recommended that the bandwidth of the photodetector/amplifier combination be at least 2.5 GHz and that it be coupled through a 1.875 GHz fourth-order Bessel-Thompson filter to the oscilloscope input.

11.1.3.2   Upper Frequency Cut-Off Measurement Method

Figure 11.9 shows the recommended test setup for the receiver bandwidth measurement.

Figure 11.9   Test Setup for Measurement of Receiver Bandwidth

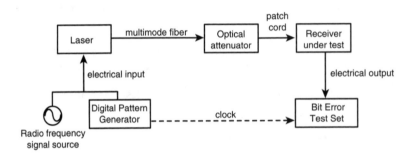

The test is performed with a linear laser source suitable for analog signal transmission. The laser is simultaneously modulated by the digital data signal and by the asynchronous analog signal produced by the frequency generator. The frequency response of the laser must be sufficient to allow it to respond to both the digital modulation and the analog modulation. The frequency response of the radio frequency (RF) signal generator, any RF combiners that are used, and the laser should be calibrated before the test. The test should be started at a low frequency (say 50 MHz). The RF power should then be increased until the center of the eye BER is degraded to a predetermined BER (say 10^{-7}).

The RF frequency should then be increased in steps (of say 100 MHz) and the power required to maintain the predetermined BER should be recorded at each step. The 3 dB bandwidth is the frequency at which the RF power, after correction for any calibration effects, has been increased by 3 dB compared to its low frequency value to produce the predetermined BER. If necessary, the 3 dB frequency can be determined by interpolation between the measured points.

11.1.4   Worst-Case Optical Power Budget Examples

This section works through the worst-case power budget for 1000BASE-SX and 1000BASE-LX through 62.5 μm MMF and 1000BASE-LX through single-mode fiber.

The discussion also covers operation with 50 μm MMF and focuses on the variation of the operating range as a function of modal bandwidth.

For MMF links, the three most significant power-budget terms are the ISI penalty (see Chapter 9, section 9.6), the cable attenuation, and the connection-loss budget. Figure 11.10 plots the variation of these terms as a function of link length for the 1000BASE-SX, 62.5 μm MMF worst-case link parameters. The connection-loss budget is fixed at 1.5 dB. Figure 11.10 plots the sum of the connection loss and the cable loss, which is called the *channel-insertion loss* in the IEEE 802.3z standard. The Gigabit Ethernet committee considered links to be ISI limited when the ISI penalty had reached about 3.6 dB (see Chapter 9, section 9.6).

Figure 11.10   Gigabit Ethernet Link Model Calculations for 1000BASE-SX, 62.5 μm MMF

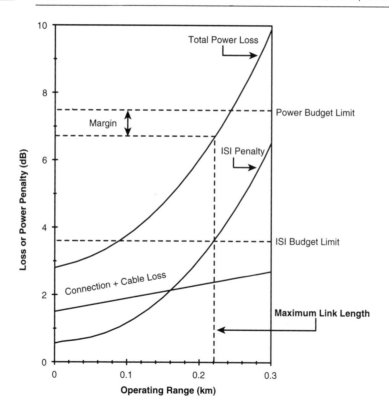

Figure 11.10 identifies both the ISI budget limit and the power budget limit on the graph for reference purposes. Because the ISI penalty curve crosses the ISI budget limit before the total power curve crosses the power budget limit, the 1000BASE-SX, 62.5 μm MMF link is ISI limited. This means that you cannot increase the operating range by increasing the power budget. A power margin 0.84 dB remains, and the link length is only 220 m. For the plot of Figure 11.10, the modal bandwidth is assumed to be 160 MHz.km. If the modal bandwidth were increased to 200 MHz.km, the link would still be ISI limited, but to a maximum operating range of 275 m, and the margin would be slightly reduced by the additional cable attenuation to 0.6 dB.

There are two 1000BASE-SX modal bandwidth cases: 400 MHz.km and 500 MHz.km for 50 μm MMF. The operating ranges for these cases are power budgets limited to 500 m and 550 m, respectively, as shown in Figure 11.3. The power margins are about 0.1 dB and 0.4 dB for the 400 MHz.km and the 500 MHz.km cases, respectively. The difference is mainly due to the increased ISI penalty for the 400 MHz.km case. However, the ISI penalty for the 400 MHz.km case is quite large at 3.2 dB and is close to the ISI-limited link length as was discovered in field testing (see Chapter 10, Figures 10.5 and 10.6).

Figure 11.11 is for the 1000BASE-LX, 62.5 μm MMF worst-case link parameters. Figure 11.1 also identifies the ISI limit and the power budget limit. Clearly, the 1000BASE-LX, 62.5 μm MMF link is not ISI limited, and a power margin of about 1.7 dB remains for the specified building backbone operating range of 550 m. Using the 1.7 dB of power margin would allow the worst-case link to operate to its ISI-limited length of 700 m (identified as *maximum link length* on the graph) and still leave a small power margin.

Figure 11.11   Gigabit Ethernet Link Model Calculations for 1000BASE-LX, 62.5 μm MMF

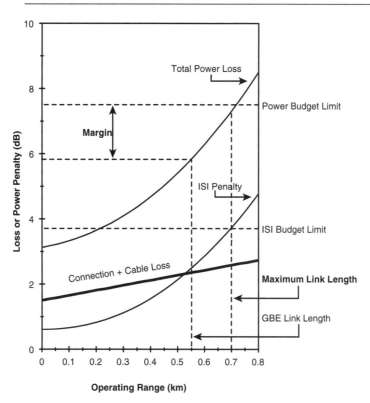

The Gigabit Ethernet committee only specified 550 m for 1000BASE-LX on multimode fiber because this is the relevant distance as far as ISO/IEC 11801 is concerned. A modal bandwidth of 500 MHz.km is assumed for Figure 11.11. For the case of 50 μm MMF, the modal bandwidth can be either 500 MHz.km or 400 MHz.km. For the 500 MHz.km case, the power margin is reduced by about 0.5 dB, compared to the 62.5 μm MMF case, due to increasing the modal noise allocation from 0.5 dB to 1 dB (see Chapter 9, sections 9.2 and 9.13). For the 400 MHz.km case, the power margin is reduced still further to around 0.1 dB due to an additional 1 dB of ISI penalty on top of the modal noise allocation increase of 0.5 dB—this case is ISI limited, as the ISI penalty is 3.6 dB.

Figure 11.12 plots the operating range versus modal bandwidth for the worst-case 1000BASE-LX and 1000BASE-SX scenarios (where every parameter apart from modal bandwidth is at its worst-case value). The dotted lines illustrate the ISI asymptotic limit and the attenuation asymptotic limit. The ISI limit is approached for very low modal bandwidths, and the attenuation limit is approached for very high modal bandwidths.

Figure 11.12   Operating Range Versus Modal Bandwidth According to Gigabit Ethernet Link Model

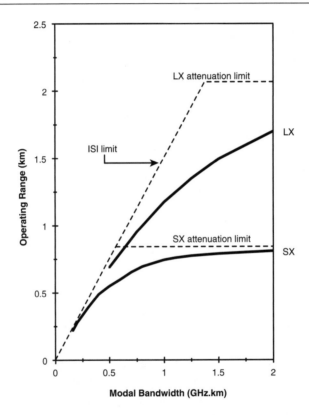

The attenuation asymptotic operating ranges are 2 km and 0.8 km for the LX and SX operation, respectively. In the limit, for the same worst-case power budget, the LX operating range is 2.5 times that for the SX. If the worst-case modal bandwidth (WCMB) of a cable to be used for a Gigabit Ethernet link has been measured or is known, then its operating range can be estimated from Figure 11.12. Although Figure 11.12 was calculated for 62.5 μm MMF, it can also safely be used for 50 μm MMF because it will slightly underestimate the worst-case operating range for that fiber.

Figure 11.13 plots the 1000BASE-LX, single-mode worst-case link parameters. Because the bandwidth of single-mode fiber is essentially infinite, ISI is not a limiting issue. The limiting penalties in this case are the channel-insertion loss and the mode partition noise (MPN) penalty. As covered in sections 9.11 and 9.14 in Chapter 9, it is very dangerous to allow the MPN penalty to grow much above 1 dB. The 1000BASE-LX, single-mode maximum operating range is therefore limited by the MPN penalty to 5 km, and for this case there is a small power margin of around 0.2 dB.

Figure 11.13 Gigabit Ethernet Link Model Calculations for 1000BASE-LX, 10 µm SMF

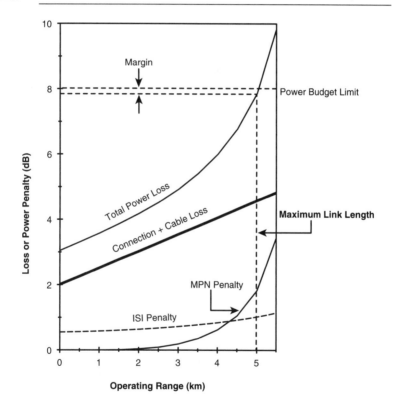

11.2 The Short-Haul Copper PMD

There is usually the need to interconnect equipment (such as repeaters, switches, bridges, and routers) within racks or wiring closets. Sometimes even network servers may be collocated within a single closet, and possibly even within the same equipment rack! Although the optical links could be used for this short distance, interconnection with a short copper link is probably more convenient and cost-effective. The 1000BASE-CX short-haul copper link was specifically developed for this purpose. It might seem like overkill to have developed this copper link specification within a LAN standard; however, Gigabit Ethernet interoperation was deemed an overriding factor that dictated the necessity for 1000BASE-CX standardization.

The 1000BASE-CX short-haul copper PMD sublayer has the following components:

- Transmitter, which consists of the following components:
  - Transmit electrical circuit
  - MDI connector receptacle
- A single continuous cable assembly, which consists of the following components:
  - Shielded, dual-pair, balanced, 150 Ω, copper cable
  - Connectors
  - If required, an integral passive equalizer
- Receiver, which consists of the following components:
  - MDI connector receptacle
  - Receive electrical circuit
  - Signal detect circuit

Clearly, the copper PMD is much simpler than the optical PMDs because, with the exception of signal detection, all functions can be implemented with passive electrical components (resistors, capacitors, and inductors).

11.2.1 1000BASE-CX Copper Link Model

Figure 11.14 shows the Gigabit Ethernet short-haul 1000BASE-CX copper PMD-link model (the signal detect output has been omitted to simplify the figure).

Figure 11.14   Gigabit Ethernet Short-Haul Copper PMD-Link Model

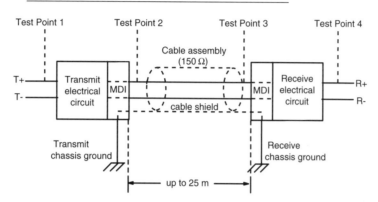

Note: Only one continuous cable assembly may be used to connect 1000BASE-CX systems

The copper link is full-duplex capable, but for clarity only one of the two contra-transmitting simplex copper links is shown. Short-haul copper PMD transceivers consist of the transmit electrical circuit, the receive electrical circuits, and the media dependent interface (MDI). Two PMDs, at either end of a link, are connected to the cable assembly via the MDI connectors. The cable assembly shield is connected to the chassis ground of the equipment through the shell of the MDI connector.

Note

For safe operation, the chassis ground of the equipment being interconnected must be connected to the same building wiring-zone ground. This is because significant and potentially dangerous electrical currents can be generated if the equipment at each end of a 1000BASE-CX link have different ground potentials. If proper grounding cannot be guaranteed, an optical link should be used.

Like the optical PMD, four link test points are defined, as shown in Figure 11.14. The physical signals at Test Points 1 and 4 are not specified, as these points would be buried within the equipment. The signal at Test Point 2 is the transmit signal, and the signal at Test Point 3 is the receive signal. These signals will be discussed in the following sections.

11.2.2 Copper Transmitter

The copper transmitter usually uses a passive transmit electrical circuit to condition the signal supplied by the PMA (typically a SERDES chip) for transmission over the cable assembly. The transmit electrical circuit will also perform any impedance matching that may be required.

The important transmit signal characteristics are defined for Test Point 2 by eye masks. Figure 11.15 shows the absolute eye mask for 1000BASE-CX.

Figure 11.15   Superimposed 1000BASE-CX Transmit and Receive Eye Masks

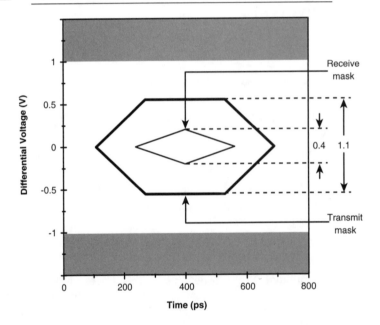

IEEE 802.3z uses an additional transmit eye mask (not shown) with normalized amplitudes to limit overshoot to less than 10 percent and the undershoot to less than 20 percent for both the logic one and logic zero signal levels. The nominal differential transmit voltage levels are consistent with the PECL levels produced by most SERDES chipsets (see Figure 11.15). The transmit signal rise- and falltimes are not defined by the eye mask, but the standard dictates that they must be between 85 ps and 327 ps. For proper operation, the differential skew of the transmitted signal must be quite low—less than 25 ps at Test Point 2.

11.2.3 Copper Cable Assembly

A Gigabit Ethernet short-haul copper cable assembly consists of a continuous, shielded, two pair, balanced cable, with a nominal impedance of 150 Ω. The cable assembly is terminated at each end with MDI shielded plug (male) connectors. The maximum allowed differential skew within a single pair of the cable assembly is 150 ps. The standard also recommends that the cable attenuation, measured at a frequency of 625 MHz, should be less than 8.8 dB, and that the near-end crosstalk (NEXT) loss, as measured with a differential time domain reflectometer, having a risetime of 85 ps, should be at least 24.5 dB.

Figure 5.15 in Chapter 5, "Fundamentals of Baseband Transmission," illustrated that typical copper cables would need equalization in order for 1000BASE-CX to operate over a 25 m link length. For this reason, cable assemblies may include passive fixed equalization circuits. This is one of the reasons that cable assemblies must not be connected or strung together. If equalizers are used as part of a cable assembly, the cable must be marked with information to clarify its operational characteristics.

The MDI connector preferred by Gigabit Ethernet is the newly developed style-2 connector shown, along with the pin-outs required by Gigabit Ethernet, in Figure 11.16.

Figure 11.16 Sketch of the Style-2 Connector Showing Receptacle Pin Assignments

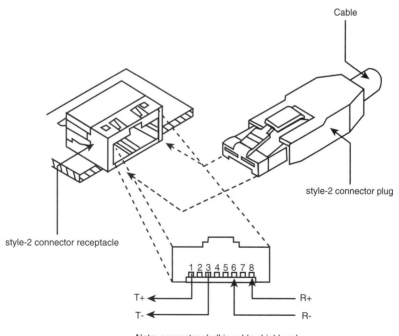

The style-2 connector is preferred by Gigabit Ethernet because there are potential inter-operation problems with style-1 connectors. The Gigabit Ethernet style-1 connector is the common 9-pin, shielded, D-sub-miniature connector. This type of connector is used for IEEE 802.5 Token Ring, 100VG-AnyLAN, Fibre Channel, and many other systems that have specified shielded twisted pair (STP) link options. Unfortunately, many existing style-1 connectors are not suitable for Gigabit Ethernet operation. Therefore, if style-1 connectors are used, they must have a specification that maintains the signal integrity of Gigabit Ethernet. Obviously, to avoid problems, both ends of the link must use high specification style-1 connectors.

Ideally, only one connector style would have been specified by Gigabit Ethernet; however, within the standards committee, consensus could not be reached on this issue. Due to the newness of the style-2 connector, the committee felt it needed a backup path. For all its potential problems, with a proper specification, the style-1 connector was known to work and so two 1000BASE-CX MDI connector styles exist.

11.2.4 Copper Receiver

The copper receiver uses a receive electrical circuit to condition the signal before it is passed on to the PMA (usually a SERDES chip). The receive circuit also performs any impedance matching that might be required. In addition, the receive circuit must perform the signal detect function.

The receive signal characteristics are defined at Test Point 3 in terms of a receive eye mask. Figure 11.15 shows the receive eye mask for 1000BASE-CX as an inset within the transmit mask. Clearly significant eye closure is allowed. In fact, the ratio of the peak eye opening (amplitude) of the inner eye mask curves defining the receive and transmit eye masks is 8.8 dB. This ratio is equal to the maximum cable assembly attenuation, measured at a frequency of 625 MHz, as recommended by the IEEE 802.3z.

Figure 11.17 shows a simulation of the output signal at Test Point 3 where a perfect transmit signal was passed through a 15 m length of relatively good copper cable. The superimposed receive eye mask clearly indicates that equalization would be required to reach 25 m with this cable type. According to the standard, for proper operation the differential skew of the received signal, at Test Point 3, must be less than 175 ps.

Figure 11.17   Simulated Unequalized 1000BASE-CX Received Eye Diagram Shown with the Receive Eye Mask

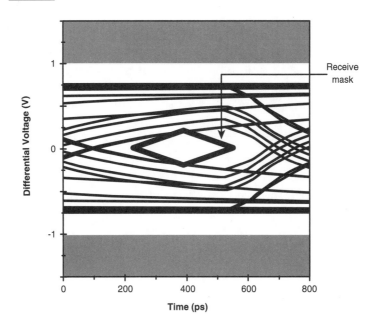

11.3 Summary

This chapter reviewed the functions and components of the Gigabit Ethernet, baseband, optical, and short-haul copper PMDs. The chapter also discussed the cable model, the link model, and the specifications for the PMDs. Figure 11.4 presented the operating ranges of the optical links and the ranges defined in the standard. It may not have been obvious, but we actually discovered that 1000BASE-LX is by far the most versatile Gigabit Ethernet PMD option for the following operating ranges:

- Operating range for 1000BASE-LX operation *without* offset launch patch cords

  - 62.5 µm MMF: 2 to 250 m

  - 50 µm: 2 to 300 m

  - SMF: 2 to 5 km

- Operating range for 1000BASE-LX operation *with* offset launch patch cords

  - 62.5 μm MMF: 2 to 700 m

  - 50 μm MMF: 2 to 550 m

The chapter also showed that, strictly speaking, using 1000BASE-LX without offset launch mode conditioning patch cords is not Gigabit Ethernet compliant. And to line up with the building backbone wiring standard link length requirement of about 540 m, IEEE 802.3z only quoted a 550 m operation length for 1000BASE-LX operation with 62.5 μm MMF. However, according to the Gigabit Ethernet link model, it has enough ISI and power budget margin to operate to 700 m. So, for the conditions stated, 1000BASE-LX links will work perfectly over the operating ranges quoted above. Although long-wavelength, 1000BASE-LX transceivers are more expensive than short-wavelength, 1000BASE-SX transceivers, they are in fact very cost-effective because of their additional versatility.

PART VI

Network Installation
and System Considerations

The purpose of this part of the book is to consolidate the material in the previous eleven chapters and to discuss the present and future systems factors that must be considered when you plan for a new network or for an upgrade to an existing network. This part of the book is also a departure from the earlier chapters in that it has more of a "how to" than "what is" emphasis.

Chapter 12: The Cable Plant: Installation and Management

Chapter 13: Upgrading Ethernet LANs: System and Topology Considerations

Chapter 14: Gigabit Ethernet in Context with Other LAN Technologies

Chapter 15: The Future: Gigabit Ethernet and Beyond

12

The Cable Plant: Installation and Management

The purpose of this chapter is to introduce and discuss the most long-lasting and, hence, the most often neglected part of the network—the cable plant. Hardware and software designers, equipment salespeople, and network users simply presume that there is (or will be) one, that it will connect the areas that need to be interconnected, and that the individual links will meet the technical criteria necessary to carry the transmitted signals for the selected network protocol.

Previous chapters spent considerable time discussing signal encoding/decoding, generation/ detection, and transmission through single-mode and multimode optical fibers and shielded twisted pair (STP) cable. We also covered the need for Gigabit Ethernet to be able to operate over existing cable plants. However, our discussions have not included coverage of the cable plants themselves, or how you would go about planning for their installation, management, and upgrade.

Yes, cable plants do indeed need to be managed. You need to know how many cables and links you have; where they go; what their length and type are; which are being used; and whether there are enough unused links of the required length and type still available in the proper locations to allow the next round of moves, changes, and additions. Furthermore, if the reconfiguration requires adding cables and links to the existing plant, you need to know what type of cables will need to be installed, where you can possibly put them, whether there is space available to do it, and if not, where else they can safely be installed with minimal disruption to current operations. And finally, you need to know where everything is so that you can warn future construction crews before they accidentally sever hidden cable runs.

This chapter begins with an overview of ISO/IEC 11801 structured cabling requirements. This overview is followed by a discussion of the cable plant infrastructure installation and documentation. The next sections look at network cables and their installation, testing/validation, and documentation requirements. The chapter concludes with short discussions on cable plant management and security. A few anecdotal examples of installations gone bad are provided along the way to prevent you from finding yourself in similar situations.

12.1 Structured Cabling

Because the life expectancy of network cable plants is in excess of 10 years, the cable plant must be designed with the possibility of intermittent changes and additions. Figure 12.1 illustrates the hierarchical cabling topology and maximum link lengths recommended for Ethernet LANs and specified by ISO/IEC 11801. Network connection points are provided at each of the following locations:

- **Campus Distributor**. The term "campus" refers to a facility with two or more buildings in a relatively small area. The campus distributor is the central point of the campus backbone and the telecom connection point with the outside world. In Ethernet LANs, the campus distributor would typically be a Gigabit switch with telecom interface capability.

- **Building Distributor**. This is the building's connection point to the campus backbone. An Ethernet building distributor would typically be a 1,000/100 or 1,000/100/10 Mbps switch.

- **Floor Distributor**. This is the floor's connection point to the building distributor. The standard recommends at least one floor distributor for every 1,000 m² of floor space in office environments, and if possible, a separate distributor for each floor in the building. An Ethernet floor distributor would typically be a 1,000/100/10 or 100/10 Mbps switch.

- **Telecom Outlet**. This is the network connection point for the end station.

One or more switches, repeaters, or routers along with their associated connection/patch panels are typically installed at each distributor location, which may also include network file servers.

The model implements a star topology with optional interconnects at the campus level between building distributors, and at the building level between floor distributors. The interconnects provide path redundancy and can be used to relieve the traffic loads on the next higher level switches, if necessary. (The Spanning Tree Algorithm and the various routing protocols will limit the interconnection between communicating end stations to a single route at any time—see Chapter 4, "Gigabit Repeaters, Bridges, Routers, and Switches," section 4.2.3.)

Figure 12.1   The ISO/IEC 11801 Cable Model

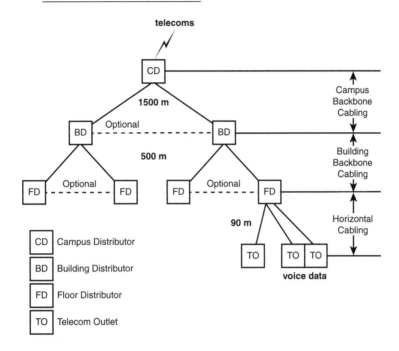

Not all distributor levels are required in every facility. A small legal office, for example, might need only a floor distributor that, in this case, would also have the telecom connection to the outside world. Similarly, an organization having a single, multifloor building would need only a building distributor and several floor distributors.

12.2   The Cable Plant Infrastructure

The cable plant infrastructure is more than just the cables that interconnect the current network. The infrastructure also includes all the facilities (conduits, cable trays, manholes, and so on) through which the cables are run, plus the connection (or patch) panels and the telecom outlets where the individual link-to-end station connections are made.

Figure 12.2 depicts an example backbone cable system that could be used on a small-to-medium campus. It contains all the elements that might be found in any backbone system: underground cable runs, manholes (or pull boxes), overhead cables, and building entries.

Figure 12.2   Example Campus Backbone Cabling

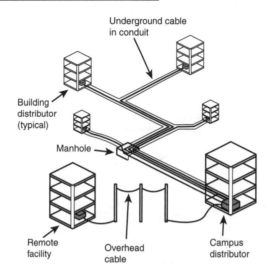

Because change is inevitable, you can either provide spare conduits or install cables with excess capacity (spare fibers) to allow for future growth. Both options are recommended (see section 13.4.6.1 of Chapter 13, "Upgrading Ethernet LANs: System and Topology Considerations").

12.2.1   *Fiber Optic Cable Installation Restrictions*

Before going any further, you need to review some fiber optic cable restrictions that can affect conduit bend radii and other design considerations during cable installation.

The outside diameter (OD) of typical inside-use fiber optic cable varies from 1/8" (~3.2 mm) to 1" (25.4 mm), depending on the number of fibers and type of covering. Outside-use cables usually have somewhat larger ODs. The actual fibers are run through a buffer tube that allows room for the fibers to move with respect to each other, as shown by the example of Siecor's FREEDM/LST cable depicted in Figure 12.3. This cable is available in 2, 6, or 12 fiber configurations.

Fiber optic cables with buffer tubes have what is known as a *loose tube* configuration. While fibers are quite strong and quite flexible, the loose tube construction allows the cables to be installed without stressing the fibers (the buffer tube may or may not be filled with a moisture-resistant gel). While Figure 12.3 shows only a few fibers in one buffer tube, larger cables with hundreds of fibers are constructed with multiple buffer tubes so that the fibers in each tube will still have room for movement.

Figure 12.3 An Example of a Loose-Tube Fiber Optic Cable

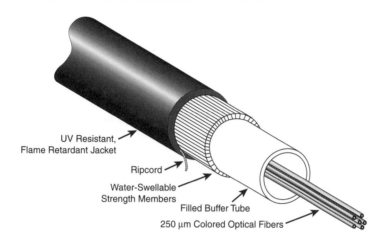

UV Resistant,
Flame Retardant Jacket

Ripcord

Water-Swellable
Strength Members

Filled Buffer Tube

250 μm Colored Optical Fibers

Courtesy of Siecor, Hickory, NC

The *maximum pulling tension* for fiber cable varies from 50 to more than 800 lbs., depending on the size of the cable and whether or not it has an imbedded strength member to support the pull. The tension required to pull a cable through a conduit depends on the total included bend angle in the conduit (see section 12.2.3.1) and whether or not a friction-reducing lubricant is used. The actual pulling tension should never be greater than the maximum specified for the cable.

Note

Only pulling lubricants that are specifically rated for fiber optic cable should be used. Some electrical-cable friction-reducing lubricants have been known to cause stress cracking in the polyethylene outer jackets used on some fiber cables.

The *minimum bending radius* for fiber cable is roughly 20X the cable OD, and care must be taken to ensure the following:

- The radii of all conduit bends and cable pulling fixtures (for example, pulleys and capstans) must be greater than the specified minimum radius for the cable.

- Cable must never be allowed to kink or knot while it is being pulled through conduit or laid in cable troughs or ducts.

- The radius of all bends anywhere in the installed cable must be greater than the specified minimum radius for the cable.

- Cable installers must never be allowed to wrap the cable around their hands to get a better grip.

Because copper cable is typically less susceptible to damage than fiber cable, any installation design that meets fiber cable requirements will also meet copper cable pulling requirements for the same cable diameters.

12.2.2 *Building Conduit and Cable Troughs*

Figure 12.4 depicts the typical inside cabling for a building. Vertical risers may be installed in a conduit or they may be secured to the wall as shown in the figure. Horizontal runs can be overhead in cable troughs, or in the case of raised floors, below the floor in cable ducts. Care must be taken in each case to ensure that the radius at each bend in each cable is greater than the minimum bend radius specified for the cable.

Figure 12.4 Building Cabling

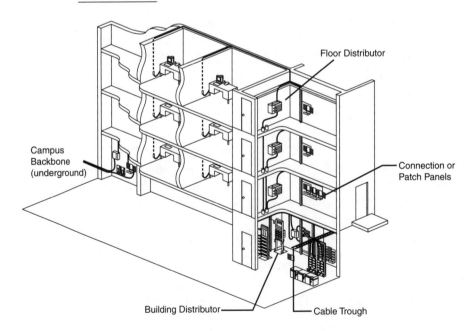

Horizontal cabling can be strung and fitted with connectors during installation or it can be purchased with factory-fitted connectors (these cables are said to be *pre-connectorized*) in fixed-length segments. Figure 12.5 shows a typical link configuration, although some companies are proposing the use of pre-connectorized, non-spliced fiber cable between the building distributor and the end station (this is sometimes called home run cabling) as an economical replacement or alternative to twisted pair copper.

Figure 12.5   Horizontal Cable Models

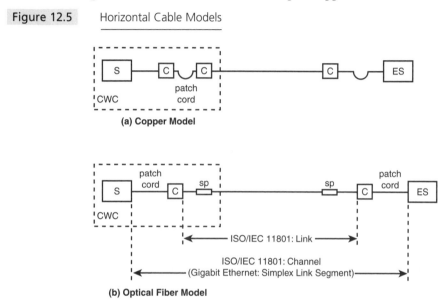

(a) Copper Model

(b) Optical Fiber Model

```
S   = Floor distributor equipment (switch)
ES  = End station
C   = connection
sp  = splice
CWC = Communications wiring closet
```

Because organizational structures (and, for that matter, office walls and cubicles) tend to be changed rather often, horizontal cables should be sized to allow at least some (probably more than you would think) flexibility in end-station location. After all, you can always connect an end station with a cable that is too long, but it is next to impossible to connect it to a cable that is too short. Provision must be made to allow for coiling the excess cable lengths somewhere out of sight and out of the way.

12.2.3   The Outside Cable Plant

Exterior backbone cables can be either installed underground or supported overhead from poles. Underground cables, in turn, can be either buried directly in the ground or run through underground conduit. Sections 12.2.3.1–12.2.3.3 consider each of these installations.

12.2.3.1 Underground Conduit

The most expensive, but the most flexible, installation is in underground conduit because it enables you to install backbone cable as needed. However, there are several caveats.

- You should never assume that you will be able to use unfilled conduits in the underground power system. National electrical codes and common sense do not allow communication cables to share the same manholes as power cables (although the conduits can share a common trench).

Note

Underground utilities should be installed in different levels with sewer lines at the lowest, water lines next, electrical conduits above the water lines, and communications conduits at the top to avoid interference when their paths have to cross. Electrical power and communications should be run in separate routes from water and sewer.

- You should never assume that you will be able to fill any conduit completely full with cables. Conduits and cable ducts cannot support long cable pulls where the cable cross-section area is much more than 50 percent of the conduit area. Furthermore, it is always very difficult to pull new cables through partially filled horizontal conduits.

- Each conduit should be installed with several inner ducts (low-friction hollow tubes) that will allow cables to be added as needed. The ducts should be sized large enough to accommodate the largest expected future cable ODs.

- Conduits should be installed in a manner that minimizes the cumulative bend angles. Horizontal and vertical conduit undulations greater than about 50 percent of the conduit diameter cause added friction during cable pulls and contribute to the cumulative bend angle. Experience with underground cable installation has shown that heavy cables are not easily pulled if the total bend angle exceeds 270° (some installation specifications limit the total sweep angle from installed bends to 180°).

- Manholes or pull boxes should be spaced close enough to ensure a successful cable pull without damage to the cable. Experience has shown that 215 m to 300 m (between 700 and 1,000 ft.) is appropriate in most installations.

Note

We have heard claims that 900 m (~ 3,000 ft.) cable pulls are possible, but we prefer to be a bit more conservative. We know of one instance several years ago where a communications group tried pulling a 1" flooded coaxial cable through ~ 1,800 ft. of 4" conduit installed under a concrete aircraft taxiway and adjacent runway. The concrete was about 20 inches thick and the cable parted less than halfway through the pull. Imagine having to tell the airfield division head that you were going to have to cut up the concrete to install another manhole or two, just when you had gotten the runway back in operation after it had been shut down for an extended period to install the original conduits!

To avoid accidental backhoe damage, the conduits should be either covered with colored concrete or guarded with a pressure-treated board that is installed at least 15 cm (about 6 in.) above the highest conduit. A wide, colored (bright orange, for example) non-degradable plastic warning sheet should also be laid along the conduit path at least 30 cm (about 1 ft.) underground and about 15 cm above the guard board or concrete conduit cover to indicate that there is a communications conduit below. Figure 12.6 shows a cross-section of a typical underground conduit installation.

Figure 12.6 Example Underground Conduit Installation

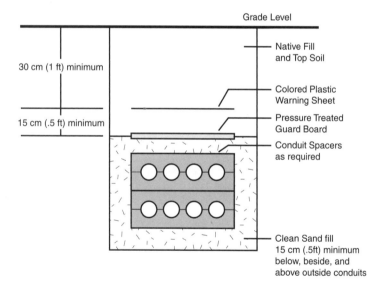

12.2.3.2 Direct-Burial Cable

Figure 12.7 depicts the makeup of a typical multipair direct-burial cable.

| Figure 12.7 | Example of Direct-Burial Optical Fiber Cable |

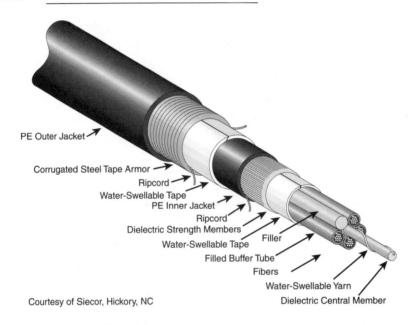

PE Outer Jacket

Corrugated Steel Tape Armor
Ripcord
Water-Swellable Tape
PE Inner Jacket
Ripcord
Dielectric Strength Members
Water-Swellable Tape
Filler
Filled Buffer Tube
Fibers
Water-Swellable Yarn
Dielectric Central Member

Courtesy of Siecor, Hickory, NC

As with underground conduit, however, there are several caveats to the use of direct-burial cable:

- Direct-burial cable should be buried below the frost line and at least 75 cm (about 30 in.) deep, if possible.

- The cable must be water-blocked (sometimes called flooded) to keep moisture from damaging the internal parts of the cable.

- The cable must be armored (covered with rodent-proof material) or installed in a plastic duct at least 3.8 cm (1.5 in.) outside diameter. (It seems that some rodents like to chew underground cables and if the cable is not rodent-proof, the cable diameter should be large enough to prevent the rodents from being able to bite into it.)

- The cable should have a metallic member to help locate the cable path should the need arise in the future.

> **Note**
>
> We know of a multipair direct-burial fiber cable that did not have a metallic member and that was not where everyone thought it was. Shortly after operational testing began, several meters of the cable became wound around a large power auger that was digging post holes for a new fence. The cable installer had taken a shortcut that was different from the planned route and no one had recorded where the cable was actually installed. The cable was severed, operational testing was interrupted for an extended period, and more than 5 km of cable ultimately had to be replaced.

12.2.3.3 Overhead Cable

Figure 12.8 shows an example of a multipair overhead cable. Overhead cable represents the least expensive, and the most visually offensive, backbone cable system. As with underground conduit and direct-burial cable, there are a few caveats here as well:

Figure 12.8   Example Overhead Optical Fiber Cable

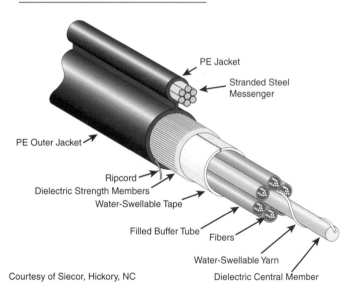

Courtesy of Siecor, Hickory, NC

- Overhead cables need to be supported, either by an integrated steel *messenger* cable, as shown in Figure 12.8, or by being lashed to an existing cable (if, and only if, the existing cable is strong enough to support the additional load and is likely to remain for the life of the backbone cable).

- Loose tube construction is highly recommended to ensure that the fibers are shielded from external stress from wind and/or ice loading on the cable.

- Pole spans should be less than the specified maximum span capacity of the supporting steel messenger (the span could be up to 90 m [~300 ft.] for the cable shown in Figure 12.8).

- The ground-to-cable clearance must be sufficient to prevent interference with pedestrian and/or vehicle traffic (at least 3.7 m [12 ft.] in pedestrian areas; 4.9 m [16 ft.] where vehicle access is allowed).

- Cable markers—for example, large orange balls like those installed on high-voltage lines crossing rivers or canyons—should be considered for overhead cables if they cross a vehicle traffic route where vehicle drivers would not reasonably expect an overhead cable.

> **Note**
>
> We know of one instance where a multipair cable with 16 ft. clearance was damaged by a crane truck because the driver had not lowered the crane and was not expecting and did not see the cable in time to stop. The vehicle was going fast enough and the cable's messenger was strong enough to break both poles as well.

12.2.4   As-Built Drawings

As-built drawings are drawings that reflect the way the cable plant is actually installed, not the way the installation was designed. Unfortunately, these drawings are frequently nonexistent or are woefully out of date. There are several reasons for this, beginning with contractors who do not want the additional expense and time required to provide them, to maintenance personnel who think it is more important to keep the system working than to document their changes, to management who often does not appreciate the importance of keeping accurate records until after something has gone wrong.

As-built drawings are needed to indicate where the campus switches, repeaters, hubs, patch panels, splices, and conduits and cables through which the wires/fibers are run are all located. There are several ways to properly place the various internal elements. One of the easiest methods is to use a grid system that defines locations by the building and floor level and by the cross-section location on the floor plan. Room numbers can also be used, but they are subject to change whenever the building is remodeled, and they are not much use in open office environments with partial-walled cubicles.

As-built drawings are particularly important in outside areas. We frequently hear of underground utilities being dug up by construction personnel because "we didn't know they were there," or "they weren't where they were supposed to be." Not knowing or not being able to accurately determine beforehand where underground utilities are located can be very expensive, very disruptive, and, depending on what gets severed, very dangerous.

Note

An example of the consequences of not doing the job right the first time and not having as-built drawings was experienced firsthand by the California half of this author team, just as this chapter was being written. I live in a rural area in the foothills of the Sierra, east of Sacramento where irrigation water is distributed by a network of ditches that were originally used to bring water to the gold mines. Because the ditch is about half a mile up the hill from us, our water is transported from the ditch to our neighborhood through a heavy 6-inch plastic (we thought) pipe that crosses several parcels on the way. Unfortunately, when it was installed, no one made an accurate map of the route, no one recorded the fact that a section of the line above the neighborhood was in reused steel pipe, and they certainly didn't indicate where the steel pipe section began and ended.

As things now stand, the steel pipe has rusted through in several places. One of the two affected parcels has been graded and recontoured—sections of the existing pipe may be more than 12 feet deep and may even be under an in-ground swimming pool. Both of the parcels have been landscaped—several trees are now growing on top of or next to the existing pipe, and in-ground sprinkler systems have been installed. Our only recourse is to reroute the pipe and take care to avoid all the obstacles that were not there when the system was originally installed (there doesn't appear to be any underground telephone or electrical power lines in the way). If we are lucky, only about 360 feet of pipe will have to be replaced and relocated.

While our system for delivering irrigation water has nothing to do with Gigabit Ethernet, replacing a pipe is no different from replacing a conduit. Our current situation is an example of what can happen when inferior construction material (in our case the old steel pipe) is substituted for the specified material, and when as-built drawings are never generated.

12.3 Network Cabling

Ethernet LANs are now typically interconnected with optical fiber, unshielded twisted pair (UTP) copper, or shielded twisted pair (STP) copper cable, as listed in Table 12.1. Coaxial cable, while it is still listed in the standard, is seldom, if ever, used for new networks or network upgrades.

Table 12.1 Cable Types Commonly Used for Ethernet Links

Media Type	Number of Conductors	Ethernet Implementation
Copper		
Category-3 UTP	4-pair (only 2-pair used)	10BASE-T
Category-3 UTP	4-pair	100BASE-T4
Category-5 UTP	4-pair (only 2-pair used)	10BASE-T
Category-5 UTP	4-pair	100BASE-T4
Category-5 UTP	4-pair (only 2-pair used)	100BASE-T2
Category-5 UTP	4-pair	1000BASE-T[a]
STP	4-pair	1000BASE-CX
Optical Fiber		
10 μm SMF	2 fibers	1000BASE-LX
50 μm MMF	2 fibers	1000BASE-LX
50 μm MMF	2 fibers	1000BASE-SX
62.5 μm MMF	2 fibers	1000BASE-FX
62.5 μm MMF	2 fibers	1000BASE-LX
62.5 μm MMF	2 fibers	1000BASE-SX

---

[a]1000BASE-T should be approved as a supplement to IEEE 802.3-1998 during the spring of 1999.

12.3.1 Cable Selection

The link lengths shown in the model in Figure 12.1 are based on 1995 technology. With the exception of 1000BASE-SX operation on 62.5 μm fiber, Gigabit Ethernet full-duplex operation meets or exceeds the ISO/IEC 11801 link length requirements. We recommend that *all new network cabling be capable of supporting Gigabit transmission rates*, which reduces the list of alternatives in Table 12.1 to those shown in Table 12.2. The initial material cost may be slightly higher, but this is far outweighed by the savings from not having to replace these cables at a future date.

Table 12.2   Maximum Gigabit Link Lengths for Interoperability

Cable Type	Half-Duplex (End Station-to-Repeater)	Full-Duplex (End Station-to-Repeater)	Half-Duplex (End Station-to-Switch)	Full-Duplex (End Station-to-Switch)
Copper				
Category-5 UTP				
1000BASE-T	100 m	100 m	100 m	100 m
STP				
1000BASE-CX	25 m	25 m	25 m	25 m
Optical Fiber				
10 μm SMF				
1000BASE-LX	Not advised	Not advised	Not advised	5,000 m
50 μm MMF				
1000BASE-SX	110 m	110 m	316 m	500 m
1000BASE-LX	110 m	550 m	316 m	550 m
62.5 μm MMF				
1000BASE-SX	110 m	220/275 m	220/275 m	220/275 m
1000BASE-LX	110 m	700 m[a]	316 m	700 m[a]

[a]IEEE 802.3 indicates 550 m to agree with ISO/IEC 11801. The worst-case 62.5 μm MMF links are capable of supporting long-wavelength Gigabit communication up to 700 m.

Cabling standards tend to reflect the installed base of cables. The predominant horizontal cabling is currently (1999) unshielded twisted pair (UTP). Ethernet, FDDI, and many other LAN standards have recommended the use of multimode fiber (MMF) with a 62.5 μm core diameter for more than a decade. For this reason, it is not surprising that current national and international structured cabling standards prefer 62.5 μm MMF. Single-mode fiber (SMF) is also recommended, especially for data rates greater than 100 Mbps where the longer campus backbone links may not always be supported with MMF.

And finally, if connecting hardware costs can be reduced enough, 10 μm SMF could become a more active player for shorter-length backbones.

12.3.2   Cable Testing and Validation

There are basically four types of cable tests that may be required before implementing a new Gigabit Ethernet network or network upgrade:

- Pre-installation tests

- Acceptance tests

- Fault-finding tests

- Conformance tests

Generally, the complexity and time involved increases in the progression from pre-installation to conformance testing (see Table 12.3). Each test has different objectives as covered in the sections that follow.

Table 12.3   Parameters and Test Instruments for Fiber Optic Link Tests

Test Parameter	Pre-Installation Test	Acceptance Test	Fault-Finding Test	Conformance Test
Loss	yes	yes	yes	yes
Return Loss	no	yes	yes	yes
Length	no	sometimes	yes	yes
Bandwidth	no	no	no	If possible
Test Instruments	ODTR[a]	OTDR & LTS[b]	OTDR & LTS	OTDR & LTS

[a]OTDR: Optical Time Domain Reflectometer
[b]LTS: Loss Test Set

12.3.2.1   Pre-Installation Tests and Test Instruments

Pre-installation tests are carried out to ensure that the cable and materials supplied for installation are not damaged or defective. Cables and materials will generally be supplied with test data that can be checked, but it is useful to test the loss of at least a sample of cables from each reel or delivered batch. These tests would normally be carried out with an OTDR and are done before cable installation.

Figure 12.9 shows a block diagram of a typical Optical Time Domain Reflectometer (OTDR). The OTDR repeatedly transmits short optical pulses into the fiber cable being tested and then measures the pulse reflections received from the fiber. The output from the ODTR is usually a graphic display of the reflected power (backscatter) as a function of distance traveled along the fiber. Numerical readouts of important measurement results can also be provided.

Figure 12.9 Illustration of an Optical Time Domain Reflectometer (OTDR)

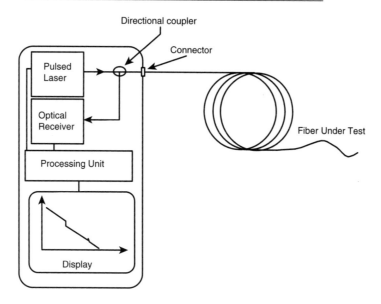

In OTDR terminology, *events* are changes in the fiber causing the trace to deviate from a straight line. Reflective events occur when some of the pulse energy is reflected (from a connector, for example). Reflective events produce a spike in the trace (see Figure 12.10, at the connector). Non-reflective events occur at parts of the fiber (such as at good splices) where there is some loss but where no light is reflected. Non-reflective events produce a dip on the trace (see Figure 12.10, at the splices). The distance to an event in the fiber is calculated in the ODTR from the time between the output pulse and receipt of the reflected signal.

Figure 12.10 Illustrative OTDR Output

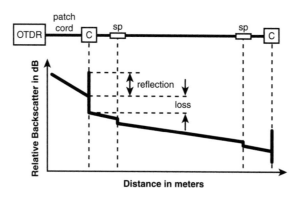

OTDRs display the relative power of the returned signal versus distance and allow the following link parameters to be determined:

- Link length

- Total end-to-end link loss

- Attenuation coefficient of the link fiber

- Distance to events on the link

- Loss due to connectors or splices in the link

- Return loss of the link connectors

Most OTDRs provide fully automatic functions for these measurements, and they will normally set themselves up to achieve the optimum results.

The transmitter of some OTDRs can also be used as a stable optical source for precision insertion loss measurements. Some OTDRs also allow power meter modules to be plugged into them for accurate insertion loss measurements, an option that converts the OTDR into a loss test set (LTS). This capability means that one compact instrument can be used to do all cable plant tests.

Modern OTDRs for LAN applications are hand-held instruments that can measure the following:

- Cable length with an accuracy of a few meters

- Connector and splice loss with an accuracy of a fraction of a dB

- Connector return loss with an accuracy of a few dB

12.3.2.2 Acceptance Tests

Acceptance tests are normally carried out after the cable has been installed. The main criteria for acceptance tests are the end-to-end link loss and the return loss from the installed connectors. Table 12.4 compares the maximum loss allowed for guaranteed multisupplier interoperation of Gigabit Ethernet fiber optic links and the maximum loss specification for ISO/IEC 11801 (1995) links. Connector return-loss specifications are the same for both cases, at least 20 dB for multimode cables, and at least 26 dB for single-mode cables.

Table 12.4	Maximum Link Insertion Loss for Short- and Long-Wavelength Operation			
Link Length	850 nm Wavelength (Gigabit Ethernet)	1,300 nm Wavelength (Gigabit Ethernet)	850 nm Wavelength (ISO/IEC 11801 [1995])	1,300 nm Wavelength (ISO/IEC 11801 [1995])
500m	3.3 dB	2.2 dB	3.9 dB	2.6 dB

Clearly, Gigabit Ethernet has a more stringent loss specification than ISO/IEC 11801. However, this observation deserves some further discussion for multimode fibers. Both the Gigabit Ethernet and the ISO link calculations assume that connectors and splices cause most of the link loss. For example, ISO/IEC 11801 assumes all loss measurements are made with optical sources that overfill the fiber and other link components. Under these conditions, the absolute worst-case loss is 0.75 dB for a connector and 0.3 dB for a splice. The worst-case ISO/IEC 11801 link has two worst-case connectors and two worst-case splices (see Figure 12.5). Therefore, the connectors and splices account for 2.1 dB of the 2.6 dB ISO/IEC 11801 total link loss. But the laser-based transceivers used by Gigabit Ethernet do *not* overfill the fiber and so they experience *less* loss at connectors and splices. For this reason, Gigabit Ethernet set the maximum connection loss to 1.5 dB. This is the maximum loss that the optical power from an actual transceiver is allowed to experience.

Therefore, Gigabit Ethernet link loss tests should be performed with a pulse source that is representative of a laser transceiver. Since the recent completion of ANSI/EIA/TIA 526-14A, test sets with these sources are becoming available. For Gigabit Ethernet, loss testing the source should be category 2 or 3 in the ANSI/EIA/TIA 526-14A classification scheme. This is appropriate even for cases where offset launch patch cords are used because even these launches do *not* overfill the fiber.

If laser sources representative of Gigabit Ethernet transceivers are not available, acceptance tests should be made to the Gigabit Ethernet link loss figures using a source that overfills the fiber. In reality, however, because the signal from Gigabit Ethernet lasers will experience less loss compared to an overfilled launch test source, a link previously qualified to the ISO/IEC 11801 specifications is very, very unlikely to cause performance problems for a Gigabit Ethernet implementation.

12.3.2.3 Fault-Finding Tests

The purpose of fault-finding tests should be self-explanatory and will not be discussed in depth here, other than to say that in addition to loss and return loss measurements, length measurements are useful for fault finding (see Table 12.3). Fault finding can usually be completed with just an OTDR.

12.3.2.4 Conformance Tests

Conformance tests are the most complex to complete and therefore, the most expensive. Acceptance tests will ensure that the overall link is within specification and that the installed cable plant is ready for use by Gigabit Ethernet. However, it is possible for the overall link loss to be acceptable, but for some of the individual components to be outside specifications (for example, in a link containing two connectors, one connector could have 1 dB loss and the other 0.5 dB loss). Because Gigabit Ethernet only specifies the total connection loss, which should be 1.5 dB or less, this example would not be an issue for Gigabit Ethernet. It would, however, be an issue in terms of ISO/IEC 11801 compliance, as the maximum allowed individual connector loss is 0.75 dB.

12.3.3 The Cable Plant Database

Obviously, when a link is down, or when changes need to be made, the maintenance personnel need to know what specific wires or fibers are involved and where they are located.

The database should include at least the following information:

- **Campus, Building, and Floor Distributors**. Their location and installed equipment ID numbers.

- **Manholes**. Their location, conduit ID numbers, and associated row and column wall locations.

- **Conduits**. Their ID number, size, termination point locations, length, and inner duct complement (with duct ID numbers) or fill status.

- **Inner Ducts**. Their ID number, size, associated conduit ID number, and cable complement (with cable ID numbers) or fill status.

- **Cables**. Their ID number, specification, design, type, length, end point locations, routing, and fiber/wire pair complement (with fiber/wire pair ID numbers).

- **Fiber/Wire Pairs**. Their ID number, type, associated cable ID, termination equipment ID, plus the performance test data from all the cable tests defined in the previous section, including:

  - Link length

  - Total end-to-end link loss

  - Attenuation coefficient of the link fiber

  - Distance to events on the link

- Loss due to connectors or splices in the link

- Return loss of the link connectors

- **Patch Panels**. Their location, ID number, size, fill status, and associated link complement (with link ID numbers).

- **Switches, Repeaters, and So Forth**. The location, ID number, ports and port capability, associated link ID numbers, and the ID number of the equipment at the other end of each link.

- **Telecom Outlets**. Their location, ID number, connector type, associated link ID number, fiber type (if applicable), the ID number of the equipment, and the port number (if multiport device) at the other end of each link.

- **End Stations**. The location, ID number, associated link ID number, the ID number of the equipment, and port number (if applicable) at the other end of each link.

12.4 Cable Plant Management

As stated at the beginning of the chapter, you need to know a number of things about the existing cable plant. Two of your most valuable tools are as-built drawings and a comprehensive cable system database. Together, they can allow you to do such things as:

- Identify which unused links meet the requirements for an add, move, or change (required route, length, performance characteristics, and so on)

- Identify currently used links with performance characteristics that exceed the service level requirement for their current use and that could be swapped for other links with lower performance characteristics

- Develop lists, plots, and/or schematics of the selected links and their specific routing before the actual repair or installation takes place

- Prepare specific fiber/wire pair connection lists and the associated link's previous performance test results to be used by technical personnel during link connection and performance validation

- Prepare up-to-date fiber/wire pair and cable connection lists for posting at connection/patch panels in each distributor location and wiring closet

- Provide other building contractors and/or maintenance personnel detailed location information regarding hidden conduits and cables

The cable plant database manager is typically responsible for monitoring conduit, cable, and link assignments to ensure that spares are actually available when needed. Empty underground conduits, for example, can be an especially attractive asset. Left on their own, they have a tendency to become used for purposes that were never intended, and worse than that, never recorded.

12.5 Cable Plant Security

Network security requires different precautions, depending on the sensitivity level of the information being transmitted, and whether or not the information has a national security classification. The discussion here will be limited to network security in non-classified environments. If your network is or will be processing classified information, you should contact the appropriate federal agency for their network security guidelines.

Earlier sections in the chapter have already emphasized the need to protect conduits and cables from inadvertent physical damage that could occur from accidents or construction projects. Networks also need to be protected from fiber and wire tapping or eavesdropping. These are activities that generally require unobserved access to some point in the link, that typically are attempted inside buildings, and that can usually be thwarted, or at least made more difficult, by the following means:

- Overhead cable troughs should be run above hallways rather than above individual offices to make unobserved access more difficult.

- Links carrying sensitive information should be run in conduits, rather than in cable troughs.

- Access to wiring closets containing building distributors and connection panels should be limited to authorized personnel only.

An operational fact is that it is very difficult to eavesdrop (even by inductive means) on any copper cable that you cannot isolate for a short distance, and it is next to impossible to tap an optical fiber without cutting through the core.

12.6 Summary

Cable plant design guides can be obtained, often free of charge, from cable manufacturers. An excellent example is the Siecor LANscape *Fiber Cabling Solutions for Premises Networks*, which covers topics from preliminary design considerations to testing and documentation in ten chapters. Siecor is a jointly owned subsidiary of Siemens and Corning. They can be contacted at Siecor, P.O. Box 489, Hickory, NC 28603 USA, telephone 1-800-SIECOR5 (1-800-743-2675).

And finally, we cannot resist a few cost-related admonitions before going on to discuss network topology and system considerations in the next chapter. The cables in the cable plant should outlast the connected equipment many times over, and the conduit structure should outlast the installed cable so long as neither are accidentally damaged. However, you need to remember the following truths about the cable plant:

- Planning for change or repair is much easier and less costly when all the information about the current cable plant is accurate and available, and when at least some conduits and cables have been maintained as spares in all critical areas of the campus.

- Prevention of accidental damage to the cable plant is usually far less expensive and disruptive than having to repair or replace whole sections. Also, the cost of lost production can sometimes even exceed the cost of the repair.

- Installing a larger capacity cable (with many optical fibers) in the beginning is much less costly than installing, and then later replacing, a lower capacity cable.

- Installation contractors typically won't provide as-built drawings and test results for the cable plant database unless it is a contractual requirement and additional funding is provided. However, the cost of obtaining this information after everything is closed up and in operation can be several times the incremental contract cost of having it prepared as the installation is taking place. In short, *you can pay a little now or a lot later.*

13

Upgrading Ethernet LANs: System and Topology Considerations

> The traditional 80/20 rule to which most networks were designed has reversed itself—traffic that remains local to the LAN has now become the exception. [An Internet White Paper—NetReference, 1998]

Gigabit Ethernet was originally developed to be a transmission rate upgrade for existing Ethernet LANs. However, it can also be a transmission rate upgrade for LANs employing other technologies and protocols.

Many of the technical considerations are the same, but the starting points (the existing networks) are obviously different. Because of this, two chapters address the separate issues and discusses these upgrade possibilities.

This chapter considers how Gigabit Ethernet can be used as either an upgrade path for existing Ethernet LANs or as the basis for entirely new Ethernet networks. Chapter 14, "Gigabit Ethernet in Context with Other LAN Technologies," considers the use of Gigabit Ethernet as an upgrade path for existing non-Ethernet LANs.

13.1 Justifying the Need for Network Upgrades

There can be many reasons why networks need to be upgraded. In some cases, the network just needs to support more people than it was designed for, or the network equipment may be out-of-date or difficult to support. However, the most common reason is rapidly increasing traffic loads. An attempt to list all the factors behind the continuing explosive growth in network traffic would be daunting; however, a few commonly stated ones are as follows:

- A rapid expansion of the World Wide Web and its related applications has led to unpredictable data patterns and greatly increased traffic both in the local networks and on the Internet.

- The continued accuracy of Moore's 1965 observation (Moore's Law) that hardware performance doubles in power and halves in price approximately every 18 to 24 months has also impacted software development:

  - Application programs and their associated file sizes have continued to grow with every software upgrade.

  - The use of presentation graphics, animation, computer aided design, desktop publishing, imaging applications, and other applications that require communication support continues to increase at non-linear rates.

  - Time-sensitive information transfer (such as audio and video) is placing new packet delivery restrictions on network operations.

13.2 Opportunities for Upgrading Ethernet LANs

Communications networks are installed for a single purpose: to facilitate the transfer of information and data. They must be designed with sufficient capacity not only to carry each user's traffic load, but also to do so in a *timely manner*.

The original Ethernet low delay goal—"At any given level of offered traffic, the network should introduce as little delay as possible in the transfer of a frame"—did not suggest that upper bounds be established for frame delay. The goal implies that no frames should be held up in preference to others. If traffic levels were low, the delay could be expected to be low; if traffic increased, delays could also increase.

Most of this book's earlier discussions have concentrated on new Ethernet capabilities that either directly or indirectly address the issues of user bandwidth and transmission delay: Gigabit Ethernet, full-duplex operation with flow control, and VLAN tagging. Each of these technologies opens new opportunities for increasing network bandwidth, decreasing transmission delay, providing more timely packet delivery, or adding flexibility to the network topology. The list that follows provides some of the beneficial characteristics of these technologies that increase the robustness of a network.

- Gigabit Ethernet

  - Provides a 10X transmission rate and bandwidth increase over Fast Ethernet.

  - Includes a packet bursting feature in which end stations, switches, and other network devices are able to send small bursts of short frames without having to contend for network access between successive packet transmissions when operating in half-duplex (CSMA/CD) mode.

  - Can be used over link lengths greater than those defined for Fast Ethernet.

- Full-duplex operation

  - Allows immediate frame transmission after an interframe gap and eliminates the need for CSMA/CD link access procedures plus any time losses that would be required for collision recovery.

  - Doubles the effective available bandwidth over CSMA/CD half-duplex operation. The instantaneous transfer rate of full-duplex Gigabit Ethernet links, for example, is 2,000 Mbps (1,000 Mbps in each direction).

  - Opens the door to extended link lengths for all transmission rates. Full-duplex link lengths are limited by the physical properties of the link rather than the network collision diameter for the particular transmission rate.

- MAC Control

  - Implements fast response, link-by-link flow control (PAUSE) capability for use during full-duplex operation at all Ethernet transmission rates.

  - Provides a structure for the future definition of control operations spanning one or more links.

- VLAN tagging

  - Creates a *Class of Service* (CoS) capability for frame forwarding that can allow time-sensitive transmission over Ethernet networks. VLAN tagging allows frames to be forwarded by intermediate network devices according to their transmission priority level instead of their port reception order.

  - Provides the capability for separating users into logical workgroups, without regard to their physical locations or assigned transmission rates.

  - Simplifies adds, moves, and changes for networks with installed network management software.

13.2.1 Quality of Service

"Timely" does not have the same meaning for all packets transferred across a network. For example, a packet that arrives so late that it causes jitter in a high resolution real-time display is *not timely*. On the other hand, a packet such as a response to a database inquiry that is delayed may be just *annoying*. The task of network designers and network managers is to ensure that packets arrive in time to prevent a change in the computational result and to keep the annoyance factors at or below acceptable levels.

In a literal sense, *Quality of Service* (QoS) is a measure of performance that reflects the transmission capabilities of a network. QoS provides an indication of how information transfer will be handled by the network. And by extension, QoS is also an indication of whether or not the information can be expected or guaranteed to reach the intended receiver(s) in a timely fashion.

The Internet Engineering Task Force (IETF) has defined three general types of traffic that may need to be considered when planning a new network or network upgrade:

- *Best-effort traffic* is the traditional type of traffic carried on LANs and IP networks. Typical applications include mail, transaction processing, file transfer, and so forth. Packet delays are a function of the link lengths and the available bandwidth at each intermediate node in the transmission path.

- *Rate-sensitive traffic* is the type of traffic where timeliness can be traded for assured reception rates (such as for video conferences). Longer end-to-end network delay can be tolerated so long as packet reception is regular enough to ensure an essentially constant received bit rate once transfer has begun.

- *Delay-sensitive traffic* requires that transmitted packets be received within a prescribed time window (for example, in video over IP). The typical CODEC-generated packet stream contains information for an entire screen display (called a *key frame*) followed by changes to the screen display (delta frames). The bandwidth necessary to transmit an entire screen can vary from ~3 Mbps for an uncomplicated display to ~7 Mbps for a complicated one. The bandwidth required for delta frames is typically much lower than that for key frames. However, both the key and delta information must be received in time for the CODEC to keep up with the display's scan rate.

Note
Frames, as used with key and delta frames, should not be confused with MAC frames. A number of MAC frames are typically required to transfer the information contained in only one key frame.

Quality of Service is not a problem in networks when sufficient bandwidth is always available. However, this is seldom the case. The available bandwidth in a transmission path is a function of both the path's segment/switch bandwidth capacities and the traffic volumes at the time.

Traditional best-effort traffic can be satisfied by simply providing enough bandwidth to ensure that annoyance delays occur infrequently and only during peak traffic periods.

Rate- and/or delay-sensitive traffic is another matter. Two things are required: high bandwidth plus a control mechanism to ensure that time-sensitive traffic reaches its destination when needed and that best-effort traffic is not delayed too long in the process. The common solution is either to reserve a portion of the channel bandwidth or to assign transmission priorities to the packets in the data stream.

As might be expected, the approach to handling the different types of traffic is different for LAN/MAN and WAN implementations:

- *Quality of Service* (**QoS**) **Transmission**. In time division multiplexed (TDM) circuit switched networks (such as ATM and SONET), a portion of each transmitted frame is assigned and reserved for exclusive use by the data stream. Once the circuit has been set up, frames are transmitted at the rate allowed by the transmission channel and timely reception can be guaranteed.

- *Class of Service* (**CoS**) **Transmission**. In packet switched networks (such as Ethernet, Token Ring, FDDI, and so forth), the packets in the data stream are assigned a transmission priority that is interrogated and used by each switch along the path to determine transmission order. For layer 2 devices, this approach is known as *Class of Service* (CoS) transmission, or IEEE 802.1p/Q priority VLAN service.

- *Type of Service* (**ToS**) **Transmission**. In layer 3, the Internet IP protocol's ToS is equivalent to layer 2 CoS service. IP ToS maps directly to and from IEEE 802.1p/Q CoS.

CoS is basically a subset of QoS. While it does not provide the guaranteed delivery of QoS, CoS is less complex and, unless bandwidth is severely restricted in some portion of the transmission path, it is typically "good enough".

13.2.2 Setting Up a CoS Transmission Path

CoS is sometimes coupled with IETF's Resource Reservation Protocol (RSVP). RSVP is not a routing protocol. It is a layer 4 Internet protocol that works with IP to set up transfer paths and to reserve bandwidth for data streams (sequences of data packets) having the same source(es) and destination(s). Each designated receiver and switch/router along each potential transmission path is interrogated to determine whether it can support the requested quality of service *(all entities involved in an RSVP-transmission must be able to support RSVP)*. The actual transmission path is chosen to minimize delay, and bandwidth is reserved at each intermediate node.

RSVP accepts requests for all three types of traffic (best-effort, rate-sensitive, delay-sensitive); however, because RSVP operates on a first-come, first-served basis, and because it is a bandwidth reservation system and not a bandwidth reallocation system, an earlier low priority request from a different source could have already been allocated some of the bandwidth needed at one or more intermediate nodes for a new time-sensitive transfer request. Should no viable paths be found, the source host(s) is (are) notified that the requested transmission service level cannot be supported at the present time.

Note

RSVP is still under development and test. It is not at all clear how to provide end-to-end CoS because routines that work well in small networks do not scale and mechanisms that appear to scale do not seem practical. It's currently an emotional battle, and while some people think they have the answer, not everyone agrees with them.

The previous 12 chapters have given you *almost all* of the basic information that you need to plan, configure, upgrade, and/or manage an Ethernet network. There is still one thing missing before putting it all together and considering Ethernet as a total system. You need to factor in the user base with its existing and projected traffic profiles.

Before you can plan a new network or a network upgrade, you need to have at least a reasonable idea of how many people the network will need to support and how it will be used. You can take several approaches to planning a new network installation or an existing network modification.

13.3 Planning for a New Network or Network Upgrade

Network planning is essentially a three-step sequential process:

1.   Determining what is needed

2.   Deciding how to do it

3.   Obtaining approval and funding

The three planning approaches covered in sections 13.3.1–13.3.3 (brute force network planning; piecemeal adds, moves, and changes; and total network planning) each represent an extreme in one way or another.

13.3.1 *Brute Force Network Planning*

The brute force network planning approach involves providing full-duplex VLAN-compatible Gigabit Ethernet access for every user, installing a number of extra links in all locations, and including spare conduits in every backbone route. This approach will definitely ensure user bandwidth availability, and will provide for future network growth, but it also ignores a couple of basic facts of network planning:

- Many network users will not (in the forseeable future) need more than 10 Mbps or 100 Mbps capability at the desktop. While the amount of information transferred across a network for each user will continue to expand, individual user traffic will continue to be bursty. Unless these transfers need to be in real time, they can be done in background mode while the user is accomplishing other tasks.

- The cost of an all-Gigabit Ethernet LAN would be several times the cost of a mixed-transmission-rate network.

Individual users should definitely have access to the transmission rates they need to do their job, but not to capabilities that they do not need or cannot effectively use.

13.3.2 *Piecemeal Adds, Moves, and Changes*

Adding, deleting, or moving users and replacing existing equipment as necessary to meet local needs and without reference to a total network plan is a typical approach in small networks and in networks where individual groups are responsible for their own subnet. The actual impact on the rest of the network is often left "to be determined". The necessary changes are made to the network management system (if one exists), and the new/revised link connections might or might not be recorded.

This piecemeal approach works for small networks and for limited adds and changes to larger networks, but there can be long-term problems, even if all the subnets utilize Ethernet protocol. Some of the problems include the following:

- End stations, repeaters, and switches that are individually added or replaced over time might or might not have the options (for example, IEEE 802.1p/Q VLAN capability) that exist or will be needed in other closely associated parts of the network. Option compatibility becomes an important factor when routing and/or priority transmission becomes a factor in network planning.

- Network equipment purchased on an individual item basis typically costs more (it is not often subject to a discount), even when a number of the same or similar items are purchased or leased in a short period of time.

- Recently purchased equipment may need to be prematurely replaced whenever the subnets are consolidated into a total network.

- Piecemeal adds of "just a few more users and maybe another switch" can have an adverse effect on higher-level backbone traffic. Unless they are monitored, these "little" additions can even lead to unanticipated saturation in other parts of the network.

13.3.3 *Total Network Planning*

The total network planning approach presumes full availability of information about the network, its cable plant, the users, and management's plans for the future. Unfortunately, this a knowledge base that is often out of date or not even available. Network planners must first verify that the information is accurate and then fill in the gaps where information is missing as defined in the list that follows.

1. Define the current network. (The following two steps are not necessary if you are planning a completely new installation. However, you will still have to determine where telecom access is available.)

   1a. Obtain or prepare as-built drawings of the cable plant.

   1b. Determine the current traffic profiles and historical load-growth trends.

2. Identify the user needs.

   2a. Survey the user population to determine their workloads, potential software requirements, and associated file sizes.

   2b. Categorize the user population and traffic trends according to transmission priority requirements and priority traffic volume.

   2c. Survey management to determine group plans for future facility expansion (or contraction) and long-term development direction(s).

   2d. Locate the current/future user populations and potential traffic levels/priority categories on building floor plans and campus maps.

3. Develop a long-range network plan

   3a. Develop a long-range network architecture and server concept, including provisions for future growth.

   3b. Identify existing/potential floor and building switch locations, and building backbone risers (conduits).

   3c. Overlay the campus backbone schematic of the current inter-facility cable routes on the campus user population map.

   3d. Identify all current inter-facility backbone cables and spare conduits and determine routings for any new inter-facility conduits and cables.

3e. Identify which current equipment and cables are reusable, which will need to be upgraded or replaced, and what additional equipment and cabling will be required.

3f. Develop a budget and define a migration strategy.

Total network planning will theoretically result in an optimized plan. However, there are additional costs associated with this type of planning effort that must be traded off against any future savings that might result from being able to implement an optimized network. These are costs for additional time needed to gather, verify, and analyze all the required information. Additional costs also exist for ongoing projects that are not able to use an updated network during the extended planning period.

13.4 A Compromise Approach to Network Planning

The network plan is developed from the bottom up. You begin with some planning objectives and the givens: the existing cable plant, the current network topology, and the user locations and applications profiles (or with just the user locations and projected applications profiles in the case of a new installation).

13.4.1 Network Planning Objectives

Local area networks (LANs) are an organization's data communication utility. An objective of the planning effort should be to provide a network with the same or better reliability and up-time levels as a public telephone utility. As such, the plan should:

- Be based on an extensible architecture that will:

  - Allow adding new users and new applications at minimal long-term cost and without disruption to the network

  - Provide automatic recovery from failure of any single switch or intermediate network interconnection

- Incorporate a comprehensive network management system for controlling the network and for collecting/maintaining operational data and network usage trends

- Include a cabling plant with sufficient capacity to support long-term growth in network size and application profiles

- Provide for uninterruptible power supplies (UPS) and/or backup power generators for network switches and critical file servers (such as mail servers) to allow continued network operation during periods of primary power failure

13.4.2   *Mitigating Factors in Planning for Ethernet LANs*

Network planning is case sensitive. No single planning procedure will fit all instances where existing networks need to be upgraded or new networks implemented. However, there are at least three mitigating factors associated with Ethernet LANs that can greatly simplify the planning process:

- Non-blocking switches both eliminate the shared-media bandwidth limitation problem and allow full-duplex transmission at 10 Mbps, 100 Mbps, or 1,000 Mbps to each connected device.

- User applications and network file servers that require full-duplex transmission rates greater than 10 Mbps easily can be supported at 100 Mbps. Providing users with higher transmission rates than they actually need is called *bandwidth over provisioning*.

- The need for VLAN and priority transmission capability is only dependent on whether time-sensitive applications are needed at a particular end station, not on how often or how long they are used.

These mitigating factors mean that *it is not necessary to determine exact bandwidth requirements for each network user*. Furthermore, if each user station and associated switch port is equipped with 10/100 Mbps network interface cards (NICs), the transmission rate will be network-management selectable. The only remaining user question is whether or not any users will need IEEE 802.1p/Q capability.

13.4.3   *Identifying Present and Potential User Populations*

While it is not necessary to do an exhaustive user survey to determine specific application profiles and bandwidth requirements, it is appropriate to determine the sizes of the various user populations (which should be located on campus maps and building plans) and to identify those that will need IEEE 802.1p/Q VLAN capability. This information will be needed later for backbone sizing and routing.

13.4.4   *Network Architecture Considerations*

Network topology and a good network management system are the keys to network reliability. The topology defines how the various switches/routers should be interconnected. The network management system provides the tools to monitor network performance, to identify links and servers that are approaching load capacity, and to reconfigure the network in case of equipment failure.

13.4.4.1 The Traditional Ethernet Topology

Traditional Ethernet requires a tree structure like that shown in Figure 13.1. To avoid network loops, there is one and only one path between any end station and another end station, network server, or the telecom connection to the outside world.

Figure 13.1   The Traditional Ethernet Topology

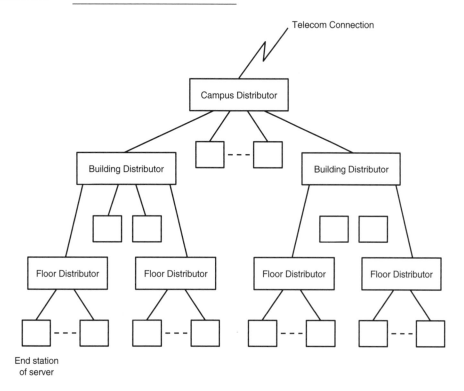

13.4.4.2 Mesh-Connected Topologies

The traditional tree structure depicted in Figure 13.1 has been very successful for Ethernet LANs over the years, but the topology has two potentially serious deficiencies:

- The network is susceptible to separation into parts in the event of a switch failure or a failure in a switch-to-switch link.

- Traffic in switches and their interconnecting links becomes more concentrated at higher levels in the network structure.

Because of the high reliability levels exhibited by Ethernet components, the first concern has seldom been a problem.

The second concern is a different matter. High traffic loads can saturate higher level switches and can cause excessive packet delays. An obvious solution is the installation of higher-speed switches and links. Another solution is to interconnect the network's switches in a mesh pattern similar to that shown in Figure 13.2 (for simplicity, end stations are not shown).

Figure 13.2   A Mesh-Connected Topology

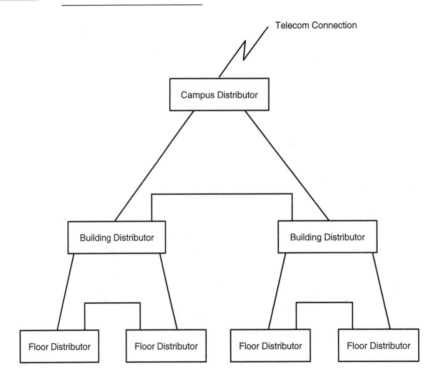

The interconnecting structure may be either partial-mesh (where some, but not all, switches have additional separate connections to other switches in the network) or full-mesh (all switches have separate connections to each other). Mesh interconnection of network switches provides two distinct advantages over the traditional tree structure:

- Alternate paths are available in case of switch or switch-to-switch link failure.

- Floor-to-floor and building-to-building traffic not destined to higher network levels can be transferred directly between peer switches without having to be passed up to and back down from the campus distributor.

The disadvantage of the mesh topology is that unless a network management system is installed to monitor the network and a proper control (such as the Spanning Tree

Protocol) is provided, the alternate paths can result in network loops and packet duplication. This means that networks with mesh interconnections must be implemented with routers that limit the transmission path between communicating end stations to a single route at any time (higher layer routing was introduced in sections 4.2.3 and 4.3.1 of Chapter 4, "Gigabit Repeaters, Bridges, Routers, and Switches," and will be further discussed in Chapter 14, section 14.1.2).

13.4.4.3 *Topologies with Redundant Links: Link Aggregation and Trunking*

Figure 13.3 shows an alternate partial-mesh interconnection that provides an important additional advantage over the example network of Figure 13.2. Redundant links between individual switches not only provide alternate paths in case of link or port failure, they can also provide additional bandwidth capability for the interconnection.

Figure 13.3   A Network Topology with Redundant Link Interconnections

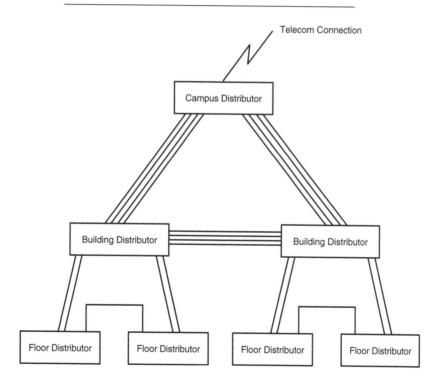

Many commercially available Ethernet switches have the capability to aggregate individual links to form higher capacity trunks. Four 100 Mbps full-duplex aggregated links, for example, could provide an aggregate transmission rate of 400 Mbps in each direction.

This capability provides an incremental transmission rate upgrade path for switch interconnections and can be a cost-effective upgrade for the following:

- Ethernet LANs that are reaching capacity with 100 Mbps systems, but that won't require Gigabit capability in the short term.

- Aggregating 62.5 µm multimode fiber (MMF) links currently used for backbones longer than 700 m (the maximum length for 1000BASE-LX operation) into higher-speed switch-to-switch trunks (the maximum length for 100 Mbps operation is 2 km).

- Switch-to-server connections. Link aggregation is quite common between servers and switches. Most servers can fully utilize the capacity offered by an aggregated link, but are not able to fully utilize a Gigabit Ethernet link.

The caveat is that there must be enough unused fibers and switch ports available to form the aggregated link.

In the longer term, Gigabit Ethernet will be the natural upgrade for these lower-speed aggregated links. The main reason is that there is likely to be a requirement for even higher throughput between inter-networking nodes. New servers, able to use a large fraction of a dedicated Gigabit Ethernet link, will have been purchased. And of course, the next upgrade will be to aggregate the Gigabit Ethernet links!

It seems safe to conclude that link aggregation, at all data rates, will become more and more important. This is not just because it increases link capacity, but also because it provides other useful features such as load balancing and alternate paths in case of link or port failure.

Ethernet link aggregation is currently under development as a draft standard by the IEEE 802.3ad task group. Section 15.2 in Chapter 15, "The Future: Gigabit Ethernet and Beyond," provides an extended discussion of this capability.

13.4.4.4 Network Server Strategies

One issue that should be addressed during development of a long-range network plan is the size and network location(s) for the various file servers that are used by the organization. The file servers can be either distributed across the network or they can be concentrated in a central location. Both approaches work, but there are several factors that should be considered before a final server location strategy is adopted:

- Installing applications software on network file servers saves end-station disk space, reduces software maintenance (new releases of the software do not have to be installed in each end station), and ensures that all users have access to the same release level (preventing a compatibility problem that arises when different release levels are not fully forward/backward compatible).

- Server locations can affect network traffic levels and backup power supply costs:

  - Centrally located file servers can provide a uninterruptible power supply (UPS) economy-of-scale cost savings for battery-based UPS and backup generators, but they will likely increase the intermediate switch and backbone traffic loads.

  - Distributed file servers, on the other hand, can decrease the intermediate switch and backbone traffic loads, but they will likely increase the UPS and backup generator costs.

- File servers that contain information used only by closely located workgroups (such as workgroups on a single floor or in a single building) can reasonably be installed near the associated floor or building distributor. Network traffic to and from the servers remains within the workgroup subnet, and because user stations are seldom provided with backup power, these servers probably do not need to be provided with long-term UPS protection either.

- File servers accessed by workgroups in multiple buildings or in other facilities should be centrally located and should be provided with backup power, particularly if the workgroup personnel needing access to these files are located in facilities that are not served by the same power source.

- File servers used for storing classified or business-sensitive information should be located in secure facilities with appropriate protection against unauthorized network and facility access. Backup power might or might not need to be provided.

There is one class of servers, however, that may need additional consideration during network upgrade and consolidation—mail servers. Individual workgroups that have installed their own small LANs have traditionally procured and maintained their own file and mail servers. Then, when the small LANs are interconnected to form a campus network, the local mail servers are often left where they are, and this can be a problem.

Experience has shown that mail server UPS maintenance is often neglected when the responsibility is left with a user department, particularly during periods with lean budgets.

Note

We know of a case where the power to half of a university campus was shut down over a weekend for electrical system modification. The UPS power to the mail servers failed and more than half of the UPS battery bank had to be replaced—the batteries had not been properly maintained because they were not a priority budget item. The result was a complete loss of the mail system in a number of departments for more than a week.

Mail servers provide a communication function. They should be administered, maintained, and provided UPS protection in the same manner as network switches, bridges, and routers.

13.4.4.5 *Establishing the Long-Range Network Architecture*

While there is no question that any of the above topologies can provide excellent Ethernet service, the choice of the final topology depends on several somewhat subjective factors, for example:

- The network's capability to recover in case of link/port failure at any level, or switch failure at the building or campus distributor levels

- The network's capability to balance traffic loads

- The capability to aggregate links to form higher-speed trunks

The choice of factors here might seem somewhat arbitrary, and it is. However, Ethernet components have typically exhibited a high degree of reliability over the years and failures, when they occur, tend to occur singularly: to a single link or port, to a single switch, or to a single end station. Table 13.1 compares several possible topologies for these four factors. Listing recovery from failure to an end station and a multiport failure to a floor distributor switch was purposefully omitted because they both represent a low level of vulnerability when compared to building and campus level switches.

Table 13.1   Operational Characteristics of Several Example Topologies

Network Topology	Recovery from Link/ Port Failure	Recovery from Single Switch Failure[a]	Traffic Load Balancing	Link Aggregation (Trunking)
Tree	no	no	no	no
Tree with redundant links	yes	no	some	yes
Partial-mesh[b]	yes	no	some	no
Partial-mesh with redundant links	yes	no	yes	yes
Partial-mesh with redundant links/switches[c]	yes	yes	yes	yes
Full-mesh	yes	yes	yes	no
Full-mesh with redundant links	yes	yes	yes	yes
Full-mesh with redundant links/switches[c]	yes	yes	yes	yes

[a]At the building or campus distributor level.
[b]Partial-mesh provides at least one alternate path for all switch combinations (see Figure 13.2).
[c]Redundant switches are defined for the building and campus distributors (see Figure 13.4).

The final choice is a trade-off between the additional cost for the extra links and/or switches versus the desired network flexibility and reliability levels. In these examples, there appears little to be gained from having a topology with any more redundancy than the partial-mesh with redundant switch interconnection and redundant switches at the building and distributor levels, as shown in Figure 13.4.

Note that the number of switch ports and backbone links are the same in Figures 13.3 and 13.4, but the network reliability level is increased by using smaller paired switches.

Figure 13.4   Example Partial-Mesh Topology with Redundant Links and Switches

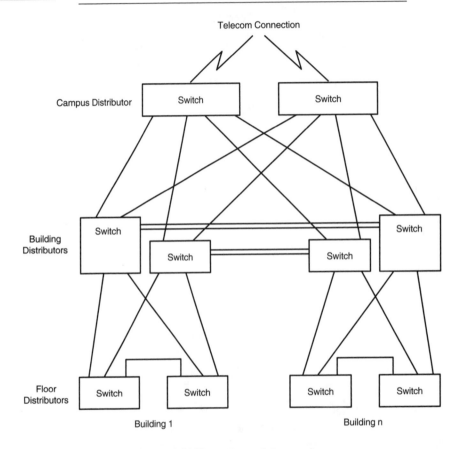

13.4.5 *Network Compatibility Considerations*

Figure 3.1 in Chapter 3, "Media Access Control," first introduced the concept of access and link compatibility dimensions. Chapter 4 alluded to a third compatibility dimension, router compatibility, now shown for the first time in Figure 13.5. Each dimension ultimately relates to how the network is configured to handle the expected traffic loads and patterns. This section reviews link and access compatibility. Chapter 14 discusses router compatibility.

Figure 13.5   Ethernet Compatibility Dimensions

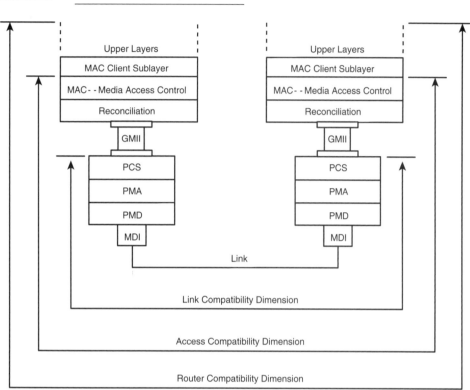

GMII = Gigabit Media Independent Interface (optional)
PCS = Physical Coding Sublayer
PMA = Physical Medium Attachment
PMD = Physical Medium Dependent Sublayer
MDI = Medium Dependent Interface

13.4.5.1 Link Compatibility Requirements

Link compatibility ensures that link partners (such as the end stations and/or switch ports at each end of a link) are able to communicate with each other. This requires that both NICs are compatible with the link media and with each other. In addition, both NICs must utilize the same operational mode (half- or full-duplex).

The capability to communicate across a link must be established when the link partners are first connected to the link. Once that is done, communication viability is verified and the operational mode is negotiated each time either link partner goes through a power up or reset cycle (see Chapter 8, "Physical Coding, Physical Medium Attachment, and Auto-Negotiation for 1000BASE-X," sections 8.1 and 8.4).

Note

Link compatibility also requires that transmitters at each end of the link are connected to the receivers at the other end of the link in systems that use multiple conductor links (as shown in Figures 5.2 and 5.3 in Chapter 5). This means that the conductors must *cross-over* each other at some point between the transmitter output and the receiver input. Unfortunately, when this requirement first arose in 10BASE-T, IEEE 802.3 chose not to make a hard rule for where the crossover function was to be implemented. Instead, the standard lists two rules and two recommendations:

- There must be an odd number of cross-overs in all multiconductor links.

- If a PMD is equipped with an internal cross-over function, its MDI must be labeled with a graphical "X" symbol.

- Implementation of an internal cross-over function is optional.

- When an end station is connected to a repeater (or other intermediate network device) port, it is recommended that the cross-over function be implemented within the intermediate network device port.

The eventual result was that the ports in most intermediate network devices (DCEs) were equipped with PMDs that had internal cross-over functions and most end stations (DTEs) were equipped with PMDs that had no internal cross-over function. This eventually led to the following *de facto* "installation rule:"

"Use a straight through cable when connecting a DTE to a DCE device. Use a cross-over cable when connecting a DTE-to-DTE or a DCE-to-DCE."

Unfortunately, this "rule" does not apply to all subsequent Ethernet versions that have been developed in the years following 10BASE-T. As things now stand:

- All fiber-based systems (10BASE, 100BASE, and 1000BASE) use cables that have the cross-over functions externally implemented in the optical fiber cable.

- All 100BASE systems using copper links use the same requirements and recommendations as 10BASE-T.

- 1000BASE-T systems provide an optional autonegotiation procedure that negotiates which PMD will enable the internal cross-over function. 1000BASE-T PMDs with cross-over negotiation capability are interconnected by straight through links.

This all means that network maintenance personnel and cable installers must be careful to use the correct equipment cable when making network connections. It also means that network managers need to understand the problem and to make sure that the appropriate personnel are properly trained.

13.4.5.2 *Access Compatibility Considerations*

After link compatibility has been established, the MAC sublayer configuration must be considered. Access compatibility only becomes a problem in a frame transfer when the transmitting MAC cannot correctly format the frame to be transferred, or when the receiving MAC cannot correctly interpret all the fields of the received frame.

Configuring a network for complete access compatibility requires that all affected devices in the network paths are equipped with compatible MACs.

The Full-Duplex/MAC Control Option

Full-duplex operation allows simultaneous frame transmission and reception between two MACs connected by a single link. Full-duplex MACs must be equipped with separate transmit and receive frame buffers as well as with the MAC Control option.

MAC Control was defined for two purposes:

- To implement a fast response local flow control (PAUSE) capability that will prevent buffer overrun and frame loss when one link partner is about to be swamped with frames being received from the other partner

- To define a format structure that will allow the addition of future (as yet undefined) control operations that span one or more links

Flow control (MAC_CONTROL.request[PAUSE]) can be invoked only during full-duplex operation and only between link partners to control transmission over a single link. Both link partners must be capable of full-duplex operation.

The PAUSE direction (which of the link partners is allowed to invoke a PAUSE operation) is determined at power-up by the Auto-Negotiation function in the PCS sublayer at the same time that the operational mode (half- or full-duplex) is determined, based on the configuration register's FD, HD, PS1, and PS2 bits (see Chapter 8, section 8.4.5). The values of the PS1 and PS2 bits represent the desired PAUSE configuration and can be set by network management.

PAUSE frames are never forwarded by a repeater, switch, bridge, or router (see section 3.1.2.1 in Chapter 3).

The VLAN Tagging Option

VLAN tagging was developed as a bridging protocol to support transmission of time-critical information across IEEE 802 LANs. Transmission priorities are identified within the VLAN tag in the MAC frame header and are used by network switches, bridges, and routers for frame selection and queuing.

In addition, the development of VLAN tagging enabled filtering services that support the definition and establishment of groups within a LAN environment as well as the forwarding of frames only to the network segments required to reach members of the group. Filtering (frame selection and queuing) is based on both transmission priority and VLAN ID.

Unlike the MAC Control PAUSE operation that affects only the link partners at each end of a single link, VLAN tagging can impact the entire network. *The end stations and all intermediate devices in the network path between end stations requiring VLAN services must be VLAN-compatible to support priority transfer.*

13.4.5.3   *Frame Transmission Between Dissimilar MACs*

It is obvious that a MAC without MAC Control or VLAN tagging capability would not be able to format either a MAC Control or VLAN-tagged frame for transmission. But it is not so obvious whether a MAC without these capabilities would be able to receive a MAC Control or VLAN-tagged frame.

With MAC Control (PAUSE) frames, if either link partner lacks full-duplex/MAC Control capability, neither local flow control nor full-duplex operation will be allowed (MAC Control frames will never be generated by either link partner).

With VLAN-tagged frames, if the receiving link partner lacks the IEEE 802.1p/Q VLAN option, the VLAN tag field cannot be interpreted. However, because the network switches are essentially multiport learning bridges, and because network management is able to determine the MAC option complement of each end station and switch port, the last switch before the non–VLAN-compatible receiving MAC will strip the VLAN tag (and the priority indication) from the frame header and will forward the frame as a non-tagged frame. The frame may be delayed, but the intended receiver will still be able to read its contents correctly.

13.4.6   *Network Infrastructure Considerations*

The key to a *future-proof* network is to provide an infrastructure (the inaccessible facilities—the conduits and links) that will support long-term network growth, future technology changes, and even greater transmission rates.

The previous chapter spent considerable time discussing installation and management of the cable plant; however, there was no consideration of where the cables should be run, how many fiber/wire pairs should be provided, or what type of link should be installed. Where to run the cables is determined in large part by the topology selected for the network. You still have to consider the size, type, and number of conduits, cables, and fiber/wire pairs that should be installed.

Sections 13.4.6.1–13.4.6.3 discuss systems issues that affect cable plant sizing.

13.4.6.1 Hidden Conduits and Cables

Although coverage of brute force planning approach was included with tongue in cheek, this approach should be considered when planning conduits, cables, and links that will be hidden after construction is complete. Holes for cable runs can be one of the most expensive items in a network upgrade. Extra conduits are easy to install in walls and under streets and sidewalks during initial construction. The additional cost is minor when compared to the future cost and disruption of installing new cables and conduits after the fact.

Sizing Underground Conduits

A rule of thumb for underground conduit installations is to plan conduit space for backbone cabling with capacity at least 10X the projected maximum bandwidth, then double the number of conduits and add at least one or two extra. The doubled conduit space is for unanticipated future growth (it can also be for other low-voltage services such as telephone cable and alarms). The extra conduits are to provide space for pulling higher capacity cables (for example, cables with more optical fibers) without having to shut down the network during cable plant upgrade. After cutover, the lower capacity cables can be removed from their conduit and that conduit then can become the "extra" for future upgrades. The installed backbone cable capacity should be at least 10X the projected bandwidth requirements. Some recommend 100X, but as you will see in section 15.5 in Chapter 15, 100X may be unrealistic because wavelength division multiplexing (WDM) provides an alternate way to increase backbone capacity of existing fibers.

Direct-Burial Cable

If direct-burial cable is installed for the campus backbone, an alternate backbone cable should be installed in a geographically separated route to avoid network shutdown in case of cable damage during future construction activities.

Building Conduits and Cabling

Accessible empty conduits should be installed in office walls to facilitate future link installations. In multipurpose facilities, the number of hidden user-to-floor distributor links should provide for a user floor-space density that would allow for office use (say, at least one link for each 10 m^2 of floor space).

13.4.6.2 Links and Link Issues

Fortunately, there is a high degree of link compatibility between the different implementations of 10 Mbps, 100 Mbps, and 1,000 Mbps Ethernet. For example, depending on the implementation of the NIC's physical layer, Category-3 UTP links can support either 10 Mbps or 100 Mbps operation; Category-5 UTP can be used for 10 Mbps, 100 Mbps, or 1,000 Mbps; and multimode fiber can be used for 10 Mbps, 100 Mbps, or 1,000 Mbps.

You can see that there is considerable flexibility in link-media selection for either new networks or network upgrades. In fact, you should consider two different strategies: one for the recycling of existing links and cables, and the other for selecting media for links that have yet to be installed. The two sections that follow, "Existing Links" and "New Links," cover these two strategies.

Existing Links

Because the network cable plant can represent a considerable investment, it is always desirable to reuse existing links wherever possible. Reusing existing links with new, higher performance network equipment takes advantage of Ethernet's *backward compatibility* design.

Tables 13.2 and 13.3 list the operational capabilities and maximum lengths defined in IEEE 802.3 for both copper and optical fiber links.

Table 13.2 Maximum Copper Link Lengths for Multisupplier Ethernet Interoperation in Switch-Based Networks

Link Media	Implementation	Half-Duplex Length	Full-Duplex Length
Category-3 UTP	10BASE-T	100 m	100 m
	100 BASE-T4	100 m	Not Supported
Category-5 UTP	10BASE -T	100 m	~180 m
	100BASE-T2	100 m	100 m
	100BASE-T4	100 m	Not Supported
	100BASE-TX	100 m	100 m
	1000BASE-T[a]	100 m	100 m
STP	100BASE-TX	100 m	100 m
	1000BASE-CX	25 m	25 m

[a]Not all Category-5 links can support 1000BASE-T operation (see section 15.1 in Chapter 15).

Table 13.3   Maximum Optical Fiber Link Lengths for Multisupplier Ethernet Interoperation in Switch-Based Networks

Link Media	Implementation	Half-Duplex Length	Full-Duplex Length
50 μm MMF	1000BASE-SX	316 m	500 m
62.5 μm MMF	100BASE-FX	412 m	2,000 m
	1000BASE-SX	220/275 m	316 m
	1000BASE-LX	316 m	7,000 m
10 μm SMF	1000BASE-LX	316 m	5,000 m

New Links

New links should be selected with *forward compatibility* in mind. While cost is always a consideration, link selection criteria should consider the media's potential for supporting even higher transmission rates in the future.

All new horizontal link installations (links with lengths under 100 m) should be able to support at least Gigabit transmission rates. New links can be either multimode fiber or Category-5, or better, unshielded twisted pair (UTP) copper. (Chapter 15 discusses 1000BASE-T UTP cabling requirements.) Single-mode fiber is not likely ever to be required for floor distribution.

Multimode optical fiber may be used for Gigabit backbone link lengths up to 700 m, but single-mode optical fiber should be considered for new links longer than 100 m to allow use with higher transmission rates (10 Gbps Ethernet, for example) in the future. The installation of cable assemblies that include a mixture of *both SMF and MMF links* is a good way to allow for this *future need*.

13.4.6.3 *Extended-Length Gigabit Ethernet Links*

This book has iterated several times that 62.5 μm MMF can support 1000BASE-LX operation at lengths up to 700 m. You should also know that single-mode fiber links are not limited to only 5,000 m.

Presently available (early 1999) commercial link extenders allow full-duplex Gigabit Ethernet transmission over single-mode fiber in lengths up to 110 km (about 68 miles) using wavelengths near 1,550 nm. The products usually include a standard 1000BASE-SX or LX interface to the local Gigabit Ethernet port and electronics to drive a proprietary transceiver that operates in the 1,550 nm wavelength band for the long distance link. The higher transceiver costs are more than offset by the longer distance capability.

At least one manufacturer is claiming validated Gigabit transmission over test distances up to 800 km (about 500 miles) by using Gigabit Ethernet extender technology in combination with WDM techniques and optical amplification.

These products can be very important for organizations that need to link facilities separated by more than 5 km link distance. In short, these products are extending the Ethernet protocol into both the metropolitan area network (MAN) and the wide area network (WAN) domains.

13.4.7   Defining the Network Plan

Once you develop an extensible long-range architecture, you are ready to define the network plan. The actual plan need only cover the areas of the network that are directly affected. Defining the network plan basically involves fitting the current network into the network topology and selecting the equipment necessary for the upgrade, as discussed in the sections that follow.

13.4.7.1   Fitting the Current Network into the Network Topology

Unless you are installing a completely new network, you will want to determine how the current network fits into the chosen topology. This requires an accurate picture of the current network and cable plant, information that should be available in the cable plant database and as-built drawings (see Chapter 12, "The Cable Plant: Installation and Management," section 12.2).

However, if there is any doubt about the accuracy of the cable plant record status, a reasonably sized random check should be made to determine its probable condition. Also, if either the cable plant database or the as-built drawings are missing or are out of date, you should survey the network and bring these documents up to date before proceeding further.

Note

We understand that many installers have not bothered to keep their cable plant records up to date, but without them, each subsequent upgrade will have to start from the essentially same place: surveying the cable plant to see what there is, what is currently in use, what is available, and what needs to be added. If this situation sounds familiar, take the time to set up the cable plant database and prepare drawings or sketches of the hidden conduits and cable runs so that next time the network is upgraded (and it will be) this task will not have to be done again.

You can now begin to prepare a set of single-line schematics and supplemental detail listings for each *affected* floor (or floor section), for their associated building backbone risers, and for the campus backbone cabling identifying what is to be added, moved, or changed.

13.4.7.2 Selecting the Equipment

Part of the add, move, and change decisions will typically involve equipment selection, including network switches. As with links and cables, switches should be selected with an eye to the future (switches have the longest useful life after cables and links; user stations are now being replaced as often as every 18 to 24 months). Consideration should be given to requiring all new switches to have the following characteristics:

- Have full-duplex/flow control capability. The added cost to this option is easily offset by the increased bandwidth and link length flexibility.

- Have VLAN capability, even if priority frame transfer is not anticipated. The capability to define VLAN groups assists routing protocols and makes network management much easier during adds, moves, and changes.

- Be non-blocking to better handle periods of intense traffic loads.

- Be capable of link aggregation and load balancing across multiple links.

- Be equipped with multirate NICs (such as 10/100 Mbps or 100/1,000 Mbps) at each port. Switch ports should be hot-swappable and should not require the switch to be powered down in case of port failure.

> **Note**
>
> A rule of thumb to ensure acceptable CoS service is to size switches and their interconnecting links with sufficient capacity to keep the peak link bandwidth utilization under 60 percent.

After establishing the switch configurations, the network manager should promulgate the network compatibility requirements for network end stations, which can continue to be procured by the different workgroups.

13.5 *Summary*

By this point, you should have a reasonably good idea of what is involved in planning or upgrading an Ethernet network. This chapter has:

- Presented several planning procedures

- Suggested some planning objectives

- Pointed out some mitigating factors that simplify planning for Ethernet networks

- Discussed possible topological alternatives

- Proposed criteria for link and equipment selection

The reason you should take the time to develop a set of network objectives, an extensible network architecture, and a maintainable cable plant database is to give you a starting point and to save time during future upgrades (many can be handled as piecemeal adds, moves, and changes).

While the discussion included references to all three hierarchical levels defined by ISO/IEC 11801 (campus, building, and floor), you should remember that these are merely guidelines. *Not all networks need to include all hierarchical levels.* For example:

- A small office would likely need only a floor distributor.

- A multifloor office building should have a building distributor plus floor distributors for each floor.

- A small facility with an office building and a detached shop or lab might have a building distributor plus floor distributors for each floor and the detached shop (if the shop required only one or two user stations, they might even be connected directly to the building distributor or one of the floor distributors).

- A facility with a number of widely scattered single-floor buildings might need only a campus distributor plus floor distributors for each building.

There are obviously more examples where not all hierarchical network levels are required, but these are enough to make the point.

And finally, before closing out this chapter, we need to stress again the importance of having a good network management system to monitor and control the configuration (and reconfiguration) of your network. Properly used, it will warn you before things get out of hand and will also save countless hours during adds, moves, and changes. The next chapter discusses Gigabit Ethernet in context with other technologies.

14

Gigabit Ethernet in Context with Other LAN Technologies

As stated in Chapter 13, "Upgrading Ethernet LANs: System and Topology Considerations," Gigabit Ethernet can be used to upgrade both Ethernet and non-Ethernet local area networks (LANs). Chapter 13 discussed upgrading Ethernet LANs. This chapter briefly reviews some non-Ethernet technologies currently deployed in LANs and then considers the use of Gigabit Ethernet as an upgrade.

There are several reasons why you also should consider upgrading non-Ethernet networks with Gigabit Ethernet technologies:

- Different divisions within the same organization may have initially chosen to implement different LAN technologies and protocols.

- Gigabit Ethernet can be the lowest cost long-term alternative for upgrading, even within a non-Ethernet environment. Over 80 percent of the nodes in the world's LANs use Ethernet technology. Furthermore, because this is a highly competitive market, costs can be expected to continue their downward trend.

- The Ethernet protocol is typically less complex, more easily understood, and simpler to implement than competing protocols.

- Ethernet can now provide previously unavailable Class of Service (CoS) transmission.

It is widely recognized that the first major application to be addressed by LAN equipment upgrades is the need for increased bandwidth between workgroup, backbone, and campus networking equipment. But, the introduction of new data types requiring CoS and QoS features means that raw bandwidth alone is not sufficient. For this reason, all new switch-based products, whether packet- or circuit-based, already have or are introducing techniques that can provide CoS and QoS features, at least to some degree.

This chapter begins with a review of commonly installed LAN technologies, then continues with a discussion of the higher layer protocols required to both support IP-based traffic on connection-oriented networking technology and to support QoS or CoS over IP-based networks. The chapter concludes with a discussion of the suitability of Gigabit Ethernet as an upgrade for each of the LAN technologies discussed.

14.1 Commonly Installed LAN Technologies

As you should be aware by now, LAN equipment is installed in a hierarchical manner. The hierarchy is related to the building wiring standard levels for horizontal cabling (for connection to desktops), building backbone cabling (for interconnection of workgroup LAN equipment), and campus backbones (for interconnection of building LAN equipment). This hierarchy has evolved because it eases the burdens associated with network design, network management, and fault isolation of both LAN equipment and the supporting cabling infrastructure.

Table 14.1 summarizes some of the important features of commonly installed Layer 2 LAN technologies. ATM is the only connection-oriented LAN technology listed in Table 14.1. All the others are connectionless (packet-based) technologies.

Table 14.1 Multimode Fiber (MMF) Link Lengths for Commonly Installed Layer 2 LANs

LAN Type	Data Rate (Mbps)	LAN Configuration	Typical Usage	Maximum MMF Link Length (m)
Ethernet	10	Shared	Desktop	2,000
Ethernet	10	Switched	Desktop	2,000
Ethernet	100	Shared	Desktop and Wiring closets	412
Ethernet	100	Switched	Backbone and Desktop	2,000
Token Ring	4	Shared	Desktop	2,000
Token Ring	16	Shared and Switched	Desktop	2,000
Token Ring	100	Switched	Backbone and Desktop	2,000
FDDI	100	Shared and Switched	Backbone	2,000
100VG	100	Shared and Switched	Desktop and Backbone	2,000

LAN Type	Data Rate (Mbps)	LAN Configuration	Typical Usage	Maximum MMF Link Length (m)
ATM	155	Switched	Backbone	2,000
ATM	622	Switched	Backbone	550[a]

[a]This distance could be increased to 1,600 m if mode-conditioned 1000BASE-LX Gigabit Ethernet optical transceivers were used for this application.

Although Table 14.1 states the maximum multimode fiber link length, you should remember that practically all desktop links use Category-5 UTP cable. Also, as noted in Chapter 13, if single-mode optical fiber is used for switched links, the maximum link length could be very long indeed—up to 110 km—with commercially available, specialized, non-standards-based, single-mode link extenders.

14.1.1 Layer 2 LAN Summary: Token Ring

Token Ring is a deterministic protocol that was developed in the early 1980s to avoid the random packet collisions that occur in Ethernet. Token Ring has been standardized as IEEE 802.5. Originally the network topology was a physical ring. However, today many Token Ring networks have their wiring installed in the normal building wiring tree or star topology.

In the ring configuration, both tokens (permission to send) and information packets are transmitted between successive stations or nodes on the ring. Only one token is allowed on the ring and only the node holding the token is allowed to transmit a data packet. After the sender has finished transmitting a data packet, it generates a new token that is then circulated around the ring. The token will be captured by the next node on the ring needing to send a packet.

The Token Ring frame format is different from the Ethernet format both in how the information is encoded and in the field definitions for the frame format. The data field length can be up to 4,500 bytes, and two additional fields provide control information that is not available in a basic Ethernet frame:

- A 1-byte access control field in the frame header contains 3 bits for packet priority designation, 3 bits to indicate a token reservation and its priority level, plus a token bit to differentiate a data/command frame from a token.

- A 1-byte end delimiter identifies the end of the frame and contains control bits to indicate whether the frame was damaged in transmission and whether this frame is the last frame in a logical sequence.

Currently available Token Ring products operate at 4, 16, and 100 Mbps (100 Mbps Token Ring is in the final stages of standardization; also, a task force has been set up to draft a Gigabit Token Ring standard). Both shared and switched versions of Token Ring are available.

14.1.2   Layer 2 LAN Summary: FDDI

The Fiber Distributed Data Interface (FDDI) is a Token Ring protocol similar to IEEE 802.5 that operates at 100 Mbps. FDDI was developed in the 1980s as a high speed backbone and desktop replacement for IEEE 802.5 and was standardized through ANSI by the X3T9.5 working group. Originally, FDDI was designed as a fiber optic network; however, copper UTP and STP versions were developed. The FDDI physical layers were reused by the IEEE 802.3 committee for 100BASE-FX and TX Fast Ethernet. The packet format used by FDDI is similar to that of Token Ring.

FDDI actually uses two counter-rotating rings to provide a high degree of fault tolerance. Comprehensive station management was developed as part of the standard and FDDI's main role has been as a highly reliable backbone LAN. Both shared and switched FDDI products are available. A higher data rate version of FDDI has not been developed.

14.1.3   Layer 2 LAN Summary: 100VG-AnyLAN

100VG-AnyLAN uses the Demand Priority Access Method (DPAM), a deterministic protocol that was developed in the early 1990s as a high speed upgrade for both 10BASE-T and 4 Mbps and 16 Mbps Token Ring LANs. As such, a single DPAM-based network can operate in either an Ethernet mode, where it transmits Ethernet frames, or a Token Ring mode, where it transmits Token Ring frames, but not in both modes at the same time. DPAM also provides two levels of packet priority. DPAM was standardized as IEEE 802.12.

100VG-AnyLAN was specifically designed to operate over the lowest grade UTP cable used by 10BASE-T: 25 pair, voice grade UTP cabling. Because of this, it has a significant operational margin on better grades of UTP, STP, and optical fiber cabling. With shared media, 100VG-AnyLAN obeys the same topology rules as 10BASE-T. Both shared and switched versions of 100VG-AnyLAN are available.

There was an initial effort to develop a Gigabit version of IEEE 802.12; however, with the advent of switch-based networks, it was recognized that Gigabit Ethernet would be a very effective upgrade for 100VG-AnyLAN. Gigabit activity within IEEE 802.12 was terminated, and many of the contributors from that committee transferred to the IEEE 802.3z committee, where they played key roles in the development of Gigabit Ethernet.

14.1.4 Layer 2 LAN Summary: ATM

Asynchronous Transfer Mode (ATM) is probably the best known alternative to Gigabit Ethernet. For this reason, this section provides more coverage than is provided for the other LAN examples. ATM was developed by the telecommunications industry as part of the Broadband Integrated Services Digital Network (BISDN). It provides a means to integrate various data types having disparate transmission requirements, such as computer data traffic, voice traffic, and video traffic. In contrast to the examples considered thus far (Ethernet, Token Ring, FDDI, and 100VG-AnyLAN), ATM is connection-oriented.

ATM transmits a continuous stream of small fixed length packets called *cells*. An ATM cell is only 53 bytes long, consisting of a 5-byte header and a 48-byte payload field. ATM cells were purposely kept short to reduce transmission delay variations and to enable efficient switching.

The header contains the control and next destination routing information for the cell, including:

• A generic flow control (GFC) field that is seldom used, but typically set to a default value

• A virtual path identifier (VPI) that is used with the VCI to identify the next route destination of the cell

• A virtual channel identifier (VCI) that is used with the VPI

• A payload type (PT) field that indicates whether the cell contains data or control information

• A congestion loss priority (CLP) bit that indicates how the cell should be treated with respect to other cells in cases of network congestion

• A header error control (HEC) field containing a checksum for the header information

The purpose of the ATM layer is to provide transparent transfer of cells across pre-established network connections according to a pre-arranged traffic contract. ATM systems generally use a Synchronous Optical Network (SONET) physical layer. When this is the case, the ATM layer must insert unassigned (idle) cells into the stream of cells during times when there is no data to transmit. The result is a continuous stream of cells, a process called *cell rate decoupling*.

The VPI and VCI are used by ATM switches, which form part of the ATM layer, to manage connections across the ATM network. Because ATM is a connection-oriented protocol, end-to-end signaling must be used to establish a virtual circuit before any data is transmitted. The signaling establishes the path through the ATM switching network and any required QoS agreements.

Another important part of the ATM layer is the ATM adaptation layer (AAL). The ATM adaptation layer usually resides in end stations. The AAL layer in the transmitting station segments frames received from higher protocol layers into cells for transmission; the peer AAL layer in the receiving station collects the cells and reassembles them into frames for forwarding to the higher protocol layers. Various types of AAL have been standardized for use with different traffic types. AAL5 is commonly used for packet-based communication.

14.1.5   *Higher Layer Protocols for IP-Based Networks*

The discussion in sections 14.1.1–14.1.4 was limited to issues relating to layer 1 (the physical layer) and layer 2 (the data link layer). For a more complete comparison of Gigabit Ethernet with the other networking options, you need to consider some of the higher layers. This discussion begins with a brief review of the most commonly used LAN model: the TCP/IP suite. The TCP/IP protocol suite doesn't have the same layered model as the OSI reference model. Roughly speaking, however, IP can be associated with the network layer and TCP with the transport layer, although TCP also includes some of the OSI session layer functionality. In Ethernet implementations, the bottom two layers consist of the IEEE 802.2 LLC and IEEE 802.3 MAC (data link layer) and the IEEE 802.3 physical layer, as shown in Table 14.2.

Table 14.2   The Relationship of the TCP/IP/Ethernet Protocol Stack to the OSI Model

OSI Layer	OSI Layer Name	Protocol Implementation
4	Transport	TCP
3	Network	IP
2	Data Link	IEEE 802.2 LLC and IEEE 802.3 MAC
1	Physical	IEEE 802.3 PHY

Because IP is a connectionless protocol, no end-to-end signaling or control information needs to be exchanged before packet transmission begins. Also, because IP only provides a *best effort* service, no QoS or CoS is provided. TCP is the transport layer protocol of the TCP/IP suite and it provides connection-oriented reliable transmission (see Chapter 4, "Gigabit Repeaters, Bridges, Routers, and Switches"). TCP is a protocol that is best suited to data communications applications. TCP/IP is not a good choice for real-time video transmission.

An IP-based network has two types of nodes: *hosts* and *routers*. A router is a node with at least two network interface connections and is capable of forwarding packets from one network to another network. A host is simply a node that is not a router.

Three other important protocols that support the IP protocol are the Internet Control Message Protocol (ICMP), the Internet Group Management Protocol (IGMP), and the Simple Network Management Protocol (SNMP), all of which are standardized. ICMP is used mainly for fault diagnosis, error reporting, and control messages. IGMP is used to form and manage multicast groups. SNMP enables network administrators to manage the network.

In an IP-based internet, routes are calculated by the network routers in a distributed fashion. The IP protocol does not define how the routers should do this. However, there are standard *routing protocols* for this purpose. Some well-known examples of standards-based IP routing protocols include the following:

- Routing Information Protocol (*RIP)*

- Open Shortest Path First (*OSPF)*

- Border Gateway Protocol (*BGP)*

QoS and CoS in IP-Based Networks

Until the advent of multilayer switching, routing was performed by general purpose processors under software control. But because software routines are typically slower than ASIC hardware routines, software-based routers can be congestion points in a network. As such, software-based routers could make it difficult to provide QoS/CoS service; however, IP doesn't provide either QoS or CoS anyway.

As section 13.2 in Chapter 13 stated, the Internet Engineering Task Force (IETF) has been working for some time to define standards-based mechanisms and protocols for providing QoS and CoS—especially for switch-based networks. They are also finalizing the Resource Reservation Protocol (RSVP), which will enable networks to reserve dedicated bandwidth. In addition, the IP-based multicast backbone (Mbone), which was based on the Real-time Transport Protocol (RTP), has proven that real-time, multicast video conferencing is possible over the Internet—the Mbone was originally designed to broadcast the meetings of the IETF.

continues

Even before these standards are finalized, many manufacturers of high-end multilayer switches have implemented the common IP-based routing algorithms (RIP, OSPF, BGP, and so forth) in hardware to produce *routing-switches*. These routing switches can process packets at the line rate of each port (even for Gigabit Ethernet!). Usually, each port has dedicated routing hardware so that packets entering the port can either be switched, based on layer 2 information or, if need be, routed, based on layer 3 information. Many of these routing switches can also provide CoS and QoS features based on some or all of the following: IEEE 802.1p/Q, IP datagram Type of Service (ToS), and the source or destination TCP/UDP port number. But not all protocols are routed in hardware. Those that aren't are usually forwarded to a software-based router. However, the network performance for these other protocols is also greatly improved because the software-based routers are only required to deal with non-IP traffic.

Several manufacturers are using *cut-through* switches to gain performance improvement, compared to software routing. Cut-through switches usually gain performance improvements by switching based on the examination of only the packet header of each packet in a transmission. However, some routers gain a further increase in performance by only examining the first few packets of an identified transmission. Several of the schemes used for IP cut-through routing actually involve using a switch with an underlying ATM-based switching fabric. Cut-through switch-routers tend to use proprietary methods, although standards are beginning to emerge.

14.1.6   Higher Layer Protocols for ATM-Based Networks

As stated in section 14.1.4, ATM is a connection-oriented switch-based layer 2 technology that requires end-to-end signaling before any data packets are transmitted. However, the end-to-end signaling can also be used to set up connections with guaranteed levels of QoS and CoS.

While ATM is ideal for voice and video applications, it has some difficulties when transmitting IP-based data. These difficulties arise because IP was predicated on a connectionless service model. Broadcast and multicast traffic is commonly used in Ethernet and IP-based networks for functions such as address discovery and routing table updates. ATM requires additional higher layer protocol support to cope with these broadcast and multicast requirements, but because over 80 percent of the world's network connections are through Ethernet ports, support of IP traffic is no longer optional.

Even before the growth of the World Wide Web, it would have been difficult to change the software associated with networking to a connection-oriented model simply because most applications assume a connectionless network model.

Table 14.3 compares the TCP/IP/ATM layer-2 protocol stack to the OSI model.

Table 14.3   The Relationship of the TCP/IP/ATM Protocol Stack to the OSI Model

OSI Layer	OSI Layer Name	Protocol Implementation
4	Transport	TCP
3	Network	IP, LANE, MPOA, MPLS, or RFC 1477[a]
2	Data Link	ATM AAL5 and ATM switching layer
1	Physical	SONET

[a]MPOA is Multiprotocol over ATM, LANE is LAN Emulation, MPLS is Multiprotocol label switching, and RFC 1477 is the IETF's classical IP-over-ATM standard. To simplify the table, ATM end-to-end signaling protocols are not shown.

So, it seems we've discovered a Catch-22 situation:

- ATM has native QoS, but requires complex higher layer protocol support for traditional IP-based traffic.

- Ethernet is ideal for IP-based traffic, but requires complex higher layer protocol support in order to provide CoS for emergent multimedia traffic.

In general, there is no solution to this Catch-22 situation. The best that can be done is to use the appropriate technology for the situation at hand. However, it is now widely recognized that Ethernet technology is best suited for the LAN, and ATM is best suited for the WAN; it is expected that both will compete for use in MANs. The next few sections introduce some of the higher layer protocols commonly used to support IP traffic on ATM-based networks.

14.1.6.1   LANE

The LAN emulation (LANE) protocol defines the operation of a *single* emulated LAN (ELAN). LANE uses ATM connection-oriented switches in a way that *emulates* a traditional connectionless LAN. For example, in the case of an Ethernet emulated LAN, the LANE interface behaves the same as a standard Ethernet layer 2/3 interface. This means that all data sent through the ATM network consists of ATM-encapsulated Ethernet packets.

Multiple ELANs can be simultaneously operated on a common ATM network. However, a separate ELAN must be dedicated to each traditional LAN protocol in operation. LANE was intended to accelerate the introduction of ATM networks. A disadvantage of LANE is that because it emulates a traditional connectionless layer 2/3 LAN interface it cannot use ATM's native QoS features.

LANE is based on a client-server model. The LAN emulation client (LEC) is an end-station function that performs data forwarding, address resolution, and registering of the MAC address with the LAN emulation server. For traditional LANs, the LEC also provides a standard layer 2/3 network interface to higher layer protocols. If an ATM end system is connected to multiple ELANs, there must be a separate LEC for each ELAN supported.

LANE requires three servers as follows:

- **LAN Emulation Server (LES)**. One LES is required for each ELAN. It is a central point that controls the admission of LECS to the ELAN. It is also responsible for registering client MAC and ATM addresses, and for address resolution.

- **LAN Emulation Configuration Server (LECS)**. One LECS serves all ELANs within an administrative domain. It maintains a database of the LECs and the ELANs to which they are registered. When queried by an LEC, the LECS will respond with the ATM address of the LES that serves the ELAN appropriate to that LEC.

- **Broadcast and Unknown Server (BUS)**. Each LEC is associated with one BUS per ELAN. The BUS is responsible for delivering broadcast frames and multicast frames. Additionally, unicast frames containing addresses that are unregistered or as yet unresolved are delivered by the BUS.

As illustrated in Figure 14.1, the LANE protocol is deployed in two types of ATM equipment: ATM network interface cards (NICs) and internetworking equipment—a layer 2 LAN switch is shown in the figure. Because an ELAN emulates a specific traditional LAN (Ethernet, Token Ring, FDDI, and so on), it can support various higher layer protocols such as IP, IPX, SNA/APPN, and NetBIOS.

Figure 14.1   Example of How LANE Protocol Can Be Implemented in ATM Network Devices

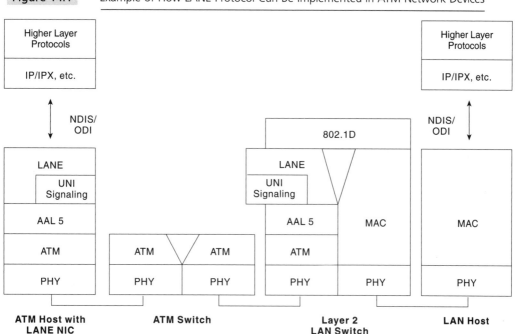

14.1.6.2   *Classical IP over ATM: RFC 1477*

Because IP over ATM as specified in RFC 1477 does not change the basic nature of the IP protocol, it is called *Classical IP over ATM*. Classical IP over ATM has the following characteristics:

- It is based on the concept of a logical IP subnetwork (LIS).

- An LIS contains hosts and routers having the same IP subnetwork mask (the bits of an IP address that are being used for the common subnetwork address) and the same subnetwork address.

- Any two hosts of the same LIS may communicate directly using virtual channels (VCs).

- Hosts from different LISs may only communicate through a router.

- The maximum transmission unit (MTU) is the same for VCs in an LIS and is a maximum of 9,180 bytes.

- Within a single LIS, IP addresses are resolved to ATM addresses by an ATM address resolution protocol (ATMARP) server. The inverse resolution is also performed by the inverse ATMARP on the server.

Classical IP over ATM has the obvious advantage that it allows IP data to be routed over an ATM LAN or WAN. However, its main disadvantages are that it only supports IP routing, it has no multicast support, ATM's intrinsic QoS properties may be lost passing through routers, and it is difficult to scale to a large number of LISs.

14.1.6.3 *Multiprotocol over ATM (MPOA)*

In an MPOA environment, connectionless LAN traffic is directed to shortcut ATM paths. For this reason, MPOA is classed as a *shortcut* or *cut-through* routing scheme. MPOA uses three technologies or concepts:

- LANE protocol

- IETF's Next Hop Resolution Protocol (NHRP)

- The concept of the virtual router

LANE is basically used for configuration purposes, NHRP is used to determine shortcut paths through the ATM switch-based network, and the virtual router concept allows partitioning of routing functions among various physically separated elements of the network.

The routing calculations are performed by the MPOA Servers (MPSs), while traffic forwarding is the responsibility of the MPOA Clients (MPCs) and the ATM switching layer. An MPS could be a standalone ATM attached route server, or it may reside within an ATM switch-router. MPCs reside in network edge devices and in ATM attached hosts. Traditional (non-ATM) hosts connect to the ATM network through the edge devices that support traditional LANs on the LAN side of the device and ATM on the backbone side.

Native ATM devices may be directly connected to the ATM layer. The MPOA routers or route servers within the ATM network provide routing information to the edge devices. The edge devices transmit data from their connected hosts to other edge devices using the shortcut ATM layer paths identified by the route servers. Again, although QoS is available to all ATM-attached devices, traditional connectionless-oriented LAN devices may not be able to take full advantage of this feature.

14.1.6.4 *Multiprotocol Label Switching (MPLS)*

MPLS is a form of tag switching. Tag switching was introduced in Chapter 4 and will not be discussed here. In an ATM context, VCs would be identified with particular labels or tags.

14.2 *Network Upgrade Comparisons*

Section 14.1 introduced commonly installed LAN technologies: Token Ring, FDDI, 100VG-AnyLAN, and ATM. This section briefly discusses the use of Gigabit Ethernet as an upgrade for these technologies. In many cases, ATM would be an upgrade alternative to Gigabit Ethernet for existing LANs. However, in this chapter, ATM will be discussed separately as an upgrade in section 14.2.4.

14.2.1 *Higher Speed Token Ring*

If a network is currently based on the Token Ring protocol, higher speed Token Ring may seem to be a natural upgrade choice. Further increases in capacity could also be achieved by using switched Token Ring. However, it must be remembered that switch-based Token Ring implementations bypass Token Ring's native deterministic MAC protocol. At the desktop level it may be advantageous to maintain Token Ring links just to avoid changing network interface cards or software "tuned" to Token Ring. This would be especially true in large Token Ring based networks. However, within the network core there is no real requirement to maintain the Token Ring protocol or packet format.

In the backbone, 100 Mbps Token Ring has limited advantages when compared to FDDI, 100 Mbps Switched Ethernet, Ethernet Link Aggregation, Gigabit Ethernet, or ATM. In addition, it will be some time before Gigabit Token Ring becomes widely available. Gigabit Ethernet is likely to be used to interconnect workgroup Token Ring hubs and switches. However, because of the different packet formats used by Token Ring and Ethernet, bridging or routing Gigabit Ethernet-to-Token Ring switches will be required. Native Token Ring fairness and priority mechanisms will not be directly supported by switch-based networks. However, the use of switches that have implemented the QoS and CoS features discussed in Chapter 13 will provide similar performance.

14.2.2 *FDDI*

In section 14.1.2, you discovered that FDDI only operates at 100 Mbps. You also learned that the capacity of an FDDI network can be upgraded using switch-based implementations. However, the introduction of switching accelerates the need for higher data rate connections between switches. It must also be remembered that switch-based FDDI implementations bypass the deterministic MAC protocol used by shared versions of FDDI.

Gigabit Ethernet is a good, economical upgrade path for FDDI networks because it provides the required higher data rate links. However, if native FDDI devices are to be interconnected by Gigabit Ethernet, then Gigabit Ethernet-to-FDDI bridging or routing switches are required because the packet formats of the two networks are different. Native FDDI fairness and priority mechanisms will not be directly supported by switch-based networks (FDDI or Ethernet). However, the use of switches that have been implemented with the QoS and CoS features discussed in Chapter 13 will provide similar performance. In addition, FDDI has been popular as a highly reliable network. Gigabit Ethernet switches that provide for dual homing redundant links will be required to emulate the reliability of FDDI.

14.2.3   100VG-AnyLAN

Many of the points discussed in section 14.2.2 regarding the use of Gigabit Ethernet as an upgrade for FDDI are relevant to the case of upgrading 100VG-AnyLAN. However, because the packet format of 100VG-AnyLAN is usually the same as Ethernet, Gigabit Ethernet is even more suitable as an upgrade for 100VG-AnyLAN. 100VG-AnyLAN already provides a high level of reliability by using redundant links. Again, Gigabit Ethernet switches that provide redundant links will provide the same level of reliability.

14.2.4   Asynchronous Transfer Mode

This section begins where the discussion of ATM left off with the following Catch-22 observation:

- ATM has native QoS, but requires complex higher layer protocol support for traditional IP-based traffic.

- Ethernet is ideal for IP-based traffic, but requires complex higher layer protocol support in order to provide CoS for emergent multimedia traffic.

So, as with many things in life, there is no best solution. The network designer must determine what is really important for users. If integrated real-time video, voice, and data are vital business-critical applications for the majority of LAN users, then ATM would be the safe choice. However, to access ATM's native QoS features, *every* desktop would require an ATM-based network interface card with software drivers and real-time applications. Because most computer workstations and personal computers don't have ATM connectivity as standard, this would be an expensive optional extra.

Because the highest available ATM data rate for LAN applications is 622 Mbps (if all campus backbone links were specified to use 1000BASE-LX transceivers and mode conditioning patch cords) in place of the normal 622 Mbps SX-based ATM transceivers, worst-case multimode fiber link lengths of up to 1,600 m would be supported. This would allow all the important LAN backbone link lengths to be supported using multimode fiber. This could be viewed as an advantage compared to Gigabit Ethernet.

However, it also must be recognized that a high performance ATM system is likely to be much more expensive than a switch-based Ethernet solution. In the local area, a switched Ethernet hierarchy (10/100 to desktops, 100/1,000 in the backbone, possibly with link aggregation) allows a network designer to inexpensively over-provision the bandwidth available to every user and to design a highly reliable LAN at the same time. Bandwidth over-provisioning in itself will greatly improve network performance. Then, if real-time applications are vital for some users, this can easily be provided by most switch-based Ethernet systems in the campus LAN environment.

On the other hand, it must be recognized that ATM comes into its own in wide area networks—not surprising since that was its principal design target.

14.3 Summary

This chapter reviewed some of the reasons for upgrading existing non-Ethernet based LANs with Gigabit Ethernet. Many user issues perceived to relate to QoS and CoS were addressed by the ability to cost-effectively over-provision bandwidth using Ethernet technology. However, Gigabit Ethernet does not in itself guarantee CoS or QoS. Ethernet requires complex higher layer protocol support to provide CoS and QoS for emergent multimedia traffic.

ATM has native QoS, and at first glance, this appears to be a major opportunity for LAN-based ATM technology. But ATM is connection-oriented, which causes problems for IP-based data communications. Therefore, to support IP-based data communications, ATM requires complex higher layer protocol support.

There really is no best solution to the QoS/CoS problem. However, for LANs, it seems that most users have already chosen to use switch-based Ethernet, to over-provision the bandwidth, and to incrementally introduce emergent IP-based CoS features as required. For WANs, ATM remains popular because bandwidth is still precious and issues such as service contracts and billing are business-critical.

15

The Future: Gigabit Ethernet and Beyond

A turtle is an animal that makes no forward progress without sticking his neck out. [Anonymous]

This is the chapter where we get to wrap up the book—"stick our necks out"—and predict what the future may or may not bring to the world of Ethernet LANs. This chapter considers three types of "futures":

- Current Ethernet development projects that are likely to result in supplements to IEEE 802.3-1998, including:

  - Project 802.3ab: Gigabit Ethernet over 4-pair Category-5 or better UTP (1000BASE-T).

  - Project 802.3ad: link aggregation.

- Emerging technologies and non–standards-compliant commercial products that may or may not be considered for future standardization, but that are likely to impact future Ethernet LANs and LAN upgrades. These technologies include:

  - Commercially available extended-length Gigabit Ethernet links.

  - Wavelength Division Multiplexing (WDM): A way to support very high transmission rates with lower-cost laser-based transceivers.

  - Combining link extenders and WDM with routing switches: An economical alternative to ATM/SONET and SONET/SDH MANs and WANs.

- Some issues relating to what is needed to make the next 10X jump in the Ethernet transmission rate progression include:

- Line coding: Several possible options for use at 10,000 Mbps (10 Gbps).

- Full-duplex operation: Should higher transmission rate links be limited to full-duplex operation only?

- The optical layer: Is a new lower physical layer needed at the bottom of the Ethernet reference model, particularly for MAN- and WAN-based routing switches?

We realize that some of the content of this chapter may be speculative and that we may be pushing the envelope in some areas. But isn't that what the future is about? The purpose of this chapter is to raise some issues that we think are important, to emphasize that local area networking is a rapidly evolving technology, and to get you thinking about what is likely to be possible, as well as what is currently available.

We will begin with the most certain futures, the projects already officially under way or nearing completion by the 802.3 standards group.

15.1 1000BASE-T: Gigabit Ethernet over UTP Copper Cable

1000BASE-T (IEEE 802.3ab) defines a new media-dependent physical layer (see Figure 15.1) that will support 1,000 Mbps operation over a 100 m link consisting of 4-pair, Category-5 or better, balanced, unshielded twisted pair (UTP) copper cable. The purpose of this new physical layer is to provide an upgrade path for current 100BASE-TX networks and to extend the life of existing Category-5 UTP cable, the most common inside cable in use. IEEE 802.3ab should be approved as a supplement to IEEE 802.3-1998 sometime during the spring of 1999.

Figure 15.1   1000BASE-T Ethernet Reference Model

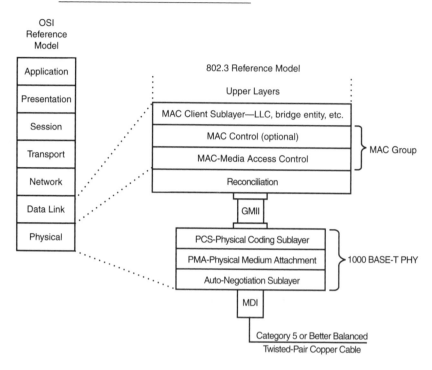

GMII = Gigabit Media Independent Interface (Optional)
MDI = Medium Dependent Interface

15.1.1 1000BASE-T Signal Transmission and Reception

The 1000BASE-T PHY sublayers and signal transmission procedure is different from the PHY sublayers and transmission procedures described for 1000BASE-X in previous chapters. Instead of using two simplex links (two optical fibers or two wire pairs) to form one full-duplex link, 1000BASE-T sends encoded signals simultaneously in both directions on the same wire pair, as shown in the 4-channel link topology of Figure 15.2.

Figure 15.2   1000BASE-T Link Topology

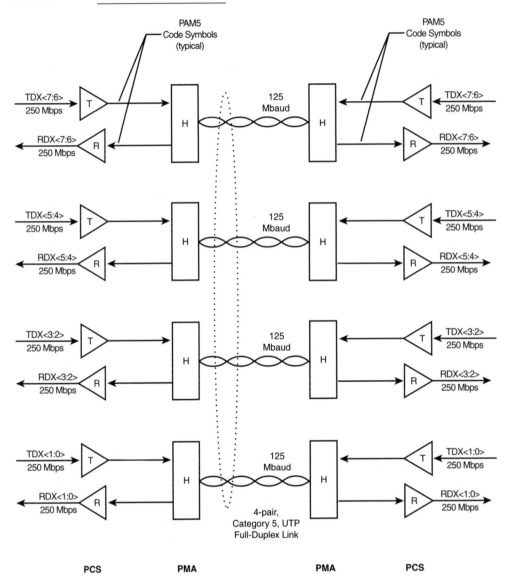

H = Hybrid Canceller Transceiver
T = Transmit Encoder
R = Receive Decoder
Four PAM5 Code Symbols = One 4D-PAM5 Code Group

This means that the signal at the MDI is the sum of the just-transmitted signal and the signal being received from the entity at the other end of the link. It also means that the receiver must be more than an amplifier and signal detector. The transmitted signal that is added to the received signal at the MDI must be removed (canceled) before any amplification and detection of the received signal can take place.

Figure 15.3 shows a simplified block diagram of the PCS/PMA data circuits. The PMA hybrid transceiver consists of the following:

- A normal Transmit function with four independent transmitters

- A special Receive function, with four independent receivers where the inverse of the transmitted signal is added to the composite signal from the MDI to cancel the transmitted signal

- A clock recovery unit to recover the clock from the received signal sequence

Figure 15.3   PHY Data and Clock Circuits

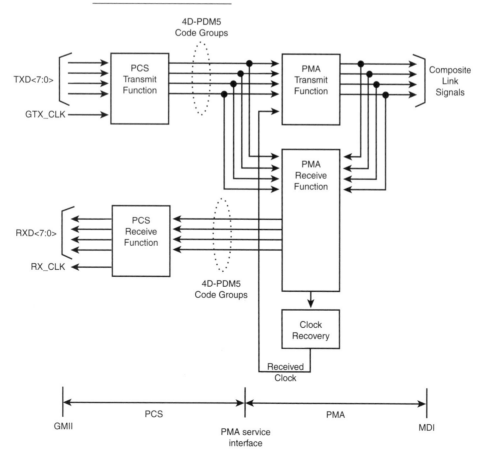

The actual transmitted signal on each wire pair is a 5-level (+2, +1, 0, –1, –2) pulse amplitude modulated symbol (PAM5). Four symbols, transmitted simultaneously on the four wire pairs, form a code-group (4D-PAM5) that represents an 8-bit frame octet. The 4D-PAM5 coding allows an aggregate 1,000 Mbps data rate to be achieved with a transmission rate of only 125 Mbaud per pair (baud is the transmission rate in symbols/second). Transmitter pulse shaping and receiver equalization are used to compensate for the spectral characteristics and signal distortion of the link.

A continuous stream of Idle symbols (from a restricted set of values [+2, 0, –2]) is sent whenever regular transmission is not in progress to maintain continuous clock synchronization between the two link partners. During Auto-Negotiation, one partner is chosen to be *master* (typically the multiport partner) and the other to be *slave*. Subsequent transmission from the master is then timed by the master's local clock, and transmission from the slave is synchronized by the clock that is recovered from the received symbol stream, as shown in Figure 15.4. This form of synchronization is known as *loop timing*.

Figure 15.4   1000BASE-T Master/Slave Loop Timing

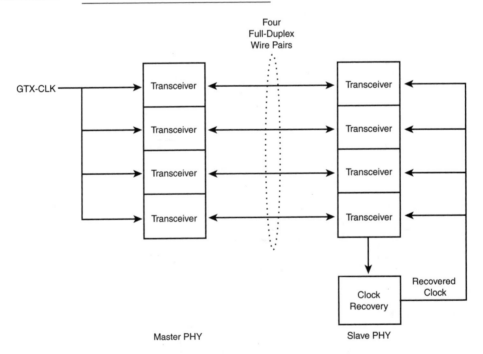

Encoding of the outgoing frame octets and decoding of the received 4D-PAM5 code groups occurs in the PCS sublayer. The 1000BASE-T coding procedure was chosen for several reasons:

- Four-Dimensional 8-State Trellis Forward Error Correction coding (this is the 4D of the 4D-PAM5 code designation) enables the system to operate as if the signal-to-noise ratio at the analog-to-digital converter in the receiver had been improved.

- Encoding an octet as four 5-level PAM5 symbols allows the entire octet to be transmitted in one symbol (baud) period, and reduces the symbol rate to 125 Mbaud on each pair.

- Separate scramblers for the master and slave PHYs randomize the symbol sequence, reduce the spectral lines in the transmitted signal, and create essentially uncorrelated data symbols between the two opposite travelling symbol streams on each wire pair. All of these aid in symbol recovery.

15.1.2   1000BASE-T Cabling Considerations

While 1000BASE-T is designed to operate over existing Category-5 cabling, all cables should be tested before they are used for Gigabit operation. The Gigabit Ethernet Alliance has estimated that up to 10 percent of the existing Category-5 cables may not be able to pass two critical performance parameters that were not established when Category-5 cabling initially became available:

- **Return Loss**. Return loss refers to the magnitude of the signal power returned to a test point as a result of reflections that are caused by cabling impedance mismatches at the connection points.

- **Far-End Crosstalk (FEXT)**. Crosstalk is noise coupled onto the wire pair by signals on adjacent pairs in the cable (see Figure 15.5). FEXT is noise induced at the far end of the cable from the transmitter. FEXT can be exacerbated by the use of non-standard connectors and also by incorrectly installed connectors (such as connections where the wire pair has been untwisted more than necessary).

Figure 15.5   Typical FEXT Noise Induction for One Wire Pair

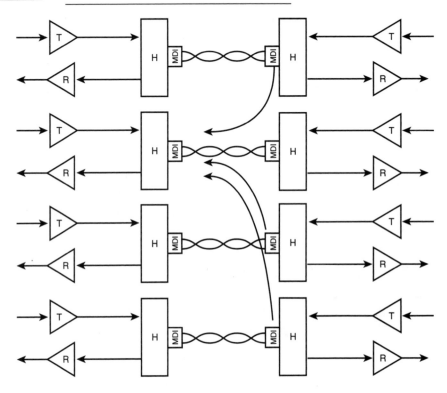

H = Hybrid Canceller Transceiver
MDI = Media Dependent Interface
T = Transmit
R = Receive

The problem arose quite innocently. The early Category-5 cable installations were used for 10BASE-T. However, because 10BASE-T operates at much lower frequencies than either 100BASE-TX or 1000BASE-T, return loss and FEXT were not a critical problem (remember that 10BASE-T was originally designed to operate over ordinary telephone twisted-pair cable).

While the cable was available earlier, Category-5 installation instructions were not specified and agreed upon until 1995 (see ANSI/TIA/EIA 568-1995), the same year the first versions of Fast Ethernet were approved. Category-5 connectors were also not available until 1995, and, as a result, Category-5 cables installed before then were typically installed with Category-3 connectors. Therefore, 1995 is a calendar benchmark and any pre-1995

Category-5 cable will not have standards-compliant hardware unless new connectors have been retrofitted.

The return loss and FEXT problem was not fully recognized until 100BASE-T2 was being developed (100BASE-T2 was approved in 1997). As things stood in late 1998:

- The Telecommunication Industries Association (TIA) was developing a technical service bulletin to define new cabling practices, new return loss, and FEXT measures that will be published as ANSI/TIA/EIA-TSB-95 for an *Enhanced Category-5* cable (Category-5E).

- The International Organization for Standardization (ISO) was adding return loss and FEXT measures to ISO/IEC 11801 for Category-5 cabling (which ISO will continue to call Category-5 rather than Category-5E).

- TIA was developing performance, installation, and testing specifications for Category-6 cabling with a specified bandwidth of 200 MHz (Category 5 has a specified bandwidth of 100 MHz). Because Category-6 specifications are still in development, not all currently available Category-6 connectors are interoperable.

- ISO had begun development of performance, installation, and testing specifications for a Category-7 cable with a 600 MHz bandwidth. The expected completion date for this category cable is sometime in 2000.

That is all well and good, but what do you do with existing Category-5 cabling? How can you tell whether or not it will support Gigabit operation? What can you do if it doesn't?

If the current cabling supports 100BASE-TX operation, it is likely to support 1000BASE-T operation. However, because 100BASE-TX uses only two of the four wire pairs, the cable should still be tested to determine whether or not it is suitable for 1000BASE-T operation.

If the current cabling is not being used for 100BASE-TX operation, it will definitely need testing to determine whether or not it is suitable for 1000BASE-T operation.

Note

Basic cable testing procedures are defined in ANSI/TIA/EIA-TSB-67, and a number of suppliers now have new Category-5 test equipment and/or retrofit upgrades for existing test equipment that will perform the tests specified in ANSI/TIA/EIA-TSB-95.

If the current cabling does not pass the return loss and FEXT tests, modifying the link configuration may still bring the cable into compliance (see the sidebar, "Modifying Category-5 Link Configurations for 1000BASE-T Operation").

Modifying Category-5 Link Configurations for 1000BASE-T Operation

Figures 15.6 and 15.7 show the range of link configurations that may be used for 1000BASE-T. All 1000BASE-T link configurations should be at or between the maximum and the minimum shown.

Figure 15.6   Maximum 1000BASE-T Category-5 UTP Link Configuration

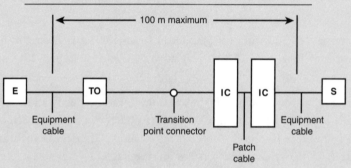

E = End station
TO = Telecom outlet
IC = Interconnect panel
S = Switch port

Figure 15.7   Optimized 1000BASE-T Category-5 UTP Link Configuration

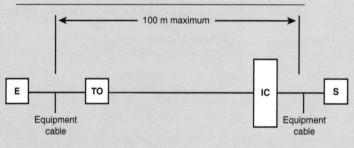

E = End station
TO = Telecom outlet
IC = Interconnect panel
S = Switch port

The following list provides the corrective actions recommended for links that do not meet the return loss and FEXT requirements. (There is no implied order to the action list. We listed those that would likely cause the least disruption to area activities first. Remember that the link should be retested after each action is taken.)

- If the link has a cross-connect, reconfigure it as an interconnect.
- If the interconnect connectors do not meet Category-5E specifications, replace them with connectors that do.
- If the telecom closet equipment cable does not meet Category-5E specifications, replace it with a cable that does.
- If the work area equipment cable does not meet Category-5E specifications, replace it with a cable that does.
- If the work area telecom outlet connector does not meet Category-5E specifications, replace it with a connector that does.
- If the transition point connector does not meet Category-5E specifications, replace it with a connector that does, or better yet, if sufficient slack exists in the link, connect the transition point end of the link directly to the telecom outlet connector.

What if you are not able to correct problems with some of the cables? Does this mean the cables will have to be replaced? The answer is usually a resounding no! Remember that most networks will have a mix of 10 Mbps, 100 Mbps, and 1,000 Mbps services. The problem cables will still support 10BASE-T and 100BASE-T2 with two pairs, and will also support 100BASE-T4 so long as four pairs are available, even if they won't support either 100BASE-TX or 1000BASE-T.

15.2 Link Aggregation: Project 802.3ad

Section 13.4.4.3 in Chapter 13, "Upgrading Ethernet LANs: System and Topology Considerations," first mentioned link aggregation as a feature contained in some commercially available switches. We noted there that link aggregation could be used as a cost-effective way to provide higher-speed trunks in Ethernet LANs that are reaching saturation with 100 Mbps transmission rates but that won't require Gigabit capability, at least in the short term.

Likewise, link aggregation could also be used as a cost-effective way to provide higher-speed trunks in Ethernet LANs that have existing 62.5 μm multimode fiber (MMF) backbone links longer than 700 m (the maximum 1000BASE-LX length according to the Gigabit Ethernet optical link model). Because the maximum length for 62.5 μm MMF links operating at 100 Mbps is 2 km, aggregating n existing MMF links that are too long to support 1000BASE-LX, for example, will support an aggregate transmission rate of $(100\ n)$ Mbps.

Link aggregation is a proven capability. It is also technology that can be applied to any transmission rate implementation. However, currently available link aggregation schemes are proprietary, and they are not all interoperable.

The Project 802.3ad working group has been formed within 802.3 to develop a standard link aggregation protocol that is both interoperable and backward compatible with existing Ethernet devices. The primary goal of the project is to provide a means where several links can be combined into one logical trunk to increase the effective connection capacity (in unit multiples of the individual link transmission rate rather than a 10X step).

Note

An individual communication over a trunk can only access a maximum communications bandwidth equal to that of *one* of the links forming a trunk. However, throughput is improved by trunking as other communications can be carried by other links of the trunk.

Some of the more important objectives of the project are to define link aggregation in a manner that will do the following:

- Apply to full-duplex links and any Ethernet transmission rate so long as all links in an aggregated trunk operate at the same rate (link aggregation will specifically not apply to CSMA/CD links)

- Not require change to the existing Ethernet MAC format

- Support existing 802.3 MAC clients without change to higher-layer protocols

- Contain a low risk of frame duplication or reordering

- Allow rapid configuration and reconfiguration, including very rapid automatic detection and reconfiguration in the case of link failure

- Provide a means for network management to monitor link operation and control link aggregation

While the draft of the link aggregation standard is currently (early 1999) in the initial drafting stages and is subject to change, we can provide some indication of the current status and direction.

15.2.1 Link Aggregation Logical Model

There appears to be general agreement and acceptance of the logical reference model shown in Figure 15.8. Because the link aggregation sublayer will be required to control transmission and reception through multiple ports, it must be positioned between the MAC (or the MAC Control) and the MAC client sublayers.

Figure 15.8   Proposed 802.3 Logical Reference Model

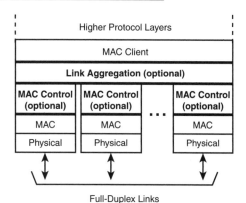

Full-Duplex Links

> **Note**
>
> Because link aggregation and MAC Control are optional sublayers, logical compatibility must be maintained at all 802.3 MAC service interfaces (indicated in bold).

There is also agreement that to maintain backward compatibility, the new sublayer will need to appear to the MAC client as an individual MAC (or MAC Control) and to the MAC in each port as the MAC client. This means that *all* the MAC service interfaces shown in bold in Figure 15.8 must be logically compatible.

15.2.2 Link Aggregation Functional Model

The details of how link aggregation will be defined are less certain at this time. Figure 15.9 shows the proposed link aggregation functional block diagram.

Figure 15.9   Proposed Link Aggregation Sublayer Functional Block Diagram

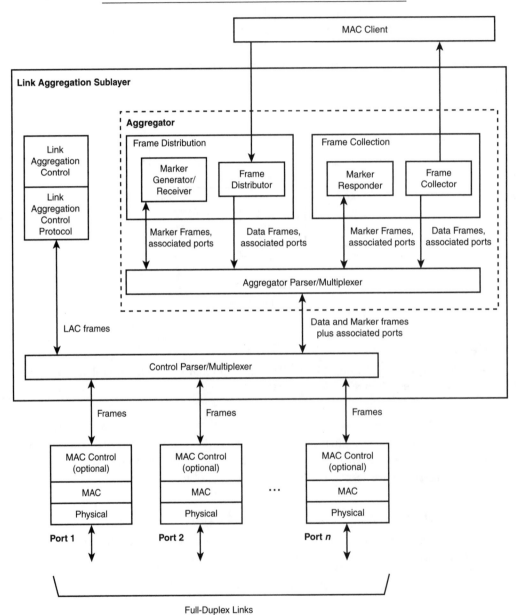

Full-Duplex Links

Five major functions (described in sections 15.2.2.1–15.2.2.5) are currently proposed, but even these are still subject to change.

15.2.2.1   The Control Function

The Control function will generate and accept link aggregation control (LAC) frames that are exchanged with its peer link aggregation sublayer in the link partner. This function incorporates a Link Aggregation Control Protocol (LACP) that is responsible for:

- Establishing and controlling link aggregation groups (LAGs—groups of links that appear as if they were a single link between pairs of link partners)

- Monitoring the links in each LAG to ensure they remain viable members of the group

- Reconfiguring LAGs as conditions change or as requested by network management

Determination of whether or not a link is appropriate for inclusion in or removal from a LAG is based on information about the link and link partner's capabilities contained in the Link Aggregation Control Protocol Data Units (LACPDU). LACPDUs are exchanged in LAC frames both before LAG establishment and periodically during LAG operation.

15.2.2.2   The Frame Distribution Function

The Frame Distribution function will be responsible for ensuring that frames are not duplicated and that frame ordering is preserved, particularly during transfer of frames that are part of an ordered sequence. Ordered frame sequences are called *conversations*. They may be either monologues (where all the information transfer is in one direction) or dialogues (where the information flows in both directions). Multiple conversations may occur simultaneously between the same link partners, at either the same or different priority level.

The frame distributor is not allowed to segment, label, or modify outgoing frames. It selects which port will be used to transmit each frame prior to passing the frame to the aggregator parser/multiplexer. The same port must be used for all frames in a conversation, and the frames must be transferred in the order they are received from the MAC client.

15.2.2.3   The Frame Collection Function

The Frame Collection function accepts incoming data frames from the aggregator parser/multiplexer and passes them on without reordering to the MAC client. Frame order will have been maintained because all frames associated with a conversation will have been transferred across the same physical link (see the sidebar, "Changing Links During a Conversation").

Changing Links During a Conversation

If changing links becomes necessary during a conversation, the frame distributor must ensure that no frames are lost during the changeover. The frame distributor can do this by allowing a specified time period to elapse (to ensure sufficient time for the last transmitted frame to be received by the link partner). Likewise, the frame distributor can send a marker frame to indicate that the last data frame has been sent and then wait for a marker response frame acknowledging receipt of the marker frame.

Once the link has been "flushed" (the timer has expired or a marker response frame has been received from the link partner), the remaining portion of the conversation can safely be assigned to another link in the LAG and the conversation can resume.

15.2.2.4 The Aggregator Parser/Multiplexer Function

The Aggregator Parser/Multiplexer function separates incoming data and marker frames and passes them on to either the marker receiver or the frame collector. Outgoing data and marker frames are associated with their selected ports and are passed to the control parser/multiplexer.

The aggregator and control parsers both determine where to send incoming frames based on the value contained in the Length/Type field, similar to the way data frames are separated from MAC Control or VLAN-tagged frames:

- Data frames are identified by a Length/Type value ≤1,500 and are passed from the Control parser to the Aggregator parser, which passes them on to the frame collector.

- Marker frames are identified by a reserved Length/Type value = *Flush Protocol Type* and are passed from the Control Parser to the Aggregator parser, which passes them on to the marker responder or marker receiver.

- LAC frames are identified by a reserved Length/Type value = *LAC Type* and are passed to the control function.

The reserved values for LAC Type and Flush Protocol Type will not be made public until after IEEE P802.3ad is approved as a standard.

15.2.2.5 The Control Parser/Multiplexer Function

The Control Parser/Multiplexer function separates incoming frames and passes them on to either the Control function or the Aggregator Parser/Multiplexer. Outgoing frames are passed to their associated ports for transmission.

15.3 *Extended Length Gigabit Ethernet Links*

Fundamentally, the full-duplex Ethernet protocol has no distance limits. Link lengths are limited by the particular physical layer technology and the characteristics of the link media. IEEE 802.3 guarantees that *all* 1000BASE-LX compliant single-mode fiber (SMF) links will *interoperate* over link lengths up to 5 km. This is the *baseline* performance requirement for the relatively low-cost technology that was the focus of the Gigabit Ethernet standard.

However, as suggested in Chapter 13, it is possible to greatly extend link distances and still allow fully compatible Gigabit Ethernet operation:

- Matched high-performance 1000BASE-LX transceivers (one at each end of a link) can allow operation over link lengths of about 20 km.

- Commercially available link extenders (one at each end of a link) can increase link lengths to about 120 km (about 75 miles) without optical amplification.

- Commercially available link extenders used in conjunction with inline optical amplifiers appropriately spaced along the link can increase link lengths into the 1,000 km (about 620 miles) range (see the sidebar, "Inline Optical Amplifiers").

The availability of these options means that Gigabit Ethernet is a very respectable alternative to MAN or WAN technology. Consider the distributed campus sites in the example of Figure 15.10. Sites 1 and 2 are within 5 km of each other, but Site 3 is about 120 km distant. The Ethernet LANs in Sites 1 and 2 are interconnected by a standard 1000BASE-LX link, and both of these two sites are connected to Site 3 by extender-based links. The link extenders at each end of the extended links are connected to the local campus distributors by short 1000BASE-SX or 1000BASE-LX links.

Figure 15.10 Example Gigabit Ethernet Metropolitan Area Network (MAN) with Link Extenders Connecting Three Remote LANs

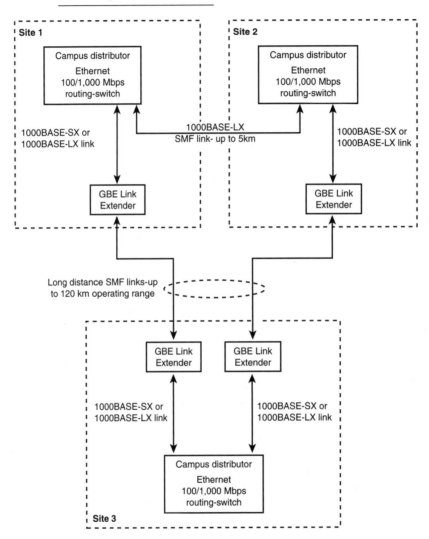

GBE= Gigabit Ethernet

Figure 15.11 shows the essential parts of a Gigabit Ethernet link extender incorporating a single frequency, distributed feedback (DFB) laser operating in the 1,550 nm band. The long distance link can be either one fiber or two as shown in the figure, depending on which type of link extender is chosen:

- If two fibers are used for the long distance link, both transceivers can be identical.

- If only one fiber is used, each transceiver will also need to be equipped with an appropriate optical splitter/combiner to enable bidirectional operation.

Figure 15.11   A Gigabit Ethernet Link Extender

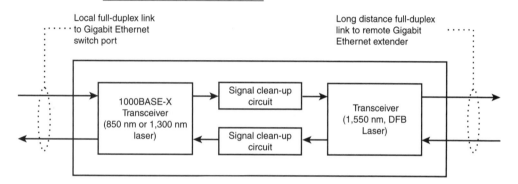

Some link extenders also include quite complicated electronics, ranging from a basic network management counter set to a full two-port bridge capability.

Inline Optical Amplifiers

Section 6.4 and Figure 6.29c in Chapter 6, "Fundamentals of Fiber Optic Communication," explained how stimulated emission can amplify light. That description was based on semi-conductor lasers.

Although inline optical amplifiers could be made using semiconductors, it has become more common to use Erbium-doped fiber amplifiers (EDFA). An EDFA usually consists of many meters of single-mode optical fiber that has been doped with Erbium.

As we saw in Chapter 6, there must be more ions in a higher state compared to a lower state for stimulated emission to occur, a condition known as *population inversion*. In EDFAs, we take advantage of the fact that Erbium atoms actually exist in an ionized state within the glass. Consider the simplified energy level diagram for Erbium ions shown in Figure 15.12. The population inversion between states 2 and 1 can be created by exciting ions from state 1 to the higher fast-decaying state 3 (state 2 is a state that would naturally decay very slowly compared to state 3).

continues

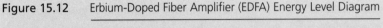

Figure 15.12   Erbium-Doped Fiber Amplifier (EDFA) Energy Level Diagram

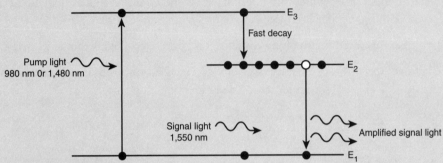

In semiconductors, the atoms were excited into a higher state by absorbing energy from an applied current. A different excitation procedure is used in EFDAs. Erbium ions in glass can be excited to move from state 1 to state 3 by a light source (called the pump). In EFDAs designed to amplify 1,550 nm wavelength signals, the pump light usually has a wavelength of either 980 nm or 1,480 nm, and this light is coupled into the Erbium-doped fiber using a simple wave division multiplexer.

Amplification is similar to the optical amplification we saw in a semiconductor laser. The signal light shining on ions in unstable excited states stimulates them to fall back to their lower states and to emit additional light in the process. For very small signal levels, the amount of stimulated emission, and therefore the optical gain of the EDFA, is proportional to the difference in the number of excited state ions in state 2 compared to the number of ions in state 1 and is proportional to the intensity of the 1,550 nm signal light.

However, it is usual to operate EDFAs in a saturated gain mode where the gain is relatively independent of the input signal level.

15.4   Gigabit Ethernet Implementation in MANs and WANs

Many institutions and Internet service providers (ISPs) have discovered that Gigabit Ethernet is a very cost-effective plug-and-play technology for MANs and WANs. The implementation cost for Gigabit-Ethernet–based MANs and WANs is routinely less than 25 percent of that for a comparable POS/SONET/SDH or ATM/SONET system. A primary reason is the availability of very competitively priced Gigabit Ethernet routing switches. Another reason is the economy of scale inherent in Ethernet technology, plus the added bonus that currently installed Ethernet LANs can be readily interconnected as Gigabit Ethernet MANs or WANs.

However, you should also know that telecom companies and ISPs argue that the issues of Quality of Service (QoS), billing, network management, and link protection and restoration are not adequately addressed by Ethernet technology.

15.4.1 QoS

You should be aware by now that QoS is very quickly disappearing as an issue for switch-based Ethernet. Interestingly, however, many telecom providers are still expressing concerns about the QoS of a physical link (for example, they would like to be able to monitor its performance and BER). Fortunately, most QoS performance factors are physical layer issues and these are not major stumbling blocks for Gigabit Ethernet. Many of the physical link performance measurements can already be deduced by monitoring the existing network management counters that are routinely included in most switches.

15.4.2 Billing

Billing is a new issue, but not an insurmountable one. LANs have been corporate owned and have traditionally provided connectionless packet transmission service that is not charged back (billed) to the users. On the other hand, WANs provide connection-based service over commercial communication links that are subject to usage charges.

The solution to the billing problem could require extended negotiations to establish a new billing model with new rate structures and methods for measuring usage, but this might be closer than some would think. Change is already happening because ISPs have had to find ways to bill for their data communications links differently (and typically at lower cost) than voice links.

15.4.3 Network Management

Network management might be a larger issue than billing, but it is also not an insurmountable one. Ethernet was developed as a LAN technology, and commercial MAN providers would like more features than are commonly available with current LAN network management protocols. However, work is underway and some Gigabit Ethernet switch providers have already started providing additional features such as out-of-band network management and performance monitoring to satisfy this concern.

15.4.4   Link Protection and Restoration

Another commonly stated concern relative to SONET/SDH is link protection within the MAN or WAN. Combinations of redundant hot-standby links and link aggregation techniques can be used to provide comparable (or at least appropriate for IP-based traffic) protection at the layer 2 level. Layer 3 routers have the additional capability to reconfigure the network topology to restore connectivity.

15.5   Wavelength Division Multiplexing and Gigabit Ethernet

It is now possible to precisely control the wavelengths of DFB lasers. The output of many such lasers, each having a different wavelength, can be launched into a single fiber. This operational mode is called *wavelength division multiplexing (WDM)*. The different wavelengths are then separated and individually detected at the receiving end of a WDM link. Many hundreds of wavelengths have been combined in a single fiber in laboratory tests.

Lasers used in today's telecommunications links can be modulated at transmission rates up to 10 Gbps, although 2.5 Gbps is more common. Commercially available systems can typically be configured for up to 32 separate wavelengths. This means that commercially available links can transmit about 320 Gbps if the lasers are modulated at 10 Gbps, or 80 Gbps if the lasers are modulated at the more common rate of 2.5 Gbps.

WDM technology can also allow different networks to exist within a single fiber by assigning different wavelengths to each type of service. Furthermore, it is possible to build optical demultiplexers that can remove a selected wavelength from the incoming fiber and pass it to a local detector, as shown in Figure 15.13. The same wavelength can then be simultaneously added to the outgoing fiber from a local transmitter. This type of optical demultiplexer is called an optical-add-drop-multiplexer (OADM).

Figure 15.13 A Conceptual Diagram of an Optical WDM Add/Drop Multiplexer

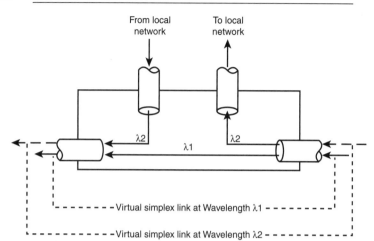

OADMs are important because they enable you to form WDM optical networks using existing fiber backbones. This is just another way to create virtual networks, but now each network can have a different modulation technique, a different packet (or cell) format, and a different access protocol, all simultaneously supported on the same fibers within the backbone!

Figure 15.14 shows a simple WDM network based on OADMs, WDM transponders, and standard Gigabit Ethernet and ATM/SONET routing switches. In this example, WDM technology is used to create two virtual networks: one Ethernet and one ATM network.

Figure 15.14 Example Ring Connection with Separate GBE and ATM Networks via WDM Optical Network Layer

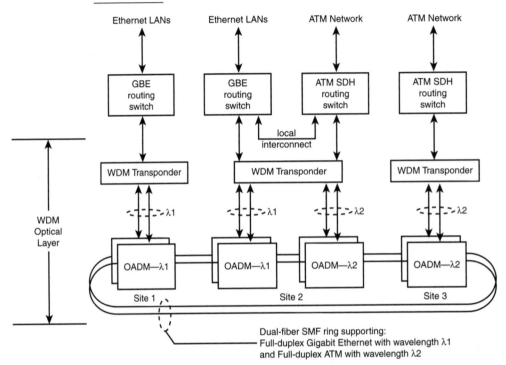

The *WDM transponders* in Figure 15.14 are devices that convert local non-WDM signals to and from controlled-WDM wavelengths and signals. Figure 15.15 shows the essential functions of a very basic Gigabit Ethernet WDM transponder. A basic SONET transponder would have the same structure except the local transceiver would be a SONET transceiver. In this example, two different wavelengths are used to carry the Gigabit Ethernet traffic and ATM/SONET traffic. The WDM transponders are connected to the links in the fiber ring by OADMs. The WDM transceiver must be specifically chosen to be compatible with WDM system wavelengths.

Figure 15.15   A Basic Gigabit Ethernet WDM Transponder

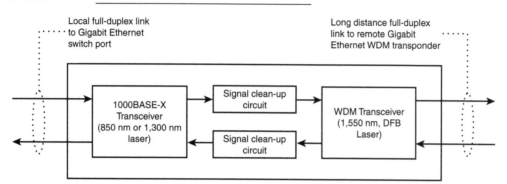

> **Note**
>
> If the WDM transponder in Figure 15.15 looks amazingly similar to the Gigabit Ethernet link extender in Figure 15.11, it is because it is. The difference is that the link extender in Figure 15.11 uses an ordinary transceiver and the WDM transponder uses a WDM transceiver. Both are link extenders.

If OADMs were programmable, or if optical cross-connect switches were available, the optical channel could be reconfigured to route around faults at the optical level. In the near term, while the optical topology can be changed on command, the change-time is slow and it is not yet practical to do optical packet switching. This currently limits the optical layer to optical topology changes, link protection switching, and connectivity restoration, all of which are still very useful functions!

We feel that sometime in the future there will be a WDM optical network sublayer below the current physical layer. Many higher layer services will be carried by such networks. Figure 15.16 is a quasi-layered model for a WDM-Optical-Network showing how different traffic types could be transported. Figure 15.17 shows a possible layered model for a WDM-based network. The important point to note is that *raw ATM cells and IP datagrams cannot be carried directly over the WDM layer because a physical layer and a data link layer are required between the WDM and IP or ATM layers!*

Figure 15.16   Quasi-Layered Model for WDM-Optical-Network-Based IP Network

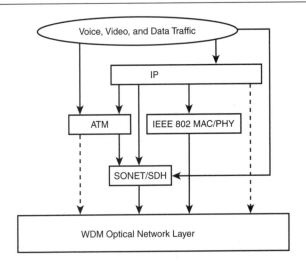

Figure 15.17   Layered Model for a WDM Network Using Different Layer 1, 2, and 3 Technologies

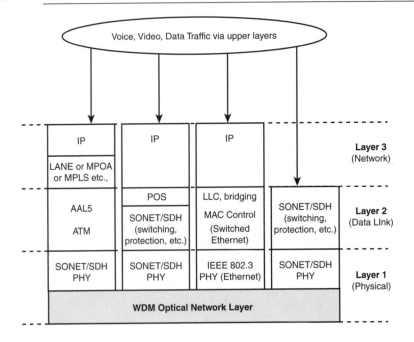

15.5.1 Optical-Layer, Physical/Data Link Layer, and Layer 3 Link Protection and Restoration

Because WDM allows virtual networks to be constructed, a simple method for link protection and restoration would be for each virtual network to use its own layer 2 and layer 3 protection and recovery mechanisms. The optical (WDM) layer would then only be used to provide redundant virtual paths that could be used in the event of a link failure. If load balancing schemes are desired, then some of the redundant links could even carry low priority traffic when the network is operating normally. The low priority traffic could be either dropped or delayed to allow protection of the higher priority traffic in the event of a failure.

Currently, there is an ongoing industry debate as to whether protection and restoration should be done in the optical layer, the physical/data link layer, or layer 3. A major question is how the various protection functions in each layer will interact.

15.6 Ten Gigabit Ethernet

The next logical data rate upgrade after Gigabit Ethernet is 10 Gbps: Ten Gigabit Ethernet. In fact, even during the writing of this chapter, preparations were in progress to create an IEEE 802.3 study group on Ten Gigabit Ethernet.

15.6.1 The Need for Ten Gigabit Ethernet

One of the first concerns that such a study group will have to consider is the need for Ten Gigabit Ethernet:

- Why is Ten Gigabit Ethernet needed?

- When will it be needed?

- What will be the major technical challenges during its development?

Possibly, the main reason that Ten Gigabit Ethernet will be required is because of the hierarchical nature of switch-based networks. As we have said before, the amalgamation of traffic from lower layers in the switching architecture means that each higher layer requires higher bandwidth. The simplest way to provide for this is to have a hierarchy of data rates. For the foreseeable future (at least the next five years), aggregation of Gigabit links is probably sufficient in building backbones as a data rate upgrade for Gigabit Ethernet LANs. We expect that the first need for Ten Gigabit Ethernet will be for the campus backbone (the highest level in the LAN network) and for MAN/WAN implementations.

However, if Ethernet is to compete effectively in the MAN/WAN markets, it must also compete with or augment wide area ATM/SONET or POS/SONET links and networks. The highest SONET data rate currently in use is 10 Gbps. Thus, there is pressure to develop a 10 Gbps Ethernet physical layer. In addition, there is an emergent need for a relatively low-cost local connection to WDM-based transponders—a need that Ten Gigabit Ethernet could address.

15.6.2 Technical Considerations

Some of the major technical questions that will need to be addressed during the development of Ten Gigabit Ethernet are likely to be:

- Should CSMA/CD be included in the standard?

- Should multimode fiber be supported and how?

- Which physical layer line codes will be used?

15.6.2.1 CSMA/CD or Full-Duplex Only?

To the authors, it seems clear that CSMA/CD is not useful as a LAN protocol at 10 Gbps, because:

- The network diameter would be reduced to only a few tens of meters.

- The trend throughout the industry is toward switch-based LANs and full-duplex links.

- CSMA/CD cannot be used for link aggregation.

Because Ten Gigabit Ethernet will be primarily limited to backbone links, it seems inappropriate to try to invent new ways to stretch CSMA/CD to 10 Gbps. For these reasons, it is likely that Ten Gigabit Ethernet will be full-duplex only.

15.6.2.2 Multimode Fiber

It will be also difficult to support multimode fiber within Ten Gigabit Ethernet. For example, at 10 Gbps with non-return-to-zero (NRZ) encoding and a multimode fiber having a modal bandwidth of 500 MHz.km, the Gigabit Ethernet model shows that the maximum link length would be about 100 m. Thus, unless new multimode fiber having much higher bandwidth is developed, it is unlikely that multimode fiber will be useful for single channel 10 Gbps systems.

However, multichannel systems might be able to support longer link lengths with currently installed multimode fiber. For example, four lasers, each operating at 2.5 Gbps on different wavelengths, would allow the link length to be increased to about 350 m. This is a useful distance and it has been shown to work. A proof of the principle of a four wavelength WDM 10 Gbps link was demonstrated by Hewlett-Packard Laboratories at Networld-InterOp 1998.

However, with offset launch, at least 75 percent of today's installed MMF links would have bandwidth greater than about 750 MHz.km (see section 10.11 in Chapter 10, "The Gigabit Ethernet Modal Bandwidth Investigation"). Because we know this statistic, and because cable companies are releasing better quality MMF, it seems more reasonable to project link lengths based on 750 MHz.km. The worst-case link length would then be about 500 m for a four wavelength WDM 10 Gbps link. This length is sufficient for the building backbone as well as some shorter campus backbones. (By comparison, the 10 Gbps single frequency calculation with the Gigabit Ethernet model for a 750 MHz.km MMF link shows that the link length would still be only 150 m.)

15.6.3 Single-Mode Fiber

Link lengths of 5 km should easily be achieved at 10 Gbps with SMF using single frequency lasers operating at wavelengths near 1,300 nm or 1,550 nm. A major issue that could impact cost is back-reflections (from the link connectors). Most single frequency lasers are very sensitive to reflections, and the link bit error rate (BER) can be severely degraded by them. Optical isolators (to stop reflections from getting into the laser) might be needed and this could increase the cost of the transceivers. Operation at wavelengths near 1,300 nm is a low-cost option, and it seems likely that a specification at that wavelength will be developed. However, given that some vendors will want to use Ten Gigabit Ethernet as a MAN or WAN, they are also likely to want IEEE 802.3 to give consideration to a 1,550 nm-based specification, simply because it is the common low-loss wavelength band used by telecom WDM-based MAN/WAN systems.

15.6.4 Physical Layer Electronics Issues

Low-cost Complimentary Metal Oxide Semiconductor (CMOS) electronics can be used for multifiber WDM-based systems. However, single-fiber systems operating at the full line rate of 10 Gbps will require new Germanium/Silicon-based technologies. Silicon or GaAs technologies could also be used for either the multifiber or the single-fiber systems but with higher power dissipation. It is unclear how the choice would be made between these options.

15.6.5 *Single Channel Line Coding Issues*

There are two obvious choices for a Ten Gigabit Ethernet line code: 8B10B and SONET line coding (SONET framing with scrambled NRZ). Both alternatives have several advantages and disadvantages, as shown in Tables 15.1 and 15.2.

Table 15.1   8B10B Advantages and Disadvantages

Advantages	Disadvantages
No DC content	25% coding overhead
Short run length	
Excellent transition density—makes clock recovery easy	
Excellent error detection—especially with the Ethernet frame check sequence (FCS)	
Good control word space	
PCS and Auto-Negotiation sublayers would remain the same as Gigabit Ethernet (except for rate scaling)	

Table 15.2   SONET Advantages and Disadvantages

Advantages	Disadvantages
Very little coding overhead (just framing and control bits?)	New PCS and Auto-Negotiation sublayers would have to be developed (which could be complicated and time consuming).
10 Gbps chip sets are available	Rigid frame-based coding that can increase latency of control signaling (not an ideal match for bursty Ethernet traffic, but because this will be used at a higher switching level, it may be all right).
	No native control words (but some of the bits in the frame could be used for control).
	Run length is practically unlimited (opto-electronics can have problems with long runs and physical layer can be more expensive because of this).

Recently, however, one of the authors of this book, David Cunningham, proposed a third option—the use of a very simple block code with less overhead than 8B10B. Because most SONET hardware is tested for runs of 72 bits, the code limits the run length to a relatively long length of 42 bits. This means that opto-electronics developed for SONET should always operate well within their specifications.

It can be shown that a 16B18B code is quite satisfactory for this [Coles and Cunningham, 1998]. The code operates on two data bytes and would be simple to implement, only requiring logic to invert data (when needed), to add two label bits, and to compute the running digital sum (RDS). Clock recovery would be more complex compared to 8B10B coding but less complex than SONET line coding. A 16B18B code would have many of the benefits of the 8B10B code stated in Table 15.1, and would decrease the coding overhead to 12.5 percent. Furthermore, because the code is not frame-based, both control words and packets could be transmitted as required.

Codes similar to 16B18B are a very good compromise between the SONET and 8B10B line codes. They are very suitable for both bursty and non-bursty traffic. If there were a blank slate, a new code like the 16B18B would be the best option. However, all things being considered, the choice will likely be between 8B10B and SONET.

15.7 Summary

We began this chapter with a review of two ongoing IEEE 802.3 standards projects:

- 1000BASE-T, which is designed to provide an upgrade path for Ethernet LANs with existing Category-5 UTP cabling, should be an approved standard by the time you read this and should be considered as an alternative to 1000BASE-X for links under 100 m.

- Link aggregation is still in the early drafting stages and is not yet complete enough to allow us to be rigorously specific. We hope, however, that you have at least a reasonable idea of how link aggregation will likely work.

We next discovered that network providers have already demonstrated that Gigabit Ethernet can be used to build cost-effective and relatively large MANs that can support both IP and multimedia (for example, IP-telephony) traffic. Furthermore, if link extenders are installed, Gigabit Ethernet can also be used to interconnect Ethernet LANs as WANs.

We also saw that wavelength division multiplexing can allow many different network technologies to be multiplexed onto the same physical fiber. This allows each technology to form its own virtual network. It is already possible for network providers to supply Gigabit Ethernet at one wavelength and ATM/SONET and POS/SONET on other wavelengths. In fact, as the WDM technology matures, new service providers are likely to enter the market to provide such choices. For the longer term, it seems that the never-ending debate about whether Ethernet or ATM-based technology is best is somewhat irrelevant. Both technologies can be provided, and the user can choose based on the cost and their desired service levels.

Since SONET designs are available, there will likely be pressure to reuse them for Ten Gigabit Ethernet. However, to achieve a MAC data rate of 10 Gbps, the line rate will need to be greater than 10 Gbaud (the higher line rate compensates for the framing and control overhead). Also, the data scrambler for a SONET-based system will need to be carefully chosen to ensure all data sequences can be transmitted. Methods for choosing the data scrambler are well known for packet transmission over SONET.

15.8   Final Thoughts

We have talked a lot about standards and interoperability during the development of the book, and in this last chapter, we have also talked about several commercial products that are "not standard compliant" but that are still "fully compatible" with Ethernet networks. We probably should revisit what we mean by these terms before ending the book.

Standards compliant means that the product has met all of the electrical, mechanical, optical, and logical requirements specified for the appropriate interface and that the unit will operate according to the defined protocol. The Ethernet standard does not imply how a product should be implemented (that is the task of the product designer). Rather, the standard defines what the product shall do and how it shall act when interconnected in a network with other standards compliant products.

Consider the link aggregation functional block diagram shown in Figure 15.9. The link aggregator sublayer will typically be completely internal to a switch or network server. The actual circuits in the chip set and/or the software routines that implement this sublayer may even be organized into different functional blocks, but they will still be standards compliant if they are functionally equal to the operational requirements defined for the sublayer and the logical requirements for MAC service interface.

Ethernet compatible means that the product will operate as though it is standards compliant, even though it may not be defined by the standard. Gigabit Ethernet, for example, specifies a worst-case maximum link length where interoperability is guaranteed. As we said earlier, this is a baseline requirement that has been specified in a manner that will enable many manufacturers to enter the market.

Gigabit Ethernet link extenders provide an example of an Ethernet compatible product. They are not even considered in the standard. However, they can be standards compatible if they meet the optical characteristics and timing requirements for the signals at the media-dependent interface.

It is important when you are contemplating a new network or a network upgrade to select equipment that you know will interoperate with other devices on your network and that will provide the features necessary for the desired types of services. We hope that we have provided you with the knowledge necessary to ascertain for yourself whether or not this will happen.

Appendixes

References and Other Sources of Additional Information

IEEE 802.3 Standards and Supplements

You can access the complete IEEE standards at *http://www.ieee.org/prod_svcs.html.*

IEEE Std 802.3-1998: "Information technology—Telecommunications and information exchange between systems—Local and metropolitan area networks—Specific require-ments—Part 3: Carrier Sense multiple access with collision detection (CSMA/CD) access method and physical layer specifications." (This is the base standard. It is a revision of ISO/IEC 8802-3:1996 and incorporates IEEE 802.3r, 802.3u, 802.3x, 802.3y, 802.3z, and 802.3aa.)

IEEE Draft Std 803.3ab: Supplement to Carrier Sense Multiple Access with Collision Detection (CSMA/CD) Access Method and physical Layer Specifications: Physical layer specification for 1000 Mbps operation on four pairs of Category 5 or better balanced twisted pair cable (1000BASE-T)

IEEE Std 802.3ac-1998: Supplement to Carrier Sense Multiple Access with Collision Detection (CSMA/CD) Access Method and physical Layer Specifications: Frame Extensions for Virtual Bridged Local Area Networks (VLAN) Tagging on 802.3 Networks

IEEE Draft Std 803.3ad: Supplement to Carrier Sense Multiple Access with Collision Detection (CSMA/CD) Access Method and physical Layer Specifications: Link Aggregation

Other Standards

You can access the complete EIA/TIA standards at *http://www.tiaonline.org/standards.*

EIA/TIA-526-14A-98: Optical Power Loss Measurement of Installed Multimode Fiber Cable Plant

EIA/TIA-568-A-95: Commercial Building Telecommunications Wiring Standard

EIA/TIA-568-A-1-97: Propagation Delay and Delay Skew Specifications for 100 ohm 4-pair Cable

EIA/TIA-568-A-2-98: Correction and Additions to TIA/EIA-568-A

EIA/TIA-TSB-67: Transmission Performance Specifications for Field Testing of Unshielded Twisted-Pair Cabling Systems

EIA/TIA-TSB-95: Currently under development

IEEE 802-1990: Information Technology—Telecommunications and information exchange between systems—Local and metropolitan area networks—Overview and Architecture

IEEE 802.1D: See ISO/IEC 15802-3

IEEE 802.1p: See ISO/IEC 15802-3:1998

IEEE 802.1Q-1998: IEEE Standards for Local and Metropolitan Area Networks: Virtual Bridged Local Area Networks

IEEE 802.2-1994: See ISO/IEC 8802-2

IEEE 802.12-1995: See ISO/IEC 8802-12

IEEE 1394-1995: IEEE Standard for a High Performance Serial Bus

IEC 60825-1:1993: International Electrotechnical Commission Standard Publication, "Safety of Laser Products—Part 1: Equipment Classification, Requirements and User's Guide," 1st edition, 1993

ISO/IEC 8802-2:1994: Information technology—Telecommunications and information exchange between systems—Local area networks—Specific requirements—Part 2: Logical Link Control

ISO/IEC 8802-12:1998 Information technology—Telecommunications and information exchange between systems—Local area networks—Specific requirements—Part 12: Demand-Priority access method, physical layer and repeater specifications

ISO/IEC 15802-3:1998 [IEEE Std 802.1D, 1998 Edition], Information technology—Telecommunications and information exchange between systems—Local area networks—Media access control (MAC) bridges (This is a revision of ISO/IEC 10038: 1993, IEEE 802.1j-1992 and 802.6k-1992. It incorporates IEEE Std 802.11c-1998 and IEEE projects P802.1p and P802.12e.)

ISO/IEC 11801:1995: Information Technology—Generic Cabling for Customer Premises, Global Engineering Documents, July 1995

ISO/TC97/SC16 N227: International Organization for Standardization (ISO), "Reference Model of Open Systems Interconnection," Document no. ISO/TC97/SC16 N227, June 1979

Books and Papers

Agrawal et al, 1988: Govind P. Agrawal, P. J. Anthony, and T. M. Shen, "Dispersion Penalty for 1.3-mm Lightwave Systems with Multimode Semiconductor Lasers," *Journal of Lightwave Technology*, Vol. 6, No. 5, May 1988, pp. 620-625.

Bates et al, 1995: Richard J. S. Bates, Daniel M. Kuchta, and Kenneth P. Jackson, "Improved Multimode Fiber Link BER Calculations due to Modal Noise and Non Self-Pulsating Laser Diodes," *Optical and Quantum Electronics*, No. 27, 1995, pp. 203-224.

Brown, 1992: Gair D. Brown, "Bandwidth and Rise Time Calculations for Digital Multimode Fiber-Optic Data Links," *Journal of Lightwave Technology*, Vol. 10, No. 5, May 1992, pp. 672-678.

Coles and Cunningham, 1998: Alistair Coles and David Cunningham, "Low Overhead Block Coding for Multi-Gb/s Links," HP Laboratories Technical Report, HPL-98-168, October 1998. (This report is available at *http://www.hpl.hp.com/techreports/98/ HPL-98-168.html.*)

Folts, 1981: Harold C. Folts, "Coming of age: A long-awaited standard for heterogeneous nets," *Data communications*, January 1981.

Ford et al, 1997: Merilee Ford, H. Kim Lew, Steve Spanier, and Tim Stevenson, *Internetworking Technologies Handbook*. Cisco Press: 1997.

Gimlett and Cheung, 1986: James L. Gimlett and Nim K. Cheung, "Dispersion Penalty Analysis for LED/Single-Mode Fiber Transmission Systems," *Journal of Lightwave Technology*, Vol. LT-4, No. 9, September 1986, pp. 1381-1392.

Goldstine, 1972: Herman H. Goldstine, "The Computer from Pascal to von Neumann." Princeton University Press: 1972.

Gowar, 1983: John Gowar, *Optical Communication Systems*. Prentice Hall: 1983.

Hakki and Bosch, 1989: B. W. Hakki and F. Bosch, "Dispersion and Noise of 1.3-um Multimode Lasers in Microwave Digital Systems," *Journal of Lightwave Technology*, Vol. 7. No. 5. May 1989, pp. 804-812.

Hanson, 1996: Delon C. Hanson, Private communications.

Intel, 1980: "The Ethernet: A Local Area Network—Data Link Layer and Physical Layer Specifications, Version 1.0," Intel Corporation, 1980.

Isaacson, 1997: Walter Isaacson, "The Passion of Andrew Grove," *Time*, Vol. 150, No. 27, December 29, 1997.

Kazovsky et al, 1996: Kazovsky, Leonid, Benedetto, Sergio, Willner, and Allen, *Optical Fiber Communication Systems*. Artech House: 1996.

Kreshav, 1997: Srinivasan Kreshav, *An Engineering Approach to Computer Networking— ATM Networks, the Internet, and the Telephone Network*. Addison Wesley: 1997.

Lasky et al, 1995: Ronald C. Lasky, Ulf L. Osterberg, and Daniel P. Stigliani, *Optoelectronics for Data Communications*. Academic Press: 1995.

Metcalfe and Boggs, 1976: Robert M. Metcalfe and David R. Boggs, "Ethernet: Distributed Packet Switching for Computer Networks," *Communications of the Association for Computing Machinery*, Vol. 19, No. 7, July 1976.

Midwinter, 1979: John E. Midwinter, *Optical Fibers for Transmission*. John Wiley & Sons: 1979.

NetReference, 1998: "Upgrading the Network with Routing Switches," an Internet White Paper, NetReference, *www.netreference.com*, April 1998.

O'Malley, 1998: Chris O'Malley, "Computing's Outer Limits," *Popular Science*, March 1998.

Senior, 1992: John M. Senior, *Optical Communications Principles and Practice*, Second Edition. Prentice Hall: 1992.

Smith and Personick, 1982: R. G. Smith and S. D. Personick, "Receiver Design for Optical Communication Systems in Topics in Applied Physics," Volume 39, *Semiconductor Devices for Optical Communications*. Editor, H. Kressel, published by Springer-Verlag, 1982.

Zimmermann, 1980: H. Zimmermann, "OSI Reference Model—OSI Model of Architecture for Open Systems Interconnection," IEEE Transactions on Communication, COM-28 No. 4, April 1980.

B

8B10B Code Table

Table B.1 contains the valid code 8B10B code-groups, their code-group names, and their equivalent octet values. The rules for determining whether to use the RD minus or RD plus code-group in a particular code conversion are listed in Chapter 8, section 8.6.1.

Table B.1 Valid 1000BASE-X Data Code-Groups

Code-Group Name	Octet Value	Octet Bits HGF EDCBA	RD (–) abcdei fghj	RD (+) abcdei fghj
D0.0	00	000 00000	100111 0100	011000 1011
D1.0	01	000 00001	011101 0100	100010 1011
D2.0	02	000 00010	101101 0100	010010 1011
D3.0	03	000 00011	110001 1011	110001 0100
D4.0	04	000 00100	110101 0100	001010 1011
D5.0	05	000 00101	101001 1011	101001 0100
D6.0	06	000 00110	011001 1011	011001 0100
D7.0	07	000 00111	111000 1011	000111 0100
D8.0	08	000 01000	111001 0100	000110 1011
D9.0	09	000 01001	100101 1011	100101 0100
D10.0	0A	000 01010	010101 1011	010101 0100
D11.0	0B	000 01011	110100 1011	110100 0100
D12.0	0C	000 01100	001101 1011	001101 0100

continues

Table B.1   Continued

Code-Group Name	Octet Value	Octet Bits HGF EDCBA	RD (−) abcdei fghj	RD (+) abcdei fghj
D13.0	0D	000 01101	101100 1011	101100 0100
D14.0	0E	000 01110	011100 1011	011100 0100
D15.0	0F	000 01111	010111 0100	101000 1011
D16.0	10	000 10000	011011 0100	100100 1011
D17.0	11	000 10001	100011 1011	100011 0100
D18.0	12	000 10010	010011 1011	010011 0100
D19.0	13	000 10011	110010 1011	110010 0100
D20.0	14	000 10100	001011 1011	001011 0100
D21.0	15	000 10101	101010 1011	101010 0100
D22.0	16	000 10110	011010 1011	011010 0100
D23.0	17	000 10111	111010 0100	000101 1011
D24.0	18	000 11000	110011 0100	001100 1011
D25.0	19	000 11001	100110 1011	100110 0100
D26.0	1A	000 11010	010110 1011	010110 0100
D27.0	1B	000 11011	110110 0100	001001 1011
D28.0	1C	000 11100	001110 1011	001110 0100
D29.0	1D	000 11101	101110 0100	010001 1011
D30.0	1E	000 11110	011110 0100	100001 1011
D31.0	1F	000 11111	101011 0100	010100 1011
D0.1	20	001 00000	100111 1001	011000 1001
D1.1	21	001 00001	011101 1001	100010 1001
D2.1	22	001 00010	101101 1001	010010 1001
D3.1	23	001 00011	110001 1001	110001 1001
D4.1	24	001 00100	110101 1001	001010 1001
D5.1	25	001 00101	101001 1001	101001 1001

Code-Group Name	Octet Value	Octet Bits HGF EDCBA	RD (−) abcdei fghj	RD (+) abcdei fghj
D6.1	26	001 00110	011001 1001	011001 1001
D7.1	27	001 00111	111000 1001	000111 1001
D8.1	28	001 01000	111001 1001	000110 1001
D9.1	29	001 01001	100101 1001	100101 1001
D10.1	2A	001 01010	010101 1001	010101 1001
D11.1	2B	001 01011	110100 1001	110100 1001
D12.1	2C	001 01100	001101 1001	001101 1001
D13.1	2D	001 01101	101100 1001	101100 1001
D14.1	2E	001 01110	011100 1001	011100 1001
D15.1	2F	001 01111	010111 1001	101000 1001
D16.1	30	001 10000	011011 1001	100100 1001
D17.1	31	001 10001	100011 1001	100011 1001
D18.1	32	001 10010	010011 1001	010011 1001
D19.1	33	001 10011	110010 1001	110010 1001
D20.1	34	001 10100	001011 1001	001011 1001
D21.1	35	001 10101	101010 1001	101010 1001
D22.1	36	001 10110	011010 1001	011010 1001
D23.1	37	001 10111	111010 1001	000101 1001
D24.1	38	001 11000	110011 1001	001100 1001
D25.1	39	001 11001	100110 1001	100110 1001
D26.1	3A	001 11010	010110 1001	010110 1001
D27.1	3B	001 11011	110110 1001	001001 1001
D28.1	3C	001 11100	001110 1001	001110 1001
D29.1	3D	001 11101	101110 1001	010001 1001
D30.1	3E	001 11110	011110 1001	100001 1001
D31.1	3F	001 11111	101011 1001	010100 1001

continues

Table B.1   Continued

Code-Group Name	Octet Value	Octet Bits HGF EDCBA	RD (−) abcdei fghj	RD (+) abcdei fghj
D0.2	40	010 00000	100111 0101	011000 0101
D1.2	41	010 00001	011101 0101	100010 0101
D2.2	42	010 00010	101101 0101	010010 0101
D3.2	43	010 00011	110001 0101	110001 0101
D4.2	44	010 00100	110101 0101	001010 0101
D5.2	45	010 00101	101001 0101	101001 0101
D6.2	46	010 00110	011001 0101	011001 0101
D7.2	47	010 00111	111000 0101	000111 0101
D8.2	48	010 01000	111001 0101	000110 0101
D9.2	49	010 01001	100101 0101	100101 0101
D10.2	4A	010 01010	010101 0101	010101 0101
D11.2	4B	010 01011	110100 0101	110100 0101
D12.2	4C	010 01100	001101 0101	001101 0101
D13.2	4D	010 01101	101100 0101	101100 0101
D14.2	4E	010 01110	011100 0101	011100 0101
D15.2	4F	010 01111	010111 0101	101000 0101
D16.2	50	010 10000	011011 0101	100100 0101
D17.2	51	010 10001	100011 0101	100011 0101
D18.2	52	010 10010	010011 0101	010011 0101
D19.2	53	010 10011	110010 0101	110010 0101
D20.2	54	010 10100	001011 0101	001011 0101
D21.2	55	010 10101	101010 0101	101010 0101
D22.2	56	010 10110	011010 0101	011010 0101
D23.2	57	010 10111	111010 0101	000101 0101
D24.2	58	010 11000	110011 0101	001100 0101

Code-Group Name	Octet Value	Octet Bits HGF EDCBA	RD (−) abcdei fghj	RD (+) abcdei fghj
D25.2	59	010 11001	100110 0101	100110 0101
D26.2	5A	010 11010	010110 0101	010110 0101
D27.2	5B	010 11011	110110 0101	001001 0101
D28.2	5C	010 11100	001110 0101	001110 0101
D29.2	5D	010 11101	101110 0101	010001 0101
D30.2	5E	010 11110	011110 0101	100001 0101
D31.2	5F	010 11111	101011 0101	010100 0101
D0.3	60	011 00000	100111 0011	011000 1100
D1.3	61	011 00001	011101 0011	100010 1100
D2.3	62	011 00010	101101 0011	010010 1100
D3.3	63	011 00011	110001 1100	110001 0011
D4.3	64	011 00100	110101 0011	001010 1100
D5.3	65	011 00101	101001 1100	101001 0011
D6.3	66	011 00110	011001 1100	011001 0011
D7.3	67	011 00111	111000 1100	000111 0011
D8.3	68	011 01000	111001 0011	000110 1100
D9.3	69	011 01001	100101 1100	100101 0011
D10.3	6A	011 01010	010101 1100	010101 0011
D11.3	6B	011 01011	110100 1100	110100 0011
D12.3	6C	011 01100	001101 1100	001101 0011
D13.3	6D	011 01101	101100 1100	101100 0011
D14.3	6E	011 01110	011100 1100	011100 0011
D15.3	6F	011 01111	010111 0011	101000 1100
D16.3	70	011 10000	011011 0011	100100 1100
D17.3	71	011 10001	100011 1100	100011 0011
D18.3	72	011 10010	010011 1100	010011 0011

continues

Table B.1	Continued

Code-Group Name	Octet Value	Octet Bits HGF EDCBA	RD (−) abcdei fghj	RD (+) abcdei fghj
D19.3	73	011 10011	110010 1100	110010 0011
D20.3	74	011 10100	001011 1100	001011 0011
D21.3	75	011 10101	101010 1100	101010 0011
D22.3	76	011 10110	011010 1100	011010 0011
D23.3	77	011 10111	111010 0011	000101 1100
D24.3	78	011 11000	110011 0011	001100 1100
D25.3	79	011 11001	100110 1100	100110 0011
D26.3	7A	011 11010	010110 1100	010110 0011
D27.3	7B	011 11011	110110 0011	001001 1100
D28.3	7C	011 11100	001110 1100	001110 0011
D29.3	7D	011 11101	101110 0011	010001 1100
D30.3	7E	011 11110	011110 0011	100001 1100
D31.3	7F	011 11111	101011 0011	010100 1100
D0.4	80	100 00000	100111 0010	011000 1101
D1.4	81	100 00001	011101 0010	100010 1101
D2.4	82	100 00010	101101 0010	010010 1101
D3.4	83	100 00011	110001 1101	110001 0010
D4.4	84	100 00100	110101 0010	001010 1101
D5.4	85	100 00101	101001 1101	101001 0010
D6.4	86	100 00110	011001 1101	011001 0010
D7.4	87	100 00111	111000 1101	000111 0010
D8.4	88	100 01000	111001 0010	000110 1101
D9.4	89	100 01001	100101 1101	100101 0010
D10.4	8A	100 01010	010101 1101	010101 0010
D11.4	8B	100 01011	110100 1101	110100 0010

Code-Group Name	Octet Value	Octet Bits HGF EDCBA	RD (−) abcdei fghj	RD (+) abcdei fghj
D12.4	8C	100 01100	001101 1101	001101 0010
D13.4	8D	100 01101	101100 1101	101100 0010
D14.4	8E	100 01110	011100 1101	011100 0010
D15.4	8F	100 01111	010111 0010	101000 1101
D16.4	90	100 10000	011011 0010	100100 1101
D17.4	91	100 10001	100011 1101	100011 0010
D18.4	92	100 10010	010011 1101	010011 0010
D19.4	93	100 10011	110010 1101	110010 0010
D20.4	94	100 10100	001011 1101	001011 0010
D21.4	95	100 10101	101010 1101	101010 0010
D22.4	96	100 10110	011010 1101	011010 0010
D23.4	97	100 10111	111010 0010	000101 1101
D24.4	98	100 11000	110011 0010	001100 1101
D25.4	99	100 11001	100110 1101	100110 0010
D26.4	9A	100 11010	010110 1101	010110 0010
D27.4	9B	100 11011	110110 0010	001001 1101
D28.4	9C	100 11100	001110 1101	001110 0010
D29.4	9D	100 11101	101110 0010	010001 1101
D30.4	9E	100 11110	011110 0010	100001 1101
D31.4	9F	100 11111	101011 0010	010100 1101
D0.5	A0	101 00000	100111 1010	011000 1010
D1.5	A1	101 00001	011101 1010	100010 1010
D2.5	A2	101 00010	101101 1010	010010 1010
D3.5	A3	101 00011	110001 1010	110001 1010
D4.5	A4	101 00100	110101 1010	001010 1010
D5.5	A5	101 00101	101001 1010	101001 1010

continues

Table B.1 Continued

Code-Group Name	Octet Value	Octet Bits HGF EDCBA	RD (–) abcdei fghj	RD (+) abcdei fghj
D6.5	A6	101 00110	011001 1010	011001 1010
D7.5	A7	101 00111	111000 1010	000111 1010
D8.5	A8	101 01000	111001 1010	000110 1010
D9.5	A9	101 01001	100101 1010	100101 1010
D10.5	AA	101 01010	010101 1010	010101 1010
D11.5	AB	101 01011	110100 1010	110100 1010
D12.5	AC	101 01100	001101 1010	001101 1010
D13.5	AD	101 01101	101100 1010	101100 1010
D14.5	AE	101 01110	011100 1010	011100 1010
D15.5	AF	101 01111	010111 1010	101000 1010
D16.5	B0	101 10000	011011 1010	100100 1010
D17.5	B1	101 10001	100011 1010	100011 1010
D18.5	B2	101 10010	010011 1010	010011 1010
D19.5	B3	101 10011	110010 1010	110010 1010
D20.5	B4	101 10100	001011 1010	001011 1010
D21.5	B5	101 10101	101010 1010	101010 1010
D22.5	B6	101 10110	011010 1010	011010 1010
D23.5	B7	101 10111	111010 1010	000101 1010
D24.5	B8	101 11000	110011 1010	001100 1010
D25.5	B9	101 11001	100110 1010	100110 1010
D26.5	BA	101 11010	010110 1010	010110 1010
D27.5	BB	101 11011	110110 1010	001001 1010
D28.5	BC	101 11100	001110 1010	001110 1010
D29.5	BD	101 11101	101110 1010	010001 1010
D30.5	BE	101 11110	011110 1010	100001 1010

Code-Group Name	Octet Value	Octet Bits HGF EDCBA	RD (−) abcdei fghj	RD (+) abcdei fghj
D31.5	BF	101 11111	101011 1010	010100 1010
D0.6	C0	110 00000	100111 0110	011000 0110
D1.6	C1	110 00001	011101 0110	100010 0110
D2.6	C2	110 00010	101101 0110	010010 0110
D3.6	C3	110 00011	110001 0110	110001 0110
D4.6	C4	110 00100	110101 0110	001010 0110
D5.6	C5	110 00101	101001 0110	101001 0110
D6.6	C6	110 00110	011001 0110	011001 0110
D7.6	C7	110 00111	111000 0110	000111 0110
D8.6	C8	110 01000	111001 0110	000110 0110
D9.6	C9	110 01001	100101 0110	100101 0110
D10.6	CA	110 01010	010101 0110	010101 0110
D11.6	CB	110 01011	110100 0110	110100 0110
D12.6	CC	110 01100	001101 0110	001101 0110
D13.6	CD	110 01101	101100 0110	101100 0110
D14.6	CE	110 01110	011100 0110	011100 0110
D15.6	CF	110 01111	010111 0110	101000 0110
D16.6	D0	110 10000	011011 0110	100100 0110
D17.6	D1	110 10001	100011 0110	100011 0110
D18.6	D2	110 10010	010011 0110	010011 0110
D19.6	D3	110 10011	110010 0110	110010 0110
D20.6	D4	110 10100	001011 0110	001011 0110
D21.6	D5	110 10101	101010 0110	101010 0110
D22.6	D6	110 10110	011010 0110	011010 0110
D23.6	D7	110 10111	111010 0110	000101 0110
D24.6	D8	110 11000	110011 0110	001100 0110

continues

Table B.1   Continued

Code-Group Name	Octet Value	Octet Bits HGF EDCBA	RD (–) abcdei fghj	RD (+) abcdei fghj
D25.6	D9	110 11001	100110 0110	100110 0110
D26.6	DA	110 11010	010110 0110	010110 0110
D27.6	DB	110 11011	110110 0110	001001 0110
D28.6	DC	110 11100	001110 0110	001110 0110
D29.6	DD	110 11101	101110 0110	010001 0110
D30.6	DE	110 11110	011110 0110	100001 0110
D31.6	DF	110 11111	101011 0110	010100 0110
D0.7	E0	111 00000	100111 0001	011000 1110
D1.7	E1	111 00001	011101 0001	100010 1110
D2.7	E2	111 00010	101101 0001	010010 1110
D3.7	E3	111 00011	110001 1110	110001 0001
D4.7	E4	111 00100	110101 0001	001010 1110
D5.7	E5	111 00101	101001 1110	101001 0001
D6.7	E6	111 00110	011001 1110	011001 0001
D7.7	E7	111 00111	111000 1110	000111 0001
D8.7	E8	111 01000	111001 0001	000110 1110
D9.7	E9	111 01001	100101 1110	100101 0001
D10.7	EA	111 01010	010101 1110	010101 0001
D11.7	EB	111 01011	110100 1110	110100 1000
D12.7	EC	111 01100	001101 1110	001101 0001
D13.7	ED	111 01101	101100 1110	101100 1000
D14.7	EE	111 01110	011100 1110	011100 1000
D15.7	EF	111 01111	010111 0001	101000 1110
D16.7	F0	111 10000	011011 0001	100100 1110
D17.7	F1	111 10001	100011 0111	100011 0001

Code-Group Name	Octet Value	Octet Bits HGF EDCBA	RD (−) abcdei fghj	RD (+) abcdei fghj
D18.7	F2	111 10010	010011 0111	010011 0001
D19.7	F3	111 10011	110010 1110	110010 0001
D20.7	F4	111 10100	001011 0111	001011 0001
D21.7	F5	111 10101	101010 1110	101010 0001
D22.7	F6	111 10110	011010 1110	011010 0001
D23.7	F7	111 10111	111010 0001	000101 1110
D24.7	F8	111 11000	110011 0001	001100 1110
D25.7	F9	111 11001	100110 1110	100110 0001
D26.7	FA	111 11010	010110 1110	010110 0001
D27.7	FB	111 11011	110110 0001	001001 1110
D28.7	FC	111 11100	001110 1110	001110 0001
D29.7	FD	111 11101	101110 0001	010001 1110
D30.7	FE	111 11110	011110 0001	100001 1110
D31.7	FF	111 11111	101011 0001	010100 1110

Glossary

Numerics

1BASE5: IEEE 802.3 Physical Layer specification for a 1 Mbps CSMA/CD LAN over two pairs of twisted pair telephone cable.

3B4B decoder: A device for decoding the four left-most bits in an 8B10B code-group back into the three left-most bits of the data octet.

3B4B encoder: A device for encoding the three left-most bits of the data octet into the four left-most bits in an 8B10B code group.

4D-PAM5 decoder: A data decoding device that uses the 4D-PAM5 transmission code.

4D-PAM5 encoder: A data encoding device that uses the 4D-PAM5 transmission code.

4D-PAM5 transmission code: The data encoding used by 1000BASE-T. Each 8-bit octet is converted into a code-group of four 5-level symbols that are transmitted in parallel during one symbol period.

5B6B decoder: A device for decoding the six right-most bits in an 8B10B code-group back into the four right-most bits of the data octet.

5B6B encoder: A device for encoding the four left-most bits of the data octet into the six left-most bits in an 8B10B code-group.

8B10B decoder: A data decoding device that uses the 8B10B transmission code.

8B10B encoder: A data encoding device that uses the 8B10B transmission code.

8B10B transmission code: The DC-balanced byte-orientated data encoding specified by 1000BASE-X.

10BASE-F: IEEE 802.3 Physical Layer specification for a 10 Mbps CSMA/CD LAN over fiber optic cable.

10BASE-FB port: A port on a repeater that contains an internal 10BASE-FB MAU that can connect to a similar port on another repeater.

10BASE-FB segment: A fiber optic link segment providing a point-to-point connection between two 10BASE-FB ports on repeaters.

10BASE-FL segment: A fiber optic link segment providing a point-to-point connection between two 10BASE-FL MAUs.

10BASE-FP Star: A passive device used to couple fiber pairs together to form a 10BASE-FP segment. Optical signals received at any input port of the 10BASE-FP Star are distributed to all of its output ports (including the output port of the optical interface from which it is received). A 10BASE-FP Star is typically comprised of a passive-star coupler, up to 33 fiber-optic port connectors, and a suitable mechanical housing.

10BASE-T: IEEE 802.3 Physical Layer specification for a 10 Mbps CSMA/CD LAN over two pairs of twisted pair telephone cable.

10BASE2: IEEE 802.3 Physical Layer specification for a 10 Mbps CSMA/CD LAN over RG-58 coaxial cable.

10BASE5: IEEE 802.3 Physical Layer specification for a 10 Mbps CSMA/CD LAN over coaxial cable (i.e., thicknet).

10BROAD36: IEEE 802.3 Physical Layer specification for a 10 Mbps CSMA/CD LAN over a single broadband CATV cable.

100BASE-FX: 100BASE-X over two optical fibers.

100BASE-T: IEEE 802.3 Physical Layer specification for a 100 Mbps CSMA/CD LAN.

100BASE-T2: 100BASE-T over two pairs of Category 3 or better balanced, unshielded twisted pair cabling.

100BASE-T4: 100BASE-T over four pairs of Category 3, 4, or 5 balanced, unshielded twisted pair cabling.

100BASE-TX: 100BASE-T over two pairs of Category 5 UTP or shielded twisted pair (STP) wire.

100BASE-X: IEEE 802.3 Physical Layer specification for a 100 Mbps CSMA/CD LAN that uses the PMD sublayer and MDI of the ISO 9314 group of standards developed by ASC X3T12 (FDDI).

100VG-AnyLAN: 100 Mbps Fast Ethernet and Token Ring media technology using four pairs of Category 3, 4, or 5 UTP cabling. This high-speed transport technology, developed by Hewlett-Packard, can operate on existing 10BASE-T Ethernet cable plants.

1000BASE-CX: 1000BASE-X over specialty shielded balanced copper jumper cable assemblies.

1000BASE-LX: 1000BASE-X using multimode and single-mode optical fiber and laser-based transceivers operating at long wavelengths near 1,300 nm.

1000BASE-SX: 1000BASE-X using multimode optical fiber and laser-based transceivers operating at short wavelengths near 850 nm.

1000BASE-T: IEEE 802.3 Physical Layer specification for a 1,000 Mbps LAN using four pairs of Category-5 balanced copper cabling.

1000BASE-X: IEEE 802.3 Physical Layer specification for a 1,000 Mbps LAN using optical fiber or specialty shielded copper cabling.

A

AAL (ATM adaptation layer): Service-dependent sublayer of the data link layer. The AAL accepts data from different applications and presents it to the ATM layer in the form of 48-byte ATM payload segments.

application layer: Layer 7 of the OSI reference model, this layer provides services to application processes (such as email) that are outside the OSI model. The application layer identifies and establishes the availability of intended communication partners (and the resources required to connect with them), synchronizes cooperating applications, and establishes agreement on procedures for error recovery and control of data integrity.

as-built drawings: Drawings that reflect the way a cable plant is actually installed rather than how it was initially designed.

ASIC (application specific integrated circuit): An integrated circuit made for a specific application.

ATM (Asynchronous Transfer Mode): International standard for cell relay in which multiple service types (such as voice, video, or data) are conveyed in fixed-length (53-byte) cells. Fixed-length cells allow cell processing to occur in hardware, thereby reducing transit delays. ATM is designed to take advantage of high-speed transmission media such as E3, SONET, and T3.

ATM ARP: The ATM address resolution protocol between an end system and an ATM address resolution server. The ATM ARP is used to resolve IP network layer addresses to ATM addresses.

attenuation: A decrease in power (usually by a length of optical or copper cable); usually stated in dB.

AUI (Attachment Unit Interface): IEEE 802.3 interface between a media attachment unit (MAU) and a network interface card (NIC).

Auto-Negotiation: The physical sublayer that negotiates the link operational mode during link initiation.

B

back-reflection: Power reflected in the opposite direction to the direction of signal transmission.

baseline wander: The low frequency wander introduced into the envelope of a digital pulse sequence by the removal of a direct current path.

baud: The transmission rate in symbols/second.

BER (bit error rate): The ratio of number of errored bits received to the total number of bits received.

Bessel-Thompson filter: An electrical filter having a Bessel-Thompson transfer function.

best-effort traffic: The traditional type of traffic carried on LANs and IP networks. Provides no guarantee of delivery or delay time.

BGP (Border Gateway Protocol): An Internet inter-domain routing protocol.

bit-serial communication: Transmission of one bit after another.

block coding: The coding of groups of binary digits into longer groups of binary digits to facilitate some operation, such as error detection or baseline wander control.

bridge: Device that connects and passes packets between two network segments that use the same or different communications protocol. Bridges operate at layer 2 of the OSI reference model. In general, a bridge will filter, forward, or flood an incoming frame based on the MAC address of that frame.

building backbone cable: A cable that connects the building distributor to a floor distributor. Building backbone cables may also directly interconnect floor distributors.

building distributor: A distributor (switch and connection panels) in which the building backbone cable(s) terminate(s) and at which connections to the campus backbone cable(s) may be made.

bus: A communication medium in which the communicating entities are connected to the communication medium in parallel. A bus may be comprised of one or more conductors.

BUS (broadcast and unknown server): Multicast server used to flood traffic addressed to an unknown destination and to forward multicast and broadcast traffic to the appropriate clients.

bus segment: In Ethernet LANs, a single coaxial cable up to 500 m long used to interconnect up to 100 Ethernet stations.

C

cable: An assembly of one or more cable units (copper wire pairs or optical fibers) typically of the same type and category in an overall sheath. It may also include a shield. Optical fiber cables may include both single-mode and multimode fibers.

cabling: A system of telecommunications cables, cords, and connecting hardware that can support the connection of information technology equipment.

campus: A facility containing one or more buildings in a single site.

campus backbone cable: A cable that connects the campus distributor to the building distributor(s). Campus backbone cables may also interconnect building distributors directly.

campus distributor: The distributor from which the campus backbone cabling emerges.

Carrier Sense function: The function that detects the presence of a carrier, usually in a CSMA/CD LAN.

Category-3: Unshielded twisted pair (UTP) copper cable designed for 15 MHz bandwidth.

Category-5: Unshielded twisted pair (UTP) copper cable designed for 100 MHz bandwidth.

cell: Basic data unit for ATM switching and multiplexing. Cells contain identifiers that specify the data stream to which they belong.

cell rate decoupling: The mechanism for inserting "idle" cells into an ATM cell stream to ensure that a continuous stream of ATM cells is transmitted.

CFI (canonical format indicator): An indicator in the VLAN Tag Control Information Field that indicates the presence or absence of a Routing Information Field in the MAC Client Data field.

channel-insertion loss: The attenuation introduced by the insertion of the channel between a transmitting and a receiving unit; usually stated in dB.

chip: A semiconductor containing integrated circuits.

chromatic bandwidth: The bandwidth of a fiber due to the effect of chromatic dispersion. Chromatic bandwidth is characterized as the 3 dB optical bandwidth in units of MHz.km. See also *chromatic dispersion* and *intra-modal dispersion.*

chromatic dispersion: The velocity of light in a physical medium depends on its wavelength. Because of this, an optical signal made up of different wavelengths will separate or disperse as it travels through a physical medium. This effect is called chromatic dispersion.

CLP (cell loss priority): A field in the ATM cell header that determines the probability of a cell being dropped if the network becomes congested. Cells with CLP = 0 are unlikely to be dropped. Cells with CLP = 1 are classed as best-effort and might be dropped in a congested network.

CMOS: Complementary metal oxide semiconductor (a technology used in fabricating integrated circuit chips).

co-directional wavefronts: Wavefronts that propagate in the same direction.

code-group slipping: A device that implements the Gigabit Ethernet Physical Medium Attachment sublayer is allowed to delete or modify at most four received code-groups during code-group alignment. This process is called code-group slipping.

CODEC (coder-decoder): Device that typically uses pulse code modulation to transform analog signals into a digital bit stream and digital signals back into analog.

comma sequence: A unique bit sequence that in the absence of transmission errors can never appear in a valid combination of encoded data characters.

Confirmation Primitive: A service primitive that is passed from a lower layer ($n - 1$) to an upper layer ($n + 1$) to provide the results from one or more previously invoked request primitives. See also *service primitives.*

conformance test: A test used to determine whether or not a network component conforms to the specified operational requirements.

connection-oriented network service: Term used to describe a communication service over a network that requires the establishment of a virtual circuit.

connectionless network service: Term used to describe a communication service over a network without the existence of a virtual circuit.

core/cladding interface: The interface between the core and cladding of an optical fiber.

CoS (Class of Service): The priority level (0-7) required by an upper-layer protocol during packet transmission. CoS is used with datagram transmission over IP networks. See also *QoS*.

CPR (coupled-power-ratio): The ratio of the power coupled into a multimode fiber compared to the power coupled into a single-mode fiber. CPR is measured in accordance with EIA/TIA-526-14A, and CPR values are averaged to eliminate variations due to laser speckle fluctuations.

CRC (Cyclic Redundancy Check): A binary polynomial value that is mathematically generated by the bit content of a data frame and appended to the end of the frame to provide a reference value when the received frame is checked for transmission errors.

cross-point switch: A switch having input paths and output paths that physically cross a point.

CRS (carrier sense): The detection of carrier in a CSMA/CD LAN device.

CSMA/CD (carrier sense multiple access collision detect): Media-access mechanism wherein devices ready to transmit data first check the channel for a carrier. If no carrier is sensed for a specific period of time, a device can transmit. If two devices transmit at once, a collision occurs and is detected by all colliding devices. This collision subsequently delays retransmission from those devices for some random length of time.

cut-through switching: A routing/switching method in which the next logical destination (the associated switch output port) is determined from the destination address information of the first packet in a packet sequence. The second and subsequent packets are switched directly to the output port associated with the first packet as soon as the packet has been identified as belonging to the sequence, and typically before the end of the packet has been received. Cut-through switching reduces the switch delay that would be required if each packet had to be processed independently. It is an implementation of the "route once, switch many" philosophy.

D

data link layer: Layer 2 of the OSI reference model. Provides reliable transit of data across a physical link. The data link layer is concerned with the physical addressing, network topology, line discipline, error notification, ordered delivery of frames, and flow control. The IEEE divides this layer into two sublayers: MAC and LLC.

datagram: A self-contained packet that includes all the information necessary to transfer the packet to its intended destination. A datagram is the electronic equivalent of a telegram or a letter.

datagram network service: See *connectionless network service.*

DCD (duty cycle distortion): The fraction of time the signal is on during a periodic waveform is called its duty cycle. Gigabit Ethernet has a nominal duty cycle of 50 percent so that the pulse width of an "on" pulse equals the pulse width of an "off" pulse. However, distortions in the performance of link components can cause the duty cycle to be reduced or increased during a measurement period. This is called duty cycle distortion.

DCE (data communications equipment): An intermediate network device such as a repeater, bridge, router, or switch.

deference: The action during CSMA/CD operation in which a station needing to send a frame waits until the network has been quiet for a short period (the interframe gap time) before beginning transmission.

delay-sensitive traffic: Requires that transmitted packets be received within a prescribed time window (e.g., in video over IP). The typical CODEC-generated packet stream contains information for an entire screen display (called a key frame) followed by changes to the screen display (delta frames). The bandwidth necessary to transmit an entire screen can vary from ~3 Mbps for an uncomplicated display to ~7 Mbps for a complicated one. The bandwidth required for delta frames is typically much lower than that for key frames. However, both the key and delta information must be received in time for the CODEC to keep up with the display's scan rate.

delta frames: Frames that include only the changes in a screen display rather than the entire screen display.

deterministic jitter: Jitter that is not random and that is dependent on the transmitted data sequence. Repetition of any given transmit data sequence will produce the same repetitive jitter pattern. See also *jitter* and *random jitter.*

DFB (distributed feedback) laser: A laser in which light is fed back into the laser cavity in a distributed manner.

DMD (differential mode delay): The difference in the propagation delay time between the modes of a multimode fiber.

DPAM (Demand Priority Access Method): Media access method specified by IEEE 802.12 (100VG-AnyLAN).

E

EDFA (Erbium-doped fiber amplifier): An optical amplifier formed by doping single-mode optical fiber with Erbium and by providing an auxiliary light source to cause a population inversion in the Erbium ions. See also *population inversion*.

edge emitting laser: A laser that emits laser light from its edge(s).

ELAN (emulated LAN): ATM network in which an Ethernet or Token Ring LAN is emulated using a client/server model. ELANs are composed of an LEC, an LES, a BUS, and an LECS. Multiple ELANs can exist simultaneously on a single ATM network.

EMBI (Effective Modal Bandwidth Investigation): The first ad hoc committee formed by members of IEEE 802.3z and TIA FO 2.2 during the Gigabit Ethernet standardization process to investigate the modal bandwidth of laser-based multimode fiber links.

EMI (electromagnetic interference): Interference by electromagnetic signals that can cause reduced data integrity and increased error rates on transmission channels.

encapsulation: Wrapping of data in a particular protocol header. Ethernet data, for example, is wrapped in a specific Ethernet header before network transit. Also, when bridging dissimilar networks, the entire frame from one network is simply placed in the header used by the data link layer protocol of the other network.

EPD (End_of_Packet Delimiter): Delimiter indicating the end of a packet.

EWRAP (enable wrap-loopback): A PMA signal. If EWRAP is enabled, the output of the TBI transmitter function will be connected to the input of the TBI receiver function via the loopback path. Otherwise, the transmitter will pass the bit stream out of the serial interface to the PMD. See also *TBI*.

extinction ratio: The ratio of optical energy emitted by a laser during a zero-bit period to the energy emitted during a one-bit period.

extinction ratio power penalty: In an optical transmission link, the power penalty associated with transmitting a non-zero power level for a zero (no light) code bit.

eye diagram: The diagram displayed on an oscilloscope when it is triggered by the bit clock and many received waveforms, from a digital transmission, are overlapped on the oscilloscope display. Usually the time base of the oscilloscope is adjusted so that the display width in time is equivalent to a few bit periods. Eye diagrams are useful for assessing the quality of the transmission link—the more open the center of the eye, the better the quality of the link.

eye mask: Defines the allowed boundaries of an eye diagram.

F

Fabry-Perot laser: A laser having a Fabry-Perot cavity—a cavity formed by two parallel mirrors, one at each end of the laser.

falltime: The time required for a signal to fall from a high signal level to a low signal level. Usually the signal levels are measured as a percentage of the level of a one.

FCS (frame check sequence): Extra characters added to a frame for error control purposes. Used in data link layer protocols.

FDDI (Fiber Distributed Data Interface): LAN standard that specifies a 100 Mbps token-passing network using fiber optic cable, with transmission distances of up to 2 km.

fiber mode: A standing-wave electric-field pattern perpendicular to the z axis of the fiber formed by light propagating in the fiber.

floor distributor: The distributor used to connect between the horizontal cable and other cabling subsystems or equipment.

FOIRL: Fiber optic inter-repeater link. The optional fiber optic link used to interconnect 10BASE5 repeaters. (See IEEE 802.3, subclause 9.9.)

frame: The unit of information transmitted over a LAN. The length of a frame can vary from a defined minimum to a defined maximum length. The minimum and maximum frame lengths may vary from protocol to protocol.

frame bursting: A standard feature included in the Gigabit Ethernet MAC that allows users to send a series of frames in half-duplex mode without relinquishing control of the network medium after each frame.

full-duplex transmission: Simultaneous bidirectional data transmission between a sending station and a receiving station.

full-mesh network topology: A network topology in which each intermediate network node (bridge, switch, or router) is connected by a physical circuit to every other intermediate network node.

G–H

GFC (generic flow control): A field in the header of an ATM cell.

GMII (Gigabit Media Independent Interface): An optional interface defined in the IEEE 802.3 Gigabit Ethernet standard. The GMII makes the differences among the various Gigabit Ethernet physical layers transparent to the Gigabit Ethernet MAC sublayer.

graded-index multimode fiber: Multimode fiber having a core with a graded refractive index profile. The multimode fiber used by Ethernet has a core refractive index that has a parabolic profile.

half-duplex transmission: Bidirectional data transmission, but in only one direction at a time, between a sending station and a receiving station.

HEC (header error control): Algorithm for checking and correcting an error in an ATM cell.

home run cabling: A cabling system that connects telecommunications outlets directly to a building distributor, bypassing the floor distributor. See also *floor distributor*, *building distributor*, and *telecommunications outlet*.

horizontal cable: A cable connecting the floor distributor to the telecommunications outlet(s).

horizontal eye closure: The closure measured in time of an eye diagram. See also *eye diagram*.

I

ICMP (Internet Control Message Protocol): Network layer Internet protocol that reports errors and provides other information relevant to IP packet processing.

IDLE ordered_sets: These ordered_sets are transmitted when the GMII is idle. The IDLE ordered_sets are used as keepalive signals for both the clock recovery electronics and the electro-optics of a link.

IGMP (Internet Group Management Protocol): Used by IP hosts to report their multicast group memberships to an adjacent multicast router.

in-phase wavefronts: Wavefronts having the same phase.

index of refraction (also known as the refractive index): The ratio of the velocity of light in a vacuum to the velocity of light in a medium.

Indication Primitive: A service primitive passed from a lower layer (n) to an upper layer ($n + 1$) to indicate an event or condition significant to layer ($n + 1$). The event may be logically related to a remote request primitive or it may have been caused by a condition that is internal to the layer (n). See also *service primitives*.

integral passive equalizer: A signal equalizer, requiring no electrical power, that is permanently built into another component.

inter-frame control signals: Control signals transmitted when frames are not being transmitted.

inter-modal dispersion: Pulse spreading (in time) due to the DMD of a multimode fiber.

inter-symbol interference (ISI): The spreading of power of transmit symbols into adjacent receive symbol periods.

interferometric noise: Multiple reflections caused by fiber connectors in an optical link will optically interfere and cause optical interference induced noise within a laser. This noise is usually called interferometric noise.

intra-frame control signals: Control signals transmitted during frame transmission/reception.

intra-modal dispersion: See *chromatic dispersion.*

IP (Internet Protocol): The Layer-3 datagram protocol of the Internet suite.

IP address: The 32-bit (four octet) address used to identify a network node during an IP packet transmission.

IPG (Inter Packet Gap): The required minimum time period between successive frame transmissions.

ISO (International Organization for Standardization): International organization responsible for a wide range of standards, including those relevant to networking.

J–K

jabbering: Error condition in which a network device continually transmits random, meaningless data onto a network.

jitter: Analog communication line distortion caused by the variation of a signal from its reference timing positions. Jitter can cause data loss, particularly at high speeds. See also *random jitter, deterministic jitter.*

joule (J): The Systeme International (SI) unit of energy.

keepalive signals: Signals that maintain the operation of a component or function within its specified limits.

key frame: A special type of frame associated with digital video transmission.

L

LACP (Link Aggregation Control Protocol): The protocol used for implementing and controlling link aggregation.

LACPDU (Link Aggregation Control Protocol Data Unit): The transmission data unit used by LACP.

LAG (link aggregation group): Group of links that appear as if they were a single link between a pair of link partners.

LANE (LAN emulation): Technology that allows an ATM network to function as a LAN backbone. The ATM network must provide multicast and broadcast support, address mapping (MAC-to-ATM), SVC management, and a usable packet format.

latency: The time it takes for a packet to travel from one network point to another. Network latency represents the packet travel time between the source to the destination. Switch or router latency represents the time between receipt and retransmission of a packet.

Layer-2 Switch: A switch with Layer-2 protocol capability.

Layer-3 Switch: A switch with Layer-3 protocol capability.

Layer-4 Switch: A switch with Layer-4 protocol capability.

LEC (LAN emulation client): Entity in an end system that performs data forwarding, address resolution, and other control functions for a single end system within a single ELAN. An LEC also provides a standard LAN service interface to any higher-layer entity that interfaces to the LEC. Each LEC is identified by a unique ATM address, and is associated with one or more MAC addresses reachable through that ATM address.

LECS (LAN emulation configuration server): Entity that assigns individual LANE clients to particular ELANs by directing them to the LES that corresponds to the ELAN. There is logically one LECS per administrative domain, and this serves all ELANs within that domain.

LED (Light Emitting Diode): Semiconductor device that emits light produced by converting electrical energy. Status lights on hardware devices are typically LEDs.

LES (LAN emulation server): Entity that implements the control function for a particular ELAN. There is only one logical LES per ELAN, and it is identified by a unique ATM address.

link aggregation: The method of combining multiple links between the same two network entities (such as two switches or a switch and a file server) to operate as one logical higher capacity trunk.

link compatibility: The condition that exists when the entities at either end of a link are able to communicate with each other.

link optical power budget: The primary analysis tool used for the specification of the Gigabit Ethernet optical PMD is based on the simple power transfer relation "power-out equals the power-in minus power losses." The power losses are of two types: loss of average optical power and loss of modulated signal power (due to system power penalties).

link optical power margin (link margin): The amount of optical power remaining in the link power budget after all link power penalties and power losses have been accounted for.

LIS (logical IP subnetwork): A subnetwork whose members share the same IP subnetwork address. See also *subnet*.

logic zero/one signal level: The signal level representing zero or one.

Logical Link Control (LLC) sublayer: The upper of the two sublayers in the data link layer in an end station.

loop timing: A synchronization procedure in which the slave is synchronized by the clock recovered from the master's transmitted symbol stream. Loop timing is used by 1000BASE-T.

LSDU (link service data unit): The unit of data passed between the network layer and the logical link control sublayer (the MAC client sublayer). See also *PDUs*.

M

MAC client sublayer: Upper of the two sublayers of the data link layer defined by the IEEE. The MAC client sublayer may be an LLC or a bridge entity. See also *Logical Link Control (LLC) sublayer*.

MAC Control frame: The frame used to transfer MAC Control information in an Ethernet LAN, such as the PAUSE operation. MAC Control frames are recognized by the reserved value 88-08 in the Length/Type field.

MAC frame: The frame used to transfer data in a LAN.

Manchester line code: The name of a type of 1B2B line code.

MAU (Medium Attachment Unit): Device used in Ethernet and IEEE 802.3 networks that provides the interface between the AUI port of a station and the common medium of the Ethernet. The MAU, which can be built into a station or can be a separate device, performs physical layer functions, including the conversion of digital data from the Ethernet interface, collision detection, and injection of bits onto the network.

MBI (Modal Bandwidth Investigation): The second ad hoc committee formed by members of IEEE 802.3z and TIA FO 2.2 during the Gigabit Ethernet standardization process to investigate the modal bandwidth of laser-based multimode fiber links.

MDC (Management Data Clock): A management data interface signal of the GMII. Provides the clock for the management data interface.

MDI (Medium Dependent Interface): The interface connector specification that connects the PMD to the physical layer cable. See also *PMD.*

MDIO (Management Data Input-Output): Serial management input/output interface of the GMII.

meridional rays: Optical rays in a multimode fiber whose paths are confined to a meridional plane of the fiber core.

MIB (Management Information Base): Database of network management information used and maintained by a network management protocol.

MII (Medium Independent Interface): An optional interface defined in the IEEE 802.3 Fast Ethernet standard. The MII makes the differences among the various Fast Ethernet physical layers transparent to the Fast Ethernet MAC sublayer.

MMF (multimode fiber): Optical fiber supporting propagation of multiple frequencies of light. See also *single-mode fiber (SMF).*

modal bandwidth: The bandwidth of a multimode fiber due to the effect of inter-modal modal dispersion. Modal bandwidth is characterized as the 3 dB optical bandwidth in units of MHz.km. See also *inter-modal dispersion.*

modal noise: Imperfect connectors, splices, or optical couplers create mode selective loss. Mode selective loss combined with changes in the optical spectrum of a laser can create a form of noise known as modal noise (sometimes also called speckle noise).

modal noise power penalty: The (optical) power penalty due to MPN. See also *optical power penalty.*

MPLS (Multiprotocol Label Switching): Emerging industry standard that is a form of tag switching.

MPN (mode partition noise): Fluctuations in the signal arrival time at the fiber output due to partitioning of the signal power in the differently colored laser modes.

MPOA (multiprotocol over ATM): ATM Forum standardization effort specifying how existing and future network layer protocols run over an ATM network with directly attached hosts, routers, and multilayer LAN switches.

msdu (MAC service data unit): The unit of data passed between the MAC client layer and the MAC layer. See also *PDUs*.

MSL (mode selective loss): Optical loss of a multimode fiber component that is different for different modes of the fiber.

MTU (maximum transmission unit): Maximum packet size, in bytes, that a particular interface can handle.

MUX (multiplexer): Device used by which multiple logical signals can be transmitted simultaneously across a single physical channel.

N

network layer: Layer 3 of the OSI reference model that provides connectivity and path selection between two end systems.

NEXT (near-end crosstalk): Crosstalk noise originating from near-end transmitters.

NHRP (Next Hop Resolution Protocol): Protocol used by network routers to dynamically discover the MAC address of other network routers and hosts connected to a non-broadcast multiaccess (NBMA) network.

NICs (network interface cards): Boards that provide network communication capabilities to and from a computer system.

NRZ (non-return-to-zero) modulation: A bi-level modulation format in which one symbol nominally has an amplitude equal to zero and the other symbol has a non-zero amplitude. Each symbol is transmitted for the full duration of a symbol period. If a series of non-zero symbols is transmitted without any intervening zero symbols, the signal remains at the level representing the non-zero symbol.

nsdu (network service data unit): The unit of data passed between the network layer and the data link layer. See also *PDUs*.

null: Electric field and light intensity equal to zero.

Nyquist class one pulses: A pulse of the class defined as class one by Nyquist.

O

OADM (optical-add-drop-multiplexer): An optical device that allows optical signals to be removed (dropped) from a fiber link and simultaneously allows other optical signals to be injected (added) into the same fiber link. OADMs are commonly used in WDM systems. See also *WDM*.

OFL (overfilled launch): A launch that excites all modes of a fiber with approximately equal power.

opcode: A parameter associated with the MAC_CONTROL.request primitive.

optical attenuator: A device that attenuates optical signals.

optical gain: Refers to an optical amplifier. The ratio of the output modulated optical signal power to the input modulated optical signal power.

optical power budget: See *link optical power budget*.

optical power penalty: Some link impairments such as ISI cause a loss of modulated signal power. To maintain the eye opening, the signal must be increased. Because some of the optical power budget has to be used to increase the signal power (to maintain the desired eye opening) this is called an optical power penalty. It is usually measured in dB.

ordered_sets: Sets of special 8B10B code-groups, sometimes combined with data code-groups, can be used to construct control signals (such as packet delimiters) or to exchange non-packet data for link configuration. These sets of special code-groups are known as ordered_sets.

OTDR (Optical Time Domain Reflectometer): An instrument for measuring various fiber link parameters (attenuation, return loss, etc.) by launching optical pulses into the fiber and measuring the reflections from the fiber link as a function of time.

P

packet: Unit of data transferred across a LAN. See also *frame*.

partial-mesh network topology: A network topology in which each intermediate network node (bridge, switch, or router) is connected by a physical circuit to some, but not all, other intermediate network nodes.

PCS (Physical Coding Sublayer): A subgroup of the physical layer that is responsible for coding data to be transmitted and decoding received data.

PDUs (protocol data units): OSI term for the data passed between layers in the OSI protocol.

PECLs (positive emitter coupled logic levels): The voltage level for each logical value in a positive emitter coupled circuit.

PHY (Physical Layer Device): A complete physical layer device.

physical layer: Layer 1 of the OSI reference model. The physical layer defines the electrical, mechanical, procedural, and functional specifications for activating, maintaining, and deactivating the physical link between end systems.

physical sublayer group: A subgroup of the physical layer.

PIN photodiodes: Photodiode structures incorporate p-type, intrinsic (non-doped), and n-type semiconductor layers.

Planck's constant (h): $6.626 \times 10 - 34$ J s.

PLS (Physical Layer Signaling): A sublayer of the physical layer of 1 Mbps and 10 Mbps versions of IEEE 802.3. The PLS defines the signals passed to the physical layer from the MAC and from the physical layer to the MAC. In 100 Mbps and 1 Gbps IEEE 802.3 the RCS sublayer maps signals at the MAC/PLS interface to physical layer MII and GMII signals. See also *MAC client sublayer*, *MII*, *GMII*, and *PCS*.

PMA (Physical Medium Attachment) sublayer: A sublayer of the IEEE 802.3 physical layer. The PMA provides a medium-independent means for the PCS to support the use of a range of serial-bit-orientated physical media. See also *PCS*, *PMD*, and *TBI*.

PMD (Physical Medium Dependent) sublayer: A sublayer of the IEEE 802.3 physical layer. The PMD defines the physical layer signaling, the MDI, and the supported media types.

population inversion: When an excited state(s) of a quantum system has a larger population than the lower states(s) of the system, a population inversion exists. A population inversion must be created to produce an optical amplifier or a laser.

pre-connectorized cabling: Cabling that has had connectors fitted in the factory.

presentation layer: Layer 6 of the OSI reference model. This layer ensures that information sent by the application layer of one system will be readable by the application layer of another. The presentation layer is also concerned with the data structures used by programs and therefore negotiates data transfer syntax for the application layer.

primitive: See *service primitives*.

pulse-code modulation (PCM): A modulation scheme in which transmission symbols are transmitted in the form of pulses. Different pulse amplitudes are mapped to different symbols.

pulse-shaping filter: A filter used to modify (shape) the time-amplitude response of a pulse.

PVC (permanent virtual circuit): Virtual circuit that is permanently established. See also *VC*.

Q–R

QoS (Quality of Service): Measure of the performance for a transmission system that reflects its transmission quality and the level of service availability.

radial-over-filled launch (ROFL): ROFL is created when an approximately circularly symmetric single-mode laser beam, having a small beam divergence, illuminates a large portion of the core of a multimode fiber. The axis of the laser beam must be approximately coincident with that of the fiber.

random jitter: Jitter that is random and independent of the data being transmitted. See also *jitter* and *deterministic jitter*.

rate-sensitive traffic: The type of traffic in which timeliness can be traded for assured reception rates (for example, for video conferences). Longer end-to-end network delay can be tolerated so long as packet reception is regular enough to ensure an essentially constant received bit rate once transfer has begun.

RD (running disparity): The sign of the RDS.

RDS (running digital sum): The running sum of the transmitted code bits in which one is represented as +1 and zero as –1.

Reconciliation Sublayer: A sublayer of the IEEE 802.3 Fast Ethernet and Gigabit Ethernet physical layers that translates MAC terminology into MII or GMII terminology.

refractive index: See *index of refraction*.

repeater: Device that regenerates and propagates electrical signals between two network segments.

Request Primitive: A service primitive passed from a layer (n) to a lower layer ($n – 1$) to request that a service be initiated. See also *service primitives*.

resonance light: Light with a wavelength equal to the characteristic wavelength of a transition in a quantum system.

Response Primitive: A service primitive passed from a layer (n) to a lower layer ($n - 1$) to complete a procedure previously invoked by an indication primitive. See also *service primitives.*

return loss: Return loss refers to the magnitude of the signal power returned to a test point as a result of reflections caused by cabling impedance or refractive index mismatches at the connection points.

ridge laser: See *edge emitting laser.*

RIN (relative intensity noise): Optical intensity noise resulting from fluctuations in the output intensity of a laser. RIN can be defined as the mean square intensity fluctuation divided by the square of the average intensity at the laser output.

risetime: The time required for a signal to rise from a low signal level to a high signal level. Usually the signal levels are measured as a percentage of the level of a one.

router: An intermediate network device that operates at Layer-3 or Layer-4 of the protocol to determine a path between the source and destination node (station) in a network. In LANs, routers typically determine which is the "best" connected node to get the packet closer to its destination.

RSVP (Resource Reservation Protocol): A Layer-4 Internet protocol that enables Internet applications to request and obtain predictable levels of service for their fragmented packet streams.

RZ line code (return to zero line code): A bi-level modulation format in which one symbol nominally has an amplitude equal to zero and the other symbol has a non-zero amplitude. The symbol having a non-zero amplitude is transmitted only for a fraction of the duration of a symbol period.

S

saturation: The condition that occurs when the packet transfer rate of a network component (such as a link, switch, or repeater) reaches the carrying capacity of that component.

scrambler: A device used to randomize the symbol sequence so that the running digital sum is maintained near zero.

SERDES chip (serializer/deserializer chip): An ASIC that implements the Gigabit Ethernet TBI.

service primitives: An abstract method of describing the information flow between the layers in the protocol model and identifying the particular service that is requested or that has been provided. Each primitive may have one or more parameters that convey any information required to provide the service, and a particular service may have one or more primitives that are related to the desired function.

session layer: Layer 5 of the OSI reference model, which establishes, manages, and terminates sessions between applications and manages data exchange between presentation layer entities.

short-haul copper PMD: See *1000BASE-CX*.

simplex transmission: Transmission limited to one direction only.

single-mode fiber (SMF): A fiber that only allows one mode to propagate through it.

skew rays: Rays that follow approximately spiral paths about the optical axis of the core of an optical fiber as they propagate along the fiber.

Snell's Law: The law of refraction at a plane interface between two media having different refractive indices.

SNMP (Simple Network Management Protocol): Network management protocol used almost exclusively in TCP/IP networks. SNMP provides a means to monitor and control network devices, and to manage configurations, statistics collection, performance, and security.

SNR (signal-to-noise ratio): A measure of the quality of the received signal.

SONET (Synchronous Optical Network): High-speed (up to 2.5 Gbps) synchronous network specification designed to run on optical fiber.

Spanning Tree Algorithm and Protocol: A protocol used by IEEE 802 bridges and switches to detect multiple paths (loops) in an 802 LAN and block redundant paths so that only one logical route exists between any two nodes on the network.

SPD (Start_of_Packet Delimiter): The SPD indicates the start of a packet. In Gigabit Ethernet, an SPD ordered_set is generated when the GMII indicates Start-of-Frame.

speckle noise: See *modal noise*.

step-index multimode fiber: A multimode having a step index refractive index profile.

step-index single-mode fiber: A single mode having a step index refractive index profile.

subnet: A network sharing a particular logical subnet address.

subnet mask: 32-bit address mask used in IP to indicate the bits of an IP address that are being used for the subnet address.

subnetwork: See *subnet*.

SVC (switched virtual circuit): Virtual circuit that is dynamically established. See also *VC*.

switch: An electronic or mechanical device that allows a connection to be established as necessary and terminated when there is no longer a session to support.

T–U

TBI (Ten Bit Interface): An example implementation of the Gigabit Ethernet PMA that is used as a reference model within the Gigabit Ethernet standard document. See also *PMA*.

TCP (transport control protocol): The Layer-4 transport protocol of the Internet protocol suite.

TDM (time division multiplexed) networks: Shared media networks in which communicating nodes are assigned a fixed segment of time in each transmission period.

telecommunications outlet (telecom outlet): A fixed connecting device where the horizontal cable terminates. The telecommunications outlet provides the interface to the work area cabling.

TIA: Telecommunications Industry Association.

TIA FO 2.2: A subcommittee of the TIA that is responsible for developing fiber optic systems test procedures.

ToS (Type of Service): A field in the IP header indicating the level of service being requested. ToS maps directly to/from CoS.

transceiver: A physical layer device (the PMD including MDI) that can transmit and receive. See also *MDI* and *PMD*.

transition time: The rise or fall time.

transport layer: Layer 4 of the OSI reference model, which is responsible for reliable network communication between end nodes. The transport layer provides mechanisms for the establishment, maintenance, and termination of virtual circuits, transport fault detection and recovery, and information flow control.

trunking: Aggregating parallel links between the same pair of nodes to form a logical group with higher capacity than is available with a single link. See also *link aggregation*.

TSDU (transport service data unit): The unit of data passed between the transport layer and the network layer. See also *PDUs*.

UTP (unshielded twisted pair): A type of copper cable used in links up to 100 m. See also *Category-3* and *Category-5*.

V

VC (virtual channel): See *virtual circuit*.

VCI (virtual channel identifier): A 16-bit field in the header of an ATM cell. The VCI, together with the VPI, is used to identify the next destination of a cell as it passes through a series of ATM switches.

VCSEL (vertical cavity surface emitting laser): A type of semiconductor laser fabricated such that it emits laser light vertically to the wafer surface it was made on.

vertical eye closure: The amplitude closure of an eye diagram. See also *eye diagram* and *horizontal eye closure*.

virtual circuit: Logical circuit created to ensure reliable communications between two network devices. A virtual circuit is identified by a VPI/VCI pair, and can be either permanent (a PVC) or switched (an SVC). In ATM, a virtual circuit is called a virtual channel. See also *PVC*, *SVC*, *VCI*, and *VPI*.

VLAN (virtual-bridged local area network): Group of devices on one or more LANs that are configured so that they can communicate as if they were attached to the same shared LAN segment, when in fact they are located on a number of different LAN segments.

VLAN-tagged frame: A MAC frame that has a VLAN tag field in the header. VLAN-tagged frames are recognized by the reserved value 88-00 in the Length/Type field.

VPI (virtual path identifier): An 8-bit field in the header of an ATM cell. See also *VCI* and *VC*.

W–Z

WCMB (worst-case modal bandwidth): The bandwidth of a fiber is measured for OFL and for ROFL. The WCMB is the lowest of the two measured bandwidths.

WDM (wavelength division multiplexing): The process of multiplexing optical signals having different frequencies into the same fiber.

wire rate: The link baud rate. See also *baud*.

Index